HEARTBEAT

AN AMERICAN CARDIOLOGIST IN KENYA

by Dr David Silverstein
with Mary Anne Fitzgerald

Copyright © 2023 Dr David Silverstein.

All rights reserved. No part of this book may be reproduced, photocopied or otherwise used in any way without the prior written approval and consent of Dr David Silverstein.

ISBN: 979-8864-0591-4-2

Cover design: Julia Seth-Smith
Back Cover Photograph: Mary Anne Fitzgerald

*This book is dedicated to my wife Channa,
my sons Nahum, Joshua and his wife Taylor,
Aaron and Jeremy and
my grandchildren Benjamin and Max.*

SYNOPSIS

David Silverstein arrived in Kenya in 1974 to take up what was intended as a brief posting teaching at the University of Nairobi's School of Medicine. Fifty years and many adventures later he is still in private practice as one of East Africa's foremost cardiologists.

In 1983 David was appointed as the former President Daniel arap Moi's personal physician. In the course of travelling with him all over the world, the two men became close friends. David's privileged position gave him a unique fly-on-the-wall perspective of many of the seminal events in recent Kenyan history. His memoir recounts much more as well. Stories of exceptional patients such as Nelson Mandela and Diana Delamere are interspersed with tales of treating Marburg (green monkey) disease, plague and other strange diseases. David handles all he encounters with aplomb, be it Libya's Muammar Gaddafi deep in the Sahara or the victims of terrorist attacks in the wake of bombings in Nairobi and Mombasa.

Heartbeat is a fast-paced memoir of a man who has enjoyed life to the full and who has had the courage to put it down on paper with profound honesty.

FOREWORD

The title of this long-anticipated memoir, Heartbeat, might suggest little more than crowded clinics, daily ward rounds and regular emergencies in ICU. This alone would have been a stirring story in the company of Dr David Silverstein, the most experienced and sought-after cardiologist in Kenya and, indeed, in surrounding countries. However, a glance at the chapter headings shows there are many stories between these covers that are not associated with cardiology.

For much of this book the reader is taken through the history, politics and personalities of Kenya, Dr Silverstein's adopted homeland of almost fifty years. He shares with us his Eastern European roots and childhood in Chicago before taking us to Taiwan where he served in the U.S. Airforce during the Vietnam War. In due course the reader is taken to Kenya in the 1970s where he first lectures at the University of Nairobi but soon establishes his own cardiology practice. This is the story of a man's life, written with humour and at a pace that never flags whether it concerns the grand sweep of global politics or shares with us deeply personal insights into his friendships, family and romances.

My husband, Charles, and I had the great privilege of sharing much of this remarkable and inspiring journey with Daktari and his wife Channa, a journey so vividly described in this most compelling of memoirs.

I am confident that *Heartbeat* will enjoy a wide and appreciative readership.

- Margaret Njonjo

ABOUT THE AUTHORS

David Silverstein has lived in Nairobi, Kenya as a cardiologist for the past fifty years. He is an Elder of the Order of the Burning Spear in recognition of his medical services to Kenya. In 2023 he was a recipient of a University of Chicago Medical and Biological Sciences Distinguished Alumni Award for his outstanding contribution and leadership in the field of medicine. David is a pillar of Kenya's Jewish community and its longest-serving rosh kehilla (president).

He is married to Channa Commanday and has four sons. Their farm by Lake Naivasha is their place of peace.

Mary Anne Fitzgerald has covered eastern Africa for *The Economist*, the *Financial Times* and *The Sunday Times* of London. She is the author of twelve books on Africa, including the bestselling *Nomad: One Woman's Journey into the Heart of Africa*. She lives in Nairobi, Kenya.

PROLOGUE

I don't think a lot of people would know that a highlight of my life and friendship with David, was the privilege of being the 'flower girl' when he married Channa over twenty years ago. And it is in these corners of time and friendship that I find much to celebrate in this book.

Reading David's book on his life journey gave me the opportunity to learn even more of what I know to be a rich life and medical career, nuanced in a way that even I, without the medical background, found much to relate to and understand.

On the many occasions when I was working as a Foreign Office official and we traveled around the world in the company of his famous patient, David's knowledge of the world often helped to resolve difficult situations. He could also be trusted to find historical sites for us to visit whenever there was time; or at the very least a good restaurant to dine at when we were off duty. On numerous occasions David would humor members of our delegation with their requests for urgent medical care. Many of these ailments turned out to be longstanding problems. He treated all these people for free. He is and has always been the consummate gentleman.

I look forward to reading this book many times so that I can gain more insights into my dear friend David as well as travel back to those times that shaped so many of us.

- Sally Kosgei

CONTENTS

1	Tragedy and Romance	1
2	My Parents in a World of Chaos	8
3	Growing up in Lawndale	14
4	College and Medical School	23
5	Days of Terror, Nights of Passion	30
6	The Vietnam War	40
7	Choosing a Specialty	52
8	Karibu Kenya	62
9	Setting Up Shop	70
10	The Blue Baby	78
11	Operation Thunderbolt	88
12	The Kenyatta Succession	101
13	Private Practice	112
14	Emergency Evacuations	120
15	None of the Usual Suspects	129
16	Creatures That Bite	137
17	Green Monkeys	147
18	White Mischief, My Own and Others'	154
19	A Very African Coup	165
20	Snakes and Ladders	175
21	Libyan Delusions	186

22	Romeo Nine	195
23	Bwana Simba	205
24	Nelson Mandela	210
25	A Place Under the Sun	218
26	The Circle of Life	225
27	The Slim Disease	239
28	Diplomatic Dilemmas	249
29	Two More Sons	263
30	Death on the Farm	266
31	Trips to China and Israel	279
32	Travels in Iran	287
33	The Chesoni Saga	295
34	Channa Makes Us Whole	311
35	Unusual Bar Mitzvahs	323
36	On the Frontline of the War on Terror	333
37	Rosh Kehillah	343
38	Moi's Last Days	352
39	Another Mysterious Disease	368
40	The Next Great Pandemic	379
41	Charles Njonjo Says His Last Shalom	391
42	Looking Back on It All	400
	Epilogue	406
	Acknowledgements	407
	Index	412

1

TRAGEDY AND ROMANCE

At ten o'clock on the morning of 7 August 1998, a two-vehicle convoy emerged from behind the security walls of a four-bedroom villa in Nairobi's upmarket Runda Estate. The lead vehicle was driven by Fazul Abdullah Mohammed, twenty-three, a Comoros Islands native. Close behind him came a Toyota Dyna truck carrying two tons of TNT, ammonium nitrate and other explosive material. All of it was carefully packed into hundreds of cylinders arranged inside wooden crates to create what the U.S. military calls a vehicle-borne improvised explosive device. This one had unprecedented power to maim and kill. The Toyota's driver was Jihad Mohammed Ali, known as Azzam, twenty-four, a citizen of Saudi Arabia. Next to Azzam sat British-born Mohamed Rashed Daoud al-Owhali, twenty-one, who was armed with a 9 mm semi-automatic Beretta pistol and some homemade stun grenades the group liked to call 'potatoes'.

The convoy's destination was the U.S. Embassy, a half-hour drive away at the corner of Haile Selassie and Moi avenues in the Kenyan capital's central business district. Fazul Abdullah carefully led the other two vehicles through traffic to their target then drove on. His role in the operation was now complete. After some moments of apparent confusion over how to proceed,

Azzam pulled the Toyota truck into a small parking lot behind the embassy via the exit lane.

Mohamed Al-Owhali later told the FBI that at that moment he was supposed to jump from the truck and toss several grenades in the direction of any bystanders in order to scare them away. He said he had expected to be killed in the attack. Instead he panicked, lobbed a single ineffectual grenade at an embassy guard and fled on foot. Azzam in the meantime detonated the bomb. The huge blast incinerated Azzam and almost everything and everyone around him. Moments later 670 kilometres to the southeast in Dar es Salaam, the capital of neighbouring Tanzania, a second bomb of the same size and general construction exploded outside the American embassy there.

Meanwhile back in Nairobi, Al-Owhali had yet to put any distance between himself and the Toyota truck when it detonated. He suffered lacerations to his face, hands and back in the blast and went for treatment to the M.P. Shah Hospital. There he discarded keys and bullets, raising the suspicions of the staff. Two days later he was arrested and interrogated by the Kenyan police. A federal judge in New York would later sentence him to life imprisonment for his role in this terrorist act of mass murder.

I was in my office at Nairobi Hospital seeing patients when the explosion happened. Even though I was three kilometres away, its *ka-boom* rang loud in my ears and the aftershock vibrated through my body. I looked out the window to see a great plume of dense smoke billowing hundreds of feet into the air. I couldn't tell for certain how far away it was. State House, the official presidential residence, was in the approximate direction of the cloud so I reached for the special white telephone – a hotline – that connected me instantly to the State House comptroller, Abraham Kiptanui. As President Moi's personal physician, I had good reason to be concerned. Abraham assured me that State House had not been hit and President Moi was safe. He thought the target must have been the U.S. Embassy about a mile further on. He knew nothing more.

Horrified and angered at the thought of the carnage I knew was headed our way, I ran to the Accident and Emergency Department. When I got there, I encountered Channa Commanday, a highly skilled emergency nurse from Portland, Oregon. Channa had first come to Nairobi Hospital in 1994 as a patient herself. She had been on vacation in the Maasai Mara, riding a horse at a gallop when it swerved to miss a stump, and horse and rider crashed to the ground. Channa had fractured her pelvis and several ribs and was concussed. She had spent a week as a patient at our hospital. Because of her great experience with emergency medicine, Sue Carr-Hartley, our director of nursing, had asked her to return to Kenya to teach emergency nursing and to develop and implement a disaster plan for the hospital. This was going to be the first opportunity to test her system.

Channa later told me that as soon as she saw the huge cloud of smoke from her office she pulled on her white lab coat and loaded her pockets with trauma gear: scissors, eye glasses, stethoscope, pens, notebook and other items. She locked her door as she left knowing it would be a long time before she returned. 'I need a triage officer,' she said when she saw me, 'and it's you.' Channa assigned her two best nurses, Naomi Ngugi and Sylvia Atieno, to work with me.

Though calm and focused Channa obviously was in a high adrenaline state as was I. She hoped everyone was prepared. This was going to be the moment of truth for our largely untested staff. As if she needed a reminder that not everyone would be up to the challenge, on her way to the director of nursing's office Channa encountered the unflappable chief pharmacist racing down the hallway toward her, arms up and panic in her eyes.

Channa later wrote in a report that would be read into the record at the sentencing phase of al-Owhali's trial at a federal court in New York, 'Maybe three minutes from the explosion a sudden wall of broken bodies began descending from buses and cars, charging through the open doors wide-eyed and bleeding into our emergency department. My first thought was *This is a nightmare. My God! How will we cope?*

'Battalions of cleaners kept mops and buckets in full swing to stem the progressive reddening of our floors and pale green walls. Not small groups of people but crowds pushed endlessly through the doors into the halls and rooms of the emergency department, leaning, limping, dragging and carried on top of each other with no end in sight.'

As the first casualties reached us, we only knew what our senses told us, not why the bomb had exploded or by whom. Not until later did we learn that 7 August was the eighth anniversary of the launch of Operation Desert Shield in Iraq and the arrival of U.S. troops in Saudi Arabia. This American incursion onto Muslim soil was a gross violation in the view of militant Islamists such as Osama bin Laden, a man whose name was yet to make headlines. Neither had any of us yet heard of a terrorist organization called Al-Qaeda.

Despite my close contacts in the upper echelons of the Kenyan government, I had never heard discussion of a possible terrorist attack. Nairobi was taken by surprise just as New York City and Washington, D.C. would be little more than three years later on 9/11. We did learn after the fact that the American ambassador to Kenya, Prudence Bushnell, also injured in the bombing, had repeatedly and unsuccessfully requested that the embassy security be upgraded.

The embassy incurred heavy damage from the explosion as did the seventeen-story Cooperative Bank building next door. On the other side of the embassy Ufundi House collapsed to the ground causing the majority of deaths. Most of them were staff and students at a secretarial college there. The heat from the blast also incinerated a passing bus packed with passengers. The death toll was 213. Only twelve were Americans. Another 4500, nearly all of them Kenyans, were injured. Eleven people were killed in Dar es Salaam and another eighty-five were wounded. Al-Owhali's stun grenade had caused many people on the street and in surrounding buildings to turn towards the embassy just as Azzam exploded his bomb. The result was a high incidence of lacerations and eye injuries from flying glass.

As Nairobi had no disaster plan, the civil authorities had no clear idea what to do. The great majority of first responders at the scene were Kenyan pedestrians, brave Good Samaritans who pulled people from the rubble and carried them to matatus, pickups, trucks and cars. There were some people helping in white lab coats, but most doctors headed for duty at their hospitals when they heard the explosion. Nairobi also had next to no ambulances. Instead of dozens of sirens splitting the air as would happen elsewhere, the city was eerily quiet. Some people came to us on foot from the embassy. Others drove themselves. Most came by public transport.

One of our emergency doctors, Vera Wekullo, happened to be in the vicinity at the time. She was thrown against a wall by the blast and showered with falling glass. The man who had been walking next to her was decapitated. She later recalled bending over him saying, 'I'm a doctor. I can help.' Then she thought *No*.

He has no head. I can't help him. Vera ran until she found a dazed woman seated at the wheel of her car. 'I'm a doctor!' she shouted. 'Take me to Nairobi Hospital!'

The best organized and most helpful among the volunteer first responders were the drivers of matatus, garishly painted minibuses with names like Citi, Jesus Saves, Sony Classic and Adonai that careen around the city deafening their passengers with high-decibel reggae. The matatus ferried some 500 blast victims to Nairobi Hospital. We attended to them wherever we could - in the ER, in the hallways and offices, even the library. We only lost one person, a man who died from his blast wounds just as he entered the hospital. Two others arrived dead.

I recognized one of the injured as Frank Presley, a communications officer on the U.S. Embassy staff. Frank was lying awake on a gurney on the ER floor. He had suffered glass cuts to his neck and chest, and a fractured and dislocated humerus. He was in shock from blood loss, which made it difficult to get an IV line into him. Presley was among the ten or so victims who were evacuated by air the next day to a U.S. medical facility in Germany.

While I was stabilizing patients and assessing their wounds before sending them on to critical-care areas such as surgery or the ICU, Channa was stepping over and around bodies, checking respiration, pulse and consciousness. One of the victims she treated was a man with eyes swollen shut from corneal lacerations. The blast had amputated his fingers and torn his clothes from him. When he felt her fingers at his pulse, he said, 'I'm okay. You go help the others.' She later told me about two ward nurses so terrified of a woman's gruesome eye injury that they ran away.

It was well past nightfall when we saw our last patients. I was physically exhausted and emotionally drained. My head ached and I was hungry. I asked Channa if she had had dinner yet. She laughed. 'I haven't even had breakfast. Let me take a shower and change first.'

Nothing was open at 10.30 pm save for one of the very best restaurants in Nairobi, the Mandhari in the Serena Hotel. As we walked in, I asked the *maître d'* if the kitchen was still open. '*Pole kwa kazi* (Sorry for all the work). Hang on. Let's see what we can do.' The chef had just left for the night and was called back. He produced a first-rate meal that was balm for the soul.

Channa was delightful despite the day's horrors. Of course, we reviewed the grim hours at length with despair in our hearts for all the broken and maimed. Yet we weren't altogether solemn. Her beauty and wit had a relaxing effect. As I escorted Channa back to her flat at the hospital, I wondered if the day's dreadful events had perhaps catalysed something unspoken between us. That was too big a question to address just then, but I was sorely in need of a life-affirming gesture. I kissed her lightly and was delighted that she kissed me back. Then I said good night and went home, tired and troubled but with hope in my heart.

Channa and I had met in a time of extremis then shared a gourmet dinner and a bottle of wine. We were barely acquainted yet I got the feeling that she saw right through me. It came as something of a relief. Although successful in medicine, my personal life was a mess. She was mischievous yet wise - a woman you could trust, who would never be boring. It was absurd to think this, but it struck me she was my last chance at something I had been avoiding. I didn't have a word for it then. I do now. It's intimacy. We married two years later when I was fifty-five. That was more than twenty years ago. As it turned out, I was right on every count with a bonus thrown in. Not only did I get to know Channa, I got to know myself.

2

MY PARENTS IN A WORLD OF CHAOS

Children are regarded as the hope of the future in every society. Among Jewish people this concept is emphasized by the view that children are considered a divine trust as written in Proverbs 1:8. 'Listen my son to your father's instructions. And do not forsake your mother's teaching.' The values of a Jewish home are centred on family, tradition, education and charity. Just as these values had been instilled in the generations that came before me, so they shaped me too. My family practiced what they had learned. We had a long tradition of serving as rabbis and teachers. With these foundations I became, as my parents were, educated in Judaism and fluent in Hebrew; knowledgeable about the rituals of Jewish life; and proud and confident as a Jew and an American.

My parents raised us in a post-war environment of an economy expanding against the backdrop of a fast-developing Cold War. As the world's industrial, political and military leader, America provided seemingly limitless opportunities for an emerging middle class. And we were part of it.

My father was born into a perilous world in 1905 at Grajewo, a tiny Polish *shtetl* (Jewish village) that straddled the main road from Warsaw to St. Petersburg. Poland had been a province of the Russian Empire for nearly forty years. Then in the year of my father's birth the Russian Revolution began. Much of it was fought on Polish soil as peasants and workers took up arms to demand better living conditions and autonomy for Poland. The unrest spread like a firestorm throughout imperial Russia. It was the beginning of the end of the Romanov Czars who had ruled Russia and its dependencies for centuries. They were finally overthrown during the Communist Revolution in 1917. Jews were sucked into the chaos when their *shtetls* were targeted in a series of organized pogroms. Poland at last won her independence at the close of World War I only to be invaded again in 1920, this time by the Russian Bolsheviks. It was the year my father emigrated to the United States. The death and destruction and the family's uncertain future if they stayed where they were no doubt triggered their decision to seek their destiny elsewhere.

Dad's given name was Nochem. He was one of two sets of twins. There were nine children in all with Dad and his twin sister Chana Gitel in the middle. The first of our family to arrive in the U.S. was a cousin, a rabbi, who changed his name from Brzoza to Silverstone because it sounded more Jewish. He settled in Arizona.

Dad's eldest brother and sister, Joe and Rochel, came next and settled in Chicago where Joe opened a newspaper stand. They saved enough money to bring over the next two siblings, Ruth and Eva. The four of them helped bring their parents and the two sets of twins, Dad and Chana Gitel and Alec and Rubin. One of the brothers died in Poland and never got the chance to see America.

Our family name was also Brzoza. We borrowed Silverstone from the Arizona cousin but soon switched it to Silverstein as it sounded even more Jewish. When my father entered the United States on the eve of his fifteenth birthday, he became Norman Silverstein. My paternal grandfather was a respected Jewish scholar who went blind in his old age. My paternal grandmother died within a few years after her arrival.

Norman was intelligent and had no trouble in mastering fluent, barely accented English in Chicago's public schools. To please his father he also enrolled in the Chicago Yeshiva, an Orthodox Jewish theological seminary, the year it opened. The experience seemed to have engaged his head but not his heart. After he qualified as a rabbi, Dad entered a rebellious period during which he turned away from Judaism. He took menial jobs, dated non-Jewish women and ate non-kosher foods. He didn't tell me much about this period. At some point he thought about ending his life, but the idea of becoming a doctor and helping delay the inevitability of death gave him reason to live. He entered medical school at the University of Illinois College of Medicine. He was the first in his family to receive a higher education. The unspoken darkness in Dad's soul was something that I became aware of in myself as I got older. I think that from time to time that darkness seeped into my soul too. Thankfully, those times have been brief, and for most of my life I have managed to keep any feelings of negativity at bay.

Not long after becoming a general practitioner, he met my mother. I believe Mom steered him back into being a life-affirming, practicing Jew though his faith in Judaism was perhaps less intense than it had been. Her maiden name was Sarah Peshe Kahn. She was from a tiny village in Lithuania called Plotl. It was a couple of hundred miles from Grajewo where my father was born. If you look for Plotl on modern maps, it may appear as Plautilus or Plotaius or it may not appear at all. Mom was born in 1918 into a poor but religious Jewish household. She had none of the things American couples believe are essential for a normal childhood. If she wanted a doll, she fashioned one herself from marsh reeds.

There had been rabbis on both sides of her family for generations. Her father was Rabbi Moshe Zeev Kahn. He was known to us as *Zedi*, which is Yiddish for grandfather. He was a brilliant Talmudist who had studied at the famous Telze Yeshiva in Lithuania. Sarah was nine when her family emigrated to Chicago in 1928. In due course she graduated from the College of Jewish Studies and became a Hebrew teacher. When she was in her fifties, she went to Roosevelt College to get a bachelor's degree. After that she said to my father, 'Nochem, now I want to study for a master's degree.' My father wasn't very keen on the idea and said with a smile in his eyes, 'Honey, you can't serve two masters.' She continued to take courses in many subjects throughout her life.

My parents married in 1939. Sarah, who was never on time for anything, was three hours late to her own wedding, but nobody minded. People always forgave her for her pathological tardiness, particularly my father, who was in thrall to her charm and good looks. She had high cheekbones and dark hair long enough to roll into a bun at the nape of her neck. The perfect figure she had as a bride remained with her for the rest of her life even though she never exercised. She said she didn't need to. She got her workouts getting down on her knees and scrubbing the floors. Like many beautiful women, she was aware of the effect she had on others and always made the effort to look her best. I subconsciously absorbed her preoccupation with the aesthetics of beauty and applied it to myself and later to girls I dated.

From time to time my father insisted on lavishing expensive gifts on her. One was a mink coat. She dutifully brought it out to wear once, maybe twice, a year. He loved Sarah deeply. She, in turn, worshipped him. They were married for thirty-seven years, and their passion for one another never dulled. It made a strong and lasting impression on me, but their secret lay beyond my reach for decades. It wasn't until much later in my life that I was emotionally ready for that sort of relationship.

My parents' wedding came just six weeks after Hitler and Stalin had devoured Poland, leading France and Britain to declare war on Germany. And so the horrors of World War II began. Nearly all the Silversteins' and Kahns' extended family members were killed in the Holocaust. A few managed to escape. Some ended up in Israel and South Africa but most settled in the States. Norman and Sarah's first child, my elder sister Rochelle, arrived in November 1940. By then Dad had set up his practice and was seeing patients. Then came the surprise attack by the Japanese on Pearl Harbor on 7 December 1941. Until then America - and Dad - had stayed out of the war. In due course his medical skills were required in the Pacific Theatre. He was drafted in 1943.

He had chosen to sign up with the Army because he disliked flying and was leery of being on water. To his dismay he was assigned to the USS *Hope,* which was operated by the Navy for the Army. It was one of three hospital ships built for duty in the South Pacific. It could accommodate 400 patients. Dad was to be the chief medical officer. Mom and Rochelle moved with him when he was sent for basic training at Camp Stoneman in Pittsburg, California. It was during that time I was conceived. By the time I was born in August 1944, he was already aboard ship. He distributed cigars to all the officers on hearing the news. The *Hope* was stationed in Leyte Gulf off the island of Leyte in the Philippines. The American and Australian naval vessels congregated there were the support for Operation King Two, General Douglas MacArthur's amphibious invasion that liberated the Philippine Archipelago from nearly three years of Japanese occupation. The ferocious four-day sea battle was possibly the largest naval battle in history. It was also the first time the Japanese employed kamikaze pilots to execute suicide missions by flying their airplanes into the ships.

In the spring of 1945 the Hope and her sister ships, Mercy and Comfort, were stationed off Okinawa to support the invasion of Japan. The Hope weathered repeated attacks without damage, but Comfort was not so fortunate. A kamikaze pilot crashed his plane through three of her decks into a surgical theatre, killing twenty-eight and wounding forty-eight more. The Japanese surrender was announced on 15 August 1945.

3

GROWING UP IN LAWNDALE

When Dad enlisted, Mom moved in with my grandfather Zedi Kahn near Wicker Park in North Chicago. In 1946 Dad reappeared one day unannounced with a duffel bag over his shoulder. Rochelle opened the door and called out, 'Mom, the laundry man's here with Daddy's clothes from the army.' I was one year old and he was a stranger to me. My first memory of him was his salt-and-pepper hair and well-trimmed moustache.

As I grew older, he became my role model. He was a learned doctor, an ordained rabbi and a dedicated family man. His wardrobe was immaculate. Every day of the week without fail he appeared in a suit, tie and a starched white shirt that had been lifted out of its laundry wrapping that morning. He was a serious man who enjoyed a good joke though he was seldom the one to initiate it.

Despite his short stature, my father's absolute moral and intellectual authority made him appear huge. Dad was five feet, three inches. Mom was three inches shorter. When his thoughtful gaze fell on me, I felt the weight of his expectations. He has served as my superego throughout my life. Even now, many years after his death, I still seek his approval and wince when I know my actions have fallen short of his exacting standards.

Dad, his twin sister Aunt Chana Gitel and her husband Uncle Harry soon bought a three-story apartment building in Lawndale in Chicago's old west side. The area was sometimes referred to as Chicago's Jerusalem. There were more than seventy synagogues in a community of mostly Russian and Eastern European Jews. We lived there for ten years. Abe Skolnik, one of my mother's uncles, also lived with us for a time. Uncle Abe's preferred tongue was Yiddish. I learned it from him as a second language. In those days it was not unusual for three generations to live in one house. Uncle Abe's girlfriend had been killed by the Nazis. He never married, and he lived with us until he died in his 80s.

Allan, the third and last of the young Silversteins, was born two years after me in November 1946. We were inseparable as children, playing baseball games together and having friendly wrestling matches as breaks from our homework. When my mother scolded us, saying we'd get hurt, we told her we were just getting exercise. Her retort invariably was, 'If you want exercise get on your hands and knees and scrub the floor.' When we were five and seven, Allan and I began to steal Uncle Abe's untipped English Ovals and smoke them in the bathroom. Uncle Abe would bang on the locked door and rattle the handle as we choked on the smoke and tried to stifle our giggles.

Allan, Rochelle and I have always enjoyed a close bond that started in the bedroom the three of us shared until we left Lawndale and moved into a larger house. Looking back, it was high time we were given more personal space. Rochelle was already sixteen. I was on the cusp of becoming a teenager, and Allan was ten. He and I had shared a bed, lying side by side in the darkness, whispering stories to each other until Rochelle told us to shut up. Did we fight and kick each other? If we did, I have no memory of it.

My parents raised us on a rich diet of love and affection, and there was hardly ever discord in our house. Jewish family values emphasize moral obligations. In my family this was expressed by practicing medicine. There was an uncompromising parental expectation that all three children would excel at some vocation for which the intense and sustained application of brainpower was a *sine qua non*. Little else associated with child-rearing seemed to matter to them. Sport and exercise and the healthy outdoor life didn't interest Mom and Dad one bit. The only exception was the family two-week vacation every summer at Zipperstein's Resort in Michigan's wooded hills that were billed as the Catskills of the Midwest. Mr and Mrs Zipperstein had been running their strictly kosher establishment since 1911. They offered 'good health and pleasant surprises' to the Jewish families who faithfully returned each year. Like the other family resorts of the time, there were organized sports, drama competitions, a swimming pool and enough rich food to jeopardize the advertised 'good health'.

Dad's most strenuous undertaking was shuffleboard. He preferred playing card games, although he tried to hide this from his children. The closest he ever got to spectator sports was during the summer Sundays when he'd sit reading a medical journal in our living room as he surreptitiously listened to the White Sox baseball game on the radio before he fell asleep.

Dad's idea of recreation was to attend scholarly lectures or debates. Politics was another indoor interest. He was a lifelong Democrat and an avid supporter of Adlai Stevenson for both his presidential bids. On the flip side, my father deplored the Wisconsin Republican Senator Joseph McCarthy for his right-wing demagoguery. McCarthy's skill at oratory contributed to his success in his witch hunt for suspected communists. When Dad heard him on the radio, he'd say, 'I pray he gets a toothache.' If

Dad detected any flaws in his presentation, he'd say, 'My prayers have been heard.'

One Father's Day we bought Dad a pair of Bermuda shorts and a garden lounge chair. We were very pleased with ourselves because it was a new-fangled thing that had only just come onto the market. We couldn't wait to see him relaxing in it, enjoying a little fresh air and sunshine. When we returned to the house later in the day, we found him sitting on the lawn in his new chair dressed in his new shorts and a white shirt and tie. He was reading *The New England Journal of Medicine*.

My parents spun a sheltering cocoon around us, filtering out all distractions in order to keep our schedules free for study. Allan and I were excused from almost all household responsibilities – cleaning our rooms, helping around the house, acquiring basic self-sufficiency. They acquired their first TV after all three of us had moved away. They wanted to keep our attention focused solely on our studies to strive for that pinnacle of perfection, the straight-A report card. Mom made sure we sat down and did our homework as soon as we got back from school. Only when we had finished it could we go out and play – if there was time. Due in large part to Mom's assiduous supervision of my homework and some extracurricular tutoring, I was well ahead of my classmates, particularly in reading and arithmetic. The result was I got bored in class. The remedy, for which Mom relentlessly lobbied the school administration, was to bump me up to a higher class. This happened twice at Bryant Elementary School, in the fifth and seventh grades. These promotions had the unintended consequence of separating me from all my friends. I was isolated in other ways too. During my school years the neighbourhood's sizeable Jewish community moved elsewhere.

Our parents disapproved of us 'wasting time'. Anything that wasn't schoolwork or studying the Torah fell into that category. Dad always questioned us about our day, wanting to know what we had accomplished, what we had studied, and what we had read. He'd then ask Mom for her input before letting us know what he thought. If she said, 'They were out playing baseball all day,' he frowned. If she said we'd received straight A's, he'd beam with pride, and we'd bask in his approval. When our performance fell short of expectations – an A minus fell into this category - he'd admonish us with a gentle, 'Okay, tell me about it.' We then had to explain ourselves and discuss how we could achieve perfection next time round. Dad never really gave us permission just to be kids and goof around. All three of us still feel guilty doing something just for fun.

'Go and study,' was Mom's daily injunction. She often sat down and hit the books with us. She was a dedicated advocate of memorization from age five onward, especially the Torah (the Old Testament) in Hebrew. I credit her with nurturing my own prodigious powers of recall. This later came in handy when learning new languages such as Mandarin, German, Swahili and medical Gujarati as well as when I was preparing for my bar mitzvah. My subject was a *pilpul* (a critical analysis of the ancient debates around Jewish law and tradition) written by Grandfather Kahn for one of his sons. The subject was a hypothetical question of the sort much beloved among Talmudists but of no practical value except to sharpen the mind. Many Talmud-trained Jews excel in law and the sciences. Dad translated the document from Hebrew into English. It was ten pages of dense text, which Mom typed up and insisted I memorize in its entirety. Simply reading it wasn't good enough.

Dad had an authoritarian streak, and in no area were his

views more rigid than in his absolute reverence for medicine. He considered it the highest possible calling and presumed all three of his children would follow in his footsteps. It was a choice so obvious to him that it scarcely required discussion. One of my earliest toys was a stethoscope, placed in my crib where perhaps a rattle or stuffed animal might have been more appropriate. When I was eight or nine, I somehow came into possession of a toy skeleton for Halloween. When he saw it, Dad said, 'It's a good thing you brought this home,' and proceeded to use the skeleton as a visual aid to teach us the bones of the body. I never seriously considered any career but medicine.

My brother Allan, who became a pediatrician, was less tractable and to some degree resentful, although most of his skirmishing was with Mom, who was the family enforcer. I guessed he was rebelling against the pressure he sensed coming from Dad about going into medicine. Nothing else ever ruffled his tolerance. He was quieter and more reserved than Rochelle and me. I remember Allan always failed the routine hearing tests we had at school. In the way of children, I never questioned this. Neither did Mom. When the teachers talked to her about it, she replied he seemed to understand everything she said perfectly well. I must say, our mother was not one to speak in a soft voice.

Allan's hearing loss was probably caused by measles. Even though our father was a doctor, no one in the family paid any attention to his disability. It wasn't until he was in Chicago Medical School that his problem was solved. Allan couldn't understand what the professors were saying during lectures and got his hearing tested again. The audiologist was amazed he had been able to get the marks he had. He got a hearing aid, and it changed his whole life. Allan went on to become a successful pediatrician who was chair of his group practice. He was perfectly suited for the job. He loved caring for children although medicine was not the passion that it was for Dad and me. He had a twinkle in his eye and a fatherly air that relaxed the children and their mothers too.

My sister Rochelle was not subjected to the same pressure to go into medicine, perhaps because expectations for girls were different in those days. She was as beautiful as Mom and kept up with the latest hairstyles and fashion. She was into acting and performed in English, Hebrew and Yiddish. She had a quick wit and a way with children. She majored in literature at Barnard College in New York City. She later went into teaching Hebrew to children in grades one to three.

As a family we kept kosher but did not regularly attend religious services. At home we celebrated Shabbat, which begins on Friday evening and lasts until Saturday evening. Dad always said *kiddush*, blessing the wine and the bread before the Friday night meal. He didn't wear a *yarmulke* (Yiddish, skullcap) except for the Shabbat meal and in the synagogue. He drove his car on the Sabbath just like he did every other day of the week so that he could see his patients in the hospital or at home. In Jewish law, saving a life is prioritized over many of the prohibitions of the Sabbath, including driving. When I was young, I used to say I too wanted to be a doctor so I could drive on the Sabbath.

Meanwhile our Lawndale neighbourhood was in transition. The Jews began migrating north out of the community not long after we arrived. From what I remember the move later took on the look of a full-fledged evacuation. The community's character began to change as Black families moved in to fill the vacuum. At Bryant Elementary School I ended up as the only white kid in my class. I got chased a couple of times by kids from other classes but managed to get home safely. I was touched and grateful when classmates took it upon themselves to protect me.

Dad wasn't yet forty-five when he suffered his first episode of chest pain. It was the early 1950s. He and Mom had driven Rochelle to catch a train for summer camp. Because Mom was late leaving the house as usual, he had to rush down the platform carrying Rochelle's bags. Suddenly he experienced sharp chest pains and he had to be hospitalized. His next episode was in the autumn of 1960. This time it was a major heart attack that caused significant damage to his heart muscle. I was shaken by how vulnerable he looked lying in bed in an oxygen tent with an IV drip in his arm. It was an intimation of mortality that I found deeply disturbing.

Dad had survived a sobering brush with death and was now at risk. Perhaps because I identified so deeply with him, after the heart attack I lost some of my carefree attitude toward life as well as a youthful assumption that I was bulletproof. I was shadowed by a new fear that I might not live as long as I had assumed or hoped. I have never completely shaken that dread. Certainly my father's heart disease and concern about my own mortality contributed to my choice of cardiology.

The family all mobilized in response to Dad's emergency. Mom in particular rose to the occasion. Previously this quintessential Jewish mother had been exclusively concerned with running the household and looking after us kids. She took driving lessons so she could chauffeur Dad to the hospital and on house calls. I had just turned sixteen and learned to drive as well to help keep Dad mobile. Dad had a nephew called Leroy Sterling (changed from Silverstein) who owned the Sterling Harris Ford dealership. Dad took me down there and bought me a bright red, brand new Ford Falcon. This was when Chicago was famous for being a mobster city. We later learned that Leroy had sold about a dozen cars to

Frank Sinatra so we suspected he might have mob connections. Sinatra paid for the cars but didn't take delivery of any of them as the FBI was onto it. Leroy fled to Canada where his body was found in a ditch riddled with bullets. Dad said it was a Mafia job but didn't elaborate. I remember seeing the disappointment in his eyes. This was not what he expected of the family. That was our one and only connection to the underbelly of the city.

By contrast my life was as placid as a mill pond. It was all study, study, study laced with the hormonal longings of an adolescent boy. At school I was mixing with students who were two years older than me. They were beginning to have sexual experiences, but I was not. The girls were not interested in this socially awkward younger kid. While the other boys ventured into a new and exciting world, I was left to figure things out on my own. Looking back on it now, I realize that this contributed to my painfully slow emotional development.

My parents were unaware of my inner turmoil. We didn't discuss feelings and doubt at home. Instead, they gave me the priceless gift of unwavering, unconditional love. It instilled in me the confidence to set my sights high later in life when I was making my way in the world. To this day I hear Dad's voice gently chiding me, 'If you want to achieve anything you must study and work.' Mom and Dad also made sure I had a strong sense of my Jewish identity which has enabled me to lead and represent the Jewish community here in Kenya for so many years.

4

COLLEGE AND MEDICAL SCHOOL

By the end of 1960 I had enough credits to leave high school six months early and begin pre-med studies. I felt I had to prove myself to my classmates. I was always on the sidelines and didn't fit in. Going to university seemed like a good way to show I could keep up with them. I opted to stay in Chicago and enrol in the excellent pre-med program at the University of Illinois at Navy Pier, starting in the spring term. Going into the summer term the dean told me they had no record of my graduating high school. This was true, of course. What's more, there was an American history course I was still required to do. I managed to wriggle my way into and through a history correspondence course during a three-week holiday and finally got my high school diploma.

While at Navy Pier I discovered to my surprise that I was reasonably good at athletics. At fifty-six kilos I was strong for my size and already had some untutored experience in wrestling. I competed all the way to the championship in my weight division before finally losing to someone who went on to join the university team. I began dating properly too. Sandra, my first steady girlfriend, was Japanese. It was the start of a new and exciting phase of my life as I came to realize how much I had missed in those cloistered years under my parents' roof. I was determined to do some catching up.

After finishing the pre-med course, I was accepted at the prestigious University of Chicago. I was nineteen and the summer stretched ahead of me. It was the first time since I was nine years old there was nothing penned into my schedule. Until our bar mitzvahs our parents sent us for six weeks to Camp Massad, a summer camp at Dingman's Ferry in the Pocono Mountains of Pennsylvania. It wasn't particularly religious, but a strong Zionist theme ran through everything we did. We were expected to speak Hebrew while playing sports, during meals and even in our cabins when we bunked down for the night. Our teams had names like *Tzonchanim* (Israeli paratroopers), *D'gania* (one of Israel's first kibbutzim) and *Ma'pilim* (the Jews who immigrated to Israel before World War II). The reward for speaking the most Hebrew during the week was a blue felt flag and perhaps an ice cream or an outing to the local bowling alley. We thought Camp Massad was cool. We always looked forward to it because it promised the most fun we would have all year. We played ball games and hiked through the woods and canoed and swam in the lake. I liked soccer best and loved the bonfires and singing Israeli songs at night.

Now there was no camp and none of the extracurricular tutoring Mom and Dad always arranged for us during school vacations. I was attracted to the idea of being independent and earning wages. I began looking for a job. Dad was not happy about this. 'The important thing is studying,' he told me. 'I earn the money to educate my children. You can earn your own money once your education is finished.'

Between college and the start of medical school I wanted to see how I'd fare working with my hands rather than using my brain all the time. I was taken onto the payroll at a cable factory thanks to my sister Rochelle's Israeli boyfriend who knew the owner. My job was to go through all the discarded wires with a magnet and extract the ferromagnetic metals like iron and steel from the copper because copper had a good resale value. I stayed at the cable factory for two months until med school started. I had another job too. I worked one or two nights a week, usually on the weekend, at a clinic operated by a wealthy surgeon. Dad didn't complain because he thought the practical experience would be good for me. In those days lawyers employed 'ambulance chasers' who listened in on police band radios and rushed to accident scenes. They would offer their services to the victims, promising to help them sue for damages for personal injury and to get immediate medical care. Then they brought their victims to us. The outside door was locked against intruders. If anyone wanted to come in, they first had to ring the emergency bell by the front door. Since I worked exclusively at night and was usually on my own, the job dovetailed nicely with the needs of a young man determined to make up for lost time with the opposite sex. Sandra and I got to know the clinic intimately.

I was still the proud owner of the Ford Falcon bought from my cousin Leroy, but I had no intention of commuting from home, which was now in the northern suburb of Lincolnwood, to the University of Chicago on the south side. I lived in a dorm and later rented an apartment in order to give full attention to the business of dating. My zeal in this area landed me at the bottom third of my class. I was all hormones and no sense. By my second year I had regained a foothold on the academic ladder. By my third year I was fully recovered. I still dated a lot, but I had established a better work-life balance. At last I was focused on becoming the best doctor I could be.

When it was possible, mostly on weekends, I'd accompany my father on his patient rounds. Dad had an excellent bedside manner. He was caring and gentle and gave the impression he had all the time in the world to listen to complaints and explanations. His patients adored him and welcomed him as they would a family friend, offering him coffee and snacks as they chatted. He didn't like discussing money and left payments to be handled by his secretary. After his heart attack Mom took over this side of his practice. Like Dad, I have an aversion to talking openly about money.

Dad invited my thoughts and answered my questions without pretension or judgment. As I progressed in my clinical acumen, he asked me more and more often to participate in the examination, and our discussions became more erudite. Eventually he would have me examine patients and present the cases to him. He solicited my suggestions and weighed them up with a considered, 'That's a good thought.' If he didn't agree he would explain why. But usually he acted on my diagnosis and recommendation.

Later, when I started my internal medicine residency, he recognized that my knowledge had overtaken his as a family practitioner. Sometimes he would call me to seek my advice on his cases. We were proud of each other. Dad was the perfect role model as a doctor and teacher. To this day I try to emulate Dr Norman Silverstein's kind mentoring technique with my medical students, residents and younger colleagues as well as my son Aaron, the youngest doctor of the family.

In November 1965 I flew to England to spend three months at the Royal London Hospital in an elective program overseen by Professor Michael Floyer, a nephrologist and expert in hypertension. In a strange twist of fate, he was my first boss when I relocated to Kenya some ten years later. I was just twenty-one and had never lived overseas. My family was concerned I wouldn't be able to look after myself and diligently consulted their networks in search of suitable accommodation. They found a rabbi's widow in the East End who had a room to let. What could be more proper than that? Nevertheless tongues wagged. Members of her congregation were concerned that our living arrangement might be misconstrued as *yichud*, in unsanctioned proximity to one another. Never mind that she was four times my age. People might think that because we were living under the same roof, a Jewish law called *maarat ayiin*, perception of the eyes, was being violated.

So I said good bye to 19th-century Jewish puritanism in the hopes of finding accommodation with a more contemporary spirit. This time the family came up with a cantor's widow with a spare room. She was even older than the rabbi's widow and generally regarded as being beyond the possibility of any monkey business. She was a sweet old lady, and we got along nicely. She had one of those British pay-as-you-go heating arrangements where you fed coins into a meter to get a few hours of warmth. It was winter and her flat was freezing cold most of the time. I quickly came to appreciate American central heating.

I liked England. For the first time my classmates were my age. Unlike the American system, the British one did not require an undergraduate college degree before starting medical school. This was exciting because I could relate to them emotionally. They were as immature as I was. I loved the experience of living in a different culture where everyone ate roast beef and Yorkshire pudding on Sundays and spoke English with a strange accent that made it sound as if they had lockjaw. Best of all I enjoyed having the independence to make my own decisions without consulting anyone else.

Possibly because they liked having a Yank among them, the students made me a member of their club, the Old Dionysians. The initiation was to down a yard of ale. I managed, barely, and then vomited. As reward I was allowed to wear the club necktie. I later discovered that Professor Floyer also was a Dionysian, dating back to his medical school days. He still wore his tie every Wednesday when we met for drinks at a local pub. Any Dionysian who forgot his tie on those occasions was obliged to pick up the bar tab for us all.

My best times, however, were during the third and fourth year of medical school back in Chicago when it felt like we were launched at last on the adventure we had signed up for. By then we were referred to as 'doctor'. When I introduced myself as Dr Silverstein, patients would often smile and say, 'You look like my grandson.' Patients were more comfortable asking questions of younger doctors in case their queries were too inconsequential to ask the attending physicians. I enjoyed responding with authority. I finally felt part of a medical team.

Although I seemed to be all thumbs as soon as I got into the operating theatre, I even enjoyed my surgical rotation. Deciding whether or not someone needed an operation and dealing with the immediacy of emergencies was exciting. However, the reality of the operating theatre put me off. As the most junior member of the team, I was responsible for the surgical retractor, a forklike tool with a long handle used to pull the surgical wound apart so that the surgeon can get inside to operate. I had to stand stock still squeezed between the other medical personnel crowded around the table while making sure the wound stayed open. If I scratched an itch or moved in the slightest, I was yelled at. It wasn't even a good learning experience as I could never get a clear line of sight to what the surgeon was doing. Operations tended to last for hours and hours which made it even more unbearable. Surgery was definitely not for me.

About one week before my graduation in June 1967, the allied Arab forces of Egypt, Jordan, Syria and Iraq prepared to annihilate Israel. This was the beginning of the Six Day War. It was one of the most emotional, nerve-wracking experiences of my life. During the buildup, I spent every spare moment listening to the radio for news. Israel, with its population of one million, had deployed 100,000 troops to defend itself. It was being attacked from all sides by nearly a quarter of a million enemy soldiers. Israel seized the advantage by striking first and taking Egypt by surprise. It launched a series of airstrikes that almost entirely destroyed the Egyptian air force. At the same time a ground offensive pushed the Egyptian troops out of the Sinai. I was deeply stressed as tensions heightened prior to the attacks and throughout the short course of the war. It started on the 5 June and ended on 10 June, the day of my graduation.

On the morning of 7 June I turned on the radio as soon as I woke up and heard the blowing of the *shofar* (a ram's horn traditionally blown during high holidays) by Rabbi Goren, the chief rabbi of the Israeli Defense Forces. He was standing by the Western Wall, the *Kotel*, heralding the recapture of Old Jerusalem. I cried with joy, surprised at how intensely relieved I felt. Since the War of Independence in 1948, the Jordanian government had broken its promise that Jews could pray at this section of the large wall made of Herodian stone that surrounded the Temple Mount complex. I now could look forward to one day praying at the Kotel and touching this last surviving wall of the Jewish Temple in Jerusalem. My class graduated three days later. It was anticlimactic after the emotions of the previous days.

5

DAYS OF TERROR, NIGHTS OF PASSION

I wanted to do my internship away from my home town. I'd always lived in a city and never experienced outdoor adventure. Or any adventure at all, come to that. I decided I should try the West Coast. The traffic and smog in Los Angeles made it a non-starter. I was taken by the beauty of the San Francisco Bay Area and seriously considered Stanford and University of California, San Francisco.

I was twenty-one and staying in student accommodation on the Berkeley campus outside San Franciso. Then I met Ellen at the campus swimming pool. I still remember clearly how she got out of the water and walked over to pick up a towel lying on a chaise lounge not far from where I was sitting. She turned away and began rubbing her back briskly with the towel. From time to time I caught a glimpse of a perfect profile. I was transfixed by every move she made. When she straightened and turned, she saw that I'd been watching her. She inclined her head slightly and ran her fingers through her hair. She had a habit, I was to discover, of doing this when she was nervous. She was the most beautiful girl I had ever seen in the flesh. I struck up a conversation and to my delight she came and sat beside me on the grass. Ellen lived in the Berkeley Hills with her parents. Her father was a research scientist at the Lawrence Berkeley National Laboratory for the U.S. Department of Energy. She was eighteen and still in high school. We agreed we wanted to see each other again.

Then I flew north for an interview at the King County Hospital in Seattle. It was part of the University of Washington program. It was typically grey and rainy when I arrived, but the air was soft and pollution-free. The interviews went well. One of the doctors took the time to point out the state of Washington's attractions such as its wild ocean, magnificent mountain ranges and the high desert to the east. He even made a point of mentioning there were several wondrous days of sunshine every year. The place was unlike anything I had ever known. It might as well have been on the other side of the world. It was the start of a love story with the Pacific Northwest.

I got accepted and loaded up my Pontiac Tempest, which had replaced the red Ford Falcon, and bade farewell to Mom and Dad. I was twenty-two and consumed with excitement at the prospect of my first solo road trip. Like many of my generation I had read Jack Kerouac's *On the Road* and John Steinbeck's *Travels with Charlie*. The West – the Rockies, the Pacific Ocean, the small towns in between where I'd stay in rundown motels – all of it was mine. Driving the open road beneath Montana's big sky for hours at a stretch, I inhaled an intoxicating mix of promise and freedom at every breath. Finally, I reached King County Hospital, which afforded a clear view of the peaks of both the Cascade and Olympic ranges as well as the Puget Sound. I unloaded the Pontiac and checked out my temporary hospital living quarters. Then I grabbed a taxi to catch a flight to San Francisco to deepen my acquaintance with the gorgeous Ellen.

After a four-month hiatus we reunited for a few days of youthful passion and agreed she would fly to Seattle for a longer visit before starting college. She did and was staying with me in my apartment overlooking Lake Washington when Dad phoned from the Seattle airport. 'Surprise! Mom and I thought we'd come and visit.' Ellen and I looked at each other in horror and without a word went into action. We grabbed her toothbrush, makeup and clothes and stuffed it all into her backpack. Then we made the bed and washed the coffee mugs left over from breakfast. Fifteen minutes later Ellen and her possessions had been installed next door at a friend's house. When I got back to my place, I did a quick audit for any tell-tale signs of my libidinous life. The living room and kitchen were spotless. The bed was pristine. The closet bare of feminine garments. There was nothing to indicate Ellen's presence. Or so I thought until I went into the bathroom to wash my hands. There it was. Written in red lipstick on the mirror. *Take the pill.* I was still washing it off when I heard the cab draw up outside and Dad's voice saying, 'Thank you very much, sir. Enjoy your day.'

I wouldn't normally have taken my parents camping given Dad's performance at Zipperstein's every year. He didn't have a cosy relationship with the great outdoors. But I thought it might break the ice with Ellen if we all got together under canvas. I drove us to a campground on Mt Rainier, the tallest mountain in Washington. I was pretty sure they had never been on a mountain let alone slept in a tent. I know for certain they didn't truly relax for even a minute. I told Mom I was going fishing and she said, 'What, no fish in Seattle? I should have packed some kosher fillets from the deli.' I do know they spent the entire trip trying to decide whether I was serious about my girlfriend. My parents' relationship with outdoor adventure was even shorter than my relationship with Ellen.

Like all hospitals, King County adhered to a rigid hierarchy. The department head was at the pinnacle. Beneath him were the attending physicians. These fully qualified doctors were studying to specialize in subjects such as cardiology, geriatrics, infectious diseases, oncology, hematology, pulmonology and critical care. Under the attendings were the fellows and beneath them the residents. They were still students, responsible for the daily care of the patients. They supervised the interns, who carried out the more basic daily care of the patients. The intern was the first to meet new patients, sometimes in consultation with a ward resident. As the patient arrived on the ward, usually from the emergency room, the intern took a history and drew blood while the resident did a physical. King County operated by the old principle that shit flows downhill. Interns were at the bottom of the hill.

The schedule at King County consisted of thirty-six-hour shifts with twelve hours off. We were rotated through the various medical departments: gastroenterology, cardiology, neurology, rheumatology, infectious diseases, hematology, endocrinology and pulmonology. We also did a psychiatric rotation for a month when we were on call every fourth night. We were sent to the emergency room for a month as well. The schedule was twelve hours on, twelve hours off. These were considered our easy rotations.

The resident on my first day at work was Dr Larry Altman. He would later enjoy a rewarding career as a practicing physician as well as the chief medical writer for *The New York Times*. Our paths were to cross again in Kenya when he was writing about the AIDS epidemic. Larry made a name for himself there with his groundbreaking stories. *The Lancet* medical journal was to bill him as 'the unofficial dean of medical correspondents'.

The adrenalin-filled days of the intern were exhilarating. I never knew what to expect when I took a call from the nurses' station. One minute I was dealing with a cardiac arrest and the next I was chasing a hallucinating psychotic patient along the corridors trying to jab him with a sedative. It reminded me of *The Interns*, a popular TV show at the time, with its days of terror and nights of passion. On my first twelve hours off duty I was lucky to find a terrific apartment in Leschi Park, a neighbourhood that fronted onto Lake Washington. My building extended over the water's edge and had a little jetty where I moored the canoe that I soon acquired.

In those days we started the IV drips and did the phlebotomies (drawing blood) in the early morning. We also performed laboratory tests such as blood counts and blood smears and urinalyses in the small laboratories attached to each ward. All this had to be completed before we followed the resident physician on the first round. Another round later in the day was with the attending physicians. I enjoyed the steep learning curve, especially when I played what was called 'roundsmanship'. This consisted of singling out the patients I knew we would visit and reading up all I could on their conditions. This way I impressed the patients and also the attending physician by answering all the questions he threw at me.

These were the early days of intensive-care units before critical care was an established specialty. Ventilators were still a new thing and comparatively primitive. We had just started doing arterial blood gases: tests for acidity, dissolved carbon dioxide and oxygen. Our tools for treating heart attacks were limited to intravenous lidocaine, which is used to suppress arrhythmias. Ventricular fibrillation, a chaotic and ineffective heart rhythm that is fatal unless reversed, was treated with the application of direct-current electroshock as it still is now. We were still in the early stages of decreasing the mortality from heart attacks. But more of that later.

I remember with fondness a patient who required critical care so frequently that we joked he was in danger of becoming a permanent resident of the ICU. Mr Smith was a delightful gentleman lacking any pretension. He was short and chubby, a retired blue-collar worker with a self-deprecating sense of humour. He suffered from multiple problems and a host of accompanying complications. He was in his late fifties and had severe lung disease from smoking as well as coronary artery disease. Despite this he continued to be a dedicated chain smoker and refused to quit. He often asked to be disconnected from the ventilator long enough to have a cigarette. In those days smoking was not only accepted but encouraged. Actors posing as doctors advertised cigarettes for the big tobacco companies, and complimentary sample packs were handed out on airplanes. Many doctors and nurses smoked, even in the hospital.

One morning Mr Smith said there had been a black bird flying around the ICU during the night. Whenever the bird landed on a patient's bed, a team quickly gathered and started pumping on the patient's chest, and after thirty minutes the patient was wheeled out of the ICU with a sheet covering him. He was terrified that the black bird was going to land on him. That night we had three deaths in our ten-bed unit, which was highly unusual. In the morning when he told me about it, he begged me to make sure all the windows were closed. During my twelve months of internship, Mr Smith was a patient in the hospital for at least three of those months. I became extremely fond of him and he was known as 'Dr Silverstein's patient'. His complexity of illnesses and multiple complications taught me more about critical care than I learned at any other time in my career.

It was not uncommon for young doctors and nurses to experience a psychosomatic response to their patients. I treated a patient with scabies and immediately afterward began itching all over my body. Conversely sometimes an illness was real and went unrecognized as happened when I contracted hepatitis B and was seriously ill. I had probably been infected by accidentally jabbing myself when drawing blood from a drug abuser. Hepatitis B was not then treatable. Nor was it distinguishable from the hepatitis A virus. Its symptoms included dark brown urine, light feces, jaundice, nausea, vomiting, low fevers, general malaise and an overall lack of interest in anything. I had all these symptoms for two weeks. You would have thought it might have occurred to me that I was ill, but it didn't. Instead, I grew concerned that for some strange reason I was getting bored with medicine. It was almost a relief when I began to turn yellow. I was seen by Dr Petersdorf, the guru of infectious disease, who was also chief of medicine. He concurred with the diagnosis, discharged me and gave me an additional ten days off duty.

GOMER stands for Get Out of My Emergency Room. Usually this unfortunate label is given to elderly men with poor hygiene, depression, anger and sometimes dementia. They are frequently drunk. My wife Channa, who has practiced in emergency medical settings for decades, believes that this acronym is the result of burnout. Emotionally exhausted doctors and nurses resort to a bit of dark humour to distance themselves from their patients' distress. Were they to stop and consider that the smelly, demanding man in room four who had just messed his pants could be someone's loved one, it would break their hearts. At King County we assigned GOMER points. One for being admitted drunk and unconscious; a second for incontinence and foul smells; a third for falling out of bed. I recall a GOMER who arrived in the ER drunk, stoned and confused. An intern placed a specimen bottle on a shelf for his urine sample, but he chose to use the doctor's bag beside it. He was awarded ten points for that champion performance.

We presented the case to the cardiac surgeon. Surgery was pointless, he said, because drug addicts usually reinfected artificial material such as a replacement valve. Perhaps it was my youthful naivety, but I felt the patient should be accorded every opportunity for survival regardless of his chronic addiction. I researched heart surgeons and discovered Dr J.H. Kay. He was at the University of Southern California and had enjoyed great success operating on candida endocarditis cases. I persuaded the hospital administration to allow me to contact him. To my delight he agreed to take on the case as long as the patient was transferred to the hospital where he worked. It was a complex and expensive undertaking that caused some commotion as King County was going to have to underwrite the entire bill. However, just as I had packed and was set to accompany the patient to California for this dramatic intervention, he threw an infected blood clot to his brain, probably from another valve on the left side of his heart. He died within two hours.

I was outraged by the delays that cost him his life. In my idealism I believed everyone should always be given the best treatment available regardless of their socio-economic profile and the natural history of the disease. If he had not been a drug abuser, they would not have delayed so long. Looking back now after decades of experience I believe that the surgeons' refusal to operate was the right decision. As a drug abuser he would undoubtedly have gotten a prosthetic valve infected in short order and died despite our best efforts.

I took my first small step up medicine's hierarchical ladder in

1968. Forty of us entered the residency program that year. Only two were women. None were people of colour. The doors were not yet open to ethnic, racial and gender diversity. I was still undecided as to which specialty to choose, but a spark was lit during my time in the cardiac and the coronary-care units. Specialties such as endocrinology and rheumatology were intellectually stimulating, but patient care tended to be hands off as effective treatments and procedures had yet to be developed. By contrast, cardiology offered direct involvement in the care of acutely sick patients. The first time I saved someone's life was in a coronary-care unit. After that I had the opportunity to resuscitate patient after patient. It was an empowering feeling to restore life to someone whose heart had stopped. Of course, most of the time our resuscitation attempts were futile. I could accept this knowing that we had made every effort we could to save the patient's life.

What little free time I had was devoted largely to an outdoor world I'd never known in Chicago. Often I invited the girl I was dating to come along. I had many girlfriends and enjoyed being with them, but none of these relationships went anywhere. When I finally got married for the first time at forty-five, I was still not ready to commit to someone.

I enjoyed being far from home and at liberty to do as I pleased. I loved the academic stimulation and attending patients. I enjoyed the companionship of an ever-changing roster of young women, taking the athletic ones canoeing and camping in the mountains beneath a dark green canopy of giant fir trees. I avoided dating Jewish women as I knew this would elicit family pressure to marry. It was the first sign of a commitment phobia that endured well beyond my first marriage. It was a happy and carefree period that ended in July 1969 at the conclusion of my first year of residency.

I was about to be twenty-five and the Vietnam War was at its height. I had enlisted so that I would not be drafted as a private. Signing up voluntarily gave me more rights and freedoms than conscription would have done. I entered the military through the Berry Plan with the rank of captain. It allowed physicians to defer obligatory military service until they had completed medical school and, on the basis of a lottery system, all or part of their residency training.

I had two months to spare before reporting for duty, so I applied for volunteer work in Israel. The state health service, Kupath Cholim, sent me to be a locum for a doctor in Upper Galilee who was going on summer vacation. I was based at Kibbutz Kfar Hanassi and also served as the doctor for three other kibbutzim, a nearby Moroccan village and in a small town called Rosh Pina. I held clinics in each place at least twice a week.

It was an enjoyable time. I had studied Hebrew all my life, and my family spoke it on occasions at home. But this was daily immersion. My command of the language improved by leaps and bounds. My commitment to Zionism became stronger too. The 1967 Six Day War was still fresh in everyone's memory. Israeli patriotism and national confidence were running high. I used my Saturday and Wednesday afternoons off to explore the area, visiting Safed, a centre of Kabbalistic practice (Jewish mysticism), Tiberias and Jerusalem. Israelis are famously informal, and it was easy to strike up friendships in passing. Europeans often comment that Americans and Israelis are similar. There is not much subtlety in the way we communicate. We say what we mean and mean what we say. This isn't such a bad thing.

6

THE VIETNAM WAR

By the time I signed up in the summer of 1969 there were ominous signs that the fighting in Vietnam wasn't going our way. The 1968 Tet Offensive of North Vietnamese attacks on South Vietnam had escalated the war precipitously. Thousands of U.S. soldiers were getting wounded and killed on the battlefield. A lottery had assigned me to the Air Force, which I was happy about as it was my first choice. I requested Southeast Asia as it was inevitable I would be sent there. I also could put in a request where I wanted to be based. A colleague who had recently returned from active duty recommended the U.S. Air Force Hospital at Ching Chuan Kang (CCK) in Taiwan. It was 160 kilometres south of the capital Taipei on the western side of the island. The hospital was under construction and about to come onstream. Few people knew of its existence. For those who did, it was unappealing because spouses were not allowed on the base. I wasn't surprised when the computer found a match between my request and the Air Force's staff for CCK.

The U.S. had entered the war on the basis of the Cold War domino theory that surfaced during the presidency of Dwight D. Eisenhower. If we let the communists take power in Vietnam it would be one of a series of dominos that would fall the wrong way allowing communism to sweep through

Southeast Asia. I respected the opinion of those who didn't support the war on moral grounds. They believed that the U.S. should not get entangled in foreign wars as it resulted in death and destruction. Others opposed the war because its goals were unclear and it was unwinnable. Conscientious objectors sacrificed much to protest. Many went to jail for their efforts. Others sought exemption or deferment, some legitimately and some less so. Young men of means and privilege successfully dodged the draft on flimsy medical pretexts such as bone spurs. As more and more troops were needed, the draft became harder to avoid.

I regarded the draft as an instrument that was imperfect but necessary for equitably distributing the burden of fighting America's wars. As citizens we must step up to the responsibilities of our citizenship. A volunteer military pivots enlistment away from affluent whites toward the poor, the poorly educated and the unduly brave. It also serves to sideline the public from the decision-making process and to still dissent. For all its failings the draft democratizes what is often an undemocratic business.

By 1969 Vietnam had escalated into a conflict with no end in sight. It was the poor who went first. The draft board turned its attention to the young middle class only after there were no longer significant numbers of volunteers to fight. I was one of them. People like me, who were not financially dependent on a job in the military or morally committed to the war, sought meaning in what we were doing. Instead of finding purpose we stumbled over fallacy. We were the ones who informed the journalists and the families back home that this war was wrong.

My induction physical was an intimation of how medics would be treated on active duty. All the recruits had to strip to their underpants and line up. Except for us doctors, that is. We were told to keep our clothes on. We gave blood and urine samples and got an X-ray before being examined by an Air Force doctor.

After a brief chat he asked, 'Do you have cancer?'

'No.'

'Then welcome to the Air Force.' Just about all of us passed, even a pathologist who had cerebral palsy. The thinking was that they could make use of him somewhere.

I was given orders to appear in September for a month's basic training at Sheppard Air Force Base in Wichita Falls. It was a part of Texas so flat it looked ironed – a perfect spot for aviation. Housing on the base was limited so we were put in a Ramada Inn. We had to buy our uniforms with our own money. Part of the wardrobe was a mess dress – the military version of a tuxedo - with its clip-on bow tie, jacket and epaulets, suspenders, formal shirt and studs, cummerbund, slacks and patent-leather shoes. It cost $150 and was to be worn on one occasion only – a formal dinner with the top-ranking officers to mark our graduation from basic training into service. On that particular night I was walking through the bar at the Ramada Inn to get to the dining room when a customer called out to me, 'Waiter, bring me a double scotch.'

Enlisted men were issued 5.56 mm M16 rifles with twenty-round magazines. As captains, doctors were shown how to use a .38 revolver instead. I was never issued a firearm as I was going to be stationed in Taiwan rather than Vietnam. This was just as well as the half-day training was cursory. I had never touched a gun before let alone fired one.

The day before our graduation everyone was taken to the shooting range for a final test. A master sergeant told us we each had to put thirty-four bullets into the target. We would be timed while doing it. This was 'all we had to know' about handling our weapon. He raised his left hand to get our attention. 'But for you doctors I don't have a watch. I count every hole in the target as many times as necessary until I reach thirty-four. The only way you can fail is if you harm yourself or your colleagues while shooting. So please, whatever you do, be careful and welcome to the Air Force.'

One weekend I got a pass to visit Bill Porcher, a roommate from medical school who lived in San Antonio. He was doing his internship there. The first evening I was on my own waiting for him to come home. I was bored so I fetched the radio on the table by his bed. When I picked it up, I found a handgun lodged behind it. A week earlier I would have been petrified even to look at it. Now that I had some target practice under my belt in the company of trained killers, I was emboldened. I picked it up and started playing with it. It was different from the revolver I'd been handling on base, probably a .22 pistol. I figured out it had an ammunition clip, which I removed, but I didn't think to check the chamber. I started fooling around, pretending the Vietcong were coming up the hill after me. I pointed the gun down at the bed and pulled the trigger. *Bang!* The noise reverberated in my head for what seemed to be minutes.

My first thought was of the elderly woman in the apartment below. Had I killed her? Bill was not at home, thank goodness. I called him to apologize for what had happened and to announce my immediate departure on any form of transport that would take me back to Wichita Falls. He wasn't too concerned because, he explained, I had discharged a .22 low-velocity cartridge that couldn't do much harm. He asked me to locate it before I left. After much fruitless searching I cut open the box spring mattress to find it lodged inside. I was ecstatic as visions of being shackled on a charge of manslaughter retreated.

I was sent to Taiwan not long after that. Like many young men of that era, I didn't believe in the war and would never have enlisted had I been given the choice. In my heart of hearts, I believed we were in the wrong. Perhaps because I didn't have skin in the game, throughout my time there I took short cuts where I could. I enjoyed the company of many beautiful women and focused on returning home in one piece. I was not the only one who gamed the system. Because CCK was in Taiwan, President Nixon did not include its personnel in the official number of troops committed to fight the Vietnam War. He used the same trick to obfuscate the personnel based in Thailand and the Philippines. It was illegal. It was immoral. It was war.

CCK served as a rear base for the action in Vietnam. C-130 Hercules transport planes with four-engine Lockheed turboprops, the workhorses of Asia, flew on eighteen-day missions into Vietnam ferrying personnel, supplies, the dead and wounded, and anything else that needed to be moved around the Southeast Asia theatre. Those of us on the hospital medical staff were tasked with tending to the wellbeing of the troops who were stationed on the base. I had been expecting to perform lifesaving procedures dislodging bullets and shrapnel from severely wounded airmen. The reality was the only war-related problem I treated was post-traumatic stress. I was put in charge of the venereal disease clinic and began a research project to determine how best to treat gonorrhea in the face of antibiotic resistance. I wrote a paper on the findings. It appeared in *Military Medicine (1973)*. It was my first publication.

I was eager to discover the delights of Taiwan and Thailand, the favorite R&R destination for servicemen. However, there was a fly in the ointment. Planes were the only way to get around Asia, but I suffered from aviophobia, otherwise known as the fear of flying. On more than one occasion I ended up making a fool of myself because of my crippling anxiety in the air.

According to military rules if I travelled to Vietnam or even flew over it, the first $500 of my salary wasn't liable to tax. The snag was that the pilots had to certify that we had come under enemy fire. I would fly out of CCK to Thailand a couple of days before the end of the month and return at the beginning of the following month thus chalking up a tax-free $1000. Direct military flights were comparatively infrequent while a one-stop trip via Saigon's Tan Son Nhat Airport was much easier to arrange. It was invariably a terrifying experience. One time we landed at Tan Son Nhat in the midst of some enemy shelling. I ordered a drink in the officers' club to steady myself. Just as my nerves were calming down, someone opened a beer can with a loud *pop*! I reflexively hit the floor, eliciting guffaws from my fellow drinkers. On the return flight from Thailand into Tan Son Nhat the captain invited me forward to sit with him on the flight deck. It turned out he wanted a private chat about his gonorrhea. He hoped I could treat it without putting it on his official medical record. I was glad to be promoted from my usual seat in the back of the plane where every little bump scared me. Up front with the crew I was reassured by the relaxed way they handled everything and I soon fell asleep.

Then we hit a storm. Lightning was flashing all around the plane. The passenger next to me, another doctor, elbowed me awake. 'Hey David! Look! There's shooting out of both windows!'

I jumped out of my seat and looked round for a parachute, telling the flight crew, 'Better MIA (missing in action) than KIA (killed in action).' Laughing, they said it was nothing but weather. Once again I felt like a fool.

I was close to dozing off again when I heard through my earphones an air traffic controller asking the pilot to do a

360-degree turn at a certain altitude. Then came, 'Condition Red! Condition Red!'

I was terrified yet again. 'What's this Condition Red business?'

'Oh, this happens every night at this time. They're just shooting up the airport,' the pilot said in a bored voice.

I looked out the window to see tracer fire below. 'What altitude are we flying at?'

'Ten thousand feet.'

'How high can their missiles go?'

'Fifteen to twenty thousand.'

'Let's get the hell out of here!' I was trying not to scream.

'Nah, Doc,' he replied, 'They're not interested in us.'

I didn't believe that for a second. I was getting really agitated when the shelling abruptly stopped. Then Condition Green was declared, allowing us to land without further incident.

I wrote to my father about my little tax scam including some details of my airborne adventures. He was unamused. 'Please work out exactly how much money you're saving by flying into Vietnamese airspace. I'll send you a check for that amount if you promise that you'll never expose yourself to such danger again.' I declined the offer and made a mental note to be more circumspect in my letters home.

The U.S. military had allocated specific bars where soldiers on R&R from Vietnam could drink in the company of the local women. A group of us decided to taste the water away from base where, as officers, we would not be recognized. We took the train to Taipei. My first foray into the delights of sanctioned sin was with two colonels who, as old hands, had offered to introduce me to the Taiwanese social scene. Had we been in Chicago, I would not have considered it for a moment. But behavioural norms fall away in foreign lands during times of war.

The rules of engagement were presented to every private and officer as he entered the premises. They had been drawn up by the U.S. military as an informal contract between bar owners and patrons to ensure everyone was happy and there were no drunken misunderstandings. A soldier was expected to buy at least two drinks for himself and two for the bar girl of his choice. His drinks were alcohol. Hers were dark tea in a whiskey glass. If things proceeded as they always did, he then paid the bar owner a fixed fee for loss of income while the pair enjoyed each other's company elsewhere until the following morning. Any further services rendered were negotiated between the man and his escort.

The two colonels said the plan was to sound out the marketplace by scouting several bars before choosing a partner. I was definitely not to approach the first girl I saw. It made sense, but I was a callow twenty-seven-year-old fresh from basic training. Even Dad's eternally cautionary voice had been stilled as we sat down at a table in the first bar. A gorgeous girl was sitting on a high bar stool a few feet away. My eyes never left her. I couldn't believe my luck. What we were doing was legal and the army was organizing it. Someone came to take drink orders. One of the colonels asked for a beer. The other wanted scotch on the rocks.

'How about you, doctor?'

The girl was smiling at me, tilting her head to one side and crossing and uncrossing her legs. 'Forget the drinks. I want that girl!'

One of the colonels gave me a quizzical look. 'You joking?'

'Certainly not.'

'But you haven't bought her a drink yet.'

'How much am I supposed to spend?'

'Thirty dollars.'

'Okay. Here's the money. I'm leaving with her.'

We all met up the next morning at the officers' club to share our stories. The colonel who had wondered at my overt lust confessed he had been drinking until 2 am and had spent a fortune on watered-down liquor. He said his escort had taken him to her place but vanished when her boyfriend turned up. The other colonel had left with a young woman who had appeared to fall asleep in a drunken stupor the moment she hit the bed. Something had startled her awake a few minutes later and she had run from the room screaming 'Rape!'

I seemed to be the only member of the group who had enjoyed himself. I had taken my date for a real drink or two and dancing before going to my hotel room. She later visited me a couple of times in Taichung in a non-professional capacity. We became friends. In fact, I became the doctor for her mother and grandmother. They both lived in Taichung not far from me.

I realized I would have to learn Mandarin in order to fully understand this new world. I enrolled in a University of Maryland extension-division language class that was offering a dozen credits. 'If you really want to learn the language, find a book with long dark hair,' my instructor advised us. I took his advice to heart. Xiao Ping was a Chinese nurse who worked at the base. She and I were to have a long and serious relationship. I made a game out of learning Mandarin with her. I would master phrases and use them in the local markets. The market people laughed along with me as I tried out new words and expressions. Xiao Ping introduced me to her mother. She spoke no English so it was Mandarin or silence when we were with her. Xiao Ping taught me a lot about Chinese culture: the performing arts, holidays, cuisine and much more. I knew that Xiao Ping was a wonderful partner, but I wasn't mature enough to sustain it. I still could not commit. Besides, she wasn't Jewish.

I hated upsetting my girlfriends by breaking up with them and so had the habit of being infuriatingly evasive about where we stood with each other. Xiao Ping wanted to work in the States. I thought if I helped her realize her dream, it would be an easy way out of the relationship. I bought her a plane ticket and helped her find a good nursing position in New York. That didn't quite conclude matters between us though.

At the end of my tour I was stationed at Travis Air Force Base in Solano County, California for six months. The inevitable happened. I reconnected with Xiao Ping. We took a train to Montana where we visited an Air Force couple we knew from Taiwan. Then we had another holiday together, this time in Jamaica. I still couldn't bring myself to meet her expectations. Despite her tears, I let it fizzle out. Eventually she married another doctor. Xiao Ping helped me grow up a little. It was not quite enough though, as I was to realize later.

One of my favourite discoveries was the trove of ancient Chinese art on display at the National Museum in Taipei that Chiang Kai-shek had 'liberated' from Communist China decades earlier. It stretched across the centuries from the Song Dynasty's sensuous 13th century Bodhisattva statues to the 18th century porcelain plates of the Qing Dynasty. I visited the collection often and came to appreciate its breadth of human faith and creativity. I started taking people from the base on tours of the museum. Since the exhibits changed every few months, there was always something new to learn and share. Until that time I had practically no education beyond medicine. This was a foray into a new and exciting cultural realm. And it was more fun than treating venereal disease.

A group of doctors, dentists, lawyers, pilots and navigators formed a book club. Many of the books we read were modern classics such as Hermann Hesse's *Steppenwolf*, *Zen and the Art of Motorcycle Maintenance* by Robert Pirsig, and *The Kandy-Kolored Tangerine-Flake Streamline Baby* by Tom Wolfe. This too opened my mind to other worlds and other people's emotions and viewpoints. Some of us, like Charlie Clements, a graduate of the Air Force Academy in Colorado Springs, read the assigned books conscientiously. They tended to lead the discussions. These gatherings never failed to be stimulating and enlightening.

Charlie was to become a lifelong friend. He was a lieutenant and C-130 pilot assigned to the 40th Tactical Airlift Squadron. He lived off base in a house he shared with several others. Charlie told me that he had serious concerns about how the U.S. was prosecuting the war. In particular, he was disgusted by the dishonesty of the generals and politicians in charge. He had no intention of publicizing his disaffection. Instead, he was looking for a way to somehow get away from the theatre of war. Meanwhile he was growing anxious about flying, not out of fear that he might crash, but because of his uneasy conscience. He didn't want to participate in what he considered to be an unethical war. His growing uneasiness had started when he saw firsthand the suffering the Americans were causing the Vietnamese without any apparent justification or goal. It came to a head when he recognized the name on the tag of one of the body bags he was loading onto the C-130. It was a friend who had been in the Air Force Academy with him.

As Charlie recounted in his book, *Witness to War*, his experiences made him question some of the assumptions that the U.S. was in Vietnam to save the free world from communism. He saw how the war was killing so many and couldn't rationalize it, declaring he was a conscientious objector. In the autumn of 1970 he was sent to the Brook School of Aerospace Medicine near San Antonio. A senior officer dismissed his moral issues as no more than a temporary slump. 'I'll have you back in Saigon in a week,' he promised.

When Charlie replied that as far as he was concerned the war was over for him, the Air Force locked him up in a psychiatric ward. The following spring an evaluation board declared him afflicted with a 'disabling depressive reaction with mild to moderate social and industrial impairment'. It recommended a psychiatric discharge from the military. As he was only 'ten percent' impaired he did not qualify for a pension. The medicalization of dissent was and is a terrible injustice. Thankfully the U.S. never went as far as the Soviets whose medicalization of dissent was common, but Charlie's case showed us how easily it could happen.

The Vietnam War is still a subject of debate on which historians cannot agree. Some say it was worthwhile as it halted communist expansion and world domination. Others saw it as a tragic waste of American and Vietnamese lives. I certainly believe it was the latter.

7

CHOOSING A SPECIALTY

I left the Air Force in the autumn of 1971 as a major, the same rank as my father when he was demobilized after World War II. My time in the military had been quite an eye-opener. It had sowed the seeds of the wanderlust that eventually led me to Kenya. I went back to academia a changed man with an exotic and exciting world colouring my recent past. It made the return to civilian life a bit dull. The gamesmanship of ward rounds and the eagerness to dazzle that had motivated previous academic years was no longer there. I rotated through various specialties and performed well, but an unwelcome emptiness lurked in the shadows. I needed something to rekindle my passion for life.

In my search for self I studied the *Gemara* (rabbinical commentary) in the Talmud with a Jewish study group led by Rabbi William Greenburg. And I spent a lot of time thinking about what to do next. In the summer of 1972 I started a two-year cardiology fellowship at the University of Washington. It was the next chapter and it buoyed me up with a renewed energy and excitement. It was a hopeful sign.

While I was in Southeast Asia treating mundane conditions such as the common cold and gonorrhea, I had a lot of time to consider what subspecialty I would pursue. I was attracted to the disciplines of endocrinology, hematology and rheumatology for their intellectual stimulation. However, I settled on cardiology because that was where the action was.

At that time adult cardiology in the U.S. was primarily coronary artery disease. So far it remains incurable. All treatment was and continues to be palliative and preventative. Even though some coronary disease is genetically determined, we will never evolve past our susceptibility to such degenerative diseases. From a Darwinian point of view, by the time we develop ischemic heart disease or heart attack problems, we have already fulfilled our biological role. We have reproduced and ensured that our offspring are old enough to survive. When I started my internal medicine residency in the late 1960s, cardiology was a vibrant discipline. The field was advancing quickly and had intriguing potential. For all these reasons, it appealed to me.

Cardiology dates back to the 17th century when William Harvey, an English physician, demonstrated the circulation of blood in the human body. The term itself did not come into general use for two more centuries. In 1816 Dr René Laennac introduced the first stethoscope in Paris. It was a simple wooden tube through which doctors could listen to their patients' heartbeat. The first binaural stethoscopes that could be affixed to both ears came along in the 1850s.

Cardiological technology and techniques advanced slowly due to one of medicine's most durable proscriptions. Larry Altman wrote in *Who Goes First?: The Story of Self-Experimentation in Medicine:* 'Well into the twentieth century, to touch the heart was to molest a sacred area of the body, its spiritual center, and most doctors feared to tamper with it. Even if they had not been afraid of incurring God's wrath, there were seemingly unsolvable physical problems. The heart constantly pumped blood: when cut it bled profusely. How could anyone survive such a hemorrhage?

Furthermore, the heart seemed inaccessible. It lies at most three inches beneath the skin, but it is enclosed by a bony cage of ribs that protects both it and the lungs.'

The first person to devise a successful means of entering the heart through a vein - dispelling its mystique as an impenetrable organ - was a twenty-five-year-old German, Werner Forssmann. In 1929 he was an intern at the Auguste Viktoria House about eighty kilometres from Berlin. His intention was to carefully manoeuvre a catheter along a vein until it reached the heart. Altman, whom the reader will recall was my first resident at King County Hospital, recounted that Forssmann's first step was to secure the necessary instruments and supplies, all of which were kept locked under the care of Gerda Ditzen, a nurse known to Forssmann for her strong interest in medicine. 'I started to prowl around Gerda like a sweet-toothed cat around the cream jug,' he later told Dr Altman. He finally enticed her into helping him with the false promise that she would make history as the first human to have a tube placed in her heart.

They met at midday in an empty operating room. The nurse unlocked the instrument cabinet and produced everything Forssmann required: sterile scalpel, sutures, a rubber urethral tube approximately thirty inches long, a hollow needle and a local anaesthetic. She then climbed onto the surgical table. Forssmann strapped down her arms and legs.

Forssmann moved out of Nurse Ditzen's sight and opened a vein in the crook of his arm. He inserted the hollow needle then threaded the tubing through it. 'The tubing slithered along,' Altman reported. 'There are valves in the veins that close when blood flows away from the heart, but because the tube was moving in the direction of the blood flow, the valves opened naturally and offered no resistance…As he pushed the tube along the course of the vein in his upper arm, he felt a slight warmth, but no pain. Forssmann was learning that nature keeps the veins devoid of pain fibers.'

Forssmann stopped short of pushing the tube into his heart until he could capture the image on the downstairs X-ray machine. To do this he needed Ditzen's help. He approached the surgical table, unstrapped her and said simply, 'It's done.'

'Gerda pushed herself off the table and stared at the tube in Forssmann's arm,' Altman wrote. 'She realized immediately that she had been duped. "She was furious," Forssmann recalled.'

An X-ray technician met them downstairs. Altman continued, 'Forssmann went behind the fluoroscopic X-ray screen and ordered Nurse Ditzen to hold up a mirror so he could look over the screen and see the position of the catheter on the fluoroscope. The two were silent, completely engrossed, as they watched the tube move through Forssmann's vein. Neither noticed the X-ray technician slip out of the room.

'Forssmann jiggled the catheter and inched it toward his heart; still there was no pain, only the continuing feeling of warmth. On one occasion the tube hit something sensitive, for he had an urge to cough. He restrained himself.'

Just then, the technician returned with Dr Peter Romeis in tow. Although Romeis was a friend and supportive of Forssmann's project, he now endeavoured to short-circuit his associate's moment of triumph.

'Romeis tried to pull the catheter from my arm,' Forssmann told Altman. 'I fought him off, yelling, "*Nein. Nein.* I must push it forward." I kicked his shins and pushed the catheter until the mirror showed that the tip had reached my heart. "Take a picture," I ordered. I knew the point was to get radiographic proof that the catheter was indeed in my heart, not in a vein.'

The technician did as Forssmann asked, memorializing the harrowing birth of cardiac catheterization and angiography. A new frontier of cardiology suddenly had opened.

By the mid-1930s Forssmann was married to another doctor and had started a family. His days of self-catheterization were over. Yet his notoriety continued to bedevil him. Seeking work as a urologist and surgeon, he was told by one prospective employer that they feared if he was willing to perform dangerous procedures on himself, what might he attempt on a patient?

There ensued an ill-considered decision to join the ascendant Nazi party where, as Altman pointed out, Forssmann could have unlimited access to 'the best available scientific equipment and plenty of human guinea pigs with whom to carry on his research.'

Forssmann declined. 'To me,' he told Altman, 'defenseless patients as guinea pigs was a price I'd never be prepared to pay for the realization of my dreams.'

Later forbidden to practice medicine because of his fascist connections, Forssmann was eventually reinstated and found work in a German community unfamiliar with his former infamy. Yet his bold success with catheterization did not fade into obscurity. Beginning in the late 1930s in New York City the doctors André Cournand and Dickinson Richards began inserting heart catheters into dogs and chimpanzees with the aim of measuring the concentration of gases in the blood as it flowed through the heart and lungs. They discovered dramatic changes. By the 1940s they had devised a way to measure these fluctuations in humans, first on the right side of the heart, then in the pulmonary artery. In 1956 Cournand and Richards, along with Forssmann, were awarded the Nobel Prize for Physiology or Medicine.

In 1952 the first commercially available closed-chest heart defibrillator was developed by Soviet cardiologist Naum

Lazarevich Gurvich of the appropriately named Moscow Institute of Reanimatology. In 1953 cardiologist Inge Edler and physicist Carl Helmuth used a so-called ultrasonic reflectoscope from the Siemens Corporation to produce the first heart images using sound waves. The age of echocardiography – today a ubiquitous diagnostic tool – was at hand.

Five years later a serendipitous error committed in the basement catheterization laboratory at the Cleveland Clinic sparked the momentous discovery of angiograms - the birth of modern cardiac imaging. Mississippi-born cardiologist F. Mason Sones Jr was at work in the lab one morning, preparing to take an aortagram of a thirty-six-year-old male patient suffering from rheumatoid arthritis. As contrast dye was being injected via a catheter into the man's aorta, the tip of the tube skipped into his right coronary artery, sending a huge amount of dye into the narrow vessel. It was a certain death sentence, or so Dr Sones believed. 'We killed him!' the doctor yelled as he prepared to open the man's chest and, if possible, hand massage his heart back into operation. Yet the patient's heart only stuttered then quickly resumed beating normally.

Sones and his assistants had suddenly and accidentally demonstrated that the small vessels surrounding the heart are susceptible to imaging thus allowing doctors to directly detect the presence or absence of atherosclerosis and to devise treatments accordingly. These include cardiac bypass surgery, the radical new intervention first performed by Argentinian Dr René Favaloro in 1967, the year I graduated from medical school. Favaloro later said, 'Without the work of Dr Mason Sones Jr – the most important contributor to modern cardiology - all our efforts in myocardial revascularization would have been fruitless.'

The early 1960s saw the proliferation of coronary-care units in hospitals everywhere. The aim was to consolidate the advances in heart imagery, surgery and drug therapy into a single intensive-care facility where the key factor of time lost between the onset of a cardiac episode and an intervention could be radically abbreviated. Thus patients who might otherwise have suffered severe, long-term disabilities or death had a good chance of survival. It was cardiology fused with emergency medicine, and I very much wanted to be part of it.

I received excellent mentoring in that first year and threw myself into the clinical work in the cath lab. No procedure, no matter how many times I performed it, became routine. There was always an adrenaline rush, especially when we were being taught some of the more complex and delicate maneouvres such as transseptal punctures in which a needle within a catheter is poked through the atrial septum from the right atrium to the left atrium. You never know whether you've done it successfully until you see the left atrial pressure curve on the catheterization monitor tracing and confirming that you've withdrawn oxygenated – bright red – blood. When performing this procedure my emotion swung from near panic to immediate elation. *Eureka!*

The chief of cardiology during my fellowship was Dr Robert A. Bruce, known for his work in treadmill testing. This standard exercise protocol bears his name, the Bruce Protocol. Dr Bruce was reluctant to let us know how much vacation we could take hoping that in the absence of guidelines we would not take any at all. That would have been my reaction before my military experience, but now I had the wonder of the world calling me.

My Air Force friend, Charlie Clements, the conscientious objector, had spent a considerable amount of time travelling alone around the Pacific as a deckhand after leaving the military. He had done odd jobs while considering what his next steps should be. He had reflected at length on the meaning of pacifism as preached by Gandhi, Martin Luther King Jr and the Quakers and how they spoke truth to power. In the midst of trying to figure it all out, he took a job teaching physics at the newly opened University of the South Pacific. The campus was in Suva, the capital of Fiji. He invited me to come over. I didn't hesitate.

We did some hiking and poled down a small river on a bamboo raft Charlie had lashed together on the spot. I remember the thrill of riding bareback in the surf. Charlie took a photo of me cantering down the beach, the horse's hooves throwing up sunlit droplets of ocean. He made it into a poster.

By far the most memorable adventure was a visit to a village in the interior. It was noteworthy in Fijian history as the site of the island's last known act of cannibalism. The villagers were welcoming and honoured us with their traditional kava ritual. The chief offered each of us a bowl of murky liquid extracted from the roots of the kava plant. We were told it had anaesthetic and sedative properties. I was worried I might vomit or start laughing, but I managed to gulp it down without embarrassing myself.

While we fell under the spell of the kava, the chief recounted how his grandfather, also a chief, had admired a missionary's comb. He had grabbed it and stuck it in his hair. When the missionary snatched the comb back he unwittingly committed the capital offence of touching the chief's head. The punishment was death – Fijian style. The missionary was summarily killed, cooked and consumed.

Charlie finished his tour of the South Pacific and went on to work in New Zealand before deciding to become a medical doctor. After taking the requisite pre-med courses, he was accepted at the University of Washington School of Medicine. To save money, he moved in with me. The deal was that Charlie cooked, I did the dishes and paid most of the rent. By the end of my first year of fellowship I was ready for another adventure and asked Charlie for ideas.

'If you want to have a good time,' he said, 'go to the Cook Islands. Try to get to the one called Aitutaki.' He left it to me to figure out the rest.

I had no idea of the Cook Islands' location and neither did the woman at the travel agency. When I at last managed to locate the islands on the map, it was easy to see why they were unknown to the rest of the world. They were a tiny bunch of dots in the vast blue of the South Pacific Ocean. They weren't near anything except each other. The Cooks were known in the West for being visited by Captain Bligh and his crew aboard HMS *Bounty* not long before the infamous mutiny. Bligh travelled 4000 miles in an open boat with a few loyal seamen to Timor. It was the nearest land. It took the desperate party six weeks.

Tourists still hadn't discovered the Cooks at the time I visited. I spent two nights on the main island of Rarotonga and was charmed to hear my name announced as the local radio station broadcast a list of the visitors who'd arrived by air that day. On the third day I boarded a Britten-Norman Islander for the fifty-minute hop north to Aitutaki. The island was eighteen square kilometres, hemmed with white sand beaches. It had an exquisite turquoise lagoon. The only car was the island's lone taxi. Otherwise everyone walked, cycled or rode a motorbike. I was the only tourist there. I took the taxi into town, sharing the ride with the local doctor. When I told him I was a cardiologist, he asked if I could hold a clinic. I said I would love to.

The cardiac clinic went well. Islanders with heart problems came to be examined. I didn't accept payment. To show their thanks many of the people dropped fresh fish off at my room at the government hostel over the coming days. I was beginning to understand why Charlie didn't elaborate on why I should visit Aitutaki. I probably would not have believed him.

The second evening I met an American in his mid-sixties who was in the company of a young Maori woman. 'Who's your girlfriend on this island?' she asked. We were at a stilt-dancing festival. Contestants had been drawn from all the villages, and a good crowd of supporters had come to cheer them on.

'I don't have one. I just arrived.'

'Is there anyone you see you find attractive?'

I found them all attractive. I pointed out one particular girl who was standing with her hand on her hip and laughing.

'No, no, no. She's too old for you! She's twenty-five.'

'That doesn't sound so terrible. I'm twenty-eight.'

'No, no. Let me introduce you to someone more age appropriate.'

She fixed me up with a twenty-one-year-old. She kept me company for the seven or eight days I spent in Aitutaki. We had a great time.

I returned to Seattle in the summer to resume my fellowship, some months before the Yom Kippur War of October 1973. The conflict created anxious moments among friends and supporters of Israel, myself included. We had naively come to believe that Israel was militarily invincible. Although the Jewish state was once more triumphant, Egypt and Syria proved to be far worthier opponents this time around.

I donated a quarter of my income that year to the cause via the Jewish Federation. There also was an appeal for doctors to stand in readiness to attend to Israel's wounded soldiers. I signed up. Dad, then sixty-eight, volunteered as well despite his age and two heart attacks. Neither of us was called, and a line was drawn under my military career. One year later I was in Nairobi.

8

KARIBU KENYA

When my cardiology fellowship finished in June 1974, I had to figure out what came next. It was a question that most fellows, eager to launch their careers, had been addressing for at least a year. I **had procrastinated**. The simplest option would have been to join a medical practice and become established as a cardiologist, maybe in Seattle where I had studied. That choice offered professional and financial security as well as interesting medical challenges.

However, my Dad's history of heart attacks shadowed my thinking and made me conflicted. I liked the prospect of a stable career where I worked my way to the top of my chosen profession. I could serve my patients while satisfying a need to achieve excellence in everything I did. On the other hand, it was the 1970s when everyone was discovering themselves. And my life might be short, I rationalized. The freewheeling spirit of the 1960s had ushered in an era of free love and political protest. People my age were dropping out and getting high to Marvin Gaye and Bob Dylan. A part of me longed to be reckless and without responsibilities for a few years before settling down.

I discussed the situation with Charlie Clements. I think he saw in me, the footloose bachelor, a chance to live out his fantasies vicariously. One evening he and I were on the back porch drinking gin martinis and reminiscing about the war. We were laughing a lot, trying to cap each other's stories of bar girls we'd known and bullets we'd missed. Late night traffic and the oboe croak of bull frogs riffed in the background. It was a perfect night for sharing unguarded thoughts and wild dreams.

Suddenly Charlie stopped laughing. 'You know David, coming home to a hot dinner and a warm bed every night is great but…' He was staring straight ahead as if he could see something moving in the darkened trees on the other side of the fence. Then he shook his head and scratched at something in his ear. 'Sometimes I feel that I'm missing out on life, you know? There's so much out there to find out about. Places and people that aren't like us. Do you ever think that?'

'You mean shedding all the stuff we grew up with and the plans I'd made for a regular, middleclass life? Are you talking about having adventures in places that are so far away we've never even heard of them? Yes, Charlie, I have.'

I pictured myself free as a bird, travelling the world with just a backpack. I wanted to make up for all those years in the shadow of my family before the early death I dreaded tripped me up. It was a seductive fantasy but only that. The dream ignored a deep-rooted feature of my personality. I'm a workaholic, and I require a structure within which to function. So with that important consideration in mind, I set out to achieve my version of youthful rebellion, creating a life and identity distinct from the family I loved and the man I admired most in the world. This did not preclude expressing my hippy yearnings. I grew long hair and a beard and dressed the part as well. No coat and tie for this creature of the counterculture.

I had two requirements. I needed a cardiac catheterization laboratory to serve as my institutional affiliation to pursue what

I believed was, and would continue to be, the most interesting work in cardiology. After some consideration and conversations with friends, I narrowed my search to three possibilities. The University of the South Pacific was hiring. It sounded like a ticket to paradise. Israel appealed for its cultural and religious pull and because I spoke Hebrew. Then there was Kenya, suggested by Dr Ashvin Patel, who was to become a dear lifelong friend. He was a cardiology fellow at the University of Washington whom I had met while he was recovering from typhoid. Ashvin was a Kenyan of Indian descent from Nairobi. He had done his internship at Kenyatta National Hospital. He was familiar with the city's medical establishment and described the professional opportunities in Nairobi in glowing terms. I'd find the medical community so relaxed, he said, it would melt the cholesterol plaque in my arteries. I sent inquiries in all three directions.

When I was eleven my parents had taken me to see the movie *South Pacific*. It had made a great impression and fired my imagination. On the way home, I'd exclaimed, 'Wow, what if I move there and marry a beautiful girl from the islands?' Mom had said, 'That would be fine…as long as she's Jewish.' Dad had taken her seriously. 'Sarah, don't get carried away!' But my childhood dream was not to be. The University of the South Pacific offered me deanships for its medical, dental and nursing schools and what was termed in the letter as 'the mosquito school'. There was no mention of a cath lab. They didn't have one and didn't plan on acquiring one any time soon.

Then there was Israel. I was a Hebrew speaker who knew the country well. I sympathized with the national imperative to safeguard the rebirth of an independent Jewish state. I was invited to the Ben Gurion University at Be'er Sheva in the south Negev Desert. I flew over to inspect the facility and meet the chief of the department of medicine. If I would be interested, he said, I could be the second in charge of the coronary unit. The university was only five years old. As yet there was no cardiac cath lab, but it was a future possibility. Be'er Sheva was not then the busy metropolis it has become, and the prospects for practicing the kind of cardiology I wanted to do were uncertain.

I was tempted but in the end the deal breaker was the climate. It was August and the heat was unbearable. I lay on my hotel bed at night sweltering next to an ineffective air conditioner as I pondered the pros and cons of living in a desert where temperatures reached 38º C and above. The culprit was the *khamsin*, a gale force wind that blew for hours on end dumping sand it had brought from the Arabian Desert. Khamsin is derived from the Hebrew word for fifty, *chamishim,* so called for the number of days it occurred each year. With some regret I crossed Israel off the list too. If you can't stand the heat, get out of the kitchen.

That left Kenya. I had applied for a teaching position at the University of Nairobi's School of Medicine because I knew they were getting a cath lab. After six months of silence, I received a telegram followed by a letter informing me that a new cardiac cath lab was en route to Kenyatta National Hospital, the teaching hospital affiliated with the university. Could I start immediately as a lecturer? This was roughly equivalent to an assistant professorship in the U.S. I would be under a two-year contract at Kenyan pounds 2500 a year (about $6200) and live rent-free in university housing. I had heard about the Milbank Foundation which awarded grants to American educators in Africa. I applied and received an additional $5000 a year. It was a welcome boost to my modest finances. This combined income was a fraction of what I might have earned elsewhere, but the excitement and challenge of living and working in Africa clinched the deal.

I was aware that nearly all African countries had once been colonies and had achieved independence during the previous two decades. Otherwise I knew little about sub-Saharan Africa. I consulted an atlas, recalling from geography lessons it was on the west coast of the continent. To my surprise, it was where it has always been – in East Africa facing the Indian Ocean. It was a sad reflection on my primary school education. At that point Africa really was the 'Dark Continent' as far as I was concerned. My misconceptions were banished when, two months later, I stepped onto the cracked tarmac of Nairobi's Embakasi Airport.

Nairobi was a fledgling metropolis with a population of less than a million. It was 1800 meters above sea level and lushly verdant. Not far out of town lay the eastern escarpment of the Rift Valley with its breathtaking vistas of volcanoes and lakes shimmering in the heat haze. The city was one degree south of the equator which meant the seasons were marked by the rains and the dry months rather than by winter and summer. Daybreak arrived at 6.30 am in the morning. Night fell like clockwork twelve hours later the year round.

The city was much quieter in those days. At the roundabouts uniformed policemen in white gloves conducted the traffic from raised podiums. They looked as if they were calling on each section of the orchestra to perform. Some of the streets in the suburbs were unpaved. Many people walked or rode bicycles. You'd also see people driving donkey carts. Volkswagens and Peugeots were popular as were Toyotas and Renaults. If they could afford it, most Kenyans travelled in public buses or privately operated minivan taxis known as *matatus. Tatu* was Swahili for three. When matatus were introduced in the 1960s, the fare was thirty cents. Arriviste Kenyan businessmen and politicians favoured the Mercedes Benz. They were referred to, with a touch of envy, as *wabenzi* (the Mercedes Benz people).

Uhuru Highway was the town's main artery delivering imported goods from the Indian Ocean port of Mombasa to Nairobi as well as people such as myself who had just flown in from abroad. It was a memorable arrival. I have a vivid picture of being driven past a profusion of lilac-coloured jacaranda trees. The highway was lined with them. The Hilton Hotel, which had only recently opened its doors, was one of the few buildings higher than three stories. Kenyans' almost universal civility was a mix of African deference and British good manners. The flip side of this proper behaviour were the night clubs and strip joints. I was introduced to them by Professor Ed Knight. He was West Indian and the only cardiothoracic surgeon in the country at the time. Once a month he held Academic Night at the Sombrero, a popular and rowdy strip joint of note. These get-togethers provided an opportunity for the hospital's senior clinical medical staff to let their hair down and get drunk while watching the show.

Nairobi National Park abutted the city. Its more than 100 square kilometres of grass plains and riverine forest contained all manner of wildlife including lion, leopard, cheetah, giraffe, Cape buffalo, zebra and different species of antelope. During droughts the Maasai drove their cattle herds into town to graze the municipal grass on the roadside. The Europeans kept horses in the suburb of Karen. It had been named for the Danish author Karen Blixen who started a coffee farm there before World War I. Her book *Out of Africa* evoked Kenya's untrammelled spirit personified in her love affair with Denys Finch Hatton, a glamorous English aristocrat and professional hunter. It was a staple for all new arrivals and had yet to be turned into the Hollywood blockbuster starring Robert Redford and Meryl Streep. Lions and leopards from time to time slipped into a suburban garden in search of a cow or dog. You could drink from the municipal water supply without worrying about typhoid. There was an air of innocence and hope about the place with the edges blurred between past and future.

It would be years before the crime rate shot up, earning the city the sobriquet Nairobbery. Kenyans were not to be held solely responsible for this. As civil war and unrest engulfed the neighbouring states of Uganda, Ethiopia, Somalia and Sudan, so small arms flowed across the border into Kenya. Over the past two decades acts of terrorism have added to the insecurity. But in 1974 there was little violent crime. Petty theft, by contrast, was common. Pole-fishers, as they were known, stuck long sticks through open windows in the hopes of retrieving a handbag or jewellery carelessly left on a table. If burglars were armed, it was with *pangas* (machetes). In those days a sign on the gate reading *Mbwa Kali Sana* (Very Fierce Dog) was considered sufficient deterrent against intruders.

Kenya had gained independence ten years earlier following an uprising led by a movement called the Mau Mau. The ranks of the rebellion were drawn largely, but not solely, from among the Kikuyu, Meru and Embu people who lived on the well-watered massif of Mt. Kenya. The British had encouraged European farmers to settle on this land during colonial times. When the British flag was lowered for the last time, it was feared there would be a bloodbath, triggered by African expectations to have their land returned. The anticipated chaos never happened. Kenyans were fortunate with their first leader. Jomo Kenyatta was a man with an unusual breadth of vision who had studied at the London

School of Economics in the 1930s. On taking over the helm of the nation, he shunned the Soviet bloc and aligned Kenya with NATO, Britain and the United States.

The mood in Nairobi was upbeat. Britain, the U.S., the World Bank and other Western donors drew up programs for development aid. The flow of capital brought with it the promise of prosperity. The future looked bright, peopled with a generation of young Kenyans eager to be trained in all sectors of the economy and essential services including, of course, the medical world.

In the last fifty years there has been significant progress, particularly in the health sector. Medical diagnosis and treatment in both the public and private sectors have greatly improved. Kenyans now have better medical care and live longer than they did during colonial times. I am proud to have played a part in making this happen. However, when I first arrived in Kenya my concerns were more immediate. I wanted to see the new cath lab that I would be running. Kenya had never had a cath lab. Neither had there been a fully trained cardiologist until I came along.

9

SETTING UP SHOP

In a strange coincidence Professor Michael Floyer, the rugby fanatic whom I'd first encountered as a third-year medical student at the Royal London Hospital nine years earlier, was now the chief of medicine at the University of Nairobi. Professor Floyer met me at the airport when I arrived and took me to the Milimani Hotel where I stayed for my first week in the city. As we became acquainted, Floyer took the time to familiarize me with the extremes to which our medical colleagues sometimes resorted to advance their agendas. I remembered this lesson years later when professional brinkmanship nearly ruined my reputation.

A senior lecturer named Dr Hillary Ojiambo had been angling for a professorship at the University of Nairobi, Floyer told me. His goal was to become the head of the Department of Medicine. The same month I had arrived his wife Dr Julia Ojiambo had won a seat in parliament and had been appointed an assistant minister in the Kenyatta cabinet. A Nigerian cardiologist named Dr Chepkwameka, who lectured in the department of medicine, had also announced his candidacy for the position. Chepkwameka soon received anonymous telephone death threats. Fearing for his life, Chepkwameka abruptly departed Kenya for a job with Ciba-Geigy in Switzerland. Ojiambo soon realized the professorship was beyond his grasp and accepted a job in Zambia. And so it was that when I started lecturing in the division of cardiology, I was the sole member of staff.

The day after I arrived in Kenya I asked Professor Floyer to show me the cath lab. I was excited to think that soon I would be doing cardiac catheterizations. With the exception of South Africa, it would be the first time this procedure could be performed in sub-Saharan Africa. I couldn't wait to see it in all its glory and open for business in its state-of-the-art, gleaming newness. I was puzzled when he suggested that first I settle in. Unpack, find someone to cook and clean for me, get a car. I would need a few lessons in driving on the left-hand side of the road. He seemed to be playing for time. I couldn't figure out why.

Mrs Floyer offered her services as an instructor. I thought I was up to the challenge until I nosed Mrs Floyer's car into the traffic jam on the Uhuru Highway roundabout where it joined Kenyatta Avenue. It was Nairobi's main intersection. Mrs Floyer screamed and covered her eyes with her hands as I made a wrong turn into the oncoming traffic. I slammed on the brakes and sheepishly shifted into reverse to a chorus of honking horns. Once I'd successfully steered us through a roundabout or two, I was irrationally confident that I had East African driving mastered. A pale Mrs Floyer enthusiastically agreed – anything to cut short the lesson – and drove me home at once.

I found a Volkswagen Variant for Kenya shillings 40,000 ($6000). It was outrageously expensive because of the stiff Kenyan import tariff. I couldn't manage the price tag so once again called on my friend Ashvin Patel. Within the hour I was drinking coffee with his sister Sureka and brother-in-law, Dr Yashvent Patel, while I explained my problem.

'*Keine taklif nati*,' Yashvent said in Gujarati, a western Indian language spoken in Kenya. 'No problem. I'll take you to meet my banker tomorrow morning at nine when the Bank of Baroda opens.'

The next morning I received a lesson in conducting business the Kenyan way. The meeting started with a ten-minute conversation in Gujarati between Yashvent and the bank manager, Mr Desai. Next Desai barked down the phone in Gujarati to an underling. The negotiations were now complete, and tea was brought. As we were being served, Mr Desai pulled a file from his desk drawer and asked me to review it. I saw at once it was a medical workup for his heart problem. I read it over and discussed it with him. Then an Indian man of about thirty, whom I presumed had been on the other end of the phone, entered Desai's office carrying several documents for my signature, ten temporary check books and a bank statement showing I had been issued a line of credit for Kenya shillings 40,000.

No one asked a single question about my finances - income, debt, investment portfolio, nothing. Desai simply welcomed me as a new customer having judged me by association alone as an honorary member of Ashvin's family. I stayed with the Bank of Baroda for the next twenty-five years.

Next on the arrival check list was getting my domestic life in order. The university provided me with a spacious three-bedroom flat across the street from the Milimani Hotel and around the corner from State House, which contained the presidential offices and residence. Typical of apartments built in the first decade of independence when land was still comparatively cheap, it was part of a three-block complex, each three stories high, with two apartments on each floor. Each unit came with a veranda that overlooked a parking lot and a large, well-kept garden of trees and bushes. My landlord was Mwai Kibaki, Kenya's minister for finance. He was later to become the vice president and ultimately the president of Kenya for two five-year terms.

I employed a man named Gradus Onyango as my cook and housekeeper. He was in his early forties, an ethnic Luo from Lake Victoria. Onyango had his eccentricities. Some were amusing, others less so. Hanging in my closet was the formal mess dress that I had worn only once at Sheppard Air Force Base. Onyango liked to wear it when washing my car. As the months and years went by the once crisp uniform became worn and torn until Onyango began to look like an outlandish cartoon character performing a skit.

Onyango liked to dip into my whiskey from time to time. Invariably this happened when I was throwing a dinner party. I had an inbuilt sobriety barometer that read his condition by the angle of the serving dishes he was carrying as he appeared through the kitchen door. Afterwards, angry and disappointed, I would call him out on being drunk on the job. Onyango was unperturbed. 'Lakini Bwana, sijaanguka. But Sir, I didn't fall over.' Onyango lived in a room behind the apartment blocks in a staff dormitory. He went home to his family for one month's leave a year. He remained in my employ until his death twenty years later. He was hard working, kind and loyal.

Finally the day came when Professor Floyer suggested he take me to look at the cath lab. When we got to the hospital, he headed toward a recently completed two-story building where a number of specialties were to be housed. As well as cardiology there were spaces assigned to general internal medicine, an electroencephalogram laboratory and consultants' offices.

The cath lab was on the first floor. It was a large, airy space with two offices and a waiting room. My God! I thought as I looked around. It was empty save for an ECG (electrocardiogram) machine operated by a hospital groundsman called Baraza. He had been promoted from tending the flower beds. In due course he was properly trained in the cardiology lab. He flourished in his new calling and eventually was sent to England to be trained as a lab technician.

Floyer whisked me away at once to the academic lounge, a large room adjoining the dean's office where tea and coffee were served. My expression must have betrayed me because my new colleagues, most of them older European men, did their best to calm me down. 'Listen David,' I was told, 'This is the Third World. Relax. Enjoy yourself.'

Appalled as I was by the phantom cath lab, lecturing to the students was a pleasure. My classes were made up of third- and fifth-year medical school students as well as the postgraduate residents working for their master's degree in medicine. They were attentive and grateful for what I taught them. I still hear from former students who remember my lectures as a high point in their medical education. I, in turn, think back on my time with those budding doctors as among the most gratifying and fulfilling moments of my medical career.

The only issue was my American accent. They were accustomed to British English and sometimes had trouble following what I was saying. They also had to adjust to my appearance, which strayed from the conventional academic garb I had been obliged to wear for work back in the States. I favoured flowered shirts picked up in the Pacific before moving on to boldly patterned Kenyan kitenge shirts. One of my outfits was a bark cloth shirt I had bought on my trip to Aitutaki in the Cook Islands. I became more hirsute too. My hair was several inches longer and the signature moustache had sprouted into a goatee that soon became a full beard. The students shrugged and put it down to being American. They enjoyed the informality as well as the jokes I cracked.

Philip Reese, a British physician specializing in tropical medicine, tried his best to raise my sartorial standards. He even took to wearing a tie as a belt to encourage me to put one round my neck. In due course when Philip and I went into private practice at about the same time, I realized that image counted a lot when you are the new boy on the block. I invested in some bespoke suits made to measure. Philip's, I believe, were off the peg.

Meanwhile I had discovered that for some reason the cath lab equipment had yet to be delivered. The machinery was to come from the manufacturer, Philips in the Netherlands, as part of a Dutch aid package. By the time I arrived, it was already out of date. It was less than state-of-the-art but adequate for our needs. It was around this time that a story appeared in the local press about a fundraiser for a young woman from President Kenyatta's Gatundu constituency. She needed money to travel to London for urgent heart surgery. Kenyatta himself presided over the occasion. According to the article, he asked the crowd a rhetorical question. 'Why can't we do this ourselves?'

If he had asked me, I would have replied, 'We can. As soon as the cath lab is up and running.' The story planted a seed in my mind. If the occasion arose, I would use the President's comment to leverage action to get the lab established.

A week later I was summoned urgently to a meeting called by Dr Jason Likimani in response to President Kenyatta's call for a cath lab. He wanted to discuss how to fast-track one into operation. Jason was a Maasai and one of the first African doctors in Kenya to be trained in England. He had practiced there for a time before returning to Kenya shortly after independence. The president had appointed him as the first African Director of Medical Services in the Ministry of Health. He was an excellent chair at meetings, offering insightful comments and suggestions. At this particular meeting Likimani turned to me. 'Why aren't we doing surgery?' I explained we couldn't without the proper diagnostics, which could only be provided by a cardiac cath lab. He directed me to get the lab up and running immediately but offered no guidance as to how a young American doctor, who had been in the country for only ten days, should go about it. Taking a tip from my time in the military, the first thing I did was examine the chain of command. I was employed by the university, but the cath lab came under the jurisdiction of the Ministry of Health. I turned for guidance to Dr Wallace Kahugu, the ministry's chief physician.

He conferred on me full responsibility and a free rein to establish the cath lab any way that I could. His only imperative was to 'proceed with vigour'. I telephoned Philips in Eindhoven. The machines had been ordered and were ready, but the company had never received shipping instructions.

'Send them!' I said and they did.

Philips sent a German engineer named Dieter Kuschel to assess the situation before the machines were installed. He said to me, 'You have a problem. Whoever designed this building didn't take into the account the weight of the machinery. The way it is now, everything you've ordered will fall through the floor.'

Undaunted I contacted a structural engineer in the Ministry of Works and asked him if there was any remedy. After examining the building, he concluded the only solution would be to build a retaining wall underneath the lab. Unfortunately, the wall would bisect the medical records office, meaning a doorway would have to be cut to allow the clerks to pass back and forth.

I made an appointment with an administrator at the Ministry

of Works and explained to him what needed to be done. He pondered the matter for a minute or two then informed me the project would require six months to a year to complete. I asked him for his name and reminded him of President Kenyatta's recent statement that Kenya needed the wherewithal to perform cardiac surgery. Beads of sweat appeared on the administrator's forehead.

When next we spoke he said the wall could be completed in a month. Much to my delight it was completed in one week. In the early 1970s, if you understood the system and knew the right people, you could cut through the tangle of bureaucratic red tape and achieve things much more quickly than in the West. That still holds true today.

By the time the cath lab machines had arrived at the airport, the wall had been completed. A team of Philips engineers took two weeks to install the machines. By the end of December, two months after my arrival in Nairobi, the cath lab was in business. It was around this time that Hillary Ojiambo, who had not been long in Zambia, renewed his campaign to become a full professor at the Department of Medicine as well as a full professor of medicine at Nairobi University. 'You're doing a great job. Keep it running for me until I get back,' he told me on one of his visits back home. These were my first lessons in working in Africa. The cath lab experience taught me that rarely do things go by the book.

10

THE BLUE BABY

Some say that much of what happens to you in life is down to luck. I would say it's a mix of skill, wisdom, hard work and chance. I couldn't know it at the time, but an encounter with a nurse in a VA hospital set in motion events that were to save several lives. I knew her only as Jimmy. We got to chatting while I was in the cath lab looking for a cardiac catheter to use on a dog as part of a research experiment. I shared with her my excitement over my new job in Kenya. Jimmy knew that medical supply shortages were a chronic problem in Africa. She began saving used catheters for me. Normally they are not to be re-used, but Jimmy washed and sterilized them so thoroughly they were almost good as new. I stashed all of them in my luggage.

I would soon learn that supply problems frequently shut down whole departments at Kenyatta National Hospital. In my case, catheters were a particularly trying problem as we used them in bulk. They were ordered from England and often took a month to arrive. At such times I was especially grateful for Jimmy's cache of scrupulously sterilized catheters.

Ischemic heart disease – the narrowing or closure of the coronary arteries that feed the heart muscle – is the most common cardiovascular illness the world over. It is characterized by chest pain with exertion, heart attacks or a type of sudden death syndrome in which changes in a patient's heart rhythm are fatal unless corrected by the administration of electric shock. Back in the 1970s my patients rarely presented with it. The exception was Nairobi's substantial Asian community. They often suffered stress-induced heart attacks in their thirties and forties, an unusually early age. When taking down the case histories, the patients talked about marriages that had been arranged by elder relatives, which was the custom among Asians. It caused emotional, social and economic complications for all involved, especially the newlyweds.

The first African Kenyan who was thought to be suffering a heart attack was a man in his early fifties in the ICU. I was called to attend him because of a 'suspicious' ECG. On examination I found he was exhibiting some ECG changes consistent with, but not diagnostic of, a heart attack. These changes can also be associated with pericardial disease in the sac that lines the heart. Echocardiograms at the time were not available in Nairobi so I carefully inserted a wide-bore hollow needle from below the diaphragm into the space between the sac and the heart muscle. The substance I removed resembled anchovy paste. It was pus from an amoebic abscess. These abscesses can appear almost anywhere in the body, even the brain. This poor fellow's abscess was in his liver. It had ruptured into the pericardium and sent him into shock.

As it happened some Japanese cardiothoracic surgeons were working in the Kenyatta National Hospital (KNH) as part of an aid program to help set up the ICU. They agreed to open him up to clean out the pus. Unfortunately, because of delays in getting him to the hospital and into the ICU for the procedure, his blood pressure had plummeted to dangerously low levels and remained there for so long that he had lapsed into kidney failure. In those early days we had no means to reverse this and he died.

Most Kenyans lived in the countryside and were habitually active. Over the course of my first three years in Nairobi, I found only ten cases in which an ECG disclosed previous heart attacks among my African patients. Three of those cases had normal coronary arteries, suggesting that the heart attack might have been due to spasm in a vessel or possibly a clot that then resolved on its own. Over the decades the pattern has changed dramatically reflecting Kenya's relentless urbanization.

Initially the heart attacks I did see in Africans invariably occurred among politicians or businessmen. Today we regularly encounter them in the middle class but rarely among subsistence farmers and herders. Lifestyle changes account for most of this shift. In the 1970s most Kenyans walked a lot even if they lived in a city, and their diet was high in fibre and light on red meat and with less salt. Modern Kenyans rely much more on cars, buses and *matatu* taxis. Their diet has changed too, in part because it became a status symbol to consume a lot of meat. Salt intake has increased too. However, I believe the biggest factor in the increase of heart disease is certain types of stress brought on by the competitive hustle and bustle of urban living.

Much more common in Kenya is rheumatic heart disease. It is caused by a streptococcal infection, usually involving a sore throat, although the disease can arise from a streptococcal infection of the skin or elsewhere in the body. The heart damage is done when antibodies attack the linings of heart valves. In the U.S. there was a significant amount of rheumatic heart disease among pregnant women in their thirties. Otherwise the disease usually appeared in men and women in their forties and fifties.

As a medical student in **pediatrics at the University of Chicago**, I sometimes saw acute rheumatic fever in children. Usually after some weeks of a strep throat, the child developed swelling in her joints which caused a limp. Occasionally she had Sydenham's chorea, an involuntary movement of the hands more commonly known as St. Vitus dance. Then came chest pain and, if a physician was listening to her heart with a stethoscope, the sound of murmurs due to leakage of the mitral valve. Follow-up blood tests confirmed whether or not the patient had suffered recent streptococcal infection.

The picture in East Africa was completely different. We almost never saw a case of acute rheumatic fever among African patients. Possibly the fevers occurred earlier in childhood and were not sufficiently severe to warrant a visit to a doctor. In the West patients didn't develop symptoms for decades after an acute rheumatic fever episode. In Kenya I saw little children five and six years old who presented with established valvular disease, usually with both narrowing and leakage of the mitral valve and sometimes the aortic valve as well. As there was no one else to run the paediatric cardiology clinic at the time, I became the de facto attending physician. I soon became practiced in diagnosing rheumatic heart disease in young children and was shocked by how often I saw established valvular disease.

When I started doing heart catheterizations on these children, I saw ten very severe cases of rheumatic heart disease in the first three months. The pressure in the pulmonary circuit was higher than that of the systemic circuit when normally it is one quarter of the systemic circuit. All of these children were younger than ten. Normally an asymmetrically misshapen chest is diagnostic of congenital heart disease. At the Kenyatta National Hospital paediatric clinic this finding was most common in young children who had established rheumatic heart disease at a very early age.

It was upsetting as there was not much I could do for these patients with the resources at hand. Once we had managed to assemble a cardiac-surgery team some years later, we made a point of targeting this group. Until then we had to use medications to treat a mechanical problem. The drugs were of very little value save for diuretics, which helped the children offload fluid and thus decongest their lungs. As a doctor, I continually strive to achieve a balance between empathy and detachment with my patients. Watching these wide-eyed little children suffer, knowing there was little I could do about it, was extremely distressing.

The other common cardiac condition among Kenyan children was congenital heart disease, which I was not trained to treat. Children with congenital heart disease usually went undiagnosed and untreated before coming to us. Typically we found holes in the patient's septum dividing the left and right atrium or between the left ventricle and right ventricle. In both cases it caused the blood to recirculate with a significant percentage of it crossing back to the right side of the heart. If the hole wasn't very large these hole-in-the-heart children usually tolerated it reasonably well. But over time the increased flow through the pulmonary circuit caused the lung arterioles to thicken. Without surgery the pressure in the lungs rose dramatically and permanently.

As we were just starting to operate on the children in 1975, surgery for the very sickest among them usually failed. We wanted to build public trust in our programme so we focused on patients who were within our powers to help. I only referred hole-in-the-heart patients if they had no complications and were low risk. Our surgeons' success rate with such cases, though not outstanding by Western standards, bolstered our team spirit and helped the program gain acceptance.

Occasionally I would be called on to look at a newborn less than a month old even though I had absolutely no experience in treating neonates. Looking down at the tiny creature cradled in the palms of my hands, I thought of the blessing of new life and how fragile it is. So imagine my apprehension when, three months after the cath lab had been operating, a paediatrician called me to treat an oxygen-starved 'blue baby' just a week old.

Blue (cyanotic) babies suffer from lack of oxygen to their blood. Generally they die within a short time, except in cases of some abnormal congenital connection – such as a hole in the atrium – that keeps them alive until the hole closes on its own. Such temporary structures allow some mixing of oxygenated blood from the two circuits. Today these babies receive corrective surgery at a very early age and recently even in utero. Not so in the 1970s.

I quickly read up on the condition's causes and reviewed the baby's ECG. It was a very complicated situation called 'the transposition of the great vessels'. The baby had been born with her pulmonary artery and aorta transposed. The blood coming to the right side of the heart flowed out into the body without being oxygenated in the lungs while blood from the left side of the heart flowed to the lungs and came straight back. It was recirculating in a closed system rather than delivering vital oxygen to the rest of the body.

This was the first time in my career I had been presented with a total transposition of the great vessels. It was a case of such complex delicacy that I feared it was hopeless. Then I remembered something Jimmy had said as she'd handed me an unfamiliar object. 'This is a Rashkind balloon. I doubt you'll ever need it, but just remember the name and that you have one.'

That balloon was in my hand luggage when I came to Kenya, along with all the other catheters that she'd provided me. Now as I was reading all the relevant literature I could lay my hands on, I came across a discussion of the Rashkind balloon and silently thanked Jimmy for her special gift. The device is advanced through the umbilical vein into the heart and through a hole in the right atrium into the left atrium. This is one of those temporary holes that you do not want to close as it allows the recirculation of blue blood with pink blood. To keep the hole open, you blow up the balloon at the end of the Rashkind catheter, after it has passed through the right atrium to the left atrium, then pull the catheter back with great force. This increases the size of the hole by tearing the surrounding membrane.

Just reading about this procedure gave me pause. I had never catheterized a baby, let alone one in the first week of life. I remembered holding my eldest niece at that age, and even that made me nervous. But this was no time to hesitate. The paediatric resident who was assisting located the umbilical vein, and I engaged it successfully. I carefully manoeuvred the catheter to the correct place, crossing through the foramen ovale, which was the hole between the right and left atria. I blew up the balloon. Theoretically I had now executed the most difficult part of the procedure. Not as far as I was concerned. I couldn't bring myself to give the catheter a good strong yank. Instead I pulled it down slowly. This was the wrong move.

It seemed as if the septum between the right and left atria was being pulled down way below the liver, almost out the umbilical vein, before it bounced back. I was seized by the irrational thought the baby's heart would emerge from the umbilical vein, inside out and still pumping feebly. I gritted my teeth and gave the catheter a good yank. It worked! Colour flushed the baby's skin indicating the hole had widened and she was receiving oxygen. My relief was palpable. But it was dashed some days later. The little girl contracted pneumonia and died.

The upshot of this harrowing experience was that after completing my first year at KNH, I spent a month at the paediatric cardiology clinic and cath lab at Children's Memorial Hospital in Chicago. It was a stimulating time that left me feeling a lot more confident in treating paediatric cardiac patients and teaching the residents. This was important until several years later when a new cadre of young Kenyan doctors with proper training in paediatric cardiology joined KNH and relieved me of my paediatric responsibilities.

The third and final type of cardiological disease I encountered in Kenya more often than I had in the U.S. is cardiomyopathy. It is a condition usually presenting in adults in their thirties to sixties where the heart muscle becomes diseased for no apparent reason while the coronary arteries remain unaffected. We often attribute cardiomyopathy to high blood pressure that was never diagnosed, which is certainly a possibility. Another cause that we could not diagnose at that time was an old or even recent viral infection of the heart muscle called a viral myocarditis. I have always been concerned whether it might have some environmental cause, such as a chemical toxin, but never have I discovered any evidence for this. Coronary angiography on cardiomyopathy patients was consistently normal. There are other conditions that can cause this, but they are relatively rare and were not known at that time.

I still see a lot of this condition in my practice. Alcohol consumption is another common associated cause. But we really don't know what causes cardiomyopathy, much less how to cure it. There was some evidence from Europe implicating cobalt, a contaminant found in some beers. Kenyans are fond of their beer so we analyzed some of the popular brands. None had traces of cobalt.

We also came across some unusual heart muscle disease such as hypertrophic cardiomyopathy. It is an abnormal thickening, usually of the septum of the left ventricle, which obstructs blood flow. When I first practiced in Kenya, I didn't realize how common it was.

One of the early patients presenting with hypertrophic cardiomyopathy was a young man in his early twenties. He was from Kisii in western Kenya. At that time Majid Warshow was my resident. He was later to become my partner in private practice. As hypertrophic cardiomyopathy usually runs in families, Majid and I offered the young man a lift home so that we could investigate his relatives.

It was during the rainy season and the trip was arduous. Nearly all of the safari was on dirt roads, most of which had turned into slippery mud. My low-slung Volkswagen saloon definitely was not made for this terrain. Once we got to Kisii, I had to negotiate several stretches of road that were completely under water. Given the car's poor clearance, it was a nerve-wracking endeavour. We also encountered a suicidal dog that ended its days by suddenly running in front of the car. Somehow, after twelve hours, we finally made it to a tiny village near our patient's home. By now the flood waters were rising rapidly, and I didn't trust the Volkswagen to go any farther. Night had fallen and a sudden rainstorm had reduced visibility to a few feet.

The young man was unfazed by all this. He said he'd continue on foot and promised to return the next day with his family members. We watched as the night closed around him then drove to the Tea Hotel in Kericho where we spent a comfortable night. We waited all the following day, but the young man didn't appear. In fact, we never saw him again. Majid and I guessed he had merely wanted a free ride home. And so I learned another valuable lesson about working in Africa. Take nothing at face value.

Heartbeat: An American Cardiologist in Kenya

I spent six exciting years working at the University of Nairobi and KNH. It was a steep learning curve that taught me to think outside the box about cardiac disease. During that time I also learned which technology would be useful and which would not. The objective was to improve my patients' lives. As machines had to be imported from Europe, I had to be certain they accomplished more than simply replacing good physical diagnosis and clinical acumen. I published papers in regional journals and international ones too with my residents and junior colleagues. Herbert Griswold, a retired professor from the Oregon Health Sciences University, visited and we collaborated on a paper on my research on left ventricular mitral stenosis at Kenyatta National Hospital. Griswold was the senior author. I was the first author. The paper included others too, even Hillary Ojiambo. It was published in the prestigious *American Heart Journal*. The recognition was gratifying. I soon realized, however, that academics would not be a lifetime pursuit. In fact, I *hated* writing papers. Teaching and treating patients were – and always will be – my passion.

11

OPERATION THUNDERBOLT

On Sunday, 27 June 1976, Air France flight 139 took off from Israel's Ben Gurion Airport, known for its notoriously tight security checks. Its next stopover was Athens where security had a reputation for being unusually lax. Among the passengers taken on board were three men and a woman carrying large black bags that held pistols, hand grenades and a submachine gun. Two were members of the Popular Front for the Liberation of Palestine. Two belonged to a little-known group called Revolutionary Cells. Within the week its name would be broadcast around the world, the prelude to gaining a reputation as one of West Germany's most dangerous left-wing organizations. On that sunny summer's day the four were driven by a common agenda – anti-Zionism.

The Airbus A300 lifted into the skies and, as the seat-belt sign switched off, the four terrorists burst into the aisles shouting and threatening the startled passengers with their weapons. Two of the terrorists ran to the cockpit to instruct the pilots to change course and head for Libya. The hijacked plane refuelled at Benghazi and took off again. Its destination was Entebbe International Airport on the shores of Lake Victoria in Uganda.

On the Monday afternoon of 28 June, when the Air France pilot called the Entebbe control tower, he was answered by a voice speaking Arabic. Three PLO terrorists were already at the airport to welcome their colleagues. Their demands were soon made known. They wanted the release of fifty-three Palestinian and pro-Palestinian militants. Forty were being held in Israeli prisons. The others were in prisons in France, Germany, Switzerland and Kenya. They were also asking a ransom of $5 million for the release of the plane. If these demands were not met, they would start killing the hostages on Thursday, 1 July.

It was a daunting situation for the Israelis. From the moment they had learned of the hijacking they had determined the hostages must be rescued at all costs. But how to do that? There were 254 on the plane and nearly half of them were Jews, the majority of them Israelis. Entebbe was more than 2000 miles from Israel. The Israelis would have to overfly hostile countries such as Egypt, Sudan and Somalia and risk being shot down before they had even reached their target. The planes could fuel at Sharm-el-Sheikh in the Sinai Peninsula during the approach, but they would have to refuel again somewhere else to make the return journey. At that time Israel was boycotted by the Organization of African Unity. It was doubtful any African country would allow the Israeli military to land on its soil.

There was an additional, unprecedented problem. Idi Amin, Uganda's mercurial and brutal head of state and the current chairman of the Organization of African Unity, was hosting the terrorists. He had been privy to the hijackers' plans ahead of time and had promised not only to welcome them but to provide military protection.

With only two days before the terrorists' deadline, time was of the essence as the Israeli government grappled with the impossible choice it faced. Prime Minister Yitzhak Rabin wanted to save lives by giving in to the hijackers' demands. The defence minister Shimon Peres argued that a rescue mission had to be mounted to discourage similar terrorist attacks in the future. The hours ticked by without a decision.

In the departure lounge at Entebbe on the night of Wednesday, 30 June, the German hijackers separated the Jews from the other passengers, invoking chilling memories of the Holocaust. The deadline for shooting passengers if demands were not met was now only hours away. The twelve-strong Air France crew had heroically refused to abandon the remaining passengers and remained with the Jewish hostages. They were 106 in all. Less than two hours before the 2 pm deadline on Thursday, 1 July, the cabinet voted unanimously to begin negotiating the release of Palestinian prisoners in exchange for the hostages on the condition the deadline could be extended until Sunday, 4 July. Amin agreed.

While the pros and cons of military intervention continued to be argued back and forth, military and intelligence chiefs were pressing ahead with preparations for a raid on Entebbe. The passengers who had been released by the terrorists had been flown to Paris. Mossad agents had interviewed them at the airport as soon as their plane touched down. This gave them sufficient information to build an accurate picture of where the hostages were being held in the airport terminal and the number of terrorists guarding them. Intelligence on the ground suggested that hundreds of Ugandan troops were guarding the airport as well. Whatever the exact strength of the military and where they were positioned was impossible to ascertain, but one thing was clear. The element of surprise would be crucial. The rescue mission was of a complexity that had never before been undertaken. It called for exceptional courage and ingenuity. It had not received government approval. There was a strong possibility that it would be a disastrous failure. It was given a name inspired by James Bond - Operation Thunderbolt.

How to reach the terminal without being detected and then extract everyone safely was distilled down to four options. One plan entailed flying into Entebbe in an Air Force plane carrying soldiers disguised as the prisoners whose release had been demanded. They would land, rush to the terminal and extricate the hostages. As the airport was only one kilometre from Lake Victoria, two other plans were based on an amphibious attack. A team of Navy Seals and commandos would parachute onto the lake with boats, sail to shore and rush the terminal. Alternatively, the same force would fly to Nairobi and cross the vast lake to Entebbe from the Kenyan side in a yacht pre-positioned by a Mossad agent. All three plans had glaring drawbacks, not least the voracious crocodiles that would have snapped up anyone who might fall overboard.

The fourth plan at first seemed to be the most impractical of all, but it was the one that was chosen. Four Hercules C-130 transport planes would fly 100 soldiers to Entebbe and land in the dark. The lead team of twenty-nine commandos would approach the airport terminal in a Mercedes Benz rebuilt as a replica of the presidential Mercedes that Idi Amin invariably travelled in. It would be accompanied by two Land Rovers. It was hoped the simulated motorcade would not arouse suspicion and thus be able to bypass security checkpoints without being stopped. It was crucial to maintain the element of surprise as the men in the motorcade rushed the terminal and extricated everyone. The other seventy soldiers would secure the perimeters and fend off the hundreds of enemy Ugandan soldiers believed to be out there in every direction. The idea was just plausible.

Amin had visited the hostages more than once so yet another visit would not be considered unusual. He claimed he had been sent by God and had provided them with mattresses and food brought from nearby hotels. He was at his charming best when playing the Big Man. On one visit he received a standing ovation.

Back in Israel that Thursday, 1 July, a clapped-out white Mercedes was located in the back streets of Tel Aviv while elsewhere a tailor ran up imitation Ugandan army uniforms. A civilian mechanic worked through the night to rebuild the Mercedes and paint it black. Someone else forged a Ugandan number plate. At the same time planes, vehicles and artillery were being organized. The medical team that would be on hand to treat injuries needed to secure a large supply of blood in case there were heavy casualties. So as not to alert the media, they created a cover story that a crisis was emerging on the northern border with Lebanon. There was even a supply of empty milk cans for the transport planes in case the hostages vomited. Everything was being thought through down to the last detail.

Needless to say, these preparations were being undertaken in top secrecy. The world looked on in ignorance of what was taking place behind the scenes. Once again dread and anxiety gripped both Jewish and non-Jewish friends of Israel. Nairobi was no exception. Saul Gordon, a fellow member of our tightknit Jewish community, was beside himself with worry. I was distraught about it too and willing to do anything I could to help. Saul owned a travel business with his brother and was an ardent Zionist. He was also excitable. Desperate to do something, *anything,* to help the hostages, he called me several times to discuss bribing Amin to release the captives. Did I know how to get in touch with him? As it happened I was acquainted with Amin's physician. He was a fellow cardiologist called Paul D'Arbela. It seemed to me to be a Hail Mary pass, but I diligently tried and failed to get hold of D'Arbela on several occasions.

Meanwhile crucial cooperation was being provided from other quarters. Without it the rescue operation could never have succeeded. Charles Njonjo, at that time the attorney general, has recalled the story to me many times. Njonjo received a visit from Eli Engel, the Mossad chief in Kenya. Engel wished to discuss Kenyan participation in the raid. It was a sensitive situation. Kenya, along with the rest of Africa, had severed diplomatic ties with Israel in the aftermath of the 1973 war. Nevertheless, Njonjo was a supporter of Israel, and he welcomed Engel and two other Mossad agents onto the outdoor terrace of his home.

The Mossad chief unfolded several maps and spread them out on the glass top of a wrought-iron table on the veranda. The men bent over them, heads almost touching, as Engel traced the route the rescue team intended to take. They were so engrossed, they barely noticed when Njonjo's wife Margaret appeared with a tray of coffee. The task force would land in Sharm el-Sheikh in Sinai to refuel. From there the planes would follow the international flight path south along the Red Sea, flying at thirty meters to avoid radar detection by the Egyptians, Jordanians and Saudis. The planes would circumvent Djibouti and continue west over Somaliland and Ethiopia's barren Ogaden region. Engel's stubby finger paused a second for effect and then crossed into Kenyan airspace and headed west over the Rift Valley until it reached Lake Victoria and came to rest on Entebbe on the far shore.

Not only did Israel need Kenya to look the other way, Engel told Njonjo, the pilots wanted to refuel the planes in Nairobi on the way home. Njonjo was silent. The minutes ticked by as he thought everything through, considering the implications if anything should go wrong on Kenyan soil. He nodded at Engel. 'If Mzee agrees, I'll see to it.'

Njonjo called Jomo Kenyatta at his Gatundu home and carefully explained everything. The president hesitated a moment then said, 'Do what you see fit, Njonjo. But I warn you, you're on your own. I have no knowledge of this matter if it leaks out.'

Three other Kenyans knew about the Entebbe raid in advance. Njonjo notified Ben Gethi, commander of the General Service Unit, a paramilitary wing of the police force, and Kenya's spymaster, James Kanyotu, who headed Special Branch. The third person was Njonjo's close friend and business partner, Bruce McKenzie, the South African-born Kenyan Minister for Agriculture, who had links to both Mossad and Britain's MI6.

Thanks to McKenzie another important part of the operation was executed. The most recent aerial photos of the airport that Mossad could provide were five years old. The Israelis needed up-to-date images of the air terminal or the success of the operation would be at risk. A pilot who was a Mossad operative flew to Kenya from London. With McKenzie's help, he hired a small aircraft at Nairobi's Wilson Airport and filed a flight plan for Entebbe. When he got there, he informed the control tower he had a technical malfunction with the landing gear and was going to circle the airport several times while he fixed it. After thoroughly photographing the ground layout, he spoke to the control tower again. He had been unable to fix the problem and so was returning to Nairobi.

By a stroke of luck, the Entebbe airport had been constructed by an Israeli company, Solel Boneh, and the blueprints were accessible in Israel. The night of Friday, 2 July, with the new deadline only two days away, the army built a partial replica of the terminal where the hostages were held. They did mock assaults on the building for the rest of the night and practiced loading and unloading the C-130s with men, vehicles and equipment to make sure the rescue could be executed as smoothly as possible. On Saturday afternoon 3 July, the Mossad photos of Entebbe airport were delivered to the Air Force base near Lod. With these in hand, the planes took off even though the cabinet still had not given the rescue mission permission to go ahead.

The lead C-130 carried men from Sayeret Metkal, the Israeli Defense Forces' elite unit charged with counterterrorism operations and hostage rescue. It was modelled on Britain's SAS. Delta Force was its American counterpart. Its coolheaded and courageous commander was Lieutenant Colonel Yonatan Netanyahu, elder brother to Benjamin Netanyahu, who later was Israel's longest serving prime minister. These were the men designated to disembark in the bogus Amin motorcade, enter the terminal, subdue the terrorists and extract the hostages. The other three C-130s were carrying support troops and their armoured cars. Trailing some way behind were two Boeing 707s. One was the command centre for several generals and senior officers. It would remain airborne, circling overhead for the duration of the operation. The other contained a field hospital for treating the wounded. Not long after taking off, the fleet touched down in the Sinai to top up fuel tanks. It was only then that the generals received word Rabin had sanctioned Operation Thunderbolt.

In the early hours of Sunday morning 4 July, the planes landed at Entebbe under cover of darkness. The Mercedes rolled down the ramp with Netanyahu sitting in the front passenger seat. As the motorcade approached the terminal, two soldiers stepped forward with raised rifles. They were shot dead instantly, one with a silencer and one with an automatic machine gun. It was discovered in the aftermath that Amin had recently exchanged his black Mercedes for a white one. Many years later, the Israelis learned that Ugandan cars are right-hand drive, unlike the left-hand drive Mercedes in Tel Aviv.

Unfortunately, the sound of the second shot stole the element of surprise. Netanyahu had been badly hurt in the crossfire, but there was no time to stop and tend to his wounds. The commandos stormed the departures lounge where the hostages were being held, shouting at everyone to lie down. In the confusion and noise two hostages were shot dead by the hijackers. A third hostage stood up and was immediately shot by a commando who had mistaken him for a terrorist. Within minutes all the hijackers were dead. Outside there was intense shooting from all sides for another fifteen minutes as the support troops fought off the Ugandans, killing twenty Ugandan soldiers. The commandos also destroyed five MiG-21 fighter jets and three MiG-17s that were parked on the tarmac. They didn't want anyone scrambling a jet and chasing after them. A child confused the noise and light of the explosions and tracers for fireworks and shouted, 'Wow! How beautiful!'

The efficient military operation now descended into temporary chaos as the commandos tried to herd the hostages into the waiting planes. Several people were dragging their luggage behind them. One passenger insisted on returning to the terminal to reclaim his duty-free purchases. An Air France flight attendant had been slightly wounded by a ricocheting bullet. She was clad only in her red underwear as she had been asleep. One of the soldiers threw her over his shoulder and raced for the plane with bullets whizzing past his head. The last C-130 lifted off one hour and thirty-nine minutes after the first plane had landed at Entebbe.

The mood in the C-130s was subdued. Everyone was relieved and thankful to be alive and safe. But they were too exhausted and traumatized to celebrate. Added to this was the great sadness of Yonatan Netanhayu's death. He had lost a large amount of blood. Despite every effort the doctors were unable to save him. He passed away during the flight to Nairobi.

Njonjo was true to his word. He had organized Kenyan soldiers to guard the planes while they were being refuelled. Three hostages who had been wounded were offloaded and taken to Nairobi Hospital accompanied by two Israeli doctors. One of them was Pasco Cohen, the hostage who had been accidentally shot by a commando. Tom Jorgensen, the surgeon on call, invited the Israelis to join him performing surgery on Cohen. They declined to scrub in, telling Jorgensen they trusted him to do a good job. Unfortunately, Cohen couldn't be saved. He died on the operating table.

In those days I was still attached to Kenyatta National Hospital, but as the only cardiologist in the country, I was sometimes asked to look after patients at Nairobi Hospital. I didn't want to tread on anyone's toes, so I developed the practice of seeing my patients very early in the morning and late at night to avoid bumping into the other doctors. I happened to be making my rounds when the Israelis were admitted. I had no idea what was going on until Tom explained what had happened. Since I was a Jew who spoke Hebrew, he asked me to attend to an Israeli casualty who had been wounded in the left shoulder. I administered the appropriate antibiotics and analgesics and took the man's history in Hebrew. Also at the hospital that night were some members of the Nairobi Jewish community. Among them was Vaizman Aharoni, a civil engineer and a family friend. They arrived with their sidearms to protect the Israeli wounded if necessary.

That weekend Charles Njonjo and his wife Margaret were in Laikipia staying with their friend Court Parfet, the American conservationist. Margaret first heard about the Entebbe rescue listening to the BBC on her shortwave radio at Parfet's Solio Ranch. She rushed to tell Charles the exciting news and was perplexed by his low-key reaction.

I, on the other hand, was in a state of high excitement. I can't recall ever being that wound up. I had the same choked up feelings as when the shofar was blown at Old Jerusalem's Western Wall during the Six Day War. My telephone rang all day with calls of concern from my friends and family in the U.S. Many of the staff at Kenyatta National Hospital also called me, thinking that I must have been involved. They didn't differentiate between being Jewish and being Israeli. Some asked, 'What was it like at Entebbe?'

Idi Amin, of course, saw matters in a different light. Humiliated by the apparent ease with which the Israelis had extracted the hostages, he exacted bloody revenge. The following week 245 Kenyans living in Uganda were killed at random. Another 3000 fled the country. Some of the Entebbe airport staff were murdered too, including Peter Kalanzi, the director of civil aviation, and Tobias Rugambi, who was in charge of air traffic services. Nails were driven into their skulls, then their bodies were pulverized beyond recognition with sledge hammers. Neither had been present during the raid.

Dora Bloch was the fourth hostage to die. She had choked on a piece of meat soon after arriving at Entebbe and had been taken to Mulago Hospital. The day of the raid, she had been dragged from her bed and was last seen screaming as she was thrown into the back of a car. Her body was later found buried in a sugar plantation.

There was one more person who fell victim to Amin's wrath – Bruce McKenzie. In May 1978 McKenzie and two colleagues flew to Entebbe in a light aircraft to discuss an arms deal with Amin. On their departure Amin's notorious British henchman, Bob Astles, presented them with a mounted lion's head. 'It's a gift from the Big Man,' he said and instructed the cargo handlers to stow it in the back of the plane. Concealed behind one of the animal's glass eyes was a pressure-sensitive bomb designed to detonate when the plane descended below 3000 meters. As the plane flew over the Ngong Hills on its final approach to Wilson Airport, it exploded. The three men and their young pilot were killed instantly.

Operation Thunderbolt inspired many with praise coming in from some unexpected quarters. The Supreme Commander of the Imperial Iranian Armed Forces wrote a letter congratulating the Israeli commandos and extending condolences for 'the loss and martyrdom' of Netanyahu. Inspired by the Israelis, four years later the U.S. military mounted Operation Eagle Claw to rescue fifty-three hostages from the American Embassy in Tehran. The U.S. Special Forces trained in the desert for six months beforehand, but their mission failed. The Israelis had achieved their goal with only a week to prepare.

As for Idi Amin, he never got his just desserts. He was overthrown three years later in 1979. The Saudis gave him sanctuary, and he lived with his family in Jeddah until his death in 2003.

There is another postscript to this story. Anyone familiar with Kenyan history will know the name John Henry Patterson and link it to the construction of the Uganda Railway at the turn of the last century. He was a British soldier commissioned to supervise the building of a bridge across the Tsavo River. At the time man-eating lions were dragging Indian workers from their tents at night and devouring them. Patterson had served in India and had a reputation as a fine shot on tiger hunts. He was called upon to eliminate the lions, which he duly did. He later wrote a book about it called *The Man-Eaters of Tsavo*.

Patterson was also a Christian Zionist. During World War I he commanded the Jewish Legion (at first called the Zion Mule Corps) and was often described as the godfather of the modern Israeli Defense Forces. He became close friends with a Jewish scholar called Benzion Netanyahu who had two sons. The elder was Yonatan and the younger was Benjamin. In 1947 Patterson was the *sandak* (godfather) at Yonatan's circumcision ceremony. The Netanyahu family still have the inscribed silver goblet Patterson gave his godson to commemorate the occasion.

12

THE KENYATTA SUCCESSION

As word spread there was a new cardiologist in town, I began to attract private patients from among Kenya's political elite even though I was still a government employee. In due course many of them became friends as well. And so I came to learn about the impact of personality on politics and politics on personalities. In other words, I was witness to the high-level power dynamics that took place behind the scenes. Fifteen years into independence, the political landscape was shifting in unpredictable ways. I soon found myself caught up in these changes. They were to influence the future course of my life.

Two weeks before my arrival in Kenya in 1974, President Jomo Kenyatta was re-elected for a third five-year term. He had overseen a peaceful transition in 1963 from British colony to nation state and was respected as the country's founding father. He had ruled with a firm grip, keeping tribal antagonism at bay even though many felt his fellow Kikuyus had benefited disproportionately from the fruits of freedom. Many of his colleagues had entrenched themselves in positions of political and economic power. But by then he was about seventy-seven and the question of succession was simmering below the surface. Kenyatta's running mate, Daniel Toroitich arap Moi, had served as the vice president since 1967. He had forsaken his chosen vocation as a teacher in 1955 when he gave up his position as a headmaster to be elected to the colonial Legislative Council. He had been appointed as the vice president at the suggestion of the attorney general, Charles Njonjo, to replace Joseph Murumbi, the former foreign affairs minister, who had resigned.

Moi was an intriguing character. He was a devout Christian born in a mud hut who rose to becoming one of Africa's leading statesmen. He belonged to a small subgroup of the Kalenjin people called the Tugen. His family were from the tiny village of Kuriengwo in Sacho location in what is now Baringo County. His father died when he was four, and he was raised by his mother. As a child he herded goats and cattle and played with other boys in the mountain streams and forests. When he was ten his uncle, the village chief, chose him as one of three boys to attend the Africa Inland Mission school at Kabartonjo some forty kilometres distant. They were the first boys in the area to be sent to get an education. They walked there clad in skins and barefoot, carrying *simis* (stabbing swords) and *rungus* (clubs) for protection along the way. Moi had a thirst for learning and excelled in his studies. He was later sent to a larger Africa Inland Mission school in Kapsabet.

Moi's Christianity was nurtured early in his life. As a teenager he walked fifty kilometres herding cattle to other missions at the request of his teachers. With the money he earned he bought his first Bible. During the holidays he preached at the local churches. When I later got to know him as a friend and saw him on a regular basis, I could see how his deep faith informed his politics. He felt God's presence as a steady hand on the tiller when navigating the crosscurrents of tribal and factional powerplay. Often he turned to passages in the Bible to help him make difficult decisions.

Even after many decades in politics, he still thought of himself as a preacher. On visits back to his rural home occasionally he would appear in church dressed in a loose shirt and slacks to play the guitar and sing hymns to an admiring congregation.

It was three years later in 1977 when I lost my political innocence. Dr Ramesh Desai, an internist in Mombasa, informed me that Moi had recently been to see him complaining of headaches. Desai said his examination showed that Moi suffered from high blood pressure. He had advised the vice president to see a cardiologist and had recommended me. Moi soon made an appointment through his secretary Mrs Smith. I was still a university employee and had no private office. It was arranged that he would meet me in the cardiology office next door to the cardiac cath lab at Kenyatta National Hospital.

First impressions remain in your memory. I can still recall vividly how Moi walked briskly into my office tall, erect and broad-shouldered. He greeted me with a firm handshake and a charming smile. He was a vigorous man, handsome in his way, who came across as someone much younger than his fifty-plus years. He was meticulously dressed in a suit. I liked him straight away.

Moi deferred to me when we talked about his heart. Had he had a problem before? *Bado* (not yet). He made it clear that I was in the driver's seat even though he was accustomed to being in charge. His English was halting and didn't flow easily. It was a habit he'd cultivated to his advantage. It gave him time to think so that often when speaking in public arenas - and behind closed doors too - his statements were intentionally ambiguous. I was to be witness to this diplomatic sleight of hand whenever he discussed Iran or Libya with the Israelis.

I did a complete assessment, including an ECG and cardiac fluoroscopy (as we still did not have echocardiography available in Kenya). He had trouble keeping his balance on the treadmill as lots of patients do. The vice president's issues, including his headaches and a thickened heart muscle, were all related to his blood pressure. I reassured him that his condition could be treated with drugs, which I would prescribe.

As I walked Moi to his car, Hillary Ojiambo saw us together and approached. I felt uneasy in his presence. Hillary had become a professor and, as chief of the department of medicine, was now my boss. He greeted Moi warmly but pointedly ignored me. I shrugged it off as just a petty gesture until I received a telephone call back at the office from Jerry Kiereini, Permanent Secretary for Defense. His wife Eunice Muringo Kiereini was Kenya's first Chief Nursing Officer in the Ministry of Health. She had also been President Kenyatta's personal nurse.

Jerry and I already had a history. Earlier that year I had treated his two-year-old son, Githae, for a heart murmur. On physical examination, I had diagnosed an atrial septal defect. There was a large hole in his atrial septum with blood shunting from the left atrium to the right atrium instead of going entirely into the left ventricle as it should. This overloaded the right ventricle, flooding the lungs with excess blood and damaging the lung vessels. This was confirmed by cardiac catheterization. I had arranged for Githae to have surgery at St. Thomas' Hospital in London with Mr Brynn Williams. It had gone smoothly.

Now Jerry was telling me over the phone Ojiambo had called to alert him that an agent for the CIA and Mossad was treating the vice president. Kiereini had told him, 'You know, the CIA and Mossad are our friends. And David is a good doctor. He saved my son's life!' I was amused and flattered that a junior doctor without his own office was thought to be working for the two most highly respected spy agencies in the world.

The anecdote gave me great pleasure. My doctoring skills had been praised and there had been the thrilling assumption I was a spy. I was so pumped up about it I decided to do a James Bond entry into my flat. I sprang up the stairs, turned the key and kicked the door open. I tried do a shoulder roll to the floor to miss the hail of bullets from the villains inside but tripped and landed heavily on my elbow instead. I was badly bruised and walked around with a stiff shoulder tendonitis for days.

In the summer of 1977 I was made a senior lecturer. Unfortunately, the promotion didn't protect me from Hillary Ojiambo. He continued to criticize and belittle me. Fed up with his bullying behaviour, I took my troubles to Dr Eric Mngola, who had replaced Dr Jason Likimani as Director of Medical Services. I told him about the abuses I'd absorbed in silence from Ojiambo. I'd had as much as I could take. I was thinking of going back to the States.

Mngola listened attentively as I poured out my woes then suggested a solution. 'Why don't you stay and work for me? I'll make you the chief cardiothoracic physician in the Ministry of Health.' He offered me a considerable raise above my current salary. The position came with a large colonial-style house and garden on Menengai Road within walking distance of the hospital. I said yes immediately. There was another good reason for accepting. I could continue to teach at the university and Eric would shield me from Ojiambo's vitriol. Many years later I am still grateful to Ojiambo for his affronts. They triggered a career change that improved my life and lifestyle enormously.

The following year in 1978 I went on vacation to Rome. With my Ojiambo issues solved and an important new job ahead, I had decided to celebrate with a brief August holiday in Italy. I arrived in the midst of high drama as Pope Paul VI had died, and the Roman Catholic College of Cardinals were gathered to elect his successor.

Waiting for me at the airport in Rome were my good doctor friends, Robert Thompson and Barney Hecker. I'd known them both at the University of Washington where Bob was an intern and Barney a medical student. They had since married and joined the U.S. Navy. Before we headed for Naples, where they were stationed, Bob and Barney took me on a twenty-four-hour tour of Rome which culminated at the Vatican. It was an interesting time to be there.

As we entered St Peter's Square we encountered a large crowd, including a number of press photographers who were aiming huge telephoto lenses at a chimney. English-speaking journalists in the crowd told us they were waiting for a signal. If white smoke poured from the chimney, the cardinals had chosen one of their number to be the new pope. If the smoke came out black, they had failed to reach a consensus on who he would be. Though by then we were hungry and keen to leave for dinner, the possibility of witnessing history in the making kept us where we stood, our eyes fixed on the chimney.

Suddenly the smoke appeared, and just as suddenly a debate began. Was the smoke white or black? When viewed against the setting sun, it was difficult to tell. After some serious squinting Bob, Barney and I decided the smoke was black as did many of the photographers, who started packing up their cameras. The majority of the crowd began to depart the plaza as well. We left to enjoy a delicious Italian dinner to celebrate my 26 August birthday and then retired to our hotel.

Next morning I found an Italian newspaper pushed under my door. Though I neither read nor spoke Italian, I saw the word '*Papa*' printed over a picture of what I correctly took to be the new pope standing on a balcony and waving to the crowd. He was Cardinal Albino Luciani from Northern Italy, a relatively young sixty-four years. He had taken the name John Paul I. I found it strange that so many of us staring at that chimney had mistaken the smoke's colour - until I learned we hadn't. Apparently the chimney was belching black smoke because it was badly in need of service. What was more, many of the cardinals, their eyes tearing from the fumes, had tossed their notes and tally sheets into the fireplace as they left the room. So we'd seen history after all. We just hadn't known it at the time. John Paul I died thirty-three days later in the Vatican's Apostolic Palace. The official cause of death was a heart attack although conspiracy buffs have advanced many alternate narratives.

On my way back to Kenya I stopped in London. It was a balmy summer day as I walked down Shaftesbury Avenue in search of a lightweight summer suit. At Piccadilly Circus I passed a news kiosk and did a double take when I saw the headlines. 'Kenyatta's death prompts fears of tribal warfare'.

The news was no surprise. The eighty-year-old president had suffered from heart problems for more than a decade. It was said by his inner circle that he had not been actively participating in the affairs of state for the past three years. His refusal to name a successor had led to intense jockeying for position behind the scenes.

The constitution stated the vice president would become acting president for an interim period on the president's death. After ninety days a presidential election would be held. Moi was from the Kalenjin ethnic group. It was feared by a clique of Kikuyu old guard his accession to power would undermine their dominant position in national affairs. Their plan was to prevent this happening through a constitutional amendment to introduce the position of executive prime minister. Moi's position was being safeguarded by another Kikuyu, Attorney General Charles Njonjo. It was a momentous – and dangerous – occasion.

I took the next flight home, eager to see how Kenyans would say goodbye to their first and only president. Would Moi navigate the shoals of succession without incident or would there be a storm of tribal violence as had been predicted? I had come to like Moi while treating him as a patient. I hoped all would go smoothly for him.

In due course I came to know the inside story of what took place. Kenyatta had been found unconscious at 3.30 am on 22 August at State House in Mombasa. Dr Eric Mngola, who was his personal physician, could not be located. Dr Joel Pinto and Dr J. Wasunna were summoned from their homes in Mombasa and rushed to State House with an oxygen tank. They tried to resuscitate him, but Kenyatta was already dead. Joel Pinto told me years later that he and Wasunna were immediately detained by the State House security detail to prevent any premature leaks about Kenyatta's death until it became public. Their families had no idea where they were.

Less than an hour after Kenyatta was pronounced dead Moi's bedside phone emitted a faint ping as it had been doing, off and on, for weeks. The vice president was at his Kabarak house in the Rift Valley 100 miles to the north of Nairobi. There clearly was something wrong with the phone, but Moi didn't know what. Usually when he lifted the receiver there was no one there, only static.

This time someone was there. Moi told me the familiar voice was Eliud Mahihu, the Coast Provincial Commissioner and a close political ally. The highly agitated Mahihu informed Moi,

'The eyes of Kenyatta have closed.' He urged the vice president to depart for State House Nairobi without delay. It was advice that undoubtedly saved Moi's life.

It had been known for months that Moi was a marked man. He held the home affairs cabinet portfolio as well as being vice president. After the 1977 elections, he was stripped of much of his power when responsibility for the Kenya Police Service, the General Service Unit (a paramilitary unit formed at independence specifically to ensure peaceful transitions of power), and Special Branch (the state intelligence organ) was given to Kenyatta's brother-in-law, Mbiyu Koinange, the Minister of State in the Office of the President. Moi was left with the prisons and the immigration department. It was a clear signal that he was in imminent danger. The instrument of his fate would likely be the Rift Valley Operations Team, known as the *Ng'oroko* (bandits), a 250-man private army organized by James Mungai, a Kikuyu police commissioner. It was funded by the same political foes who had tried to alter the constitution. They represented the Kikuyu ruling elite that had emerged during the Kenyatta presidency. Their mission was to make sure the presidency remained with the Kikuyu.

After speaking with Moi, Mahihu informed others of Kenyatta's death. Among them was Geoffrey Kariithi, the head of the civil service, who knew of the plot to assassinate Moi. Kariithi phoned the vice president as well, reiterating the message that he should get to Nairobi as quickly as possible.

Moi summoned his car and bodyguard/driver at once, and the two headed into the predawn darkness. They were over two hours away from Nairobi and only a step ahead of his assassins. The Ng'oroko were half an hour behind Moi. He passed through one of their roadblocks without being recognized and made it safely to his Nairobi residence where a General Service Unit detachment was waiting to escort him to State House.

While all this was happening, Moi's high-powered Kikuyu friend and ally, the attorney general Charles Njonjo, was in the air on an overnight flight from London. He had no clue what awaited him in Nairobi. On landing Njonjo was escorted to a VIP lounge at the airport to be briefed on the night's events. The more he heard, the greater Njonjo's conviction that Moi's enemies might go to any lengths to secure the presidency. It was later revealed a plot had been contemplated to murder scores of government officials. When Njonjo learned that Moi had made it safely to State House, he called Chief Justice Sir James Wicks and asked him to go there at once.

At 3 pm that afternoon, nearly twelve hours after Mzee Kenyatta had 'closed his eyes', the Voice of Kenya interrupted its broadcasts with the sombre announcement that the father of the nation was dead. Three hours after that a group of high-level government officials assembled at State House to witness the British-born Wicks swearing in Daniel arap Toroitich Moi as Kenya's second president. Two months later Moi named Finance Minister Mwai Kibaki, a Kikuyu from a different faction to that of the late President Kenyatta, as his vice president. It was a shrewd choice that assuaged tribal tensions.

The hallmarks of Moi's years as vice president had been his championing of education for all, his shrewd competence in discharging his duties in the face of persistent Kikuyu attacks, his comparative honesty and his unerring loyalty to Kenyatta. Yet once he began to wield the ivory baton he habitually carried in public, the former schoolteacher showed he'd also absorbed a lot about presidential politics during his ten years in the trenches.

His emphasis on reconciliation after the uproar and

dislocations of the latter Kenyatta years was well received as was his decision to release political dissidents from prison. Moi's masterstroke was to tap into the Kenyans' love and respect for Kenyatta, who was a venerated legend despite any of his shortcomings as president. His promise to follow in the great man's path helped to ratify his legitimacy as Kenyatta's anointed successor. He announced an ill-defined policy called *Nyayo*, or footsteps, implying that he would walk in Kenyatta's shoes. He later branded the Nyayo philosophy as one of 'peace, love and unity'. Nyayo became Moi's sobriquet. Sometimes people would identify me by saying, '*Yeye ni daktari ya Nyayo.*' He is Nyayo's doctor, meaning Moi.

13

PRIVATE PRACTICE

Toward the close of 1977 I was made chief cardiothoracic physician for the government. The Milbank Foundation funded me for one more year then cancelled the grant. They said it was time to give African doctors a chance to manage their national medical services. To compensate for the lost income, I started seeing private patients at Kenyatta National Hospital. In 1978 I was granted admitting rights at Nairobi Hospital. I worked out of a senior consultant's rooms after office hours, seeing patients from 6 to 8 pm, three evenings a week. I didn't realize it at the time, but this was to be my first step in a gradual transition to private practice.

Several factors were at play. Africanization was coming to the University of Nairobi Medical School. At the time there were perhaps a few more African instructors than Europeans and Americans at the school, but several Canadian and Scottish residents and attending physicians from McGill and Glasgow universities were at Kenyatta National Hospital. The government didn't have a structured plan for reconfiguring the faculty, but it was obvious that it intended to make public medicine more African. That was a good thing in my view.

As chief cardiothoracic physician, my professional prospects were limited. I could not reasonably expect to be promoted further in the public service system. I was theoretically eligible to someday become the director of medical services, but that was a political appointment. I did not want it. Nor would I have been considered for it. There were two options open to me if I stayed in Kenya. One was to stay on in my position and receive annual salary raises. The other was to go into private practice where the opportunity to advance in my profession had no ceiling.

For a brief few weeks I considered a move back to the States before deciding against it. I wasn't ready to settle down. I had hit my mid-thirties and was making the most of everything Nairobi had to offer. I was very involved in the Jewish community. If I stayed on, I would be made vice chairman. I was enjoying a great social life as well at the homes of diplomats, businessmen and my medical colleagues. I saw no reason to leave.

A doctor of my age and experience in the U.S. could never match this lifestyle, at least not in my eyes. My parents felt differently. They wanted to see me married to a nice Jewish girl and correctly believed I'd have a better chance of finding the right one in the U.S. Certainly not in Kenya. I knew I couldn't escape this knotty subject forever. I just wasn't ready to address it yet.

There was another very good reason not to go back to the States. I was learning to fly. I had decided to take a proactive approach to conquering my fear of flying. There were practical reasons for this. Kenya was nearly as big as Texas and had a road system that left a lot of room for improvement. The death toll on the main transport arteries was tragically high. Many of the secondary roads were a murram obstacle course. They were pitted with potholes and studded with rocks. During the rains they became a quagmire of glutinous mud. Flying was the preferred means of transport for crossing the country's great distances and wild terrain. Another consideration was that seven or eight time zones separated East Africa from the eastern seaboard of the United States depending on the time of year. A trip could take twenty-four hours. It was torture for an aviophobe.

To be honest, I had been given no choice about facing my fears. I had accepted an invitation to join my friend, Saul Gordon, and his wife Marcia on a holiday trip to the island of Lamu on the shores of the Indian Ocean. I was looking forward to spending a few pleasant days at the beach with them. But I was very nervous about how we were getting there. Marcia was going to pilot us in a four-seater Cessna.

Saul and Marcia ran a travel business with Saul's brother Harold. They worked with subcontractors in bulk tourism out of the States. He was a genius with a fantastic memory who was prone to mercurial moods. He spoke several languages fluently and read voraciously. He had the habit of cutting out magazine and newspaper articles and stashing them in shoeboxes or sending them to friends. I was one of the recipients. Saul agonized over the Holocaust, a subject that tended to surface a lot in his conversations. He wasn't religious but wore his Jewishness on his sleeve. Marcia was his foil. He had met her in Uganda as a beautiful Peace Corps worker from New Mexico. Sassy, independent and adventurous, she was the only person who could keep her husband in line – but not without difficulty.

Saul was at the back of the plane absorbed in a pile of magazines. I sat in the co-pilot seat next to Marcia. I was trying hard to appear calm and did okay until Marcia unwisely flew us into a cloud and had to do a U-turn to get us out of it. She got disoriented and started looking for a map so she could get her bearings. In those days GPS had yet to be invented. She turned in her seat to see if there was a map somewhere under Saul's feet and asked me over her shoulder, 'Can you take over the controls for a bit?'

I was overcome with terror as Marcia briefly explained how to keep the wings level, warning me not to touch the foot pedals, which controlled the rudder. It took her at least ten minutes to figure out where we were. It seemed like a lifetime. When she finally took over, she said I'd done well. 'You actually calmed down. That's because you're a control freak. You hate it when you're not in charge. Why don't you learn to fly?'

With great trepidation I agreed to give it a try. I signed up for lessons with the Safari Air Flying School, which operated out of Nairobi's Wilson Airport. Knowing that it was highly likely I might try to quit before getting my private pilot license, I loaded up on lessons and moved through them as quickly as possible. My chief dread was taking off and landing unaccompanied by the instructor. I'd had ten or eleven sessions when, without warning, he got out of the plane and told me to get on with it. Somehow I managed to do it. I then made it through the required thirty-five hours of flying time, including six hours of cross-country solo flights.

I had ignored ground school, but my friend Charlie Cronheim, an oil industry executive, had recently taken his ground-school exam and saved the old test papers. He went over them with me for a couple of nights. I passed the written exam easily. The practical exam was more challenging. The time had come to show what I was made of. My examiner was a former patient. He had a torticollis, meaning his neck was permanently stuck askew leaning to the right. Once we were aloft he cut the engine without warning. I'd been told about this. He looked at me. 'What are you going to do?' I pointed to a field where I thought I could land and began to circle. Then I realized I'd never reach it in time. There was another field almost right in front of me which looked pretty flat. Perhaps I could land there. I pulled up the flaps to slow the plane down and trimmed the rudder. I wasn't sure he knew what I was doing because his neck was stuck. To be honest, I wasn't sure I knew either. 'Is this the spot you intended?' I nodded, and he switched the engine back on. 'You can overshoot. You surprised me. Did better than I thought you would.' The truth be told, I'd surprised myself too.

To some extent I had overcome the terror I had known since boyhood. My confidence grew with time, but I was never totally at ease in the sky. I certainly did not like to fly solo. Nonetheless getting my license was one of the most liberating moments of self-realization I've ever known. Learning to fly opened the door to exciting adventures. It was yet another reason why I've remained in Kenya.

My introduction to aviation came at a time when my life was being redefined in major ways. Nairobi Hospital was far better equipped and better staffed than the government-run hospitals. It also supported its own nursing school and had a reputation for an excellent standard of nursing care. It was clear that despite the heroic efforts of the Ministry of Health to raise their standards, I would be able to provide better care for my patients in private practice. I also knew that I could help shape a new generation of Kenyan cardiologists as I intended to continue teaching. To my mind, there was really no better place to practice.

At first I was disinclined to go into solo private practice. I feared it would rob me of the time for other pursuits. I wanted to travel the world and use my newly acquired pilot's license to explore Kenya. I also wanted to start looking for a wife. The solution to my dilemma arrived in the person of Dr Majid Warshow. He was a Swahili Muslim from Mombasa of Omani descent. We had met shortly after my arrival when he was still a resident. The powers that be had wanted me to train a Kikuyu doctor from Majid's residency class. I had no problem with that as I had not been around long enough to appreciate the political motivation to have an upcountry Kikuyu rather than someone from the coast. However, when I assessed their relative capabilities independent of ethnicity, I insisted on training Majid. He had told me he was keen to become a cardiologist, and he was a quick learner with very good hands. After finishing his medical training, Majid went to work at Kenyatta National Hospital. It was there that we discussed the allure of private practice. In June 1981 we decided to become partners. I thought it was an excellent idea. He was smart and capable and had the drive that would see him excel in his profession. There was an added bonus. We enjoyed each other's sense of humour.

The following month we began working fulltime at Nairobi Hospital. A Peace Corps nurse, Anne Wunderlich, moved with us from Kenyatta National Hospital to Nairobi Hospital. In a previous life Anne had been a professional jockey, riding home winners at thoroughbred races in the U.S. She had been hired as a nurse, but in the early days she doubled as typist and accountant too. Anne married, had children and remains a friend of ours in Kenya.

Majid was married with two children with a third child on the way. He also had financial responsibility for a large extended family. I assumed he had plenty of motivation to work hard and get ahead, and I was correct. Our partnership lasted for eighteen years. At first we shared office space with Professor Ambrose Wasunna, a surgeon on the Nairobi Hospital staff. The arrangement suited us for the short term, but Majid and I were on the lookout for a larger space to accommodate our treadmills and other cardiology machines and instruments.

We resolved our office space problem in an unusual way. One day as I was walking past the operating theatre near the ICU, a young English doctor who was giving birth to her first baby by caesarean section suffered a cardiac arrest. It was fortuitous timing that I happened to be there. I was able to resuscitate her and all turned out well. She went home with her baby forty-eight hours later under the care of her surgeon husband. It was pure luck I was on the scene to save the patient. On any given day I more likely would have been seeing patients on the far side of the hospital. Recognizing the value of keeping me handy for such occasions, the hospital offered us the large space we needed near the ICU and operating rooms. They would own the new space. We would pay for the construction in return for ten rent-free years. I've worked out of that same office ever since.

A major difference between my old job at Kenyatta National Hospital and my private practice at Nairobi Hospital was that my patients were generally much better off financially. Although I still regarded myself as a cardiologist, I also was becoming more of a general internist. In contrast to the usual Western specialization in the private sector, where one would gradually go from a broad medicine practice to more specialization as one's reputation in the subspecialty builds, my professional path was the opposite. As attending physician in hospital-based practice, I became more involved in noncardiac critical care. This meant I was constantly honing my knowledge and skills in general internal medicine while mastering new areas such as rheumatology, nephrology, infectious disease and even tropical medicine in the ICU setting. In those days there were few subspecialists at the hospital. I had to do it all.

I enjoyed the holistic approach required by the varied needs of my patients. It required intensive research and often consulting internationally with experts. It was exciting. I'm happy to say that now in Kenya we have very capable and well-trained subspecialists in all the internal medicine subspecialties.

14

EMERGENCY EVACUATIONS

In the early days before my practice got really busy, from time to time I accompanied patients on international evacuations. Escorting a critically ill person long distances aboard a commercial aircraft to an uncertain fate in foreign lands is a prescription for drama. And drama there was with several patients. One of them was Ahmed.

He was a twenty-two-year-old Kenyan Somali who worked as a clerk for the National Cereals and Produce Board. He was married and had two small children. He had been sent to me with an abnormal aortic valve. I had done a heart catheterization and found it had narrowed significantly. It probably was abnormal from birth although the narrowing could have been due to rheumatic heart disease. There was no doubt Ahmed needed a replacement urgently.

The operation was not something that could be done in Nairobi at that time, so I sent Ahmed to England. The procedure was a success and at first he did very well. Then two years later he came to see me again over the Christmas period with congestive cardiac failure. On examination it was clear he was quite ill. The only explanation I could think of was his new disc valve. Perhaps the disc was getting stuck instead of opening properly. I catheterized him and found, as I had thought, that the artificial valve was barely opening due to some tissue overgrowth. Had echocardiography been available in Kenya in those days, the catheterization could have been avoided.

We quickly arranged for emergency surgery to be done by Mr Brynn Williams at St. Thomas' Hospital in London, the same surgeon who had conducted the initial valve replacement surgery. Previously Ahmed had been accompanied by a relative. This time he was so ill I would have to go with him. I booked economy seats on a British Airways flight leaving New Year's Eve morning. Ahmed actually looked pretty good so as soon as we were on the plane I closed my eyes and fell asleep.

I expected to wake up rested as we approached Heathrow. Instead about three hours later I was roused by a flight attendant who informed me that we were still on the ground. The flight had been delayed for some reason. I decided to take Ahmed to the ICU at Nairobi Hospital then went home. I needed some sleep. I was dozing comfortably when the phone rang. It was the hospital. Ahmed had gone into cardiac arrest. The nurses were giving Ahmed CPR (cardiopulmonary resuscitation) when I arrived. I cardioverted him to restore his heart rhythm, zapping him three times with electrodes.

Now I had a tough decision to make. Did I take Ahmed to London for lifesaving surgery or not? He was so sick the odds of his surviving the long trip were poor. Yet if I didn't take him, he was certain to die. His family arranged with British Airways to have a stretcher brought on board in case we decided to go. I also was now authorized by his employers to bring a nurse along. I postponed my decision for as long as possible, right until the last minute before driving to the airport in time to board the plane, expecting events would overtake me. They didn't. He was very short of breath and not making any urine despite the diuretics I'd administered. His kidneys had shut down. His blood pressure was low as well. But he was alert and talkative. He was a young man with his whole life ahead of him, and he had a family to look after as well. I decided to go for it. The nurse, Ahmed and I boarded first with all sorts of medical equipment. We were trying to get him stabilized when the flight attendant approached. 'The captain would like to talk to you.'

I followed her to the flight deck where she left me with the captain. 'What can I do for you?' I asked.

He gave me a look that was clearly sizing me up. 'I understand you have a very sick patient.'

'That's correct, sir.'

'We don't want any passengers dying on our aircraft. I don't think I want to take your patient on my plane.'

'I understand your feelings,' I answered cautiously. 'I wouldn't blame you. I'd be glad to take the patient off the aircraft, but you need to know that if I do, there's a 100 percent chance he will die. If we take him, we at least have some chance of getting him to London alive and replacing his heart valve so he might live. He's only twenty-four. He's got a wife and two young children.'

Seconds passed. It seemed to me that yet again that day, Ahmed's life hung in the balance. The captain looked down at his hands, looked up and gave me the slightest of nods. 'Okay. We'll take him.'

For the first two hours in the air everything went like clockwork. I even managed to get a little shuteye. Then the nurse woke me saying Ahmed was very short of breath. His heart could no longer provide the force to move his blood through the lungs to the body. Despite administering high doses of intravenous diuretics, his kidneys could not produce urine as they were not getting an adequate supply of blood. The excess fluid was building up in

Ahmed's lungs. He was drowning. Plan B was basically my only choice. I had to get some fluid out of him, and that fluid would be blood.

By this time a sense of high drama had gripped our fellow passengers. They were emotionally invested in Ahmed's desperate struggle. A flight attendant had put up a curtain to screen Ahmed from the other passengers. Far from being annoyed by the disturbance their *harambee* (coming together) spirit had kicked in. They were sincerely concerned about what was happening to this man who was hidden from view. Many offered their help. The palpable good will in the plane made me feel less guilty about the disturbance and allowed me to focus entirely on Ahmed.

By now he was going through a lot of changes in his heart rhythms. It was a troubling sign. The defibrillator could help to regulate its rhythm, but it didn't work because it was incompatible with the aircraft's voltage. The flight engineer was alerted. Miraculously he rigged up something that fixed the problem.

The next predicament was how to phlebotomize Ahmed. This was simply bloodletting, familiar to anyone who has ever given blood. Normally I would have inserted a needle into his vein that was connected to a plastic bag. I couldn't though because I didn't have the bag. I asked the nurse to fetch me two plastic cups of Diet Coke and drank them down. Then I instructed her to hold one of the containers next to Ahmed's jugular vein as I inserted the needle. I withdrew twenty ccs and squirted the blood into the Coke cup. I was using the largest syringe I had, but it was only four teaspoonful. I repeated the procedure until the cup was full. The nurse took it to the bathroom and returned with it empty while I was filling the second one. In this way we extracted about one and a half pints of blood. It was slow and painstaking work, but it relieved Ahmed of some of his distress.

We were about four and a half hours into the flight by the time we'd finished. At this point Ahmed suffered yet another cardiac arrest. We gave him a shock with our jerry-rigged defibrillator. He lost consciousness for about twenty seconds then woke up, looking mildly surprised, and said, 'I must have fainted.' His blood pressure was normal as was his heart rhythm. He actually looked pretty good.

I was again called to the flight deck.

'How's your patient?' asked the pilot.

'He's very sick. But he's still alive.'

'You know we're scheduled to make a stop at Zurich?'

I nodded.

'Would your patient have a better chance if we went directly to London?'

'He certainly would.'

'Doc,' he said with a broad smile, 'it's New Year's Eve. If we land in Switzerland I'll have to spend the night there, and my wife is in England.'

'My wife's in England too,' said the co-pilot.

'And so is my girlfriend,' said the flight engineer.

It was a done deal. We bypassed Switzerland.

Since very few of the passengers were destined for Zurich, nearly everyone was happy at the prospect of spending New Year's Eve in London. The plane broke into spontaneous applause. We touched down at Heathrow before ten that night. A cargo lift met us on the tarmac and carried Ahmed, the nurse and myself from the back of the 747 to a waiting ambulance.

'Doc,' the ambulance driver asked me, 'is this a real emergency?'

'As big an emergency as you'll ever have,' I told him.

With siren wailing and foot flat on the floor, he wove his way through the New Year's Eve traffic at 130 kilometres an hour. Brynn Williams was waiting at St Thomas' Hospital. Ahmed's heart stopped again on the way to the operating room so we zapped him once more. I stayed to observe the surgery that night. Sure enough the artificial valve was stuck as the catheterization had indicated, the overgrown tissue clearly visible. Brynn removed the old valve and replaced it with a new one then sent Ahmed to the ICU.

I drove with Brynn Williams to his house, looking forward to some badly needed sleep. The next morning, New Year's Day, I was up early and out bargain hunting. Brynn joked I always had emergency patients to bring during the seasonal sales. I checked in on Ahmed too. He was recovering nicely.

I spent two more nights at the Williams' house and stopped by to see Ahmed once more before flying home. He was in good spirits and very grateful to be alive. 'Thank you for saving my life a second time,' he said. 'I really, really appreciate it.'

London became a regular destination on my medical escort travels. In 1983 a nurse and I escorted two patients simultaneously on a British Airways overnight flight. One of the patients was a man in his sixties called Juma Boy. As the powerful head of COTU (the Central Organization of Trade Unions), he was well connected in and out of government circles. He had experienced recurrent episodes of chest pain (pre-infarction angina). He had not had a heart attack, but the heart muscle was not getting enough blood and oxygen. This condition often precedes a major heart attack. His diabetes put him in an even higher risk category. When I attended him yet again, I gave him aspirin, the blood thinner heparin and beta blockers. It was the maximum medical therapy at that time, but his pain did not abate. That was when I decided he required emergency bypass surgery in London.

The second patient was Pete. He was an English irrigation engineer working in the Nyeri-Nanyuki area around Mt Kenya. He had been in a horrific traffic accident. His head injuries were so severe he had been reduced to a vegetative state and had a tracheostomy tube in his neck to help him breathe. Irrigation Pete had been transferred to Nairobi Hospital where he became my patient. With no hope of reversing his neurological damage, his family in England had asked if I could bring him home to be with his loved ones.

Once again it was just after Christmas. Pete was brought aboard on a stretcher. Three rows of seats had been sectioned off for him behind a curtain. Two seats in each row had been laid flat to accommodate the stretcher. The aisle seat remained upright for the nurse. I arrived with Juma Boy and his family. Juma Boy was a VIP so by special arrangement we drove right out onto the tarmac, bypassing immigration control, and walked slowly up the external stairs into first class.

I made sure Juma was comfortable then walked back to see how Irrigation Pete was doing. The nurse told me there had been some mucus secretions in his lungs and at times he was becoming cyanotic (blue) from the deficiency of oxygen in his blood. When I asked a flight attendant for the bottle of oxygen I had ordered three days in advance, she shook her head. It hadn't been delivered. This presented a possibly life-threatening logistical problem. I asked to see the captain.

'What if we give you oxygen right after take-off?' he suggested.

'That would be okay,' I replied, 'He's young and stable enough. He can make it until then.'

Heartbeat: An American Cardiologist in Kenya

As soon as we were airborne I unbuckled and headed back to economy to check on Pete. He was getting bluer, due to the fact that the aircraft's altitude pressurization was at 6500 feet, 1000 feet higher than that of Nairobi. I had been promised oxygen so things were under control. I asked an attendant if she could tell the captain we were ready for it. Moments later some 400 oxygen masks suddenly dropped from their overhead compartments as a recorded message announced to the passengers, 'We have just lost cabin pressure. Do not panic. Extinguish your cigarettes. Put the mask to your face and breathe normally.'

It was a Marx Brothers moment. People were panicking all around us. A woman three rows in front clutched at her mask repeating again and again, 'I can't get enough air! I can't get enough air!' The flight attendant and I knew what had happened. The captain had pushed or pulled the wrong switch, releasing all the oxygen masks instead of just the one we needed. The two of us fell to our knees laughing hysterically as the 747 continued on its trajectory to cruising altitude.

The recorded announcement kept replaying, apparently because the captain did not know how to shut it off. That struck us as hilarious too and we began to laugh all over again. At last a calm male voice with a pronounced British accent announced over the intercom, 'Ladies and gentleman, you may have noticed we have a very sick patient who is on a stretcher in the economy section of the aircraft. His doctor requested that we give him some oxygen. I do apologize, but it appears that we gave him a bit more oxygen than he really needed. There is no emergency, and everyone should relax.'

Everyone did relax eventually. I know I did. After making certain both my patients were stable, I dozed off as the cabin crew moved from row to row, rolling up the oxygen masks and stuffing them back into their compartments. Sometimes one of the masks would get stuck or fall down again. None of the cabin crew had ever been through such an exercise so their progress was fitful. We touched down at Heathrow at dawn. I awoke to watch the last three dangling masks being carefully tucked away.

Irrigation Pete lived for several more months. He died peacefully with his family around him, surviving far longer than I had expected. Juma Boy underwent successful bypass surgery but ten days later unexpectedly died from complications caused by his diabetes. This saddened me. It can be a hard lesson to learn. Doctors must accept that ultimately outcomes are determined by powers greater than us.

The Brzoza family newly arrived in Chicago from Poland in 1916. David's father Nochem, 11, stands at the back with his parents and five brothers and sisters.

Maternal grandparents, newlyweds Rabbi Moshe Zeev Kahn and Eva.

Now the Silversteins, the family had expanded by 1935. Norman, with an anglicized name and a moustache, is third row far left.

Major Dr Norman Silverstein, a medical officer for the US Army, aboard the navy ship USS Hope in 1943.

Young David.

Norman and Sarah Silverstein in 1957.

David fresh from the Cook Islands in a tapa cloth vest with cardiology fellowship class at the University of Washington, 1973.

David overcame his fear of flying by getting a pilot's license.

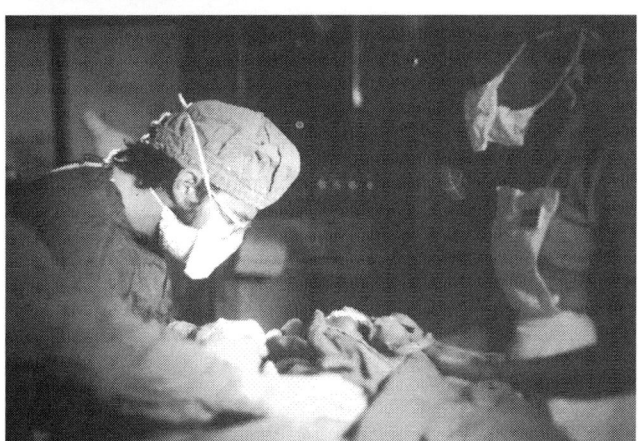

At Kenyatta National Hospital with the surgical team separating conjoined twins.

David receives his Fellow of the American College of Cardiology certification from the Deputy American Ambassador to Kenya, 1976.

President Moi as sandak (godfather) holds firstborn son Nahum at his circumcision, 1989.

Charles Njonjo, known as the Duke of Kabeteshire and Kenya's first attorney general, became David's close friend, patient and patriarch.

David's first wife Lesley with their two sons Nahum and Joshua.

Aaron (Right) and Jeremy (Left) with their mother Jackie Obare.

David and Channa attending to victims of the terrorist attack on the US Embassy in Nairobi, August 7, 1998. Afterwards he took her out to dinner, their first date.

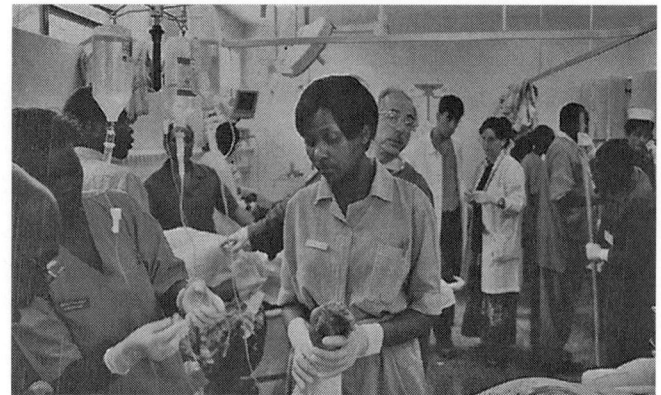

David and Channa with giraffe observing their courtship.

Channa and Sally Kosgei, her 'flower girl'.

David and Channa on their wedding day September 9, 2001 at Kongoni Game Valley, overlooking Lake Naivasha.

President Moi shakes hands with Channa and David at their wedding, while Rabbi Zeev Amit looks on.

President Moi and Charles Njonjo, guests of honour at David and Channa's wedding.

David accompanies President Moi on a state visit to Israel in 1994.

Praying at the Western Wall of the Temple in Jerusalem.

15

NONE OF THE USUAL SUSPECTS

I had come to Kenya to treat cardiovascular disease, but it was soon apparent that I had to broaden my medical horizons to encompass diseases that had not been seen in the West for a very long time. For example shortly after arriving in Nairobi, I was called to a ward to see a patient from Central Province, the fertile high country north of the capital and west of Mt Kenya. The young man had a severe headache, general weakness, gross dehydration, shortness of breath, high fever and sore swollen lymph nodes called buboes. An X-ray showed he was suffering from pneumonia as well.

I was pretty sure it was a case of bubonic plague although I'd never seen one before. It is caused by the bacterium *Yersinia pestis* which infects rats and is transmitted to humans via flea bites. Our patient had three relatives with the same symptoms downstairs in the ER. We brought them up and asked if they had a lot of rats where they lived. They did.

Bubonic plague was known as the Black Death in the 14th century when it scythed through Eurasia and North Africa killing up to 200 million people. It was the worst pandemic in history. The first known outbreak of plague in Kenya was in 1902 in Nairobi's Indian Bazaar where rats had bred in the filth that had accumulated in the overcrowded dwellings and tented shops. Dr

Rosendo Ribeiro, who made house calls astride his tame zebra, had diagnosed the disease in two Somali patients. He notified Dr Alfred Spurrier, the Medical Officer of Health. Spurrier had never encountered plague before and panicked, razing everything to the ground from the military lines and railway workshops to the Indian bazaar and nearby African villages. It cost the British government £50,000. The bazaar was rebuilt in 1904 on its present site in Biashara Street. Of the sixty-three recorded cases, twenty people had died. Today the disease is easily controlled with antibiotics, particularly streptomycin. Left untreated it is a near certain and ghastly way to die.

I immediately called Dr Wilfred Koinange, the chief of the Infectious Diseases Hospital. Blood samples confirmed my diagnosis. We put the four patients in isolation and started them on antibiotics. They recovered well. Meanwhile a medical team was dispatched to their village where an unreported plague epidemic was discovered and quickly stamped out.

On another occasion three members of a family from the town of Kisumu on Lake Victoria were brought to the hospital with the classic symptoms of botulism. Their cranial nerves were affected. They were having trouble breathing and swallowing. They had facial weakness, dilated pupils and blurred vision. None had a fever. Botulism is an exceedingly rare affliction in the U.S. and is usually associated with poorly preserved foods. It is a potentially fatal illness caused by botulinum which is produced by the common soil bacterium *Clostridium botulinum*. It is best known today for its use in Botox treatments. It is also used to treat an eye condition called strabismus as well as migraines, an overactive bladder and depression.

As I was taking a history, I figured out how the family might have been exposed. Like many Africans they prized roasted locusts as a delicacy. They told me that they had been out with plastic bags gathering dead locusts on the ground. Probably they had scooped up *Clostridium botulinum* from the soil along with the insects. In the anaerobic environment of their sealed plastic bags, the bacterium produced its neurotoxin that my patients then consumed. Botulism antitoxin was not available. We gave the patients supportive care in the ICU. Two of them required ventilators. One of the four died.

A far more complex case was that of Nancy. One day her father came to my house with his daughter. She was a beautiful young woman of twenty-six who had returned from Chicago after completing a master's degree. She was having trouble passing urine and also had developed partial paralysis of both legs. While at university she had gone to see a doctor with a rash and joint pains. He had told her she had Henoch Schonlein purpura, also called IgA vasculitis. Patients seldom develop any subsequent complications. Nevertheless, I told her father that she needed to be admitted into the hospital at once.

Laboratory tests all pointed to a diagnosis of lupus erythematosus, a chronic inflammatory autoimmune disease which is highly virulent. It was seldom diagnosed at that time among African Kenyans. We did not then have CT scans or MRIs in Kenya. There was no known association of Henoch Schonlein with lupus erythematosus. Subsequent articles decades later reported a rare association of these two conditions.

Nancy's partial paralysis was being caused by an inflammatory lesion in her spinal cord that was related to lupus. I treated her with a high dose of steroids to reduce the inflammation. I'd never before treated a lupus case involving the spinal cord. Because there were no rheumatologists in Kenya at that time to consult with, I had to decide for myself the further course of treatment. As I considered how to proceed, it occurred to me that we might try a course of cancer chemotherapy which would have the effect of knocking down her overactive immune system. This standard of care using chemotherapy was only just beginning to be introduced in the U.S. I contacted Dr Jack Klippel at the National Institutes of Health in the States. He was a leading expert on autoimmune diseases and had authored the definitive textbook on rheumatology. Once I described the situation to him over the telephone, Klippel said he felt chemotherapy was the right way to go but cautioned me that such a treatment might sterilize Nancy.

I started her off on a three-day course of high-dose intravenous chemotherapy with cyclophosphamide then three days of pulsed high-dose steroid. She responded beautifully and was able to walk out of the hospital unaided. She did very well for two years and then had a setback. The skin and joint lesions returned. I tried chemotherapy once more, this time with a once-a-week oral dose of methotrexate. It was a cancer drug that had just been introduced as a treatment for autoimmune conditions as it killed some of the cells that produce immunity. Nancy's side effects were minimal.

After an extended remission of several years, Nancy suddenly fell ill again with a high fever and cough and shortness of breath. This became galloping pneumonia within a few dramatic hours. By now she was blue, and X-rays of her lungs revealed a huge white expanse. We took her into the ICU where we treated her with broad-spectrum antibiotics. It was to no avail. She went into shock and died within hours. Losing her was extremely painful. I had pulled her through previous crises and was very close to both her and her father.

I am frequently asked if it is hard to make the difficult decisions I must face every day. My answer is no - as long as I'm certain that the course I choose represents the best practices in my profession. Like all medical personnel, I adhere to the centuries-old precept we learned as students, *Primum non nocere*. First do no harm. If I am certain I did my very best - did it correctly - then I am at peace when a patient dies even though I can feel great sadness at the time.

It is my belief that part of a doctor's duty is not to prolong life unduly when the ultimate outcome is clear. Sometimes the best choice is quality of life over endless painful and uncomfortable procedures. This was the case with Moyez, an Asian Kenyan, who was a patient of mine. He was a bon viveur who loved liquor, cigarettes, women and gambling and had the money to support his habits. He had reached his seventies by the time he came to me with unmistakable symptoms of advanced lung cancer. I wasn't the first doctor Moyez had seen about his condition. Before coming to me, he had received conflicting information and advice, most of it wrong.

Doctors must always be clear and direct with their patients at such times. When talking to patients approaching the end of life, I choose my words carefully so that the diagnosis and prognosis is clear and unambiguous but delivered with kindness. If only I could have been that expert when ending my relationships.

I told Moyez what I had found, explaining his treatment options were extremely limited, and advised him not to waste the precious time remaining with doctors and hospitals. Far better to spend the rest of his life as he pleased. That is precisely what he did, enjoying his various pursuits to the very end. Sometimes the best choice is quality of life.

My previously untested forensic skills were brought into play in the mysterious case of Sharad Maniar, a dermatologist. I was at home one evening when I received a call at about 10 pm from Hasmukh Kamdar, a general and cardiac surgeon at the MP Shah Hospital. The internist who was treating Sharad had asked if I could come in to give a second opinion. It was thought he'd suffered a brainstem stroke, but a CT scan of his head was normal. When I examined Sharad, he appeared at first to be in a deep coma. But when I induced pain, he grimaced and opened his eyes slightly for a second. His pupils were pinpoint, which is often seen with mid-brain haemorrhages.

As I was examining him, I noticed a strange odour. Sharad was certainly not a heavy drinker, and it was not alcohol. I was concerned that he might have ingested something. I asked if he had been depressed or could have taken pills for some other reason. His family quickly ruled out both possibilities. I inquired whether anybody else in the family was unwell and asked what they had eaten for dinner. Sharad and his wife had had a light meal with a cup of tea. I was told that his wife was not feeling well either, although her symptoms were not nearly as severe as her husband's. She was being attended on the ward.

That's when it dawned on me. It was most likely organophosphate poisoning. Phosphorus radicals have the specific effect of inactivating the cholinesterase in the body. This results in continuous stimulation of the entire parasympathetic nervous system causing respiratory difficulty and often diarrhoea, vomiting, seizures and loss of consciousness. Pinpoint pupils are due to unopposed parasympathetic stimulation. Organophosphates are highly toxic nerve agents widely used as pesticides. Examples of organophosphates include paraquat, DDT, the nerve gas sarin, and novichok, the poison used in the March 2018 attempted murder in Britain of the former Russian spy, Sergei Skirpal, and his daughter Yulia. These compounds are cheap to manufacture and are readily available all over the world. As a consequence, at that time in Kenya they were the most popular mode of suicide among poor, rural Africans. I saw a lot of organophosphate poisoning, both accidental and intentional, while I was at Kenyatta National Hospital. The odour was unmistakable and memorable. It seemed highly improbable that Sharad Maniar had attempted to kill himself and his wife. Nor was it likely that he'd been accidentally poisoned. The case looked like attempted murder.

I left Sharad in the ICU on supportive care with IV fluids with orders to be certain his airway was not compromised and went to see his wife on the ward. I noted the same odour on her breath. She was very sleepy and communicated with difficulty. Her pupils were also constricted. To confirm my diagnosis and find out how and why Sharad and his wife had been poisoned, I asked their daughter to return to their house and retrieve any remnants of the food or drink that her parents had consumed.

When she went back, she realized that in her panic at discovering her parents so sick she had locked their two domestic staff inside the house and left with the only key. She quickly gathered up the leftover food and drink and left again, intentionally locking the door this time so the two servants had no means of leaving.

The meal's leftovers were sent to the government chemist who discovered that an organophosphate poison had indeed been mixed in with some yoghurt. I alerted the family to contact the police right away. At the same time, I started Sharad on intravenous atropine in industrial doses. Atropine is a parasympathetic inhibitor and helps to reverse the poisoning process. By the next morning Sharad was wide awake. His wife's case was very mild as she had taken little supper. We gave her atropine in lower doses and she was also in fine shape by the morning. The following day both were ready to go home.

Fortunately the police found the two suspects still locked in the kitchen and took them into custody. At trial both servants were found guilty and sentenced to prison. As a young man I had read many stories about Sherlock Holmes by the Scottish physician, Sir Arthur Conan Doyle. Never in a life of Sundays could I have imagined that I would be solving a murder mystery too.

16

CREATURES THAT BITE

Caring for the critically ill at Nairobi Hospital meant I saw a lot of malaria. I still do. The name comes from the Italian *mal aria*, meaning bad air. It is an ancient disease described by the Chinese in 2700 BC. Even though it has ravaged populations around the world ever since, it was the turn of the 20th century when scientists identified the mosquito as the vector for transmitting the disease. It was later established the chief culprit was the female *anopheles* mosquito.

For millennia most malaria cures used substances extracted from various tree barks. Their efficacy is recognized by modern practitioners of Western medicine. The earliest of these was an extract of the bark of a type of wormwood (*Artemisia annua*) found in Chinese tombs dating back to the 2nd century BC. Today artemisinin is a first-line drug for treating malaria. Almost 2000 years later, Spanish Jesuit missionaries learned from native Americans the medicinal value of Peruvian bark taken from the cinchona tree. The active ingredient was later called quinine.

The U.S. National Malaria Eradication Program, undertaken by state and local health agencies in thirteen southeastern states, as well as by the CDC (the Centers for Disease Control and Prevention), was created in 1947. Four years later malaria was eradicated in the United States by draining swamps and spraying with the pesticide DDT. It had been discovered in 1939 and was to be banned worldwide in 2001 because of its toxicity. International campaigns against malaria, especially in Africa, have not been as successful. As far back as 1910, when malaria was the leading cause of death among expatriate soldiers and administrators in British East Africa, efforts were made to control the disease over the years by spraying mosquitos and their habitats with various compounds, the most effective of which was DDT.

Today roughly nine out of ten malaria deaths worldwide occur in sub-Saharan Africa. This includes Kenya where malaria is common at altitudes below 5000 feet. Now with global warming more cases are occurring at higher altitudes in the Rift Valley. Two decades ago a major success in Kenya's program to control malaria was the introduction of ACT (antimalarial combination therapy). Infections treated quickly with ACT reduced the plasmodia load in the blood and therefore mortality. Malaria plasmodia have developed resistance to every generation of antimalarials and continue to do so. Building on earlier efforts a program to distribute bed nets on a large scale was launched in 2006. The nets were impregnated with pyrethrum insecticide derived from the pyrethrum plant that grows in Kenya. Unfortunately, the malarial plasmodia are now developing resistance to pyrethrum too.

Complicating this uphill struggle to control malaria in Africa, only six percent of Kenya's 2020 – 2022 allocation from the Global Fund to Fight AIDS, Tuberculosis and Malaria was disbursed. The official explanation was that COVID-19 had disrupted travel and therefore the distribution of bed nets under mass campaigns. This was true but didn't fully explain the Ministry of Health's poor performance. Another reason was that communities stopped using the health facilities out of fear of catching COVID-19. So people didn't receive bed nets to prevent malaria and didn't get treated when they came down with it.

In endemic malarial areas such as the Indian Ocean coastal strip and around Lake Victoria, much of the population has developed partial immunity. When adults from these areas are infected with malaria they fall sick with fever, but their bodies almost inevitably mount sufficient defences to avert death from the disease. Those born and raised at higher altitudes are at greater risk of dying from malaria as is the expatriate community and tourists who do not take the necessary prophylaxis. Of the several types of malaria in Kenya, the most common is *Plasmodium falciparum*. This is not the malaria that lies dormant and recurs at intervals over many decades. This is the far more virulent type of malaria that can kill someone who is not immune.

Carmen was one such person. A fifty-two-year-old Peace Corps volunteer, in July 1986 she was flown from the Tanzanian capital Dar es Salaam to the Nairobi Hospital ICU and placed under my care. At that time and for some decades to come, I treated all volunteers referred by the Peace Corps medical officers because their cases were complicated and almost invariably needed hospitalization. The Peace Corps required their volunteers to take the most effective prophylactic medicine of the time against malaria. The requirement was so strict that failure to do so could result in termination of services. Carmen was loath to ingest chemicals. She felt that garlic would keep the *anopheles* mosquito away. She ate fresh garlic and slept with a garland of fresh garlic around her neck instead of taking chloroquine, the malaria prophylactic of choice in the 80s. There were cases of chloroquine resistance described in Asia at the time but none yet in our East African experience.

When Carmen fell ill with malaria in a remote Tanzanian village hospital, she was promptly diagnosed with malaria and given chloroquine. Unfortunately, the chloroquine didn't work. Despite receiving the standard treatment of the day, Carmen deteriorated and was transferred to the Aga Khan Hospital in Dar es Salaam three days later. She presented with delirium, spiking high fevers and bloody diarrhoea. She was found to be clinically dehydrated. The doctors resorted to intravenous doses of the old Peruvian drug quinine, which had been used extensively during Africa's colonial period.

It has long been suspected, but never proved, that quinine can cause a complication of malaria called blackwater fever. The patient passes very dark urine caused by the massive destruction of red blood cells (haemolysis) by the malarial parasites. According to this theory, quinine precipitates black urine by rapidly destroying all the malarial parasites living in the red cells causing cascades of haemoglobin to flood the bloodstream. This leads to kidney failure. Quinine can also cause tinnitus, a severe ringing in the ears.

The doctors in Dar es Salaam rehydrated Carmen, but her kidney function continued to falter. When the air ambulance delivered her to us, she was clearly very ill. Blood smears taken at the Aga Khan Hospital showed that sixty percent of her red blood cells were infected by the *Plasmodium falciparum*. Any infection rate above five percent puts the patient at risk of death. The tropical medicine textbooks published earlier in the 20th century stated that anything above ten percent was uniformly fatal.

When we assessed Carmen's blood results we noted the kidney dysfunction was severe. We found the levels of creatinine, a waste product normally excreted through the kidneys, three and a half times the upper limits of normal. Her liver tests showed evidence of hepatitis, which we commonly saw with malaria. Carmen's delirium and stupor indicated cerebral malaria. This occurs when so many blood cells are filled with malarial parasites they plug up the arterioles and capillaries. Small but widespread areas of the brain do not get enough blood supply, and the brain swells as a result.

Her chest X-ray showed diffuse whitish areas of infiltrates in both sides of the lungs. Although it was read by the radiologist as pneumonia, given the clinical setting it was clearly acute respiratory distress syndrome. Fluid was leaking through the lung capillaries into the air sacs just as was happening in the brain. In addition her kidney dysfunction was severe. Such a combination was almost uniformly fatal. Her malarial count had by this time plummeted from sixty to zero. The quinine had destroyed all the malaria parasites, but Carmen's blood vessels, kidneys, lungs and brain were severely damaged. Her life was at stake.

She was very dehydrated, but with aggressive fluid therapy we slowly got her kidney function to improve thus avoiding dialysis. Her lungs were a far greater challenge. The evening after her admission we inserted an endotracheal tube through her mouth into her trachea to ease her breathing and put her on a ventilator to ensure she received an adequate supply of oxygen. She also had to be fed via a tube through her nose into her stomach and subsequently had to have a tracheostomy. She was on a ventilator for twenty-eight days. As was expected Carmen also developed recurrent chest infections over this period. Fortunately, pathogenic organisms of that era weren't as resistant as today's. Nevertheless, we had to put her on three different antibiotics.

Two days after she was taken off the ventilator, with vigorous chest physiotherapy, we transferred her to the ward where she stayed for a fortnight until she was strong enough to fly home to the U.S. with a medical escort. She was behaving in a bizarre manner when she left, but without knowing her medical history I couldn't tell whether this was a personality change or if she was always like that.

Carmen's case was seminal in the treatment of malaria in East Africa. It was the first clinical instance of marked resistance to chloroquine, the traditional drug of choice for prevention and treatment. After that most doctors in East Africa stopped using the drug. In 2000 I published a paper with nurse Martha Loeffler reviewing the previous ten years' data on the treatment of malaria in the ICU. The combination of Carmen's complications - cerebral malaria, acute respiratory distress syndrome and acute renal failure - was still nearly 100 percent fatal despite the use of new drugs.

Subsequently we tried a variety of other medications (garlic was not among them) but abandoned each before long for a variety of different reasons. The drug Halfan (halofantrine) was quite effective except in cases of severe malaria. The deal breakers were the cases of sudden death related to its cardiac side effects. We moved on to a drug called Larium (mefloquin). It worked well except for one important drawback. Many of the people who took it for prevention, especially young Peace Corps volunteers, had terrible dreams and even developed acute psychosis. We also noted a higher incidence of seizures. These days we usually prescribe Malarone (atovaquone and proguanil) although there are recent reports of growing resistance to it. Our treatment regimen now is based on artemisinin, the same wormwood bark recovered from the ancient Chinese tombs. Yet there is evidence that the malaria plasmodia are evolving resistance to artemisinin as well, proving once more this centuries-old disease's extraordinary resistance to every new - and ancient - attempt to eradicate it.

Thirty-two years after I discharged Carmen, I received a letter from her sister in Fort Worth, Texas. She informed me that Carmen, then eighty-four, had just learned that the Department of Labor would no longer subsidize the treatment for her lifelong disabilities stemming from the malaria she contracted as a Peace Corps volunteer. For some reason a practitioner of sports medicine had been engaged to assess Carmen's symptoms. She suffered from joint disease, which he correctly believed was unrelated to the malaria. But he was certainly incorrect to conclude that her severe lung disease and inability to walk because of her struggles to breathe were not connected to the malaria. I wrote numerous letters to explain Carmen's medical complications to the U.S. Department of Labor. Those who read them remained unmoved. I did everything I could for her but to no avail. After that I had no more news of Carmen. Looking back on it, I wish I had mustered the courage to ask her if she still wore garlic around her neck.

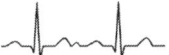

When it comes to medical crises, there is one that is nearly always fatal - rabies. The incubation period after a bite to the onset of symptoms is usually one to three months depending on the distance between the area of the bite and the central nervous system in the brain and spinal cord. This is because the virus travels via nerves not the blood stream. There are cases where the incubation has been as brief as four days and as long as six years.

Initial symptoms such as fever and headache are not alarming. As the disease progresses the rabies virus causes meningitis, an inflammation of the meninges or lining of the brain and spinal cord. Patients present with anxiety, partial paralysis, insomnia, confusion, agitation, abnormal behaviour, paranoia, terror and hallucinations progressing to delirium and coma. Another name for rabies is *hydrophobia,* the fear of water. This is seen in the later stages of the disease when patients develop difficulty swallowing. They panic when offered drinking water. Their saliva production increases and they can suffer painful throat spasms, which might be the basis of the hydrophobia.

The incidence of human rabies in the U.S. has been driven down dramatically by the mandatory vaccination of domestic animals. Most of the rabies is caused by bats. In the developing world, specifically Africa and Asia, dogs are the primary culprits in the spread of rabies to humans. There has never been a documented case of a person with rabies infecting another person by a bite, probably because people infected with rabies are admitted to hospital. There have been rare cases of human-to-human transfer from transplanted tissue such as corneas or kidneys.

This is the background for a sad episode that began 11 August 1983 when I received a phone call from my friend Dr Chandu Sheth. Chandu was the primary doctor for the U.S. Peace Corps in Kenya. He asked my help with a most bizarre case. The day before a volunteer in her early twenties working in Kikima, a small village in Makueni to the east of Nairobi, had appeared at his outpatient clinic complaining of insomnia and pain in her left arm and shoulder that had started three or four days earlier. Her neck also hurt. She said she had been healthy until then. When she returned the next morning her condition had definitely deteriorated. She was very agitated, and her upper body was in constant jerky motion. She lifted her arms a lot. At times she answered questions coherently. Other times she made no sense at all. She also had a high fever.

I treated her empirically for a bacterial infection pending the results of cultures. This had no effect. Within twenty-four hours her breathing became laboured. Her left arm appeared to be paralyzed. Her face was twisted into a grimace. She was salivating a lot. Sheila Waterman, a Peace Corps nurse, assured me that it was standard practice to vaccinate all Peace Corps volunteers with three doses of vaccine against rabies. This young woman had received her third and final dose only nine months ago, she told me.

The patient continued to deteriorate, becoming so agitated we had to chemically paralyze her and put her on a ventilator. Her high fevers persisted despite antibiotics. One of her fellow volunteers went to her house at Kikima and brought her diary back to the hospital. An entry in late April described an orphaned puppy she had discovered on her doorstep. She adopted the animal and grew fond of it. There was nothing unusual in her entries until 3 May when she wrote that the puppy was acting bizarrely and had bitten her. 'I sure hope that puppy doesn't have rabies,' she wrote. The dog subsequently ran away and presumably died.

Sixty-nine days after the bite she became symptomatic. We called in Bruce Johnson, an American virologist working in Kenya, and Peter Tukei of the Ministry of Health's Viral Research Centre at KEMRI (the Kenya Medical Research Institute). Peter had previously worked with us on two Marburg cases. We reached out to Dr Chuck Oster from the U.S. Army as well. He too had helped us on previous occasions. We knew that her rabies was fatal so we had to take precautions. We needed two confirmations, especially as she was American and a Peace Corps volunteer to boot. Together we collected the necessary tissue specimens and sent them off to CDC in the States and the KEMRI virology lab. It was no surprise when our diagnosis was confirmed.

Only six people in the world are known to have survived rabies after developing its symptoms. One of these survivors was an American who lived in Milwaukee, Wisconsin. The attending doctor devised what is called the Milwaukee Protocol, which entailed antivirals and prolonged paralysis with medication. Unfortunately, the Milwaukee Protocol proved to be a one-off success. The medical consensus is that it is not effective and not recommended.

It was frustrating and distressing to care for our young patient as we watched her deteriorate day by day. We did all we could. We administered rabies immunoglobulin and revaccinated her, hoping in vain to forestall the inevitable. She should have had a long productive life ahead of her, but we knew she would never leave the hospital. She died eighty-nine days after being bitten and just under three weeks from her arrival at our hospital. Her death was a tragedy that touched each one of us deeply.

Something positive did emerge from this sad episode. The young woman had contracted rabies and died despite being up-to-date on her vaccinations. That September we published an article in CDC's weekly bulletin, the *Morbidity and Mortality Weekly Report*, highlighting the fact that rabies patients with full pre-exposure prophylaxis still need two more intramuscular doses post-exposure - one on the day of exposure and another one on day three. I hope this new guideline has since saved lives that otherwise would have been lost.

17

GREEN MONKEYS

Ebola is a word that everyone knows. But when I started in private practice it was barely on the tongues of the doctors here in East Africa. This much feared disease has been overshadowed by another virus that has engulfed the world and changed the way we think about medicine, health systems and even our lifestyles. The COVID-19 pandemic continues to infect millions around the globe due to its high transmissibility. However, its global mortality rate is less than two percent, far lower than Ebola's current mortality rate of fifty percent. Ebola and its less known cousin Marburg haemorrhagic fever are spread via blood, faeces, body fluids and sex. They are among humankind's deadliest and most horrible afflictions. Mortality during outbreaks of Ebola has reached ninety percent or higher. Marburg outbreaks are more rare, but the mortality rates are also high.

Marburg is also known as Green Monkey Disease and is probably of African origin. Like many other diseases it was named after the place where it was first observed – Marburg in West Germany. The virus arrived there in 1967 in a shipment of monkeys from Uganda which were to be used in the development of a polio vaccine at Behringwerke, a vaccine-production facility. Thirty-one people were infected. Seven died. The first recorded case of a human infected by Ebola was in 1976 near the Ebola River in the Democratic Republic of the Congo. Both diseases are caused by filoviruses, which are named for their threadlike appearance under an electron microscope.

Marburg attacks the immune system and causes massive internal haemorrhaging, turning internal organs into bloody slush. It is deadly to a range of mammals from humans to guinea pigs. Marburg was unknown in Kenya in January 1980 when Jean Charrier, a Belgian in his mid-fifties, was brought into Nairobi Hospital's Casualty Department in a wheelchair. Shortly after Charrier reached the emergency room, he vomited a huge amount of blood, some of which went down his trachea. As medical staff scrambled to attend to him, the alarming case of a desperately ill man was set in motion. It was to make medical headlines around the world.

The sole doctor on duty that day at the modest, four-bed ICU was Shem Musoke, a young Ugandan of considerable talent and promise. On arrival in the emergency room, Musoke put a tube down Charrier's trachea to assist his breathing. Blood continued to spew from Charrier's gut into Musoke's face and onto his exposed skin. He rushed the patient to the ICU where he administered antibiotics, IV fluids and blood. Despite Musoke's every effort, Charrier continued to bleed from every orifice and needle-stick site. Unfamiliar with the filovirus and stymied by what he was seeing, all Musoke could do was provide supportive care in an effort to stabilize his patient. None of the Belgian's symptoms were unusual, but in combination they were mystifying. Hepatitis, shigellosis, yellow fever, typhoid fever and food poisoning all crossed Musoke's mind as he ministered to Charrier. Despite every effort, the young doctor was unable to save him. Fourteen hours after his arrival, Charrier's heart stopped and Musoke pronounced him dead.

Journalist Richard Preston recounted vividly what Musoke saw in his best-selling book, *The Hot Zone*. Charrier 'becomes dizzy and utterly weak, and his spine goes limp and nerveless and he loses all sense of balance. The room is turning around and around. He is going into shock. He leans over, head on his knees, and brings up an incredible quantity of blood from his stomach and spills it onto the floor with a gasping groan. The only sound is a choking in his throat as he continues to vomit blood and black matter while unconscious. Then comes a sound like a bedsheet being torn in half, which is the sound of his bowels opening, and venting blood from the anus. The blood is mixed with intestinal lining. He has sloughed his gut.'

A week or two later Dr Musoke became sick. His initial symptoms were general body aches, particularly in his back muscles, exhaustion, loss of appetite and fever. Then came jaundice, bloodshot eyes and persistent abdominal pain in the region of his liver. He went to see Dr Antonia Bagshawe, one of the hospital's visiting staff. She considered gallstones or perhaps a liver abscess as possible causes for his assortment of symptoms and sent him home with instructions to rest. When that didn't help, she ordered a variety of tests. All were negative.

Shem Musoke has a scant and fragmented memory of his Marburg ordeal. He recollects growing disoriented with distorted vision and experiencing personality changes. He became uncharacteristically abusive toward the staff and his colleagues. Antonia Bagshawe sent him to MP Shah Hospital for an ultrasound scan of his gall bladder. There were no signs of gallstones. Neither were any found during exploratory surgery at Nairobi Hospital, but his liver was red and swollen. To the amazement of the surgical team, Musoke bled and bled despite all efforts to staunch the bleeding. The lead surgeon Dr Imre

Loefler took a liver specimen, stopped the bleeding and stitched him back together.

Dr Bagshawe was personal physician to President Moi at that time and had to accompany him on an official overseas trip. I was appointed to take over Shem Musoke's care. Before she left, Antonia sent off Shem's blood and specimens from his liver biopsy to the CDC in Atlanta, Georgia and South Africa's National Institute for Virology (now the National Institute of Communicable Diseases).

Musoke was deteriorating by the hour. His kidneys began to fail. I could do little more than give him supportive treatment, as he had done for Charrier and try to keep his fever under control. Three days after I took over, at about 2 am, I received a telephone call at home from Dr Bruce Johnson, the American. He informed me that CDC had isolated the Marburg virus in Musoke's tissue samples.

I rushed to the hospital medical library to see what I could learn about this strange and powerful microorganism. There wasn't much known or much that I read to give me hope. I also had to assume that this was a highly infectious disease. By this time any number of people at the hospital could have been exposed. I explained the situation to the Kenyan health authorities, the hospital administrator Col Mike Harbage, and the doctors involved in Musoke's treatment. All agreed with my suggestion that the medical staff who were at risk, some fifteen to twenty people, be quarantined for at least two weeks or until we knew for certain whether or not they had developed the disease. A large sign was installed at the entrance to the hospital. Closed to public because of Green Monkey Disease. No new patients were accepted during that period. As it turned out, only three staffers developed antibodies to the virus and none of them became clinically ill.

Dr Wilfred Koinange, the director of medical services at the Ministry of Health, drove me to State House to brief President Moi on the situation. Attorney General Charles Njonjo happened to be there. He gave me a sceptical look. 'What's this monkey business all about?' he asked. The health minister was at the meeting too. I shared with them the little I'd learned from my morning session cramming about Green Monkey Disease. I also related the good news that two doctors with expertise in haemorrhagic fevers were being dispatched from the Institute for Virology in South Africa along with specialized equipment. I told them I was against a suggestion that had been floated to put Dr Musoke in a special capsule and fly him to South Africa for treatment. Fortunately, this plan received no further consideration.

Moi, Njonjo and the health minister James Osogo questioned me for ten minutes. Njonjo gave his word that even though Kenya did not issue visas to South African citizens in the era of apartheid, the two doctors would have no trouble securing their travel papers. Then I was sent on my way with a 'Good luck, Daktari.'

After about two weeks Musoke began to improve. He was down to a cadaverous forty-five kilos having lost fifteen kilos. He had sloughed his skin 'like a snake' as he put it. He was literally moulting. Despite this he was back at work in three months and reported no long-term medical issues except hypertension and impaired liver function. Three years later Shem Musoke and his friend and fellow Ugandan, John Masembe, joined my team. Shem has been a valued colleague and he and his family beloved friends ever since.

It is now suspected that when the Marburg virus isn't spreading it is sustained by colonies of African fruit bats – known as a reservoir - that seem largely immune to its pathogenic powers. It is also known that it incubates for about two weeks before symptoms first appear. Our first patient, Jean Charrier, was an amateur geologist. He and a friend had explored Kitum Cave, a popular tourist destination on Mount Elgon near the Ugandan border, about two weeks before he first became ill. The cave attracted many species of wild animals. Elephants had for centuries visited the cave for its rich deposits of salt crystals. Cape buffalos and leopards visited Kitum Cave too. Deep inside the cave, the salt crystals underfoot were generously covered with bat guano, deposited by various species of bats living there in the millions, including fruit-eating bats.

Seven years after Jean Charrier's anguished death, on 2 August 1987, a fifteen-year-old Danish boy named Kristian Ravn visited the cave with his parents and sister. Kristian and his mother, as Jean Charrier must have done, wandered deep into Kitum Cave. Kristian handled many stones covered with crystals. Some of these were needle sharp.

By 10 August the vacationing Ravns were at Tiwi Beach near Mombasa. Kristian was complaining of a headache. He was febrile and had no appetite. The fever persisted. Kristian grew weak. Three days later he was admitted to Aga Khan Hospital in Mombasa with suspected malaria. Sixteen days after visiting Kitum Cave, Kristian was transferred to the ICU then flown the next day by the Flying Doctors to Nairobi where he came under my care. Kristian presented with a fever, but he was alert and talkative. As I examined him, I noticed a raised patch on the boy's right arm. It looked like an insect bite. An X-ray told us he had acute respiratory distress syndrome. Fluid had collected in the lung's air sacs and was depriving organs of oxygen. Then Kristian turned blue.

I suspected we had another case of Marburg and made sure everyone wore masks, gowns and gloves. When the lab results came back from KEMRI in Nairobi and were confirmed by the U.S. Army Medical Research Institute of Infectious Diseases, we had everyone quarantined once again. It was frustrating and heartbreaking that we couldn't intervene in any meaningful way. Kristian died on 20 August, two and a half weeks after he had gone looking for rocks in Kitum Cave. His immediate cause of death was septicaemia from an opportunistic infection that he had probably acquired in the hospital.

Although it seemed fairly certain that Kristian Ravn contracted the Marburg virus at Kitum Cave, just as Jean Charrier apparently had, a large and scientifically sophisticated expedition composed of U.S Army and Kenyan scientists explored the cave a year later. They failed to confirm the virus was lurking anywhere inside or outside the cave. Large numbers of people continue to visit the cave, but none have caught Green Monkey Disease. Five years later I visited Kitum Cave. We were spooked by the swirling clouds of bats, overwhelmed by the acidic smell of their guano and awed by its vaulted magnificence.

The U.S. Federal Drug Administration released a vaccine for Ebola in December 2019. Whether it will be effective for Marburg is not yet known. Treating patients with novel diseases such as Marburg, Ebola and now COVID-19 certainly keeps a doctor humble.

18

WHITE MISCHIEF, MY OWN AND OTHERS'

As my private practice grew, I made friends with some of my more interesting patients. They were intriguingly eccentric characters who enjoyed the opportunity and adventure Kenya had to offer. Their personal lives and loves mirrored my own at the time - unconventional and emotionally messy. I was in good company.

Courtland E. Parfet – known as Court – was from Colorado. He wore a Stetson and had an accent to match. He had served in France during World War II and had taken note of how popular the American boys in uniform were when they handed out sticks of chewing gum to the French. After the war he bought a factory from Wrigley and released Hollywood gum into the French market. It was a wild success. In 1963 he sold his business for a reported $15 million to General Foods. He moved to Kenya and bought a vast ranch in the bush. Here at Solio he crossed imported French Charolais with the hardy indigenous Boran cattle. This was also a success.

His other passion was conservation. Court dedicated about 14,000 acres as a game conservancy and started an important breeding program for the threatened black rhino which continues to this day. A century ago there were so many black rhinos in Kenya they were considered vermin. For the past fifty years their horns have fetched high prices in Asia for their supposed medicinal properties. This fallacy has led to such heavy poaching that the animals are critically endangered. Court later added White rhinos, a species that is endangered. A subspecies known as Northern White rhino are on the verge of extinction. The last two northern white rhinos in the world – both female – are at the neighbouring ranch, Ol Pejeta, under the watchful eye of round-the-clock armed guards. The last male, Sudan, died there in 2018 of natural causes linked to old age.

Court was a heavy drinker and smoker, a womanizer and a hypochondriac. It was in that last capacity that I first met him in 1978. He called at all hours. 'Doc! I think this is the big one!' he shouted into the phone early on in our association.

'Court, I haven't taken your history yet, but after long experience with heart attacks I can tell you that patients suffering from one don't talk as loud as you're talking right now.'

Court was my patient and good friend until he died at the age of ninety-one. Throughout those thirty-one years he was on a 24/7 alert for 'the big one', and I was on his speed-dial. Every time he had any discomfort he called me immediately. 'Doc, I think this is really it.' The calls increased in frequency with age until Channa, tiring of his almost nightly alarms, suggested I give him a standing weekly appointment. This worked well as I saw him at the end of the day so that he could have as much time with me as he needed. He seemed to believe that having complete workups (physical exams, lab tests, ECGs, ETTs, echocardiograms) at least monthly would keep him alive forever. In the end his 'big one' came from a head injury due to a fall in his bathroom.

Court was very generous and often flew me in his private plane to stay with him and his third wife Claude at Solio. Throughout the daily game drives he peppered me with medical questions, usually triggered by having read about his latest symptoms in the Merck Manual, which was a medical reference book. I delighted in being driven among giraffe, zebra and antelope and would point out the handsome ivory tusks of the old bull elephants we came across. 'Look how big they are!' But Court would shrug off my excitement. 'Toothpicks, David. They're just toothpicks.'

Court was an avid fisherman and hunter. He carried around evidence of one hunting episode in the form of scars across one side of his face, courtesy of a wounded leopard. One claw swipe had barely missed his left eye, leaving it to droop. It required frequent medical attention.

Early on in our friendship he invited me on a fishing trip. It would be a real break, he said. 'Nobody will know where you are,' he assured me. I met him at the Malindi airport on the Indian Ocean, about seventy miles north of Mombasa. In order to get to where we were staying, we had to take a ferry across Kilifi Creek. A guard surprised us by asking if either of us was Dr Silverstein. 'No!' Court barked before I could say anything. As it turned out, I was being sought by David Partridge, the estate manager for Lady Delamere. She was desperately ill in the Mombasa hospital. I said I would get in touch.

Diana Delamere was still a prominent figure in Kenyan society even though she had retired to her home on the coast, which she called White Bear. As a widow she led a quiet life, often deep-sea fishing with David on her boat, also called *White Bear*. In her time she had been a notorious femme fatale. As the English writer Cyril Connolly noted, 'She was one of those creamy ash blondes…with a passion for clothes and jewels, both worn to perfection, and for enjoying herself and bringing out enjoyment in others. Her large pale eyes would be called cold by those on whom they had not smiled, her mouth hard by those who had not kissed it.' Diana's fate was to be forever tainted by scandal for she was the keeper of the only truly well-kept secret in Kenya.

Her story was an interesting one. She had arrived in Kenya in 1940 at the age of twenty-two with her second husband, Sir Delves Broughton. He was known to everyone as Jock and was thirty years her senior, more than old enough to be her father. Diana and Jock soon fell in with the Happy Valley set of moneyed British and European aristocrats, many of them remittance men banished to the tropics to get them out of the family's way. Their hedonistic indulgence in alcohol, drugs, wife-swapping and divorce had earned them a reputation that lives on to this day.

A month after setting up a home in the Nairobi suburb of Karen, Diana met the arrogant, rakish and twice-married Josslyn Hay, the Earl of Erroll. The attraction was instant and soon they were an item. Broughton had pledged in writing that he would not stand in her way if she fell in love with a younger man. What's more, he would provide her with a generous income of £5000 a year for at least seven years after the divorce. At first Broughton seemed to take the cuckolding in his stride, at least outwardly.

Then early one morning a little more than ten weeks after the couple's arrival in Kenya, Joss Hay was found slumped over the wheel of his Buick sedan in a country lane about a mile from the Broughtons' house. Two shots had been fired. One had missed. The other had entered behind his left ear and passed straight through his head. Delves Broughton was arrested and charged with murder. Diana, who was in court throughout the trial, brought a Queen's Counsel from London to defend him. All this was covered in great detail in the British press. Delves was acquitted for lack of evidence, and immediately afterwards Diana divorced him.

No one else was ever charged in connection with the crime. Some months later he committed suicide. Many plausible theories have circulated over the years as to who really did kill Joss Hay, most of them connected to various of his many girlfriends. It was also said that Joss had told Diana he was ending the affair, and she had persuaded a male friend to shoot him. Another theory suggests that he may have been killed by the British Secret Service as he was a member of Oswald Mosley's pro-Nazi British Union of Fascists.

Diana married Gilbert Colvile immediately after Broughton's death. He was a man who until then had preferred the company of Maasai men to that of his fellow settlers. He lived on Ndabibi, his 40,000-acre cattle ranch at Lake Naivasha, in a sparsely furnished wooden shack. It was filled with the skins of animals he had shot. They were badly cured and smelled. A man of unprepossessing looks, it was said in later life he resembled a tortoise. Diana called him Pooey. Colvile, who was probably the wealthiest man in Kenya, doted on her. He bought her a Moorish-style house on the shores of Lake Naivasha. It had a minaret and crenelated walls and was known as the Djinn Palace. Diana had probably spent time there already. It had been built by Major Cyril Ramsey-Hill whose wife Molly had divorced him to marry Joss Erroll.

All went well for twelve years until Diana fell in love with Tom Cholmondeley (pronounced Chumlee), the fourth Baron Delamere. His father, Hugh Delamere, had been one of the founding settlers who had built the Kenya colony. Tom was

Gilbert's neighbour, speaking in the relative terms of Texas ranchers. He lived at Elmentaita, one lake up in the Rift Valley, on Soysambu, his 65,000-acre ranch. Things might have become sticky if Colvile had not agreed to an amicable divorce. Tom Cholmondeley divorced too, his second wife, and Diana became Lady Delamere. Gilbert Colvile remained good friends with the couple and left his estate to Diana in his will. At the time of his death he owned 265,000 acres on which he ran 20,000 head of beef cattle.

I came to know Diana through Tom, who was a patient of mine. She was by then in her mid-sixties and still quite beautiful with those ice-blue eyes. I remember telling them both that Tom, who was approaching eighty, had chronic lung disease and needed to stop smoking. At his next appointment, he announced that he had indeed stopped because he could no longer inhale any smoke. His story sounded strange until I discovered that Diana had secretly pulled his cigarettes from their pack and painstakingly punctured each one with a pin just above the filter.

Tom died in 1979, and I began to treat Diana from time to time. She kept an apartment in London, and travelled a lot, taking months' long Mediterranean cruises. I usually saw her in the spring. When she had a facelift, she requested I be present in the operating theatre…just in case. She asked me once if I liked cufflinks. I said that I did, and she gave me an exquisite pair she'd purchased for me in England. Diamonds set in mother of pearl with white-gold trim. I still have them. She seemed to breathe different air than the rest of us. Her presence brought you back to the roaring twenties and daring thirties. When I was with her, I felt as if I was time travelling.

Diana was always punctual for appointments. After my partner Majid Warshow and I relocated our office in Nairobi

Hospital, she once failed to appear on time. Our secretary Ann Wunderlich walked over to see if she'd forgotten about the move. Sure enough, she found Diana on a bench outside the door to my old office, chatting away to a scruffy Peace Corps volunteer with long hair and a backpack. The young man told Anne that talking to Diana was 'a lot of fun' and asked who she was.

The morning after the guard at Kilifi informed Court and I that Diana was in need of her doctor, we took Court Parfet's boat down to Mombasa and I went to see her at the hospital. She was seriously ill with pneumonia, cyanotic (blue), and suffering dangerous changes in her heart rhythms. I stabilized her with antibiotics and oxygen and with medication to control her heart. Bagging the fishing trip, I arranged for the Flying Doctors to fly us to Nairobi. On the plane I was very tempted to ask her who had killed Lord Erroll but decided that would be unprofessional. On landing at Wilson Airport she was even more cyanotic, so we rushed her by ambulance straight to the Nairobi Hospital ICU.

In those bachelor days I enjoyed playing the field. Perhaps a bit too much. Serial monogamy went out the window. When I first arrived in Nairobi, I had dated a beautiful Kenyan woman with seductive eyes. There were several others too. Later I brought out Cheryl, who I had been dating in the States. She worked with me in the cath lab under the guise of Peace Corps research assistant. I happened to be seeing someone else at the time as well. Things inevitably got complicated. I remember the cardiac surgeon quipping, 'Here comes the African in our group. He has two wives.'

On one of my visits to the States I met a woman named Marilyn (a pseudonym). There was chemistry between us, and it was agreed she would fly out to see if we had a future together. She arrived a few days after I had admitted Diana to the ICU.

Lady Delamere seemed to be improving by then. So I asked Majid Warshow and Shem Musoke to take over, confident she would receive excellent care.

Marilyn and I took off for Solio to stay with Court Parfet and Claude. From there I took her to the luxurious and romantic Mount Kenya Safari Club. It had been built in the mid-sixties by the actor William Holden and the game trappers Don and Iris Hunt. It was on the equator on the slopes of snow-capped Mt Kenya. We visited Don and Iris and stroked their pet cheetah with William Holden and Stephanie Powers in attendance. John Travolta was staying at the club and kept us awake one night making a racket into the small hours of the morning pounding on the piano and singing. Others might have thought being entertained by Travolta was wonderful, but Marilyn and I had other fish to fry.

When we returned to Nairobi, I resumed Diana's medical care. While we were away, she had suffered a stroke and was on a ventilator. As Christmas approached, she improved enough to be moved out of the ICU to a private VIP room. As Diana's balance was a little iffy, she was given a tripod cane to steady her when she walked. She soon discarded it. My intention was to keep her there through the holidays until she was more stable, but David Partridge came to see me. 'Dr Silverstein, we have a problem. Lady D wants to go back to White Bear for Christmas.'

I wasn't crazy about discharging her early. David was pretty nervous about it too. He suggested that Marilyn and I spend Christmas down at the coast as her guests. Court Parfet loaned Diana his twin-engine Beechcraft and his pilot, and we all flew down to Kilifi together. When we landed, Diana's entire staff of some twenty employees were lined up on her private airstrip to greet us. Mohamed the boat captain, his crew, the butler, the maids, the gardeners, Diana went down the line greeting them like a head of state at a banquet.

White Bear was just as much fun as the Mt. Kenya Safari Club. The house gave onto a long beach of pale white sand that stretched for several miles. It was great for runs and walks. Waiters wearing Ottoman fezzes brought our meals to a green marble table on the veranda. When Marilyn and I left our guest house to go swimming in the estate's heart-shaped pool, we returned to find our clothing had been taken away to be laundered and ironed.

I enjoyed Marilyn's visit to Kenya. She was animated and full of laughter. I flew her in a rented Piper to Governor's Camp in the Maasai Mara. Then we went to Lamu Island, where one of my patients made a boat and crew available to us and we sailed around the island like Sinbad and his crew. I threw a party at my house in Nairobi to introduce Marilyn to my friends and gave her an emerald ring I'd purchased on a trip to Brazil. It wasn't exactly an engagement ring, but it was a token of serious feelings for her.

The following spring I flew to Los Angeles for a medical meeting and to meet up with Marilyn. She told me she couldn't have children. That shook me. As far as my family and I were concerned, marriage and children were almost the same concept. I suddenly found it difficult to imagine marrying Marilyn. I was still attracted to her, but something had changed. We could adopt children, of course, but somehow I couldn't picture that in my mind. I tried to tell myself it shouldn't be a deal breaker, but I was beginning to think it might be.

Not long after I got back to Kenya, Marilyn called me with the news she was pregnant, news that I greeted with ambivalence. Then to my shock and surprise, less than two weeks later I received a phone call from a man who introduced himself as Marilyn's 'other boyfriend'. He was a motivational speaker whom I had met when I had accompanied Marilyn to one of his talks. In an anxious, halting voice he said, 'I thought you should know that although the baby is probably yours, it's in the realm of possibility that it could be mine.' What had I gotten myself into?

He played me a telephone conversation with Marilyn he had taped. 'Please don't tell him we ever were together,' she pleaded. 'You know you and I are over. I want to be with David for the rest of my life.'

My heart was thumping furiously as I dialled Marilyn's number. Marilyn reassured me the child was mine. I was dubious she was telling the truth and very upset. Frankly, I was confused. I decided to wait before making any decisions. As it happened, any choice I might have had was taken away from me. At the beginning of her third month of gestation Marilyn told me that she'd suffered a spontaneous abortion. At that point I realized that I would never trust her again. I wrote her a heartfelt letter of farewell. She returned the ring.

When I told Charles Njonjo that Marilyn and I had split, he masked his disappointment the relationship hadn't worked out by teasing me. 'So Margaret and I wasted that expensive bottle of champagne and good dinner we gave you both.' I gave him a rueful smile and said nothing.

I believe Marilyn eventually got married and had children. Neither of us had been very grown up even though we had talked and looked like adults. Thinking back on it so many decades later, I realize that although I may have thought otherwise, at the time I did not have the right stuff for serious commitment. Still, my own bit of white mischief was nothing compared to that of Diana Delamere and Joss Hay.

Diana died at Ascot in England when she was seventy-four, reportedly of a stroke. Her body was flown to Kenya and buried atop a hill overlooking Ndabibi, as she had instructed in her will. She had built a small cemetery there and walled it in. Her husbands Gilbert and Tom had already been laid to rest beneath the fig trees she had planted. Diana lies between them with her dogs buried at the foot of each grave. She chose the inscription for her tombstone, 'Surrounded by all that I love'. We can just see the hill where they are buried from the veranda of our house at Ole Normani.

19

A VERY AFRICAN COUP

In the early hours of the morning of 1 August 1982, I was awoken by distant gunshots coming from the streets of Nairobi. From what I could tell, the gunfire was coming from small and large calibre weapons. There was the rat-tat-tat of automatic weapons too. It was too varied and sustained to be ordinary street violence. As I sat up in bed, wondering what the shooting was about and hoping it didn't spread to my neighbourhood, the telephone rang. It was my very good friend Dr Chandu Sheth, who was one of the top GPs in town. 'Don't go to the hospital if they call you. The military are up to something.' It turned out to be a brief but abortive attempt to overthrow the Moi government. It was quashed within twenty-four hours.

At 6 am when it came on air, I tuned the radio to the Voice of Kenya. I was expecting rousing martial tunes, the default music for African coups. Instead, an incongruous selection of reggae numbers by Bob Marley and Jimmy Cliff was coming over the airwaves. I learned later the junior Air Force men who had seized the radio station couldn't find any martial music hence the reggae. In due course a voice cut in, 'The corrupt government is overthrown. We are forming a National Redemption Council.' Soon after that the station went dead and remained off air for several hours.

It was a potentially perilous situation and a distinctly unsettling one. Anyone who has ever been on the edges of a riot or civil disturbance will understand when I say that it generates a special kind of fear. *Who or what is out there…what are they doing…will they come and get me or am I safe for now.* My mind was a tumble of thoughts. My chief concerns were my patients and my home. I had just bought a house and only moved into it two months earlier. *What's going to happen to it. Will I have to leave the country and go back to the States. I hope Moi is alive and safe. My patients in the ICU…are they okay…am I going to get shot if I try to reach them.*

By late afternoon the army and GSU had subdued the insurrection. The official death toll was 129 soldiers and civilians although the true number almost definitely ranged in the high hundreds. Three Europeans died in the crossfire while two Asian women who had been raped committed suicide. It's likely many other Asian women were raped, but they hid it for fear of bringing shame on their families. Some $50 million in merchandise was lost to looting.

That Sunday I stayed home, gleaning what news I could by flicking back and forth between the BBC and Voice of Kenya. I checked on my ICU patients at the hospital every few hours. Shem Musoke was on call. He said they were all fine and told me to stay where I was. I spent a lot of time on the phone chasing reliable information from everyone. They, like me, had none to give.

The next morning, unsure of what might have happened overnight, I peeped out from behind closed curtains. Down below me the gardener was calmly digging in a flower bed. I crept downstairs and went outside. 'What are you doing here? There's a coup on.'

'Yes, Bwana, but I still have to feed my family. You pay me by the day.'

As the full story of the failed coup came into focus, we learned that it had been plotted by members of the Air Force. The leaders were young and low level. They didn't seem to have much in the way of a coherent ideology other than their unhappiness with government corruption and what they saw as President's Moi's creeping authoritarianism. Their immediate goals were to seize Jomo Kenyatta International Airport, Wilson Airport, the main post office, the downtown VOK (Voice of Kenya) radio studio and the Central Bank of Kenya. State House in Nairobi was to be blown up as was Moi's farm in Kabarak. Charles Njonjo dismissed the rebels as 'stupid fellows who had no manners'.

Moi was at his upcountry Kabarak home that weekend. At 3 am the commander of the Presidential Escort, Elijah Sumbeiywo, had been woken in his quarters at State House Nakuru by a phone call alerting him that a coup was unfolding. Elijah immediately phoned his brother Lazaro, at that time a major in the army, who was attached to the Defence Headquarters as the Military Assistant to the Chief of General Staff but lived in Nakuru town. This was the first the two men had heard of mutiny in the armed forces. They had known Moi since his days as a teacher in Tambach. They were now highly alarmed. Their only concern was to ensure their friend and the leader of the nation was safe.

Elijah collected two submachine guns and strapped two ammunition belts in an X across his chest. Then they set off to Moi's farmhouse twenty-five kilometres away with Lazaro behind the wheel of his small Peugeot 204. They found Moi dressed in grey slacks and a blazer calmly talking on the phone in the sitting room. His agitated security detail had wanted to hide him in a next-door maize field, but he had refused. They were concerned that Air Force rebels would bomb the house. The Sumbeiywos were equally worried about this possibility. Initially the brothers' plan was to hide their president somewhere in the bush where he couldn't be detected from ground or air. Lazaro Sumbeiywo convinced Moi it was dangerous to stay where he was and persuaded him to squeeze into his saloon car. As they headed towards Rongai, to the north of Nakuru, an announcement was broadcast on VOK that the coup had been suppressed.

Lazaro turned the car around and headed back to Kabarak. From here Moi recorded a statement that the coup had been crushed. It was broadcast over VOK. Again Moi's wishes were at variance with the advice of his security. They wanted to take him to State House Nakuru to wait until everything had calmed down as there were still pockets of resistance in the capital. Moi was adamant he was going to return to Nairobi. Brigadier John Musomba arranged a military escort from the Gilgil barracks. The fifty-vehicle convoy included armoured personnel carriers and Land Rovers packed with soldiers. Moi insisted on making the two-hour journey in his Mercedes. That night he slept in his own bed at his house in Kabarnet Gardens.

Lacking Army support, the rebels had no armour or heavy arms to take and hold key installations. By early Sunday afternoon the coup was crushed save for sporadic skirmishing around the city. At 3 pm President Moi announced on the radio in English and Swahili that the uprising had failed. He sounded tired.

The next morning I reported for work and remained at the hospital around the clock for five days. A dusk-to-dawn curfew had been imposed. I didn't want to have to drive at night to deal with a medical emergency. The initial weeklong curfew was extended although the hours were trimmed back. Grim as the situation was, people began to throw toothbrush parties where guests were forced to stay on until dawn the next day. The alcohol consumption was prodigious.

In the uprising's wake thousands of Kenyans were detained. The University of Nairobi was temporarily closed. Moi called it 'a den of dissidents with foreign backing'. The president sacked a number of senior people in the military and security forces as well as in his government. His ostensible motive was to remove people who should have been aware a coup was brewing and should have spiked it. Some saw the dismissals as a way for Moi to strengthen his grip on government and to replace the Luos and Kikuyus with loyalists from his ethnic Kalenjin group. Senior Private Hezekiah Ochuka and Sergeant Pancras Okumu Oteyo, the two coup leaders, had hijacked a plane when it was clear the coup attempt had failed and forced the pilot to take them across the border to Tanzania. They were brought back, tried for treason and hanged five years later. Kenya has not conducted another execution since. Neither has there been another coup attempt.

Raila Odinga, then thirty-five, a Luo and the son of Kenya's first vice president Jaramogi Oginga Odinga, was arrested for his alleged role in the coup although he never admitted to being involved. He was charged with treason and detained without trial in Naivasha Maximum Security prison for six years. On his release he was twice detained again before fleeing to Norway in 1991. He returned the next year to resume political life as leader of the opposition ODM (Orange Democratic Movement). He served in Parliament for thirteen years as the MP for Langata, a Nairobi constituency. For part of the time he was a minister in the cabinet. He later ran unsuccessfully for president four times but did serve briefly as prime minister under President Mwai Kibaki. Kenyans can be awfully forgiving when it promotes their agenda of political pragmatism. Raila entered the fray for the fifth time in the 2022 elections, and lost by a narrow margin to President William Ruto.

The following year in 1983, Moi's personal physician Dr Antonia Bagshawe emigrated to Australia to enter private practice in Perth. Soon after that Jerry Kiereini, head of the civil service, sent me a letter announcing my appointment to replace her. I was surprised and flattered by the honour. I was to receive a monthly honorarium of Kenya shillings 4000 (about $350 at the time). I had been seeing Moi intermittently over the past five years whenever he had a cardiac concern. Antonia had already approached me to ask if I would take over her role. Naturally, I would have to be extremely discreet, she warned me. As I was to learn later from Moi himself, my big draw was being a foreigner and, by implication, apolitical. This was something that I came to appreciate sooner than expected when political events threatened to split Kenya apart.

I thought the appointment would be an interim one as Africanization was in full flow and several of my colleagues were very interested in having the job. Moi would have first call on my time and attention. This included accompanying him on all international travel. Although these duties and responsibilities would at times take me away from my patients, the experience seemed more than sufficient compensation for any professional and financial drawbacks.

Contrary to the opinion of those pundits who believed that African leaders like Moi made a public display of their faith for political reasons, I soon discovered that the president maintained a strict schedule, rising at 5 am each day to read the Bible, working ten to twelve hours and retiring early. I saw him regularly once a week, usually on Tuesday mornings between 6 and 7 am. I kept my visits brief – fifteen to twenty minutes – out of respect for his busy schedule. Unless he had a specific complaint, these sessions routinely consisted of pulse and blood pressure readings and a few questions to help me gauge how he was doing. Then we would enjoy a cup of *chai masala* together but not before he had said a silent prayer. During these few minutes we chatted about our favourite subjects. The latest medical developments, the application of the Old Testament in today's world, international politics and Israel.

He was remarkably fit for his age but, like most people, he had a few medical idiosyncrasies. One was a condition called an arcus, a white circle around the irises of his eyes. It gave him a strong penetrating gaze, which he put to good use at cabinet meetings and when addressing large crowds. Moi also had a space between his bottom teeth like many Kalenjin adults. When he was a child two bottom teeth had been removed to allow fluids to be administered should he suffer lockjaw from tetanus. Hundreds of thousands of babies used to die from it each year. It was only during his presidency that massive tetanus vaccination campaigns significantly reduced the incidence of lockjaw. Later in life when Moi needed advanced dental work, he insisted that the space between his teeth be left as it was. He did not want to be seen as indulging in the vanity of cosmetic dentistry.

When my team worked with him, he thanked each staff member after every test and check up with warmth and sincerity. He would often end his session at the Nairobi Hospital by having coffee and biscuits with the radiologists Dr Bowry and Dr Talwar and their staff as he could now break his fast. He chatted easily with them and was never at a loss for conversation. Every Christmas he gave me a sum of money to buy gifts for my staff to show his personal appreciation for their work and dedication.

He was an exemplary patient, always following my advice on medicine, diet and lifestyle. However, should politics intervene, he took his own counsel. Although a public figure, Moi was strictly private about his health. He made it clear I was not to release any information without his authorization. In 1991 Moi got an Achilles tendonitis, and an orthopaedic colleague put on a plaster cast to allow it to heal. In those days the national media covered Moi's schedule on a daily basis. When he failed to attend church that Sunday, rumours and speculation began to circulate. He was ill. He was in hospital. He had died.

I got calls from politicians and friends from all over the world asking if they should rush back to Nairobi. I suggested to Moi he give a press conference so people could see he was well. He was having none of it. 'David, I didn't start these rumours. It's not my responsibility to end them.'

The minute the cast was removed at State House, Moi underwent a Clark Kent transformation into Superman. Gone was the passive patient. Back was the assertive head of state. He jumped into his car and headed for Parliament. On the way the motorcade came to a sudden halt outside the Kenya Army Headquarters. Moi stepped out of the car and chatted to a group of people waiting at a bus stop. There was another unscheduled stop downtown when he bought some food from a roadside stand. It attracted a small crowd as he stood there eating and talking to passing pedestrians. All this was well covered in the press. It was Moi's way of sending out the message. The father of the nation was strong, healthy and in command.

Once when we were in England for medical tests Moi found out that the sister of a Kenyan medical professor was a patient in the same hospital. She was being treated for cancer. After his endoscopy, he passed by her room even though he should have first rested. In the middle of the visit, he felt ill and excused himself. He went to the washroom, vomited, washed and returned to continue the conversation. When we returned to Kenya, he invited her to State House and handed her an envelope as she left. 'You've been through financial hardship. This will help.' She told me later that Moi's kindness had made a tremendous difference to her life.

Moi never summoned me for anything trivial, and I was always put through to him promptly when I called. He valued my time as he did his own. Occasionally at his request I would attend to his family, his friends and associates. In each case he insisted on promptly paying my regular fee.

There was only one issue on which I could not sway him. He worked too many hours. I even resorted to quoting Exodus where Jethro advised his son-in-law Moses, '...the things you are doing are not right. You will surely wear yourself out. Make it easier for yourself and let them share the burden.' This did not dent his work ethic. Nor does it influence mine, much to Channa's chagrin.

In the early days of my new assignment it was usually no problem accommodating my professional schedule to his needs. During international travel with the president my presence or proximity was required 24/7. Far from being an onerous obligation, travelling with the president was one of the most fascinating parts of my life. It rekindled my interest in international studies, and I came to understand Kenyan politics much better. I watched as the coterie that surrounded him jockeyed for position, all too frequently peddling falsehoods, while he listened and nodded his head. There were sycophants saying what he wanted to hear to curry favour. Others couched difficult messages about their ambitions in compliments. Frequently politicians used an audience with the president to badmouth their enemies. He held his counsel, saying nothing. Otherwise, he would come out with a statement so obtuse that no one had any idea what it meant, but no one dared press him further for clarification. I saw it so many times that I came to realize it was his way of playing his cards close to his chest.

20

SNAKES AND LADDERS

My new position gave me regular access to the president. That first year I was a fly on the wall as political power play swirled around us. In those days tribe was everything, and close cooperation across ethnic lines was relatively rare. An exception was the harmonious working partnership enjoyed by President Moi, a Kalenjin, and Charles Njonjo, a Kikuyu. That is until tensions pulled them apart.

Njonjo's intellect and astute decision-making were widely recognized. I first came into contact with him in 1976 when he was named chairman of the Kenya Heart Foundation. I was already serving on this newly formed charity as a member and advisor. We were by no means closely acquainted, but I was in sufficient proximity to both admire and fear the man.

Njonjo had known privilege and power his entire life. He was born in 1920 into a prominent family. His father, Josiah Njonjo, was a senior chief in Kabete, now a suburb a few kilometres outside Nairobi, who had found favour with the British colonial administration.

Charles had earned a bachelor's degree in law at Fort Hare University in South Africa where Nelson Mandela, two years his senior, had also attended classes. He had completed his law degree and was called to the Bar at Gray's Inn in London. Like

Moi he was an avid Anglophile. He was sometimes referred to as Sir Charles or the Duke of Kabeteshire. He favoured dark blue, three-piece pinstripe suits from the Savile Row tailor he shared with Moi. I was to learn later that some of those suits had his initials woven into the pinstripes. The letters were so minute one couldn't notice it. He often wore a rose boutonniere in his lapel – again like Moi – and a pocket watch on a fob. He had been a legal clerk for the colonial government in its final years before becoming Kenya's first attorney general at the relatively young age forty-three. In 1972 he married Margaret Bryson, the daughter of the Irish missionary who had baptized President Moi.

Njonjo was a canny choice to chair the Heart Foundation. He was rich, dynamic, shrewd and extraordinarily well connected in the business community. Kenyan corporations loved having him on their boards. When it was announced that the foundation would be funded by private charities and overseen by Charles Njonjo, a torrent of Kenyan shillings poured into its coffers.

After my move from Kenyatta National Hospital to Nairobi Hospital, Charles served as chairman there as well. He was a man of action who took on small problems as well as big ones. The board almost always concurred with his decisions. Although I was terrified of him at first, I soon learned to trust him implicitly in the way he handled the hospital's issues.

Another serious crisis in Kenyan politics surfaced in 1983. Drawing on what I know and can confidently conjecture, President Moi was worried that Mwai Kibaki, the Kikuyu vice president, might build a sufficiently strong power base among the Kikuyu to seize the presidency, one way or the other. The idea of supplanting Kibaki with Charles Njonjo might have appealed to Moi. It might have appealed to Njonjo too as it would secure a path to the presidency when the time came. He liked power for the authority it conveyed. As the attorney general he enjoyed the efficiency of getting favours granted and injustices righted simply by lifting the phone.

In seventeen years of assiduously consolidating his power and influence as the attorney general, Njonjo never had indicated publicly any interest in elective politics. He seemed to disdain the hurly burly of political life. Yet Charles had resigned as the attorney general in 1980 and persuaded his friend, Amos Ng'ang'a, to step down as MP so he could stand in a by-election. It was widely assumed that Moi and Njonjo were jointly solving the Kibaki problem. That Ng'ang'a was then named chairman of the Tana River Development Authority did nothing to dispel this belief. Shortly after Charles won the by-election, Moi appointed him to a newly created post, Minister for Home and Constitutional Affairs. It was a position that implied broad powers in the interpretation of the nation's constitution.

Everything seemed to be in place until something happened to change Moi's mind. I don't know what it was, but it might have been the attempted coup and his mistrust of the Commander of the Air Force, who was a Kikuyu. He may have wondered, along with everyone else, just what Njonjo had in mind. According to Court Parfet, Moi once told him, 'Njonjo did some terrible things against me,' without specifying what he meant.

An early sign of what lay ahead for Charles occurred in 1983 after Moi replaced Jeremiah Kiereini with Simeon Nyachae to head the civil service. Nyachae was immensely wealthy and had a strong and loyal power base. He was one of the few politicians who could take on Njonjo in a meaningful way. He decided to do it by launching a campaign of lies designed to undermine

Njonjo's standing with the president. Moi much later told me that Nyachae had misinformed him about Njonjo.

Njonjo at first seemed unfazed by the political gossip that was swirling around him. During this period the hotelier Jack Block died suddenly on a fishing trip in Chile. The Block family asked me to say Kaddish, the Jewish memorial prayer, at his funeral. Njonjo spoke as well. Afterward he congratulated me on my recent appointment as President Moi's physician and added, 'We'll be seeing a lot of each other on state trips abroad.'

The president's change of heart soon became abundantly clear. In May Moi told the crowd at a fundraising rally that 'a traitor' was being groomed by 'foreign powers' to take over the presidency. During the weeks that followed a whirlpool of accusations and innuendo created by MPs and party officials pointed to Njonjo as the suspect. After that things moved rapidly. Elijah Mwangale, the Minister for Tourism and Wildlife, speaking in Parliament denounced Njonjo as a traitor. Njonjo immediately wrote a letter of resignation both as a member of Parliament and as a member of the Cabinet. Whether that letter reached Moi before he subsequently fired Njonjo from the Cabinet we may never know. It was always a matter of pride to Njonjo that he took the dignified initiative. He was suspended from Kenya's sole political party, KANU (the Kenya African National Union), while a judicial inquiry was constituted to examine charges that Njonjo had committed 'serious irregularities'. Njonjo denied the allegations, but by July he had been effectively stripped of any political credibility.

By this time Kenya was divided into Moi supporters and Njonjo backers, with no room to be both. Njonjo called on me with medical issues shortly before his tribunal began. My frightened receptionist told him I wasn't in the office then added as an afterthought, 'How can he help you?'

Njonjo responded 'What do you mean? He's my friend, and he's my doctor.'

Many of my patients, hospital associates and friends wondered why I didn't drop Njonjo. They pointed out his name was now poison in certain circles. When I told Moi of this and asked his advice, he grew stern with me. 'Daktari, you are a doctor, a professional,' he said. 'This is just politics. *Wacha siasa* (ignore politics). If you are his doctor, you take care of him. And don't let anybody scare you into thinking I'm upset about you going to see him. That's not the case.'

At least once or twice a week I'd visit the president in the morning and Njonjo at his home in the evening. I was one of the very few in the country who remained friends with both of them at that time. Perhaps as a trusted American Jewish doctor, they saw me as being beyond the reach of tribalism and politics. I was happy to have it that way.

The three-person commission of inquiry was headed by Justice Cecil Miller, a native of Guyana. Dusty Miller, as he was known, was also a patient of mine. The hearings were in session for 109 days. Kenyans were gripped by the proceedings and were eager to know every detail. *The Daily Nation,* Kenya's leading newspaper, ran an average of 8000 words every day of verbatim transcripts, analysis and descriptions of the participants. It was a huge story, and the paper's saturation coverage attracted thousands of new readers. Hoping to take advantage of the moment, President Moi called snap general and presidential elections in September 1983. It would 'cleanse the system' he said. It also won him and his running mate, Mwai Kibaki, another five years in power. Those who were cleansed were primarily Njonjo partisans.

At this time Charles Njonjo was chairman of the board for Nairobi Hospital. It came up during a board meeting that some of the board members had been approached by people who were close to the president and had been told the president wanted Njonjo removed as chairman. The Minister for Health, Kenneth Matiba, had also told the hospital administrator that State House wanted Njonjo removed. He had made it clear the directive came from the president.

Njonjo made his position clear too. If the president did indeed want him to step down, he would do so out of respect for the patron of the Nairobi Hospital, President Moi. Because so many people close to the centre of power regularly used their position for personal or political gain, the board felt they needed to establish the veracity of the directive. As Moi and Njonjo were both my patients, the hospital administrator asked me if I would do it.

I mustered courage and addressed the president when I next saw him. 'Mzee, there is a request that I clarify something with you that's political. I am a doctor and an American, and I do not know how to handle the politics of the day. I am not taking sides. This is what has come from the board of Nairobi Hospital. I just want to know how to advise them.'

He assured me that I was quite right to stay out of politics. 'Is Njonjo a good chairman?' he asked. I replied that he was an excellent chairman. 'Then let him continue to do a good job. Don't forget Nairobi Hospital is my hospital. I'm proud of its progress. Let the matter stop here.'

The interminable Miller inquiry subsequently found Njonjo guilty on a number of minor counts but not a traitor as Mwangale had alleged. On 12 December 1984, Jamhuri (Independence) Day, Moi short-circuited the process by granting his friend a pardon. 'He had all along endeavoured to serve the country faithfully until sometime in 1980 when he started developing and entertaining misguided ambitions. However, considering his age (Njonjo was sixty-four) and total life in public service, I have decided to pardon him on many of the confirmed allegations.'

It was masterful statesmanship. Moi had let his old friend off the hook while ensuring no one was left with egg on his face. Many other leaders would have simply arranged a few accidents. It was a ploy known as snakes and ladders, so named after the children's board game where players slither down snakes and climb up ladders on the throw of the dice. In the context of politics, the important feature is that players are never disqualified. They always remain on the board.

Moi promoted Cecil Miller to chief justice in 1986. He died of meningitis three years later. Njonjo vanished from public life for more than a decade. He had been far from inactive while out of the limelight. After years of being too busy for much family time, he began travelling with Margaret and their three children, taking them on trips to England and Europe as well as on ski vacations. In Nairobi he had an interest in many businesses including banks, airlines, travel services and farming. He remained chairman of Nairobi Hospital and major charities such as the Starehe Boys' Centre high school. He was also a regular at dog shows.

Many had revelled in his downfall. There had even been a threat of violence between Njonjo and Moi supporters. Yet I didn't get the sense that Moi saw the crisis as anything more than a power play. It may have been an expression of tribal rivalry in some way, but it was never personal. Ultimately there were no lasting hard feelings on either side. This outcome was uniquely Kenyan.

Given President Moi's respect and fondness for Njonjo despite his transgressions, real or imagined, it seemed likely that Moi in time would try to coax him back into a government position. Njonjo told me he was willing to listen, but he needed an escape route in case Moi tried to manoeuvre him into a job he didn't want. He asked me to write a doctor's letter to put in his medical record with a copy that he could keep. It read, 'Due to medical reasons I've advised Honorable Charles Njonjo not to take any government job.' I don't know whether he ever showed the note to anyone, but he often asked me to confirm that it was still in his medical record. The last time I checked it was still on file.

In August 1994, I was given a party at the house to celebrate my fiftieth birthday. It was a large gathering with more than 100 guests. They included the Kenyan diplomat Bethuel Kiplagat and his wife Honorine, Julius and Barbara Kyambi, Shem and Helen Musoke, Chandu and Pratima Sheth and the State House comptroller Abraham Kiptanui and his wife Mary.

President Moi and his former nemesis Charles Njonjo had been invited too and both were there. It would be the first time they had been seen together for over a decade. Moi arrived early and was seated in the living room when his old friend walked through the door. He called out, 'Charles! Charles! Come sit with me.' Njonjo did, and they held hands for quite a while, a common way in Africa of showing warmth and fraternity between equals.

Most of the guests went out on the veranda and into the garden to dine. Another group of us, including Moi and Njonjo, sat down to a formal Shabbat meal. I said the Kiddush, poured the sweet Kiddush wine, said the prayer on bread, and passed around the *challah* bread.

After the appetizer, Charles surprised me. 'David, this is not very respectful to His Excellency. You didn't even offer us another glass of wine.'

Normally, Njonjo drank modestly and Moi not at all. Yet

when I asked Moi if he would like some more wine, he answered, 'Yes! Yes!' with a vigorous nod of the head. I served them our Israeli sweet ceremonial wine, which they knocked back with gusto, asking for multiple refills. Moi liked it so much that he soon began sending his people to the synagogue to purchase bottles of it for his home use.

Meanwhile by the early summer of 1998, Moi and Njonjo had an open channel, but still not a public one. As Njonjo had expected, Moi started to offer him positions. He declined them all. Moi signalled his trust more substantively when he asked Njonjo to disburse relief funds after a number of people were killed in a building collapse. Moi knew that wealthy Kenyans, Europeans and Indians would donate given Njonjo's reputation for honesty. Njonjo took the job.

After this modest public debut, Moi dangled the bait of heading the Kenya Wildlife Service, knowing that Njonjo was very fond of wildlife. Moi tried to sack the director, Dr David Western, but he was reinstated six days later under pressure from international donors. He must have known this was tentative because Moi obviously wanted to get rid of him.

I conjured up a plan I thought might suit Moi, Njonjo and even the donors, especially in light of their increasing concern about the escalating rate of ivory poaching. I suggested to Njonjo he consider the job of chairman. I suspected Moi would be happy to have him there with the caveat of an appropriate replacement for Western. He would have no trouble selling the combination to international donors. Njonjo liked the idea. I relayed this to Moi. The president said that Njonjo had so far turned him down 'everywhere', but he was happy to offer him the job if he would accept. I waited until my next visit to inform him Njonjo was interested and would accept.

As these discussions were inching toward a resolution, I took our sons Nahum and Josh on a summer road trip to the American northwest. We started in Seattle where I had done my internship, residency in internal medicine and fellowship in cardiology. We then crossed into the magical rain forests of the Olympic peninsula, heading south and camping along the way. One day as I was talking on the phone to Rochelle, she told me the Njonjos were trying to get in touch. They wanted to know if there was a fax number to which they could send me a message. I drove on until I found a gas station with a fax machine and sent Rochelle the number. She forwarded it to Nairobi, and soon three pages came rolling out of the machine.

The first was a typewritten letter on President Moi's official stationery dated 13 July. 'Dear Charles, I write to formally appoint you Chairman of the Board of Directors, Kenya Wildlife Service.' The second page contained Njonjo's reply. 'Thank you very much for your letter of appointment as Chairman of the Board of Directors of the Kenya Wildlife Service.' I took a deep breath and smiled. Njonjo continued, 'In the last few days I have begun to realize how daunting a task you have entrusted to me. I consider this both an honor and a challenge…Provided I can count on your full support as I tread this minefield of vested interest and hidden agendas, I will do my best to fulfill your expectations and work tirelessly for our national heritage and our tourist industry.' He had signed it 'C. Njonjo'.

The third faxed page was a handwritten note from Charles to me on his Shavania House stationery. 'So it has happened and you were away and had no access to that letter!' he began. 'There has been so much speculation since the appointment was made last Tuesday – What next – hidden agenda – Next as VP and so on. It is a challenge. I will try and do it…I so wish you were here to commiserate with us. But there has been a lot of supportive response. I hope you are well the three of you and love from us to Nahum and Joshua...Charles Mzee.'

After Njonjo settled in and, I am sure, had a conversation or two with the president, Moi fired Western once more and less than a week later replaced him with the palaeontologist Richard Leakey. It was Leakey's second term in the job. Western's second sacking stirred some complaints from the donors. On my return from the U.S. I went to Njonjo's house where together we wrote a letter addressing their concerns. In the interest of discretion, Njonjo requested the letter be typed at my office and delivered by hand to the donors, reaching them simultaneously with the announcement of Leakey's reassignment.

Njonjo stayed on as chair until 2003 when Mwai Kibaki, who had succeeded Moi as president, appointed Colin Church, another of my patients and a good friend. During his tenure Njonjo worked the same wonders for KWS as he had for the Heart Foundation and Nairobi Hospital. He restored its credibility by virtue of his presence. His network of connections attracted new flows of money which in turn revitalized operations in the field. Charles maintained a keen interest in wildlife for the rest of his long life. But he had no interest at all in politics.

21

LIBYAN DELUSIONS

My first trip to a foreign destination with Moi took place in June 1983 not long after I became his doctor. The president flew to Addis Ababa, the capital of Ethiopia, for a heads of state summit of the OAU (Organization of African Unity), the continental predecessor to the African Union. The previous year Moi had spent a fairly successful term as its chairman. A highlight of his tenure had been a speech delivered in the United Nations General Assembly in New York where he denounced the apartheid government in South Africa as 'an anguish upon the conscience of civilized men'.

Several major issues beset the OAU and were likely to trigger lively discussion in the following days. One was the perennial question of nationhood for the Western Sahara. It was a former Spanish colony of sparsely inhabited desert sandwiched between Morocco and Mauritania. The Atlantic Ocean formed its western border. Morocco had annexed about four-fifths of the territory. The remaining one fifth was under the control of a nationalist movement called the Polisario Front. The rebels, as the Moroccan delegate referred to them, had proclaimed the Sahrawi Arab Democratic Republic and formed a government in exile in Algeria. The United Nations considered the Polisario Front to be the rightful representative of the Sahrawi people. With the UN backing its claim to legitimacy, the Polisario Front had for some years been seeking a seat at the OAU. These tall desert warriors in their flowing robes stalked the corridors of Africa Hall at every OAU meeting and were almost part of the furniture. Naturally, Morocco opposed their bid for recognition.

The second issue concerned the outcome of the civil war in Chad, where forces under Hissène Habré had defeated OAU peacekeepers to establish a U.S.-backed government that quickly had degenerated into a violent, eight-year dictatorship. The situation was just as vexing as the Polisario Front's bid for recognition. It was against the OAU charter to overthrow a country's leader and seize power.

Moi was staying with the other heads of state at the Ghion Hotel. Every morning at 6.30 am sharp I knocked on the door of Moi's tukul for the routine presidential visit. One hand clasped a Dr Doolittle black bag with stethoscope, blood pressure cuff and other basic medical equipment. In the other hand was a much bigger bag containing a pharmacopeia of medications to treat every possible disaster that might befall Moi and his delegation. As the new boy on the block, I was eager to do everything by the book. Moi was always up and ready to receive me, sitting in a chair reading the Bible in his pyjamas.

After giving him a precursory examination, tea was brought in. I was eager to know how things were progressing behind the closed doors of Africa Hall but didn't want to overstep the line. After telling him he was in the best of health, I'd say casually, 'So how are things going, Mzee?'

Moi shook his head and looked momentarily sad. Col Muammar Gaddafi was supposed to succeed him as the OAU chair. The Libyan leader had been taking a strong stand on issues, and they were usually counter to Moi's position. 'Daktari, the

OAU is in the ICU. Gaddafi is a very difficult man. I don't know if I'll be able to hand over to him.' After that he would go on to chat about Western Sahara and Morocco or Chad.

We were to visit Addis Ababa often on state visits. Moi's meetings with Mengistu Haile Mariam, the head of Ethiopia's Marxist military junta, were held at the Imperial Palace where Emperor Hailie Selassie had once presided. Memories of those times conjure up cavernous spaces sheltering dark furniture and faded velvet in a half-light gloom. I was free to walk around at will. The guards said, 'Go where you want.' One morning I poked my head into an upstairs anteroom to the emperor's bedroom. Pushed up against the wall was a Wurlitzer jukebox with 45s of Elvis Presley, Sinatra and early rock and roll. A cupboard still contained some of the emperor's clothes. In another anteroom was a small library. I idly ran my eye over the shelves and picked out one that caught my eye, *My People, the Story of the Jews*. The author was Abba Eban, an Israeli diplomat who had been an ambassador to the U.S. and United Nations. It was inscribed to His Majesty, the Lion of Judah from Golda Meir. She had visited Ethiopia as foreign minister in 1962.

Moi was easy to talk to about international events and personalities but reticent on national affairs. He downplayed any trouble I might have read about in the papers. His response was, 'You have to believe in God. If I think I've done everything right, I have no trouble falling asleep.' It amazed me how relaxed he was during stressful times.

When he handed over the reins of power to Mwai Kibaki after serving as president for twenty-two years, he told me, 'David, I did what I had to do. I succeeded and now I'm relaxing at home.' His faith in God was unwavering. I genuinely think this is why he was nearly always calm. It was when he talked fast and loudly that I knew he was truly irritated. He never showed his irritation with me, but others irritated him from time to time. Then I walked out of the room as I knew he'd be happier if I wasn't around to see it.

Because he always treated me well, I was considered to have the presidential ear. There were those who thought I was one of most influential people in Kenya. I wasn't, of course, but it was true I had good access. At the same time, if I was passionate on a subject, which was seldom, I wasn't afraid to share my thoughts with the president. Although he often didn't agree, he would thank me for being frank. His manners never left him.

A third problem at that year's heads-of-state summit was the diplomatic question of who was going to call the shots at the meeting. The idiosyncratic and flamboyant Gaddafi viewed himself as the natural leader of Pan-Africanism. Not surprisingly Mengistu had other ideas. Gaddafi had tried twice the previous year to convene a summit of African leaders in pursuit of his ambition to lead Africa. Both times he had failed to muster a quorum of thirty-four of the OAU's fifty members.

The Libyan leader flew in to Addis Ababa in the middle of the night. The uncertainty and anticipation that preceded him had created a build-up worthy of a rock star. The following morning his arrival at Africa Hall was as impressive as it was intended to be. He swept up the steps in flowing robes accompanied by a security detail of strikingly beautiful women wearing olive-drab slacks and shouldering AK-47s. It was easy to see why the colonel was rumoured to be sleeping with his bodyguards. I sauntered over to this entourage arranged in a circle around Gaddafi and said with a smile, 'Hello. I'm with the Kenyan delegation.' One of the bodyguards lifted her AK-47, and I quickly backed off. Any delusions of a liaison with an exotic desert amazon vanished instantly.

Gaddafi rarely abandoned an ambition, whether it was to support terrorism against Israel, blow up civilian airplanes over the Atlantic or fund the myriad terrorist groups that populated the Middle East. However, one that he did have to forego that year was becoming chair of the OAU. Ethiopia's Mengistu Haile Mariam took over instead. The next time I saw Gaddafi was in Libya in March 2001 when I travelled there with Moi. By this time he'd rebranded the same grandiose scheme for continental dominance. He called it the United States of Africa. He envisaged an organization not unlike the European Union that incorporated the entire African continent. It would have a common economy, constitution, justice system and so on. Naturally he intended to run the show himself from Tripoli. Once again, he was lobbying OAU members to support him as chair of the organization.

There were forty-eight of us in the Kenyan delegation. We flew out of Jomo Kenyatta International Airport aboard a Kenya Airways flight at noon and landed in Tripoli in the early evening. Our hosts ushered us into fifteen vehicles for the drive into town where the party was issued ID badges and assigned to three different hotels.

My badge didn't look any different from the others, but I believe it had some sort of special feature because every Libyan security officer I met seemed to know at once who I was. It was an unnerving reminder of a conversation I'd had with my Mossad friends. An American Jew in Libya, even as part of a Kenyan diplomatic mission, was not a good idea. They had advised me against it, but I had been determined to go on the trip and have some excitement and adventure. Was I brave or just foolhardy?

The first day's agenda began at 1.45 pm with a half-hour flight to Sirte where Gaddafi had been born into a Bedouin family in 1942. He had strong personal and tribal connections to Sirte, which had been one of his political and military strongholds prior to the revolution of 1969 when he had overthrown King Idris and nationalized the Libyan oil fields. All the national delegations, including us Kenyans, were driven in motorcades into the desert to a commodious white tent. It must have been about twenty meters long and six meters wide. Like everything he did, this was for show. Gaddafi wanted to be portrayed as a simple desert nomad who lived modestly despite the billions of dollars he had accrued from oil.

There were a lot of logistics to be dealt with. We stood under an extraordinarily hot sun, eager for even a sliver of shade, while the flags of country after country were raised. Each delegation was summoned by turn into the tent where the colonel would chat for a few minutes with the president or head of state. The various official motorcades were parked at the top of a small hill some distance away. They were brought down to deliver and then collect the delegations as they entered and left the tent and then drove away again. This bizarre version of musical chairs seemed to be proceeding smoothly enough. I was told that if a guest agreed to go along with Gaddafi's agenda to vote him in as chair of the OAU, he was issued a personal cheque made out in his name. I had thought chequebook diplomacy was just a figure of speech but apparently not. Moi was one of the leaders who refused his largesse.

As always Moi was impeccably attired. What I called his personal brand was that of a London banker from the City. His Brioni suits were from Savile Row, each worth thousands of dollars. He favoured crisply ironed white or light-coloured shirts and had a weakness for colourful ties. He always wore a rosebud in his lapel. The gardeners at State House provided a fresh one every day from the rose garden. On this occasion in the depths of the desert, his aides had still managed to provide him with his hallmark boutonniere.

When our turn came, we all trailed behind Moi into the tent. There was barely any furniture, just some two-seater couches. A picture of Gaddafi hung against one of the canvas walls but nothing else. The carpet by now was covered with a fair amount of sand. Moi hesitated, not sure where to go. There didn't seem to be any protocol. Gaddafi was standing at the back of the tent where the flaps had been lifted up to allow a breeze to come in. Beyond was a pleasing vista of a palm oasis.

Moi walked over to join the Libyan leader and the two stood side by side. Gaddafi said nothing. Moi broke the silence with some small talk. 'How are your rains?' he inquired through a translator.

'We don't need rain. We have oil.' Gaddafi replied. Moi let out a belly laugh. He was trying to be diplomatic and what could be more neutral than the weather.

Gaddafi crossed the tent to an armchair that was larger than the others and sat down. Moi followed and sat down beside him. I sank into a two-seater within earshot of the two men. Servants came in with trays of strong black tea in shot glasses and offered them around. Moi was usually comfortable with silence but not this time. Beneath his statesmanlike façade I could tell he was uneasy. The conversation was slow and going nowhere. Outside another delegation was standing in the heat waiting to be called in. An aide approached Gaddafi and whispered in his ear. Gaddafi muttered something back.

Another silence ensued then the Libyan chief of protocol announced, 'All security out!' I remained seated. He walked over and glared down at me. 'You're still here?'

'Yes, I am. I'm not security.'

'We know who you are, Doctor,' he said.

I recalled again the conversation with my Mossad friends. They had a point. I shot to my feet and hurried out of the tent.

Nearly everyone in the delegation was now standing outside under the scorching sun. The idea was that as soon as we saw Moi emerging from the tent, we would all sprint to our assigned cars. Our motorcade consisted of black Mercedes. Each had a large number on the windscreen. Mine was the last – number seven. Eventually Moi appeared and we all took off in a rush, desperate to get out of the heat. The motorcade began to uncoil like a great fat snake. I counted the car numbers. One, two, three, four, five, six and…where was seven? It was nowhere in sight. Once Moi stepped into his vehicle the entire motorcade would roar away irrespective of where I was. 'Where's seven? Where's seven?' I yelled at the driver of number six. He pointed to a car perched atop the hill some 200 yards away.

I started running as fast as I could. I was in a panic. I could hear the cars revving up behind me. Then they were passing me. The motorcade was rolling. The sand felt like treacle. I waved frantically as President Moi's limo sped past. One after another the Mercedes drove away. I seemed to be invisible. There would be none of the traditional Bedouin hospitality awaiting me if I missed my lift. I had visions of being stuck at Gaddafi's desert compound without my passport, explaining to security officials that Silverstein was a common Kenyan name. I stepped up the pace, by now panting heavily.

Suddenly number seven drew up beside me. The back door was flung open and a hand reached out. It was Lee Njiru, chief of the presidential press unit. 'Daktari! Quick! Jump in!' He grabbed my arm and I dove headfirst into the moving car.

Our destination was the Ouagadougou Great Halls Complex, an impressively sleek and modernistic conference centre in downtown Sirte, where the OAU's Fifth Extraordinary Session was about to convene. We passed a ribbon of murals as we walked along an outside wall to the plenary hall. One read in English, 'We know who our friends are.' Another depicted a European whipping a black slave. The irony didn't escape me. Arabs were the most active of slavers before Africa was colonized. To this day Libyans practice slavery deep in the southern desert. It was near to impossible to reach consensus on any of the issues tabled at the meeting. Weeks after we had left a document was circulated that lauded the assembly's achievements. It included '…a special motion of thanks to the leader of the great socialist Libyan Arab Jamahiriya Brother Muammar Al Gaddafi,' in part for his initiatives '…to strengthen the unity, cohesion and solidarity of our peoples and continents.' It didn't mention anything of consequence as nothing of consequence had been agreed on. Gaddafi was not elected chair of the OAU.

Gaddafi never lost sight of his goal of presiding over a unified Africa. He continually strove to be acknowledged as a legitimate world leader by whatever means possible. Latterly this was by taking a conciliatory line in relations with the West. In 2003 he renounced terrorism and foreswore Libya's nuclear program. In 2008 the Libyans paid in excess of $2 billion to survivors of the victims of the Lockerbie crash they had engineered. During the 2011 Arab Spring uprisings three years later Gaddafi came to an ignominious end in the desert. He was tracked down to his hiding place in a culvert in Sirte by members of the National Transitional Council. There he was beaten, sodomized with a bayonet and shot dead. His female bodyguards had long since fled.

'Arab leaders,' Moi told me on numerous occasions, 'have an unlimited capacity for deception.'

22

ROMEO NINE

My life was far from a circuit of political meetings. I had many remarkable patients whose lives I found irresistibly fascinating as I got to know them over the years. One of them was Patrick Shaw, a morally compromised man who was larger than life in every way. He was charming but ruthless, an unhesitating killer who believed in giving the disadvantaged a helping hand. He was a mystery to most Kenyans. I believe I got to know him better than most.

Shaw was the Assistant Director of Administration for Starehe Boys' Centre, a remarkable charity-based school that took boys from among the poorest of the poor and gave them a world-class education based on the British public-school model. Over the years many of the alumni have made names for themselves in business, sporting and political circles. Many more have joined Kenya's ever expanding middle class. Shaw was sponsored in this work by Save the Children. He also moonlighted in another profession that struck fear in the hearts of many. Mothers would say to their children, 'Be good or Patrick Shaw will come and get you.'

Patrick Shaw was born in 1936, the son of a prominent London doctor. He was six feet tall and weighed over 300 pounds. His weight was popularly attributed to a glandular disorder. As his doctor, I can definitively say that it was related to his compulsive eating. He was what we call an emotional eater. Because of his obesity he developed diabetes later in life. Despite his vast size, he put on astonishing spurts of speed when the occasion called for it. After a less than stellar performance at school, Shaw came to Kenya at the age of nineteen as an agricultural officer in the colonial service. Eight years later in 1959 he joined the police force as a reservist. He moved to Starehe Boys' Centre in 1965 and worked for Geoffrey Griffin, the school's founder.

Dr David Muhindi, a colleague, friend and alumnus of Starehe, had fond memories of Patrick Shaw. The boys regarded him as an uncle and cherished the intimacy of the relationship. They joked with him but were careful not to overstep the line or he became *kali* (fierce). He had no tolerance for bullies, probably because he had been badly bullied about his size when he was at school. A student who was caught bullying was expelled without discussion. However it was Geoffrey Griffin who punished the students, not Shaw. He was 'too tender' to cane a boy and cause him pain.

In due course Shaw began to lead a double life. He became more and more active as a police reservist, responding to police alerts to crime scenes in his notorious Volvo. He proved to be not only quick on his feet when chasing criminals down, but quick to pull the trigger of his .38 pistol. It became known in the underworld that if you confronted Shaw with a gun or tried to run away, you were a dead man. Those who were afraid to utter his name referred to him by his CB call sign, Romeo Nine.

It was difficult for the Starehe boys to reconcile the uncle they loved with the sharpshooter cop they read about in the newspapers. He liked to take students with him to collect the mail from the post office and would often stop on the way back to buy them snacks. One day Shaw's CB radio went off while he had a student with him in the car. He couldn't leave the boy in the street so he drove with him to the scene of the crime. A gun battle ensued and the gangsters sped away in their car. Shaw took off in hot pursuit, telling the terrified youngster to lie on the floor of the car. Although traumatized, he survived the incident without injury.

I first heard about Patrick Shaw within months of arriving in Kenya because his name had been linked to the J. M. Kariuki assassination. J.M. was known as Kenya's socialist politician. He had been Jomo Kenyatta's private secretary from 1963 to 1969 and then entered politics in 1974 when he was elected as the MP for Nyandarua. Since then he had made several statements about corruption and unfair land distribution which had soured his close relationship with Kenyatta. At independence the colonial government had given Kenya money to purchase white-owned farms on a willing-seller basis. The idea was to redistribute the land among peasant farmers who were landless. Although much of the land was set aside for settlement schemes for common citizens, President Kenyatta and other leading politicians seemed to end up with large chunks of land. J.M. Kariuki began to fight against this practice, which he felt was unfair. J.M. Kariuki became known for making trenchant statements at political rallies. 'Kenya has become a nation of ten millionaires and ten million beggars.' This was unpopular with those who had enriched themselves. He was last seen in March 1975 being escorted from a Nairobi hotel by senior police officers and Patrick Shaw. His mutilated body was later found by a Maasai boy herding goats behind the Ngong Hills. No one was ever prosecuted for Kariuki's death even though Parliament constituted a committee to investigate the murder. Its findings implicated senior police officers including Ignatius Nderi, Ben Gethi, Wanyoike Thung'u and Patrick Shaw.

Every Friday evening at Starehe School was *baraza* (get together) night, a sort of town hall meeting where students had a free pass to ask the teachers personal questions. One Friday a student asked whether Patrick Shaw was involved in the execution of J.M. Kariuki. Geoffrey Griffin sidestepped the question by saying that Shaw was a highly principled man who would only do what he thought was ethical and correct. Dr Muhindi remembers that evening clearly. He had looked through the window and saw Patrick Shaw pacing up and down in the garden. The students noticed that he was different for some months after that. He became distant and was no longer the approachable Uncle Pat they used to joke with.

The first time I experienced general panic among Kenyans was after the official announcement of J.M. Kariuki's death. Everyone was frightened there might be an uprising. The Kikuyus were especially nervous. That same week a bomb exploded at a Nairobi bus station causing several deaths and notching up the tension. On that day offices closed early and people stocked up with food. Many of the hospital staff asked permission to leave work early. There was a pervasive fear that Nairobi would erupt into violence. Fortunately the situation calmed down.

During this time Patrick Shaw's name was cropping up in the news, and I asked around about him. I was surprised to discover he was highly respected not only by Europeans but also among Africans and Asians. In those days petty theft was committed usually with *pangas* (machetes) and *rungus* (clubs). People gave the burglars what they wanted. In return most were left unscathed. However, as time went by gangs began to be armed with pistols and revolvers. Crime took a deadly turn.

This frightened everybody. Knowing there was a man like Patrick Shaw watching out for them was reassuring.

It was said that Shaw was ever watchful and barely slept. He would sleep in his car in a seated position with his CB radio and his .38 revolver ready to respond to any crisis. It made the average person in Nairobi sleep better. His informants included parking boys or youngsters who were often themselves guilty of petty theft. He helped get them out of trouble and gave money in exchange for information. In my conversations with President Moi years later, he told me how much he had valued Patrick Shaw and that he had made sure he was given enough money to keep his informants adequately rewarded for their information and to keep his Volvo fuelled. 'We have to learn from Shaw how to collect intelligence. He talks to people,' Moi told me.

Shaw was almost always the first policeman at the scene of a crime. Sometimes he would arrive there before the crime had occurred. When he apprehended serious criminals, he would often throw them into his car and drive away. Only the fortunate ones made it to the police station alive. The public didn't seem to mind the extrajudicial killings as they believed that all too often the criminals paid the judges and returned to the streets to murder and rob again. They saw Pat Shaw as Nairobi's version of Robin Hood.

Shaw did a lot of shooting, but he was only shot once. In 1979 an Asian psychiatrist called Dr Gulam Mustafa was burgled at his residence. His wife and two other household members were shot and killed. Shaw arrived at the scene of the murders so quickly that Walimba, a notorious Ugandan criminal, was still there. Shaw wasn't carrying a weapon, and Walimba shot him in the chest. He got into his Volvo and drove straight to Nairobi Hospital, slamming on the brakes outside the emergency room and honking the horn loudly. He came bounding in crying, 'I've been shot! I've been shot in the chest!' I happened to be there seeing a patient. I immediately called Mr Imre Loeffler, a Hungarian surgeon whose judgement and skill I came to rely on for many years. Shaw was hurried off to the emergency room operating theatre. He was talking about the new gang in town while we put a gown on him. We asked if he was in pain. 'No, no. Get the bullet out. I can feel it here in my chest. I need to see that bullet.'

The bullet had entered the left side of Shaw's chest and continued along the anterior surface under his skin. Fortunately, it had lodged on the other side without entering the rib cage. Imre could feel it in the layers of fat on the right side of the chest. He said he could extract it under a local anaesthetic. Shaw was all for that, he said, because he was in a hurry. Imre extracted the bullet with a pair of forceps and dropped it into a metal bowl. Shaw sat bolt upright, tore off the surgical towels clamped in place around the wound and demanded to see it. 'I knew it! Those Ugandan bastards. Put on a plaster. I need to go!' Imre managed to apply a sterile gauze dressing before he jumped off the table and rushed off. It had been a fifteen-minute pit stop during the chase.

I subsequently saw Pat Shaw for a follow-up. He casually mentioned the Ugandan gang had been 'neutralized'. 'It pays to be fat,' he told me. 'Imagine if I were thin. That bullet would have gone right into my chest. Might have killed me.'

Shaw told me what had happened to him during the attempted coup of 1982. He was in Vienna at the time. On hearing the news he took the next plane to London hoping to get on a Kenya Airways flight home. Much to his frustration all flights to Nairobi had been suspended. He then went to the Kenyan High Commission to get a brief on the chaos that was unfolding in Kenya. He was told by the anxious Kenyans there that a group of Kenyans exiled in England were about to demonstrate outside the building in support of the coup. Shaw positioned himself on the first-floor balcony and began taking photos as the crowd formed on the street below. One of the demonstrators caught sight of the dreaded Patrick Shaw wielding his camera and let out a cry of warning. The crowd dispersed within minutes. 'They're all afraid of me. They even think I'm bulletproof. You know that isn't true, David!' he said with a twinkle in his eye.

One day Shaw called to say he was having severe chest pain. I told him to come to my office immediately. It was clear from the ECG he was having a heart attack. This was confirmed with blood tests. I told him I was going to admit him into the hospital. He was reluctant but agreed under two conditions. He had to have his CB radio and his gun with him at all times. And if a call came through that he had to respond to, he was going to leave. It seemed I had no option but to agree if I was going to treat him. I reluctantly said yes.

I called the duty nurse at 10 pm that night to find out how he was doing. She reported the medications had partially settled his pain. In those days they would have been blood thinners, aspirin and a beta blocker. The nurses had wanted to give him the sleeping pill I had ordered, but he had refused.

I came in early the next morning to review him and found him fast asleep. I told the nurses I was delighted he had slept through the night. They laughed and told me what had really happened. Sometime after midnight his CB had gone off. Within seconds he was out of bed and dressed, having yanked the monitor leads off his chest. Without even a nod to the nurses, he'd run down the stairs to his car and disappeared into the night. Two hours later was back again. The nurses reapplied his monitor leads and he went back to bed. Shaw insisted on being discharged a few days later. Fortunately for him he had healed well despite his nocturnal activity.

In those early days Nairobi Hospital parties were always great fun with the doctors, casualty medical officers, nurses and student nurses all attending. When I moved into my new house, I decided to throw a party and invited everyone. There was just one problem. I might have to get police permission to hold a 'night meeting'. The attempted coup was fresh in everyone's memory and there was concern that clandestine meetings were being held to plot Moi's overthrow.

On the morning of the party I called up Pat Shaw and asked him if my gathering would be considered a night meeting. He said he didn't have a clue but offered to go with me to the Kilimani police station. When my four housestaff saw me getting into the famous policeman's car, they were terrified. It was rare for someone to do this and return unscathed. As it turned out, I did have to get a license for the party. Afterward we went to the Norfolk Hotel for a cup of tea and some of the pastries Shaw loved.

When I got home the staff gaped at me with relief but also, it seemed, in some confusion. I later found out they had taken it for granted I was a goner. In my absence they had walked through the house divvying up my possessions and deciding who got what. Were their smiles genuine when they saw me return or were they masking their disappointment? I didn't ask them because it wasn't a question that would ever get an honest answer. Nor did I really want to know.

My relations with my staff have always been good with one exception. Yet again, it was Patrick Shaw who came to the rescue.

Heartbeat: An American Cardiologist in Kenya

There was a small safe in the house that I had been stacking with cash to avoid having to go to the bank. At one point I came down with hepatitis A and was in bed for over a week. When I felt well enough to get up, I went to my safe and found it empty. I thought I'd left money in it but I wasn't sure. I let the matter pass. But when it happened again a month later, I knew for sure somebody was stealing from me. I had no idea which of the staff was the culprit, and I didn't want to accuse anyone without some evidence.

Shaw didn't hesitate when I called him. He asked me to get 400 shillings in small notes, which he collected from my office and powdered. He later returned them in an envelope and told me to put it in the safe. I checked the safe regularly and after one week, sure enough, the envelope had vanished. Shaw came over and interviewed the staff one by one. Onyango the cook went first. He was innocent, Shaw said. Next to be summoned was the gardener and house cleaner, Onesmus, who was the son of a pastor. At first he couldn't be found until Onyango discovered him in his room in the staff quarters frantically rubbing his hands together. They were bright green. Shaw strode across the lawn in Onesmus' wake and I trailed behind him until Shaw shooed me away. I heard the unmistakable sound of loud slaps and the whining voice of Onesmus pleading his innocence. It didn't work. Shaw dragged him off to the police station where he was locked up in remand until his court case. I testified that the stolen notes had been covered with a green powder and that was Onesmus' undoing. He was found guilty and given two years. One month later Onesmus popped up again. He rang to say that President Moi had issued a blanket pardon to petty thieves on Jamhuri Day, a public holiday celebrating Kenya's independence. I was so surprised words failed me. '*Pole, nimefanya makosa.* (Sorry, I made a mistake). Can I have my job back, please?' Suddenly my voice returned. 'Definitely not!'

One evening in February 1988, Shaw was at a party held by the retired police commissioner David Rowe, my next-door neighbor. He suddenly collapsed. Somebody came running to my house to call for me, but unfortunately I was in Mombasa and could only return the next day by which time it was too late to help him. As would be expected, everybody, including his Starehe student Dr Muhindi, was convinced that Shaw had been poisoned. However, his sudden death syndrome was actually related to his ischemic heart disease. He was only fifty-two.

I found it impossible to classify this man who remained an enigma even beyond his death. Was he a murderer who had the blessing of the authorities, a vigilante, a modern version of a medieval knight dedicated to protecting the poor? Or was he a righteous man who saw the inequality and injustice that was part of the modernizing process in independent Africa and thought that he just might make a difference? I am still not sure. What I do know is that Patrick Shaw was carried to his grave by Starehe Boys pallbearers. They were students and graduates and they wept openly. The criminal gangs of Nairobi, on the other hand, rejoiced.

23

BWANA SIMBA

It has long been held that cholesterol is a major factor in heart disease. The conventional medical wisdom is that a build-up of deposits in the arteries leads to heart attacks. This was challenged by Dr George Mann, an American biochemist and physician, when he published a paper on the subject in 1972. Mann studied 1500 cattle-owning Maasai whose meat-and-milk diet was rich in animal fats, lipids and cholesterol. 'They have very low levels of cholesterol in their blood, half as much as we do, and very rarely have cardiovascular disease,' he concluded. Mann theorized that because the Maasai walked long distances and were constantly on the move, their coronary arteries were considerably larger than average, so blood passed easily through the large coronary arteries despite the cholesterol plaques on their walls. By contrast, the same size plaque in arteries of a normal size can obstruct the blood flow. As a result, the study suggested, coronary artery disease was not connected to diet but to a lack of exercise.

I partially agree with Mann. Exercise is a major mitigating factor (as well as genetics and the absence of stress). Two men who bore out this theory were brothers who lived in the bush of northern Kenya walking many miles every day. Terence and George Adamson came to Kenya with their parents after

World War I. Despite a dedication to cigarettes (Terence) and a pipe and whiskey (George), they remained remarkably fit until their deaths at seventy-eight and eighty-three. George was a game warden for a vast area of northern Kenya. Terence had a number of jobs including game warden and locust officer, but he was at his best as an engineer building roads, dams and bridges in the wilderness. Even though they faced off charging buffalos and poachers armed with guns in the course of their work, they were shy by inclination, particularly Terence. He was the younger of the brothers by two years and never married, preferring to live by himself in remote outposts. He was quite happy to sleep rough on the ground with a blanket when out on foot safaris. His knowledge of plants and wild animals was extraordinary. Such was Terence's desire for a simple life that the only clothes he owned were khaki shirts, shorts and trousers. The exception was a cheap suit given to him by the army when he was demobbed at the end of World War II. He folded it up in an airtight can and buried it. On his only trip to England, he dug it up and wore it, returning it to its burial place when he came home.

In later life Terence lived in the shadow of his elder brother. George became a household name associated with his wife Joy Adamson and the orphaned lion cub Elsa that they found and reared (in what was to become Meru National Park) before returning her to the wild. Joy's book *Born Free* was followed by other books and a movie of the same name. The books and the movie were all runaway successes. The public loved the idea of a glamorous couple in the wilds of Africa living with dangerous animals they had allowed to roam free.

George and Joy separated in 1970 after twenty-seven years of marriage. Joy was a gifted artist and conservationist who did much for wildlife. She inspired generations of school children to love and protect wild animals. She donated almost all of the proceeds from the books and the film to projects such as wildlife education and developing game park infrastructure. However, she was a difficult woman to live with. George had established a camp in one part of Meru with his lions, three of whom had performed in the film *Born Free*. Joy had set up camp in another corner to study Pippa, a cheetah she had released into the wild.

In 1980 a locally hired camp employee stabbed Joy to death. She had left instructions in her will to be cremated and her ashes scattered in Meru Park, divided between the grave of her two beloved cats, the lioness Elsa and Pippa the cheetah. When George published his autobiography, *My Pride and Joy*, he expressed, in his restrained British way, an affection for his wife and her life's work that was touching.

In 1970, when Meru was gazetted as a national park, George, Terence and George's assistant, Tony Fitzjohn, moved to Kora, a remote and undeveloped area of dry bushland to the east of Meru. Their camp became known as *Kampi ya Simba*, the Camp of the Lions. For the next eighteen years George and Tony taught orphaned big cats how to hunt and survive in the wild while Terence went about the business of making dirt roads and trails cut through the thick scrub bush. By one count, George and Tony released thirty lions and ten leopards.

I knew the brothers in their sunset years. They still smoked and George still drank, but they were constantly active. The first Adamson I treated was Terence. He was referred to me by Dr Andrew Meyerhold with a bad case of pneumonia, aggravated by his smoking. We had to put him on a ventilator for a week. I met George soon after when he came to visit his convalescing brother. George was nut-brown from the sun, lean as a whippet, with a wild shock of blond-white hair and a white beard that from time to time he trimmed into a goatee. He was covered in scars, courtesy of his beloved lions. George smoked a pipe and unfiltered cigarettes. I hospitalized him twice with pneumonia. Whenever George was admitted, his coterie of friends and admirers would smuggle in bottles of whiskey. If the nurses complained, I told them George had been given carte blanche to drink. 'I'll be coming round this evening to join him for sundowners,' I added.

I visited Kampi ya Simba only once, flying in on a rented four-seater plane with Andrew Meyerhold. We brought coffee and other staples and, of course, the obligatory bottle of White Horse whiskey. It was extremely hot the afternoon we arrived. While we were served a cup of *chai* (tea), numerous red-billed and yellow-billed hornbills settled around us to be fed biscuits by hand. We were then shown to our tents. George and Terry lived in cabins.

Before a dinner of tasty game meat came showtime. A small, battery-powered spotlight illuminated George standing a distance away from us with armloads of camel meat for his lions. We could hear them roar in the distance as they approached. Six to eight lions appeared that night. George called each one by name, and it padded forward to be petted and fed. A couple of them stood on their hind legs and put their huge paws on his shoulders in affectionate greeting. There were both males and females. It was amazing to watch the relationship between this gentle man and these great wild beasts.

At dawn the next day, the birds returned en masse. For their morning snack we served the birds toast. After breakfast, shirtless and clad as usual in a pair of shorts and sandals, George drove us a short distance to visit Tony in his tent. We had been invited to Kora to give an unusual medical consultation. Tony and his girlfriend were taking care of a very young, newly orphaned lion cub and were concerned because it wasn't well. They were in bed in their tent when we arrived, the cub snuggled between them. We examined the little guy, who was clearly anaemic, and made arrangements to have him flown to Nairobi for treatment. After lunch back at Kampi ya Simba we flew home to Nairobi.

Not long after that Andrew Meyerhold called me with terrible news. George, known everywhere in East Africa as Bwana Simba, had been murdered by Somali bandits. Apparently the bandits had stopped a vehicle carrying one of George's assistants and a young female tourist. Shots were fired. George heard the gunfire from the camp and came speeding to the rescue with four camp staff. On approaching the scene George aimed his vehicle at the Somalis and put his foot flat on the floor, intending to run them over. Before he could, they shot him and two of his staff dead. He rests today at Kora, next to Terence, who had died three years earlier. Nearby is the grave of his favourite lion, Boy, who played Elsa's wild consort in the movie *Born Free*.

At the time of George's death Tony Fitzjohn moved to Tanzania to rehabilitate and manage Mkomazi National Reserve, a heavily poached area of 1,350 square miles. In the ensuing years Tony transformed it into a haven for elephants and other animals and a sanctuary for rhino and endangered African wild dog before the stewardship of Mkomazi was passed back to the Tanzanian authorities. He was in the throes of returning to Kora at the time of his death from a brain tumour in 2022. He was 76.

24

NELSON MANDELA

On 19 October 1986 a plane piloted by a Soviet crew flew into a hill in the South African low veld and burst into flames. One of the passengers was President Samora Machel of Mozambique. He and thirty-three others died. One crew member and nine people sitting at the back of the plane survived. I was housesitting next to the Nairobi National Park for my American friends Saul and Marcia Gordon. It was a quirky thatch-roof cottage inspired by traditional mud-and-wattle huts. It was perched at the top of a small ravine, and I was enjoying a herd of zebra grazing on the far side when I heard about the plane crash on the BBC.

There were two theories about what had caused it. It had been a dark and cloudy night minutes before moonrise. The plane was still in South African airspace but on its descent to Maputo. An investigation led by the South African government concluded it was pilot error with the crew failing to react to the ground proximity warning system. It had also been suggested that the Mozambican controller in the airport tower and the Russian pilot didn't understand each other properly, which is why the crew didn't follow procedural requirements for the approach. They were communicating in English, which was not the first language for either. The International Civil Aviation Organization concurred with these findings. It was the last years of South Africa's apartheid regime and relations with Mozambique were strained. The Soviets and the Mozambicans had an alternative theory. They claimed the South Africans deliberately lured the plane off course with a decoy radio navigation beacon. Speculation persists to this day. The views of both sides had substance, but I suspected the latter was probably the correct one.

The next day it was announced that President Moi would lead a delegation to Machel's funeral. Representatives from more than 100 countries were expected to attend. Maputo had few good hotels and rooms would be at a premium. It was decided that the funeral would be a day trip, leaving aboard a Kenya Airways flight by 4 am so that we could make the morning funeral on time.

We landed in an intermittent rain that would persist throughout our brief stay. We were put on a large bus and driven past beautiful Indian Ocean beaches to the Polana Hotel, the capital's once and future architectural pearl. I've since enjoyed several stays there, but in 1986 it was a dump. President Moi was whisked away at once while the rest of us, unsure of what was happening, were herded into a room filled with numerous other African delegations. We were served soft drinks imported from South Africa while we tried to communicate with the Mozambicans. They spoke no English and none of us knew Portuguese.

There was some indication that we were to watch the funeral on television, but no one could make the set work. After some hours we were loaded back on the bus and driven past Heroes Square, where Machel was to be interred, to a nearby area where we encountered serried ranks of tents. Mozambique was a relatively new country and still in the throes of a civil war. There was no chief of protocol or guidance as to what we should be doing. Most of us sat down at random in one of the tents. We presumed that someone eventually would lead us back to the bus and we would return to the airport.

Situated as we were, we Kenyans saw little of the reported tens of thousands of mourners who were standing in the rain five to ten persons deep to catch sight of the four-and-a-half-mile-long funeral procession. Many of them were clutching flowers. I did spot Julius Nyerere walking along. He had recently resigned after twenty-three years as president of Tanzania. He later sat down near me as did Kenneth Kaunda, Zambia's long-serving and only president. Somewhere among the mourners was the Reverend Jesse Jackson, the American civil rights activist, Baptist minister and politician, as well as that old rogue, Robert Mugabe, the Zimbabwean strongman.

When I turned in my chair to have a look around, I noticed Ronald Reagan's daughter Maureen was seated three rows behind me. The U.S. president had delegated her to represent him at the funeral. A few seats along from her was none other than Yasser Arafat, the PLO chairman, wearing his customary green-and-white keffiyeh. Maureen Reagan was poised and calm in a green dress with a discreet green veil covering her forehead and eyes. She didn't seem to be aware of the scruffy revolutionary and resolute foe of Israel and the U.S. seated nearby.

The funeral service continued with neither Reagan nor Arafat noticing one another. Suddenly a little gust of wind lifted her veil in one direction and pushed his keffiyeh in the other. They both reached up a hand and inadvertently made eye contact in the process. With expressions of incredulous surprise they quickly turned their chairs away from each other as if to deny that the other even existed. They never made eye contact again.

I had heard Nelson Mandela had sent his condolences to Graca Machel, Samora Machel's widow. He was still incarcerated on Robben Island. He was to endure twenty-seven years of imprisonment before his release in 1990 at age seventy-one. During that time he suffered abuse and humiliation with dignity and exceptional courage. When he became president of South Africa in 1994 and freed his country from the shame of apartheid, he was welcomed as a hero. During his time in prison his wife Winnie had acquired a reputation for brutality and corruption. He began to ease out of this toxic marriage by separating from her in 1992. The divorce became final in 1996. At some point he met and fell in love with Graca Machel. In 1998 he asked her to marry him. He had proposed to her once before, and she had turned him down. This time she accepted. Coincidentally Graca was the first, and so far the only, woman to serve as first lady for two different countries.

On becoming a free man Nelson Mandela embarked on a series of public tours to raise his profile and hone his message in preparation for becoming South Africa's first democratically elected Black president. In May 1990 he visited six African cities. In June he left on a fourteen-country world tour. The second stop was Geneva where he met with a high-level delegation drawn from major American Jewish organizations. It was headed by Henry Seligman, the director of the American Jewish Congress.

The group was seeking clarification from Mandela, in advance of his trip to the United States, of his declared support for Yasser Arafat and the PLO. Mandela had likened the Palestinian cause to the struggles of Black South Africans. South Africa had a large Jewish population, and many Jews were disturbed by Mandela's perceived position. The majority of South African Jews had either arrived as refugees from Eastern Europe before and during the

Holocaust or were their descendants. I too was uncomfortable with Mandela's leftist sympathies and shared what Seligman called his 'sense of foreboding'. Would Mandela and his African National Congress party support Israel's right to exist?

To my relief the meeting seemed to go well. 'As far as the African National Congress is concerned - and that is my view as an individual - there has never been any doubting the existence, *de facto* and *de jure*, of the state of Israel within secure boundaries,' Mandela told the *New York Times,* adding the caveat that 'secure boundaries' meant Israel's borders before the 1967 Six Day War.

The visiting delegation in turn issued a statement that the meeting had '…reinforced our respect for Mr Mandela and his reconciling statesmanship, a respect that is not diminished by any differences between us and the ANC on some aspects of the Mideast conflict.'

Two weeks later in a letter to the *New York Times,* Abraham Foxman, who had been at the Geneva meeting and who was the national director of the Anti-Defamation League, elaborated on the session. 'My colleagues and I spent two and a half hours with the African National Congress leader. It was a warm session with good personal feelings on all sides. Mr Mandela understood far more than we anticipated about the Jewish experience, about the meaning of Israel, about its genesis.

'He talked not only of his unequivocal support for Israel's right to exist and for security, but also of his respect for Israel's leaders, David Ben Gurion, Golda Meir, Menachem Begin. We were delighted with the visit.'

Mandela's multi-city visit to the U.S. was a great success. It included an event at New York's Yankee Stadium, a cordial meeting with President George H.W. Bush and an address before a joint session of Congress. He then visited Canada, Ireland and England on his way back.

In July he arrived in Addis Ababa, the capital of Ethiopia, to attend a summit meeting of the Organization of African Unity. There he developed a cough and low-grade fever. Word that he was ill leaked out, and reports appeared in the press he was suffering from pneumonia. Professor Idris Mtulia, a cardiologist friend from the Muhimbili Hospital in Dar es Salaam, was at the OAU meeting as the personal physician of the then Tanzanian head of state, Ali Hassan Mwinyi. He was asked to see Mandela and detected an irregular pulse that he documented with an ECG. He explained to Mandela that he had two options. Either he could return to South Africa for medical care or leave for Nairobi, the next stop on his itinerary, ahead of schedule. There a Dr Silverstein could take care of him. Mandela chose Nairobi.

He looked ill and frail as he slowly descended from the plane with his wife Winnie. President Moi was there to greet him along with the Kenyan cabinet. Mandela was driven away in Moi's limousine. Winnie Mandela was put in a separate vehicle. The night before his arrival I had received a call from Njuguna Mahugu, the chief of protocol, instructing me to organize an ICU bed in the VIP North Wing. It had been built with the late President Jomo Kenyatta in mind in case he might need it for a medical emergency.

Shortly after Mandela's arrival, a large and imposing security officer dressed in full motorcycle police uniform, complete with leathers and helmet, appeared in my office demanding that Dr Silverstein come with him to State House urgently. Mandela was staying in an upstairs room. He told me he had contracted tuberculosis in prison and had a previous history of an irregular pulse. I was struck by the soothing tone of his voice. He was warm and engaging, without pretense. I took an immediate liking to the man. Any negative preconceptions disappeared.

I conducted a cursory examination. Once I had established that his condition was not life threatening, I proposed he rest and come to see me after lunch at the hospital for a more detailed assessment. He appeared in my office mid-afternoon, and I did an ECG, an echocardiogram, a chest X-ray and drew blood. Winnie was with us throughout, but she showed no interest in any of the tests, asked no questions and would not make eye contact with anyone. I didn't know if this was her usual way. I remember thinking at the time she must have had other worries distracting her. Though what could be more worrying than knowing your elderly husband's health was failing him?

I later learned Winnie had been implicated in the 1988 kidnap and murder of fourteen-year-old Stompie Sepei. He was a member of her infamous Mandela United Football Club, who acted as her bodyguards. The teenager had been abducted from the home of a Methodist minister and was found dead, covered in stab wounds, in an open field. Winnie had been charged with his kidnapping and with being an accessory to his assault, and the trial was still ongoing. With this looming over her, she could be forgiven for being distracted. In due course she was found guilty and received a six-year jail sentence. It was later reduced to a fine.

The X-ray revealed pneumonia for which I prescribed an antibiotic. Then my Maasai technician Jacinta Nkoyo connected Mandela to a Holter monitor to record his heart rhythms to see if the irregularities were solitary events. If they occurred in runs it would be a more worrisome finding. Jacinta was in awe of him. 'Thank you for letting me touch your body,' she said shyly as she finished adjusting the Holter monitor.

Besides the pneumonia, I noted other factors that were contributory to Mandela's heart irregularity. The altitude in

Addis Ababa was 7726 feet above sea level. And then there was the TB. After twenty-four hours the Holter monitor recorded no evidence of ventricular arrhythmias, in other words runs of extra beats. I told him we'd found nothing ominous, but even so he should see a cardiologist as soon as he returned to South Africa.

The next night Mandela attended a state banquet in his honour in Nairobi. He greeted me warmly at the dinner and later autographed my invitation to the event. It is one of my cherished mementos from my years as Moi's doctor. My wife Channa later had it framed. It is on prominent display in our home.

It was about nine months after I treated Mandela in Nairobi that I travelled with Moi to Swaziland for a meeting of COMESA (the Common Market for Eastern and Southern Africa). The great value of these multilateral events is the chance for heads of state to meet quietly with one another in their hotel suites. As I was not involved in these private talks, I usually sat in my room reading. Sometimes I would join Moi for a cup of tea or a meal and glean what I could of the day's developments. I was in the corridor, on my way to see the president, when I encountered Njuguna Mahugu, our chief of protocol, and some security guards escorting Nelson Mandela from Moi's suite. I moved to the side to let them pass. Mandela stopped when he saw me and said, 'Dr Silverstein, you are a much better doctor than you think. I'm still alive!' We had a good laugh as we shook hands.

25

A PLACE UNDER THE SUN

Nairobi is a dynamic city. It has a music scene, an art scene, and a diplomatic dinner round that can consume your evenings. It is a continental hub for communications, IT and transport. International media tend to base themselves here. It is the *de facto* capital of East Africa. But for me, Nairobi is a traffic jam where I work.

Nairobi is imbued with the spirit of progress. Its residents want more, better, and faster. The Nairobi Hospital is like that too. The doctors who work there are among the brightest and best and deliver excellent service to our patients. Prior to the COVID-19 pandemic, I worked ten to twelve-hour days for twelve out of fourteen days. I always looked forward to honouring the Sabbath on my weekend off. And my idea of a Sabbath retreat is not Nairobi.

I spend every free weekend at my farm on the shores of Lake Naivasha. At 6.30 am I awake with the sun to the haunting calls of the fish eagles. Taking care not to wake up Channa, I pull on my jogging gear and descend a steep path toward the lake shore. Down below is the barn where we keep the cows and horses, chicken coops and a large, organic vegetable garden. Channa runs all this so successfully that she has been able to supply customers with eggs, vegetables and dairy products on a weekly basis.

Heartbeat: An American Cardiologist in Kenya

As I run across the plain and through bush and forest, I keep a wary eye out for Cape buffalos hidden in the bush. I can hear and sometimes see hippos in the lake shallows where they wallow until evening. On any given day on either side of the path there are herds of Grant's and Thomson's gazelles, warthogs, impala, eland and giraffe. There are often troops of baboons and herds of zebra. And every time, I say to myself *This is nothing short of paradise.*

I run for over an hour and come home for breakfast that I take on the veranda overlooking the lake. I eat a healthy meal while listening to world news. Then the rest of the day is my own, now and then with a call to the hospital to confer about my patients. I read, chat with friends, take an afternoon nap.

As the afternoon draws into evening, I go out onto a hill overlooking the expansive lake with my wife, dogs and often friends, for a sundowner. This is, for me, one double single malt whiskey (never more), which I sip while we watch the setting over the lake with the sky changing magical colours. We return to the house, now with the sounds of hyena and leopard and a silence in between that promises a lovely peaceful sleep after a farm fresh dinner.

I work in Nairobi, but I live in Naivasha. My house is in Nairobi, but my home is in Naivasha.

When I first came to Kenya in 1974, I noticed that my Kenyan colleagues and friends worked hard in the city, but during the holidays they returned to the villages where they were born and where, ultimately, they would be buried. In troubled times, during periods of civil unrest or other crisis, many East Africans seek refuge in their rural *shambas* where their families grow some food crops and keep poultry and a cow or two.

Growing up in Chicago, my background had been entirely urban. My knowledge of cows was from the viewpoint of the car window when we cruised through the countryside on Sunday family outings. I thought they were wild animals. The idea of having a rural home was foreign to me. But as the years in Kenya passed, my colleagues' attachment to the land seemed to make more and more sense.

There were lots of places I could have chosen, but from my first visit to Lake Naivasha, it became the focus of my hunt for a shamba in the bush. Naivasha is a large freshwater lake of more than 140 square kilometres surrounded by forested foothills. It is filled with grunting hippos that pop up from the water to regard you with periscope eyes. Giraffe, buffalo, antelope, zebra and warthog graze and browse on the plains and in the stands of yellow-barked fever trees. There are hundreds of species of brightly coloured birds.

One hundred and twenty years ago plains-dwelling Maasai pastoralists lived there and forest-dwelling hunter-gatherers called the Ogiek. Over time the British privatized much of the land and made it into farms and ranches. After independence the newly enriched Kenyan elite bought some of these farms and ranches from their previous owners.

On one visit I ran into my friend Walter Kilele. He was the managing director of ADC (Agricultural Development Corporation). I can't recall why he was in Naivasha, but I presume it had something to do with that. The parastatal ADC had been established to oversee the transfer of agricultural land from European settlers to Kenyans in the wake of independence. Once they had succeeded in this, the corporation moved on to developing and running agricultural enterprises. As it happened, one of ADC's recent acquisitions was Ndabibi Farm, which they had purchased from my patient, Lady Diana Delamere. The corporation had assumed control of the farm's approximately 40,000 acres on her death but had yet to close on the deal. The land was in a legal limbo until the complicated transfer was completed.

When I explained to Walter why I was visiting Naivasha, he talked about a part of the Ndabibi Farm on a lakeside hill that did not fit into the ADC's largescale cattle-ranching plans. It would be available for purchase, he said, and offered to show me around. He took me to the top of a rocky hill. From this vantage point the view was spectacular, stretching miles across the ever-shifting colours of the lake to the far side of the Rift Valley. Bushes and trees clung to the sides of the precipitous drop to the shoreline, which was rimmed by groves of graceful thorn trees. Down below us the open grassland was home to buffalos, giraffes, zebra, warthogs and antelopes. I knew at once this was where I wanted to be.

Walter introduced me to Des Bristow, one of those outsized characters which Kenya favours. He was deep-voiced and muscular, a native Kenyan of British descent. He lived in a little white house not thirty metres from where I hoped to build my own place. When he talked, there was the suspicion he had recently been woken from a nap, but this proved deceptive. Des Bristow was a macho brawler, alert to everything. Diana Delamere had hired him some twenty years earlier to look after her ranch.

His chief responsibility was to keep a lid on cattle rustling. Kenya's anti-stock theft unit had become lax over time, and ranchers tended to arrange their own security. Des kept order with a posse known as Bristow's Army. They were very good at tracking down the thieves, but once they had them, Des handled matters on his own.

Emboldened by the lack of proper law enforcement, the detainees would casually acknowledge their guilt to Bristow. 'No problem! Take me to the police. I'll pay them off and be out tomorrow.'

'We're in the bush. We'll settle this man to man,' Des would say. He said he would then pummel his opponent half senseless. Anyone who could still talk begged to be taken to the police. His approach to justice was a bit like that of his urban counterpart, Patrick Shaw, and equally effective.

As Bristow and I got to know one another, he shared an unusual story. Long before Lady Delamere's death, she had ordered a fine mahogany casket built for her eventual resting place and kept it at his house. Now and then when cow business brought her to Ndabibi she'd drop by to check on her casket. Des said she expected him to keep the thing dusted and polished just so against the day it would bear her into her grave. She did have quite the dramatic touch.

Walter Kilele and I settled on a parcel of land of about sixty acres. After some delay I received a letter permitting me to buy the land. The official notification also conveyed sufficient authority for me to start construction at my pleasure. It was December 1987. In late 1988 Heini Lustman came on board as the architect. He was one of the elders of the Nairobi Jewish community, a man who had escaped the Nazis by coming to Kenya. He had retired from a partnership with George Vamos and was pushing eighty. I had been Heini's doctor practically from the moment I had arrived in Kenya. Any hesitation he might have had to take on such a project in a remote location at his age vanished the moment he saw the site.

Lustman suggested a two-story structure to take advantage of the natural slope. I had no preconceptions when we discussed the design, stressing only that I saw the place primarily as a comfortable weekend retreat where I could relax and occasionally entertain. To that end we decided on three en suite bedrooms upstairs along with the general living quarters. Downstairs would be a daylight basement. Generally speaking, however, Heini's vision of the only house I'd ever build became my vision. The plans were ready within a month.

Heini brought on Bill Sayers as the contractor. He had built most of the houses in the greater area and knew the lay of the land - literally. Bill was getting a bit long in the tooth too. He drove an ancient Mercedes that somehow managed to regularly bump and clatter its way up and down the rutted and dusty road between Nakuru and Naivasha. He assembled a thirteen-man work crew who rotated in and out of the project as their various specialties, such as masonry or window glazing, were required. We housed them in *mabati* huts, fashioned from prefabricated corrugated iron sheets, which were erected on the hill above the building site. Des piped running water from his house until I could get my own pump working. There was no electricity.

Construction started in January of 1989. Since the entire Rift Valley is an earthquake zone, the first thing Heini did was bring in a structural engineer to fortify the building against tremors. He designed a cement-and-steel structure to undergird the house and permit it to sway safely in case the ground started moving beneath us. The foundation was then laid and construction was underway.

I flew Heini up once a month to monitor the work's progress. Sayers would show us around, describe what he'd been doing, raise any issues that needed discussion and then answer our questions. These sessions were always collegial, and I looked forward to them as I watched my house on the lake take form.

Then Lustman and Sayers would walk off alone for a short time to go over monthly costs. Once Heini and I had landed back at Wilson Airport in Nairobi, he'd discuss with me what he'd learned from Sayers, show me the receipts, tell me where he agreed and disagreed with the contractor, and then present me the bill for the month. Heini was meticulous. He hated to waste anything, particularly money. I trusted him without question and never had reason to alter that view. I'd write him a check. We'd say goodbye and then meet again the following month for another flying trip to the construction site.

Next on my agenda was naming my shamba. Naivasha was originally Maasai country so I thought it fitting to give it a name that acknowledged its history. When taking turns reading from the Torah in synagogue we call men up by their Hebrew first name and as the son of the father's first name. In my case, 'David, the son of Norman'. The Maa word *ole* means 'son of' so I named the farm Ole Normani, Son of Norman.

Walter Kilele repeatedly assured me that acquiring a legally sound title deed to the Lake Naivasha property was just a formality. There was no hurry in paying for the land, he said. But with construction well under way, I wanted a somewhat more secure hold on what I owned. The solution was to engage Dr Chandu Sheth's uncle, Nanalal Sheth, who was a capable and highly respected lawyer. His task was to agree on a price with Walter and secure that deed. Kilele again advised me to hang on to my money. There was no hurry. Nanalal shook his head. He was having none of that. 'My client wants to close the deal now.' Walter nodded and at last came up with a reasonable figure. Nanalal signed a check immediately. I was out of the country and reimbursed him later.

Channa and I and our four boys enjoy many Sabbaths at Ole Normani. As it says in the good book, 'By the seventh day God had finished His work, and so He rested.' And so do I.

26

THE CIRCLE OF LIFE

On 15 July 1981 the hospital's switchboard operator rang saying she was putting through an overseas call. I felt myself tensing up. In those days international communications were still difficult and costly. People didn't call each other just to have a chat. I heard my brother Allan's voice coming down the line. He was very distressed and having trouble talking. He didn't need to. I knew immediately what he was going to tell me. This was the phone call I had been expecting for years. Every August on Dad's birthday I had celebrated that he had made it through another year. Now here it was. Allan was telling me that our father had died. He was seventy-six.

I had visited my parents in Chicago at least twice a year. Each time I had observed his progressive deterioration. On Saturdays I walked with him to the synagogue for the Shabbat service. Each year the distances became shorter before he had to stop and put nitroglycerine underneath his tongue and wait for the chest pain to abate. Yet despite the pain and discomfort he soldiered on in his medical practice, making the daily hospital rounds and attending his clinic three days a week. He had made his hospital rounds as usual that evening. Later, when in bed with my mother, he suffered a sudden death syndrome and collapsed in her arms.

Once Allan had composed himself sufficiently, he confirmed what I already knew. Jewish law dictated that Dad be buried as soon as possible. I booked a ticket for the first flights to get me to Chicago. The emotional enormity of it hadn't yet sunk in. I was operating on auto-pilot as I finished my work at the hospital and handed over to Majid Warshow. I rushed home, packed and went straight to the airport to catch the British Airways flight to Chicago via London. We lifted into the sky. I unbuckled the seat belt. And suddenly the full impact of Dad's death hit me. I would never see him again. I could no longer ask his advice. Never again would I bask in his pride as I related how I was getting on in my medical career. As the elder son, Dad would have expected me to deliver an erudite eulogy at his funeral, but I couldn't go there yet. I was overwhelmed with emotion. I finally fell asleep with tears in my eyes, recalling how Dad looked when he was beaming with happiness.

On the next leg of the trip from Chicago to London I again tried to write the eulogy, but I couldn't. I kept thinking about his only request to me during my years in Africa. I remembered it word for word. 'David you're a great success as a doctor. I'm very proud of you. You've kept a strong Jewish identity. I'm proud of you for that too. However, you will not be a complete person until you marry a Jewish woman and have children.'

'I love you, Dad. I'll make you proud. I promise.' I was crying as I whispered it to myself.

I never could write his eulogy. I delivered it off the cuff, but it must have struck a chord. Several of the mourners brought out handkerchiefs.

Three years later, in the spring of 1984, Dad's words came back to me. My fortieth birthday was approaching. It was time I got serious about marriage and starting a family. My mother had been pushing me hard in that direction for some time. After some thought I decided to multitask. The considerable travel entailed in my appointment as President Moi's physician had persuaded me that I ought to be more fully informed on world affairs, particularly on issues, trends and events that impacted Africa.

I devised a plan to leave Majid Warshow in charge of our Nairobi practice for a couple of months while I went to Washington D.C. to attend classes at the Nitze School for Advanced International Studies at Johns Hopkins University. Then with my sister Rochelle's help I'd search for a beautiful and intelligent Jewish woman willing to drop whatever she was doing to become my wife, move to East Africa and raise a family. It seemed like a pretty nifty plan. That autumn I rented a room at a hotel on N Street NW near the school.

Unbeknownst to me Rochelle and her husband Sol, together with a female rabbi of their acquaintance, had already been at work by putting a notice in the personal columns of *Washingtonian* magazine. A JSM (Jewish single male), 39, M.D., was looking for a JF (Jewish female), S or D, (single or divorced). The terms of reference left a lot of leeway for interested applicants. Replies were already coming in. My brother-in-law Sol screened out everyone who submitted photos of themselves in bikinis as well as anyone else who, in his view, did not meet standards of propriety. Non-negotiable, as far as I was concerned, was beauty. Looks counted a lot to me, probably because I unconsciously made my mother the standard against which these women were to be judged.

This was one of the more interesting and fun times of my life. I was excited to be studying again. I'd never spent much time on the humanities. The other students were very different from the people I'd met in medical school. After class I'd go to the library until 8 pm. After that I'd go on a date with someone I'd picked from the list my brother-in-law and sister were preparing. It was great.

The spouse hunt started to look particularly promising when I met Lesley Meltzer. She was an attractive honey blonde about ten years my junior and from Philadelphia. Her father, Bernie Meltzer, was a well-known radio personality of the day. He and Lesley's mother were divorced as was Lesley after a brief marriage to an Israeli. She had no children.

Lesley had a brilliant mind. For me, that was a decided plus. She had taken an undergraduate degree in Israel and earned a master's in Arabic studies at Columbia University in New York. She spoke fluent Hebrew. I gathered she was some sort of spook, which I found exciting. She told me she worked for the U.S. Department of Defense but wouldn't be more specific. When I pushed her on it, she told me to read the *Puzzle Palace* by James Banford, the book about the National Security Agency. And in this circuitous way I found out she worked there as an analyst. She couldn't discuss most of what she did. This, of course, intrigued me.

This was the time of the seemingly endless civil war in Lebanon. Sixty-three people had been killed in the suicide bombing of our Beirut embassy in April 1983. Then in October a truck bomb smashed into the U.S. Marines Corp barracks, killing 241 U.S. military personnel, 220 of them Marines. Lesley was kept very busy during this period, but we saw one another whenever possible. I took her to Chicago to meet my mother, who was favourably impressed. Then from Chicago, I flew on to Los Angeles to attend an American College of Cardiology meeting, and Lesley returned to Washington. I had expected to stay in Washington about six weeks longer than I did. I had to get home to prepare for another trip with President Moi. Even so, my time there had surpassed my expectations and stirred hopes for the future.

I invited Lesley to Kenya to see how she would take to Africa. She arrived in the autumn of 1985. I rented a four-seat Piper and flew her to the Maasai Mara game reserve for a safari. Then we went to Naivasha, the lake where I would soon buy land and build a house. We spent a few days at the Lake Hotel.

The trip was a disaster. She was every bit as lovely and smart and interesting as I recalled, but she was focused on extracting a commitment to marriage. And she didn't seem comfortable in the bush. I was touched that a woman of her stature would want to spend the rest of her life with me. On the other hand, I had ill-defined misgivings. Lesley must have had serious doubts too as her farewell to me was unambiguous. 'We'll never see each other again.'

I was in Washington D.C. in the spring of 1987 visiting my sister and her family, when Rochelle surprised me with the suggestion that I contact Lesley again. Unbeknownst to me, the two of them had stayed in touch since Lesley's unsatisfactory trip to Kenya in 1985. The scars from that confrontation may have faded, but it was with some reluctance that I agreed to place the call.

'Why don't we get together for a cup of tea or something?' I said over the phone. 'I haven't seen you for a long time.'

'Why would you want to see me?' she asked.

'C'mon,' I replied. 'You know we're not enemies or anything. We all change.'

'You don't realize how much you hurt me,' she said. 'I was devastated. I went through a depression for a year.'

She was making me feel terrible. I probably deserved it so I asked her again to have a cup of tea with me at a place I knew on Dupont Circle. She walked in looking a million dollars. *Maybe we're compatible after all*, I thought. She started writing to me and soon after that we planned a two-week trip to Israel for December the following year.

Before our departure for Israel, I spoke with President Moi. 'Enjoy your holiday Daktari. You need the rest. I will send you a gift when you're there.' I had no idea what he was talking about.

When we reached our hotel in Jerusalem, Israeli friends I knew from Kenya greeted us with the wonderful news that Kenya had resumed diplomatic relations with Israel after suspending them – along with most of the rest of Africa - over the 1973 Yom Kippur War. So this was Moi's secret gift! I could not have been happier or more grateful. At the same time Yasser Arafat also announced the Palestinian Liberation Organization now recognized Israel's legitimacy. I could smell peace in the air.

But another issue soon cast a pall on our happiness. Lesley was picking up dark intimations via the National Security Agency of a serious threat involving aircraft. She became very anxious about the trip and her own safety. The threat materialized on 21 December 1988. A bomb exploded on board a Pan Am flight over Lockerbie in Scotland, killing everyone on board and eleven others in the houses the plane crashed into. In all 270 people died. The bombing had been sanctioned by Libya's Muammar Gaddafi. I was to run into him in a desert tent some years later.

From Jerusalem we went to Haifa where she once more demanded I give her a definite marriage commitment. 'Hey,' I said, trying to keep things light, 'we've been together just a few days. I'm really not there yet.'

She didn't like that at all. And Lesley's anger, I had learned, could make me so miserable that I'd say anything to appease her.

We returned to Jerusalem and celebrated Shabbat with one of my cousins. Then we were supposed to go to Tel Aviv to meet more cousins, but Lesley said she didn't want to go. We wound up the holiday by spending a delightful, romantic night in Jerusalem, and arose early for a morning flight. As Lesley stepped out of the shower, she casually remarked she hadn't taken any precautions the night before. I didn't think much of it at the time.

'Call me if you're pregnant. You never can tell. Maybe we'll get married.' I meant it as a joke.

A few weeks later Lesley rang to say she was pregnant. It was a stunner of a statement. I wondered if all the fights that had passed between us were merely due to my unwillingness to commit to her. I was forty-five, which was starting to be long in the tooth for an eligible bachelor. I dearly wanted children not only for myself but to honour my father and maintain the family tradition. It was up to me to put this right. Lesley and I started planning for a Philadelphia wedding that March.

Polish-born Charles Szlapak, a hotelier long associated with the Fairview Hotel and a leader of the Nairobi Jewish community, was my best man. He and I met in London, and we flew on to Philadelphia. I expected Lesley and her mother to pick us up at the airport, but we landed in a frigid winter storm and found no one there to greet us. Lesley's mother explained over the phone that neither of them was about to drive in such weather so Charles and I braved the wind and snow in search of an airport hotel. It was past midnight before we found a place to stay. They had one available room which we were glad to take. It had been an exhausting day.

The next day after securing a Pennsylvania marriage license, I drove south with Charles to Rochelle and Sol's place in Potomac, Maryland, where part one of the marriage celebration would take place. It wasn't a real bachelor party. More of a roast at the Sobel house with a lot of our friends in attendance including Lesley. The next morning the wedding party and all the guests boarded two buses that Rochelle had organized to take us to a fancy kosher hotel in Philadelphia. The wedding service was officiated by Rochelle's rabbi and several other rabbis from my family. There were many speeches during the meal. It was a beautiful wedding. Once again I was hopeful that everything would be all right now that I had finally committed to Lesley and fulfilled my promise to my father.

After the reception, Charlie Clements and Romeo Kassarjian, my old friends from my Air Force days, came up to our room and stayed to chat for several hours. I hadn't seen or spoken to Charlie or Romeo for a long time. I had missed their company. There was much to catch up on. Lesley was upset by their visit. Looking back on it, I can see it wasn't the most appropriate way to spend our wedding night.

We spent three days in Philadelphia shopping and getting Lesley ready for her big move to Africa. Then we flew to New York to see Lesley's father, who was divorced from her mother. He had given an excellent speech at the wedding. Now he was hosting us in his home city. He put us up at the Four Seasons while we saw the sights and took in a play.

The next stop was Kenya to enjoy a brief honeymoon as Court Parfet's guests at Solio Ranch. When we landed at the ranch airstrip, we found a Land Rover awaiting our use. There were two keys inside the vehicle. One was the ignition key. The other gave us access to Solio's private game reserve. There was a note too. 'Enjoy, Claude and Court.'

At first Lesley enjoyed meeting my friends and made an effort to adapt to her new life in Kenya. She seemed content. I was determined to make the marriage work, but the cracks began to appear soon enough. The Naivasha house was finished by the summer of 1989. I was ecstatic that we had an upcountry home to retreat to on the weekends, but Lesley said she was allergic to something in the air. It was true that she coughed and sneezed a lot whenever she visited, which she did less and less frequently.

Charles' mother Rachel Szlapak came to our house for a visit two weeks before Lesley's due date. When Lesley complained to her of getting gas every hour, Rachel immediately drove her to the hospital. I was on duty that day and told Lesley I was excited to be there for our son's birth. However, the gynecologist, Dr S.R. Patel, forgot to tell me when the time came. I didn't see him until some hours later when Lesley was back in the room. Our first child was born 27 August 1989. We named him after his late grandfather but chose to spell it Nahum instead of Nochem.

Lesley was slow to regain her vigour after Nahum's birth and couldn't produce milk. She retired to bed and more or less stayed there while preparations for Nahum's *brit*, or ceremonial circumcision, moved ahead. Two hundred people, including President Moi, had been invited.

According to tradition, the *brit* (circumcision) was held on Nahum's eighth day. Dr Paul Blumenthal, the *mohel*, performed the *brit milah* as President Moi held my son as his *sandak* (godfather). It was a very emotional and proud moment for me as it would be for any Jewish father. There were speeches on the veranda, prayers and toasts in an atmosphere of joy and goodwill and hope for the future, embodied in this tiny baby. Nahum was accorded great respect by Kenyan men at the ceremony for hardly crying as the cut was made. At eight days a baby doesn't yet have a well-developed nervous system. The gauze soaked in the kosher wine that we gave him to suck helped too. Moi said to me that my son was exceptionally brave.

Nahum's birth brought with it a brief period of peace. Caring for her infant seemed to agree with Lesley. Our household staff spared her much of the routine responsibility which can wear down any new parent. I also engaged a Kenyan nanny called Mabel. I looked forward to our little family enjoying a life together.

Then in the spring of 1990 Lesley noticed a white spot on Nahum's knee. When it became more prominent, we took Nahum to his pediatrician, Dr Colin Forbes. Colin in turn sent Nahum to Dr R.I. Patel, a dermatologist. After examining the knee lesion under ultraviolet light, he diagnosed tuberous sclerosis. It was confirmed with a CT of Nahum's head. Tuberous sclerosis is a very rare and incurable genetic disease that causes benign calcified tumours in the shape of tubers to form in the brain and other organs. It can lead to a range of horrible problems from seizures to severe retardation to a form of autism. This was the beginning of what would turn out to be a complex and difficult life journey of hope and struggles for both Nahum and our family.

Were my genes responsible for Nahum's illness? Were Lesley's? I went into a state of irrational panic. This didn't make it any easier when discussing with Lesley and Colin what to do next. By this time Lesley was pregnant again. There was a very real chance the baby she was carrying might also be born with tuberous sclerosis. Suddenly the possibility of an abortion was thrown into the mix. Just when Lesley's analytical mind should have come into play and my medical acumen was needed, we were in such emotional distress we could hardly think straight.

Our next step was to take Nahum to see Dr Goméz, who had headed the pediatric neurology department at the Mayo Clinic in Minnesota for several decades. He was the world's premier expert on tuberous sclerosis. Sensing that I could use a medical ally, I contacted my pediatrician brother Allan. Ever supportive and generous with his time, he readily agreed to accompany us to the clinic. When we got there not only Nahum was extensively evaluated. Lesley and I were too. The results of all the tests brought excellent news. Nahum's tuberous sclerosis was not hereditary. The disease was caused by a single, random mutation. Neither Lesley nor I had passed along some malevolent family condition. Our second baby was safe. Moreover, Goméz informed us, if our son were to develop any of the conditions associated with tuberous sclerosis, the impact was likely to be mild. Thankfully Nahum never developed any further symptoms as the years went by.

I was elated to know Nahum was doing well. The experience might have forged a strong bond between us, but it served to push Lesley and me further apart. Instead of taking heart at Dr Goméz's findings, Lesley grew fearful and reluctant to return to Nairobi with her child and husband. God had abandoned her, she said. I in turn became impatient. When I reminded her that she had agreed to make her home in Kenya, she answered that she hadn't thought I meant we were going to live in Kenya for the rest of our lives.

Joshua, our second son, was born 17 December 1990 at Nairobi Hospital just as Nahum had been. Gene Melzer, Lesley's mother, was there to help care for him. She helped with the preparation for the *brit* too. I was very fond of her. She was a wonderful lady. In the following months we seemed to cohere as a family as Lesley became more at ease. She enjoyed chatting to our Israeli friends in Hebrew and started to pick up Swahili. My hopes for the marriage were high.

Then other problems appeared. By the time Nahum was two, he still wasn't talking. Lesley took him to see a pediatric neurologist in Philadelphia who said there was nothing to worry about. When Lesley visited my sister Rochelle in Maryland she disagreed. Rochelle taught in a Jewish day school and specialized in early education. 'This boy's having problems. He has tremendous insights into a lot of things, but he can't express them,' she told Lesley. Together they took him for an assessment at the Washington Child Development Center. On their recommendation we enrolled Nahum in the nearby Speech and Learning Center.

After a couple of months, I brought Josh over and set him up with his mother and brother in a hotel apartment near the center. I spent about a month there then flew back to Nairobi where I arranged for our Kenyan nanny Mabel to go to the U.S. to help Lesley look after the boys. In due course I bought a house for Lesley. And as time went by the boys were enrolled in good local schools. A de facto separation had been established. I was reluctant to admit it to myself, but it was a relief. Lesley had hated everything that Africa represented. Trying to please her had been an uphill battle.

I was determined to see as much of the boys as possible. We agreed that I would come to Maryland for extended stays two or three times a year. And Lesley, Nahum and Josh would spend their summers with me in Kenya, returning to Maryland and the new school year in September. Every year we went out onto Lake Naivasha in our inflatable Zodiac boat with Hadson and fished for black bass. I always kept a fish from our catch to give to the lake's fish eagles. I would toss it into the air and, sure enough, one of these magnificent raptors would swoop out of the sky and clamp the fish in its beak before it could touch the water. I did this to show the boys about sharing. One memorable afternoon two screaming fish eagles collided in midair as they fought over the same fish. It was a lesson on sharing of a different type.

Heartbeat: An American Cardiologist in Kenya

About five years into our marriage Lesley renewed her efforts to get me to relocate to the States. She accused me of abandoning her and the boys for the president of a foreign country. I certainly didn't see it that way. Kenya had been my home for twenty years. I felt there had been no subterfuge on my part. It was clear what she was committing herself to when she accepted my marriage proposal. We spent many hours with a marriage counselor either in person or on a conference call gnawing over this and other insoluble differences. None of it helped.

The inevitable came to pass in January 1998. Lesley and I agreed on a settlement in which we divided our assets and arranged for custody and visitation rights for the boys. I welcomed the peace I hoped the divorce would bring to our little family. It turned out that was not quite the end of it though. In the wake of the U.S. embassy bombing that same year Lesley took me to court in Maryland, claiming that Nairobi was an unsafe place for the boys to visit. Her suit came to trial in July 1999 before Judge Jay Miller in the Rockville municipal courthouse.

By chance Richard Leakey was in Washington on business and agreed to a request from my attorney, David Goldberg, to sit for a video deposition on my behalf. Richard said I had a sterling reputation and talked about how safe Nairobi was for children. The headmistress of the International School of Kenya testified as did Marcia Gordon, my friend who had pushed me into flying. Samson Chemai testified that Nairobi was safe for foreigners of any age. He was the Kenyan ambassador to the U.S. Throughout the whole process Channa was by my side giving me moral support.

Lesley brought family photographs to court and some colleagues she worked with at the National Security Agency. They didn't state that Nairobi was dangerous or that no one should go there. They only went so far as to say there were safer places in the world. It was a fair point.

We submitted a video of my life in Kenya. There were shots of the Nairobi Game Park, the Nairobi Hospital, flying to and from Naivasha. Lesley's lawyer tried to have the video excluded, but Judge Miller said he wanted to see it. 'I won't let it influence me,' he assured the court. 'I like looking at pictures of animals in the bush.'

When the testimony, exhibits and arguments were over, Judge Miller read out his verdict. He said he understood Lesley's apprehension '…but from what I've heard of Dr Silverstein, I'd trust him more in Kenya than I would him taking his kids around the United States. Furthermore, he appears to have people to help him take care of the children so I'm going to rule in his favor. Everyone pays their own costs.'

Afterwards we found ourselves standing next to the judge in the elevator. 'I want to thank you for your verdict,' I told him.

'I know a fair amount about Africa,' he replied. 'My wife is from Zimbabwe.'

27

THE SLIM DISEASE

Another strange virus was emerging on the world stage at about the same time as Marburg and Ebola. In 1981 I started reading in medical literature about unusual diagnoses among the gay population in the States. There were reports of men getting opportunistic infections such as a lung condition caused by PCP (pneumocystis pneumonia). Others got unusual cancers. Kaposi's sarcoma normally occurred only in the elderly as a slow-moving cancer that seldom killed anyone. Among the young and middle-aged men who were being diagnosed with it, Kaposi's was swift and aggressive. It was believed this mysterious illness was being transmitted through anal intercourse. At first I thought this was something I didn't need to worry about in my patients.

However I was wrong. In 1983 we began to hear about Ugandans developing diarrhoea and vomiting and losing tremendous amounts of weight. According to reports, they all died after a brief period. And they were heterosexual. The first case I treated in Kenya was a Ugandan journalist who died shortly after he came to see me. This terrible new affliction was becoming known as Slim Disease. Its proper name was Acquired Immune Deficiency Syndrome. The abbreviation was AIDS. It was caused by HIV, the Human Immunodeficiency Virus.

In those early days, when the AIDS epidemic had just begun to surface in the public arena, the people at risk of contracting the disease were thought to be gay men and haemophiliacs. In Africa, it was regarded as a white man's disease and nothing for Africans to worry about. In the absence of knowledge backed by reliable research, the existence of AIDS in Kenya was masked by official complacency.

The 1970s had seen an alarming rise in STIs (sexually transmitted infections) in some Western countries and also in Kenya where the fear of stigma had discouraged sex workers from seeking treatment. Dr Allan Ronald, an infectious-diseases expert at the University of Manitoba, Canada, was contacted by Professor Herbert Nsanze to ask if he could lend a hand with Kenya's STI problem. Nsanze was a seasoned microbiologist heading the University of Nairobi's Department of Medical Microbiology. He had already conducted several studies on cohorts of sex workers and knew exactly where to direct Ronald – to Majengo, a low-income neighbourhood on the outskirts of Nairobi's central business district. Ronald was joined by his departmental colleague, Dr Francis Plummer, and in due course by Dr King Holmes from the University of Washington in Seattle and Professor Peter Piot, a Belgian researcher at the Institute of Tropical Medicine in Antwerp.

There was another person who was keen to join the team. Dr Joan Kreiss was a post-doctoral student in infectious diseases at the University of Washington. Her intuition pointed her towards the women in Majengo, even though not a single case of HIV had been documented in Kenya. It was a commonly held belief that women could not get infected through sex. Kreiss's insistence that it was worth investigating finally overrode the protests of Ronald's team. She arrived in Nairobi in 1984. It was the same year that the first case of AIDS was officially confirmed at Kenyatta National Hospital.

Kreiss tested a group of sixty-four sex workers in Majengo and a smaller cohort in downtown Nairobi for HIV. It took eight months for the results to come back from the U.S., but by 1985 Kreiss had written up her findings. They appeared in February 1986 in the *New England Journal of Medicine* under the title *AIDS Virus Infection in Nairobi Prostitutes*. Two out of three women had tested positive for HIV. It was irrefutable scientific evidence that HIV could be transmitted through heterosexual encounters, and that repeated exposure through unprotected sex accelerated the rate of transmission.

In October 1985 an article in the British medical journal, *The Lancet*, featured Uganda's Slim Disease. According to the article it was strongly associated with HIV, later to be identified as the cause of AIDS. A similar syndrome also was being seen in the Democratic Republic of the Congo. It was thought to have spread from there to Uganda along the trucking routes. Now it was in Kenya too.

No one was prepared for the outcome of Joan's research. Until then, the Kenyan establishment had refuted the existence of AIDS in the country. It was a little understood disease that was extremely frightening even though no one had yet predicted what havoc it would wreak. The publication created a furore that stretched beyond the medical world. The evidence was there for all to see. Kenya had the beginnings of an epidemic. This was reported in the *New York Times*. When that particular edition landed in Nairobi, officials confiscated all the copies.

The problems did not end there. When Piot and Plummer discussed details of the study with the British newspaper, *The Guardian,* they were accused of spreading false rumours and threatened with deportation. It took action by Elizabeth Ngugi, then the chief nursing officer in the Ministry of Health, to calm things down by meeting with the same Ministry of Health official who had summoned the two researchers to his office. 'I explained that it wasn't their doing. This was science they were reporting on, a search for truth,' she said later.

After the sobering experience of the Ugandan journalist's rapid decline and death, a red light had flashed. I had taken a week's leave to digest all the available literature. I had also begun exercising great precaution in my personal life. Now the Pumwani study, as it became known, had vindicated my premonitions. We were heading into crisis, and everyone was asleep on the job.

As there was no cure or effective therapy of any kind, the only possible approach was education. I started giving lectures at Nairobi Hospital and Rotary Club and spoke at the Hindu Club, the Goan Community Centre and the social hall of my synagogue. The core message was simple. Unless you wanted to die, the days of unprotected sex with multiple partners were over. In contrast to my efforts, the government was actively suppressing information even though it was apparent an epidemic was underway. It was feared that if word got out, it would damage the tourism sector, one of Kenya's top foreign-exchange earners.

The coming plague soon touched me personally. In 1984 Enoch (not his real name), a brilliant young Ugandan doctor who was working for me, suddenly fell ill with a fever. He self-medicated with the assistance of a colleague, treating for the obvious causes such as malaria and typhoid. But Enoch's fevers persisted. He became confused and had to be admitted to a ward in the hospital. We had no diagnosis but treated him with a variety of antibiotics. After a marked initial deterioration, he suddenly picked up on his own and recovered. A month went by and Enoch returned to work. He was as conscientious, hardworking and capable as ever. He married the following year.

Meanwhile we continued searching for the cause of his illness. We sent blood samples from his hospital admission to the CDC for further analysis. At some point in 1985, months after the onset of his illness, CDC reported back that Enoch had tested positive for HIV. It wasn't long before weight loss set in. He seemed to be shrinking before our eyes while his skin tone darkened visibly. He also developed dark spots, a finding we were soon to realize was common among Africans with AIDS.

Enoch refused to give in to what was happening to him. He had periodic anaemia which we treated with transfusions and intravenous iron administered after hours in the office by his close friend and colleague. Then along came Kemron, a medication developed at KEMRI that contained alpha interferon, a protein that regulates the activity of the immune system. Heavy doses were effective in treating certain cancers. There was some very iffy evidence that Kemron worked against AIDS too. Patients were already flying to Nairobi from the U.S. asking for Kemron even though it had not been officially released. Enoch was desperate for any weapon in his losing fight with AIDS. At great personal expense he procured an early version of the drug. It proved to be useless.

By this stage Enoch's wife had developed AIDS too. Neither Enoch nor his wife survived long enough to benefit from antiretroviral therapy, which was still in the early stages of development. Enoch's wife died in 1985, Enoch a year later. I spoke at Enoch's funeral and was there for his wife's funeral too. We were all devastated. I had lost a brilliant, talented friend who had every reason to live. Seeing what was happening around me made me afraid. In retrospect I should have been terrified because it just as easily could have been me who was being interred.

It was during this time Pope John Paul II visited Kenya. To my astonishment and disgust he told us to protect ourselves by practicing abstinence. The Catholic Church forbade the use of condoms. I was outraged. I had admired the man as a person, but to me his injunction was criminal. It was unrealistic to expect young people to abstain. They had to be given all the options so that they could make informed decisions. This fundamental guideline for medical practitioners had been drummed into us as students. The Pope had let Catholics down by giving them no choice.

In 1986 Dr Larry Altman, who had been my first resident when I was an intern, called to say that he was coming to Africa to write a series about AIDS for the *New York Times*. Larry had been my resident when I was an intern at Harborview Hospital in Seattle. We had become good friends. I picked him up from the airport and on the drive back to my house urged him to be circumspect. He would be deported if it were discovered what he was doing. He conducted interviews with doctors in Kenya, Uganda and Zambia, staying with me in Nairobi between reporting excursions. He showed me his stories before sending them off and welcomed my feedback. Sometimes he called New York at 2 am and started shouting at his editor. He subsequently won a George Polk Award for his ground-breaking coverage of AIDS in Africa.

HIV incidence in Kenya shot up dramatically as I had foreseen. Moi respected the science of medicine and wanted the policies of the country to be informed by modern science and technology, but the AIDS epidemic proved to be an exception. His administration remained mute on the subject, except to deny that HIV was an issue. As there were no government surveys to measure the prevalence of HIV in the general population, this was hard to refute. I was regularly seeing patients reporting unexplained weight loss and often Kaposi's sarcoma. The diagnosis was always AIDS. We still had nothing with which to treat them. I lost many colleagues, friends and their children to the disease.

Several doctors I knew fell ill. I didn't understand this as they knew what was going on. It was frustrating. I felt sad for them and for my patients. Many were women whose husbands had been straying. They were the unintended victims as the husbands often hid their HIV-positive status. When they came to my surgery, I told them I couldn't take care of them if they didn't tell their wives. Like other viruses, it was a disease that touched everyone. I treated many politicians, doctors and senior civil servants. In those early years they all died as there was no treatment. Many patients continued to be promiscuous after their diagnosis. That made me angry. Later on, it became illegal to knowingly infect someone with HIV. Meanwhile President Moi generally avoided speaking about AIDS.

Kemron was still under development during that period. In due course Dr Davy Koech, KEMRI's director, and Dr Arthur Obel, the chief research officer, published the results of a preliminary study of ten AIDS patients in two medical journals. They claimed Kemron had cured the study subjects. I repeatedly shared with senior Kenyan government officials, including Moi, my doubts about its legitimacy. I warned them that research published in available literature and the evidence I had seen in my surgery strongly suggested that Kemron would not be effective against AIDS.

Moi nevertheless launched Kemron on 27 July 1990 at the Kenyatta International Conference Centre. It was billed as a miracle cure, a wonder drug and a victory of African science.

I attended the gathering but made myself scarce. Once it was officially sanctioned I was put in a difficult position. I was besieged with people wanting me to obtain the drug for them. I always refused to do it.

That October a long and embarrassing exposé of the Kemron fiasco appeared in the *New York Times* under Jane Perlez's byline. The drug had been vigorously promoted by Koech, who was a member of the president's inner circle, she wrote. Subsequent trials showed no evidence of the drug being effective. The World Health Organization conducted clinical trials in five African countries then summoned Koech to a meeting where he was told Kemron was an experimental drug with no proof of any benefit for treating AIDS. It was subsequently withdrawn.

By that time the medical profession had seen first-hand it was useless and were not using it anyway. Koech was a personable character with an infectious enthusiasm, and he was my friend. He no doubt believed in what he was promoting. But I never saw a publication by KEMRI of a proper clinical trial with placebo groups. His career was later marred by several scandals. The 1990s were notable for research collaboration between Kenyan and foreign epidemiologists and infectious-diseases scientists. Initially, the more seasoned foreigners took the lead, drawing on their previous AIDS investigations in North America and Europe. As the years went by, these working relationships evolved into collegiate collaboration as the Kenyans gained more and more hands-on experience. The researchers were working in an environment where contracting AIDS was regarded as a death sentence as there was no cure. Thus the emphasis was on the epidemiology and the prevention of transmission. Sex workers and long-distance truckers were among those who attracted the researchers' attention. The message was that multiple sex partners combined with STIs were the principle causes of HIV transmission and that condom use was critical to prevention.

A discernible change in public awareness was taking place too. Civil society became involved in countering the epidemic, and HIV/AIDS was being reported in the media. For the first time in Kenya's history, sex workers and gay men formed advocacy groups. In due course they assumed a leading role in trying to contain the spread of HIV while ensuring their peers enjoyed the right to quality healthcare.

By 1994 the HIV prevalence among urban adults aged between fifteen and forty-nine had peaked at thirteen percent. But political will and government commitment did not take root until the turn of the millennium. In 1999 the National AIDS Control Council was formed. That same year President Moi declared war on HIV/AIDS, more than a decade into the full national epidemic.

When ARVs (antiretroviral drugs) were released into the market in the late 1990s, it triggered a sea change in how the AIDS pandemic was regarded. While at first costly and inaccessible to the great majority of women and men, ARVs started the disease's transition from fatal to manageable. President George W. Bush's initiative of PEPFAR (The President's Emergency Plan for AIDS Relief) in 2004 was the tipping point, bringing affordable antiretroviral therapy to women and men in countries around the world. The AIDS scourge at last was being addressed intelligently across the continent with the resources and expertise to make a dent in Africa's ongoing disaster. By the end of that year HIV prevalence in the general adult population had dropped to six percent.

The lesson we learned from the AIDS pandemic is the moment we know the mode of viral transmission, we have to inform everybody so that the epidemic is stopped in its tracks. Transparency is vital as life and safety are far more important than tourism, GDP growth and the fear of social stigma. We also learned that the rapid approval of drugs is essential. Once proven to be effective they must be made available to everyone.

Vaccines must be made available worldwide, even to those in the Third World who cannot afford to buy them. Unfortunately, the richer nations were slow in taking this message on board when the COVID-19 pandemic engulfed the world. The Pfizer vaccine became available in the United States in December 2020 by way of a federal mechanism that allowed its emergency use before full FDA (Food and Drug Administration) approval. The Astra Zeneca vaccine was authorized for use by the European Union the following month. Yet Kenya did not receive vaccines (Astra Zeneca) until March 2021, more than a year after approval for use. The first batch was 1.02 million doses. That was precious little for a country of 55 million people. The first Pfizer vaccines arrived in Kenya two years after Pfizer had received an emergency approval for use.

28

DIPLOMATIC DILEMMAS

By 1991 a series of foreign events and domestic circumstances were converging to create a seismic social change. Soviet influence had faded away after the fall of the Berlin Wall. The West, led by the U.S., was at last in a position to call the shots when it came to geopolitics. Both Americans and Europeans saw the time was ripe to sweep Communism aside and push for democracy. Western donors and the World Bank had suspended aid in the hopes of forcing reform. Meanwhile at home a major drought had caused food shortages and triggered inflation. Foreign debt was ballooning too. The economy was in crisis.

Kenyans were experiencing straitened times. They had long chafed under the restrictions of KANU's rule. Now some were openly questioning the competence of Moi's administration. The president was feeling the squeeze from above and below. He was a pragmatic leader and reluctantly had agreed to abolish the one-party state in favour of multiparty elections. This concession came with a caveat. Moi predicted that tumult and bloodshed would ensue. On numerous occasions he told me, 'David, I fear for my people. It will take a very strong leader to hold the country together and prevent civil war.'

With his customary prescience Moi had already begun loosening the Kikuyu grip on power. Mwai Kibaki was a leading Kikuyu politician who had been vice president until Moi demoted him to head the Ministry of Health in 1988. In December 1991 Kibaki was removed from that position too, even though he had stated that trying to dislodge KANU was like trying to cut down an old oak tree with a razor blade. Kibaki was wrong. That same month Moi managed to push through an amendment to the constitution against strong opposition from KANU stalwarts. It allowed parties other than KANU to compete in elections, effectively introducing multiparty politics. It also limited presidents to serving a maximum of two five-year terms. After twenty-six years of single-party rule, Kenyans were about to have a choice of a range of politicians representing a variety of platforms. And their vote would be cast by secret ballot. Presidential and general elections were scheduled for a year later – December 1992.

Inevitably, violence erupted. In March some sixty Kenyans died as a result of violence on the western escarpment of the Rift Valley. I was with President Moi in Austria when he received the urgent call that informed him about the disaster. He was enraged. Rarely have I seen him so angry and upset. We returned to explosive tensions and incendiary oratory, much of it directed at him.

The Catholic Church blamed the killings on the government, saying it was part of a strategy to discredit political reform. Kalenjins were accused of terrorizing Kikuyus near the town of Molo, a traditional Kikuyu stronghold situated not far from the fault line separating Kikuyu and Kalenjin farming communities. The Kikuyu politician Njenga Mungai warned, 'You have taken on the wrong tribe. The Kikuyus will never sit down and watch their children and wives being massacred for no apparent reason.' He was later arrested for this statement.

Heartbeat: An American Cardiologist in Kenya

The brewing tensions could have been managed soberly if Smith Hempstone, the U.S. ambassador, had not inserted himself into the mix. When I first met him shortly after his arrival, he struck me as the antithesis of a good diplomat. The government protocol at that time was for the diplomatic community to greet the president at Jomo Kenyatta International Airport on his return from foreign trips. Either Hempstone had not been briefed or he didn't care about the rules of conduct because his first appearance was not for Moi's return from a foreign trip but on his departure. Perhaps there was a message there.

Already aboard the aircraft, I glanced out to see Hempstone advancing toward us on foot accompanied by a police officer. As he was my ambassador, I walked down the external staircase to greet him and politely set him straight on protocol. Just then Moi disembarked and approached us. I introduced the two men. Moi liked the West, particularly Britain and the States. He loved Margaret Thatcher and George H.W. Bush and was to get on well with George W. Bush too. When Bill Clinton took office in January 1992, it was the start of a solid friendship. Moi admired Clinton and couldn't understand when later he was impeached by the House of Representatives simply for having an affair.

Moi and Hempstone greeted one another with some warmth. I took it as a positive sign that recent strains in U.S.-Kenya relations were about to ease. Hempstone's predecessor, Elinor Constable, had inadvertently ruffled feathers through no fault of her own. The problem had been the male chauvinism that is embedded in African culture. For the Americans to send a woman as their highest-level representative was seen as a deliberate snub. I have no idea whether the Reagan administration had realized beforehand that Constable's gender would be perceived as demeaning to Kenya, but it was unlikely their intentions were anything but honest.

In his previous career Hempstone had been a foreign correspondent for the *Chicago Daily News* covering Africa and then Latin America and Europe for the *Washington Star*. In the 1980s he was appointed as executive editor of the *Washington Times* and latterly as its editor. He had a good grounding in politics and world affairs but no experience as a diplomat. Nor was his confrontational and outspoken style in any way conventionally diplomatic. Hempstone was a great admirer of Ernest Hemingway, who had spent time as a hunter in Kenya decades earlier and to whom he bore a distinct physical resemblance. Rarely did you see him without a glass of whiskey in one hand and a cigarette in the other. His garrulous nature and sharp wit would have taken him far in Nairobi government circles had it not been for his utter lack of tact.

He was also an unabashed enemy of President Moi. He devoted most of his time and effort to attacking Moi's policies while advocating to end the one-party state. He lambasted Moi in the public arena instead of broaching tricky issues on a one-to-one basis with Moi behind the closed doors of State House. It got so bad that Wilson Ndolo Aya, the Kenyan foreign minister, accused the ambassador of racism, saying he had the perspective of 'a slave owner'.

Hempstone's bull-in-a-china-shop approach earned him the enmity of his fellow American, Court Parfet. Court was a member of the Eagle Forum, an influential right-wing political interest group in the U.S. All previous ambassadors had rightly considered him a useful informed source on African business matters and had profited from his long experience in Kenya. That was until Hempstone came along. Parfet was on cordial first-name terms with many of the country's influential elite. He was a close friend of both Moi and Charles Njonjo. Njonjo and his wife Margaret were frequent visitors at his Solio Ranch. He had no affiliation with any particular ethnic group, which should be the default position of all expatriates who make Kenya their home. When Hempstone began harassing Moi, Parfet was so incensed he wrote to his contacts in the U.S. State Department complaining about his behaviour and adding the barb that Hempstone was a drunk. The letter got him dropped from the embassy guest list. I managed to have him reinstated after Hempstone's departure.

Moi was still very pro-American and eager as ever to cooperate when asked. Hempstone's thoughts on strengthening democracy obviously were vetted and approved by the State Department. Moi was certainly astute enough to take heed and appear amenable. As the ambassador repeatedly reminded him, the U.S. devoted a fair share of its annual economic support in sub-Saharan Africa to Kenya. The U.S. had a vested interest in Kenya. It had long been regarded as an island of stability in a politically volatile region. Moi was not deaf to this kind of talk. I believe Moi would have engaged with Hempstone and accommodated the Americans as best he could. But the authoritarian in him bristled as Hempstone openly aligned himself with political dissidents, spoke at their gatherings and publicly denounced Moi as a dictator. Moi hit back. Hempstone found himself caricatured as a bigot on the front page of the KANU newspaper. An article in the *Kenya Times* was headlined, 'Shut Up, Mr. Ambassador'.

I was invited to an embassy cocktail party in honour of Herman Cohen, a distinguished American diplomat who was deeply knowledgeable about Africa. At the time he was the Assistant Secretary of State for African Affairs. I wanted to discuss with Cohen the alarming rise of violence in Kenya, which was particularly bad in Nairobi. Automatic weapons proliferated thanks to civil wars and uprisings on Kenya's borders. They were available on the street for a comparative pittance. Criminals were growing increasingly bold and dangerous, and I was troubled by it. There was no particular class or ethnic component to the violence. The bad guys were after anybody or any place with money. They robbed houses, hijacked cars, stole from banks. The murder rate soared.

What had begun as a crime problem quickly metastasized into an economic issue. Merchants, many of them wealthy Indians, were leaving the country. Non-profit organizations and United Nations offices were said to be rethinking their presence in the economic capital of East Africa, now derisively known as Nairobbery. Corporate regional headquarters were relocating. Other multinationals that had shown an interest in coming to Nairobi changed their minds. Tourism was a vital foreign-exchange earner, and it was faltering. I told Smith Hempstone I'd like to discuss these issues with the guest of honour and to make some suggestions. Though clearly sceptical, the ambassador brought me together with Cohen before the party started.

Cohen was polite and listened carefully as I explained how I thought American forensic technology and other crime-fighting expertise might be brought to bear to retain an international presence in Kenya. I steered clear of the multiparty election discussion. I thought multipartyism was a good idea, a necessary step in the transition to true democracy. But that wasn't the time to hold forth with political opinions. I heard nothing more from Cohen, but I did receive a message from Hempstone. The U.S. government was not interested in assisting Kenya in the way I proposed for fear it would look as if it was propping up a dictatorship and promoting a police state.

In December 1992 Moi ran for re-election in the first multiparty elections in twenty-six years. He was vying against seven other contenders including his former vice president Mwai Kibaki, Kenneth Matiba and Raila Odinga's father, Oginga Odinga. Moi won by a comfortable margin. KANU retained 100 seats in Parliament and lost eighty-eight to six opposition parties. The elections were marred by widescale intimidation of opponents and allegations of rigging the returns.

George H. W. Bush's loss to Bill Clinton in the 1992 U.S. presidential election ushered in a changing of the guard. Hempstone departed Kenya in February 1993 disillusioned by the opposition's inability to unite behind one candidate. Clinton appointed Aurelia Brazeal as his successor, ignoring the chauvinist sensibilities of Kenyan men that had proved so trying to Elinor Constable. She was a career diplomat and Harvard alumna who had been in the State Department since 1968. Brazeal was versed in the art of gentle persuasion and went on to pursue a far less combative and, in my view, far more productive course during her three-year tenure in Nairobi. She later acknowledged that dialogue with the government had 'atrophied' during her predecessor's time.

Brazeal proceeded judiciously, exchanging views with the president and his senior counsellors while also keeping channels open to the opposition. She listened to everyone and established multiple contacts in the countryside as well as the capital. The streams of refugees pouring into Kenya from Somalia and South Sudan were a front-burner problem throughout her term, as was the genocide in Rwanda. Things were heating up locally too. Kenya's sporadic bursts of political violence along ethnic lines were a prelude to the fighting that erupted in the run-up to the 1997 elections. Reflecting on her Kenya posting she later said, 'Perhaps because of the emphasis I gave these issues, we were able to do a lot of things that pushed Kenya toward further development, both politically and economically, and we rebalanced our relationship so we could talk with both parties, opposition and government.'

Aurelia became a good friend to me as did her equally charming mother. I was often invited to embassy parties as well as to more informal gatherings at her residence. In turn I invited her for the weekend to my farm on Lake Naivasha where I was also entertaining friends from the States. It turned out to be an unforgettable occasion.

Aurelia took the road that followed the lake's southern shore as I had instructed her. She was running about three hours late and so stopped at the Kongoni police station to call me. I had dispatched the farm manager Hadson to meet her there and show her the way to my house. After waiting for several hours, he had given up and returned to the farm. Shortly before Aurelia's arrival at the police station, coincidentally an entourage of Kikuyu politicians led by Ngengi Muigai, Jomo Kenyatta's nephew, marched into the station. They announced that they were there to distribute food at the village of Maela to the Kikuyus who had been thrown off the land they had settled in Enosopukia. This forced eviction was led by the Maasai, who looked on the area as vital dry-season grazing, assisted by the resident Okiek hunters. It seemed the eviction of the Kikuyu was also backed by local KANU leadership, to ensure their election victory in the region. The turnoff to Maela, about 100 yards beyond the Kongoni police station, had been the scene of recent fighting between Kikuyu and Maasai youths and men. Both groups considered Maela their territory. Reporters had been alerted that a demonstration was planned and were on hand as the police informed the politicians they would not be permitted to go forward. The scene was rapidly becoming a potential political firestorm.

Aurelia wanted nothing to do with it, but the Kikuyu politicians seized on the opportunity to make capital out of her accidental presence. In front of the reporters they thanked her for her support. Meanwhile Aurelia discovered she had misplaced my number. The officer in charge, unnerved by the influx of people and the sudden arrival of an important diplomat, asked Aurelia to return to her car while he phoned State House for instructions. He was put through to the chief of the presidential escort. 'Let her through. Daktari is one of us.' The policeman found my number and called me. I sent Hadson back to lead her home. Her stay at the Kongoni police station had lasted about two hours.

I poured the ambassador a much-appreciated cup of tea when she arrived and introduced her to my other guests, Charlie and Ruth Cronheim. Then I took them down the hill to the farm to show them the dairy cows and crops and to watch the hippos from the lake shore.

Just before dusk, as we walked back to the house, I saw what I at first took to be three dust devils in the distance, not an unusual occurrence around Naivasha during the dry season. These dust devils, however, were odd in that they appeared to be moving in formation toward us. Soon enough we realized they were in fact black government Mercedes. The cars drew to a halt beside us. All the doors were thrown open almost simultaneously and out jumped a posse of plainclothes policemen. They greeted us with broad smiles. '*Jambo Daktari*. His Excellency sent us to make sure that you are all safe.'

Apparently the presidential security team had received conflicting descriptions of the incident outside the police station and wanted to sort out the matter. I thanked them for their concern and asked them to relay my warmest greetings to the president. We then returned to the house for a drink and dinner and were all in bed by nine.

The next morning we arose in the dark and climbed the hill behind my house to watch the sun rise over Mt Longonot, one of the Rift Valley's several dormant volcanoes. It was a stunning moment which we enjoyed with our coffee and scones. After that we went on an early morning game drive in the neighbouring Crater Lake wildlife sanctuary and were treated to herds of buffalo and impala, warthog, giraffe and eland.

On the way back to the house we passed a hippo out grazing. Hippos kill more people in Africa than any other wild animal. The reason? A hippo on land hates anyone or anything getting between it and its retreat to the safe haven of water. When this one saw us approaching, she panicked and charged the Land Rover. 'Reverse! Reverse!' Charlie yelled. I switched gears and hit the accelerator. As I did so the hippo veered away and ran into the lake.

Aurelia seemed to be enjoying herself despite the hiccups, but I could tell something was distracting her. By the time we returned to the house, she was looking quite concerned. She confided that with all the confusion over the previous day's events, President Moi might possibly misconstrue what had happened at the police station. To allay her anxieties, I called the president and explained the happenings of the previous day. He was neither confused nor upset and asked to speak to the ambassador. He wished her a wonderful evening and encouraged her to enjoy the beauty of Lake Naivasha.

All seemed well until the next morning when Aurelia received a phone call from her deputy, who read to her the inflammatory frontpage headlines in both the *Nation* and *Standard*. 'U.S. ambassador detained!' Aurelia at once called for her driver and rushed back to Nairobi. Back in Washington the wheels were already in motion. Aurelia was unable to stop the Assistant U.S. Secretary of State for Africa, Prudence Bushnell, from initiating an official complaint to the Ministry of Foreign Affairs. However once everyone got their facts sorted, cordial U.S.-Kenyan relations were restored. The weekend's missteps and misunderstandings were no more than a storm in a teacup. And this, you must agree, is preferable to having a bull in a china shop.

In December 2002 the third round of multiparty elections were held. For the first time in twenty-four years they did not include Daniel arap Moi as a candidate as he had already served two five-year terms. This restriction was a constitutional change that had been made prior to the 1992 elections to ease the path for multiparty elections.

Moi had been impressed by Jimmy Carter's gracious transition from politician to elder statesman and wanted to emulate the U.S. president. He was looking forward to retirement and to starting a charitable foundation. He had chosen Uhuru Kenyatta, the founding president's forty-year-old son and heir apparent, as his successor to lead KANU to victory. Uhuru ran against the politically seasoned Mwai Kibaki, who by then was seventy-one. Kibaki was at the helm of a group of opposition parties that had coalesced to unseat KANU. It was known as NARC (the National Rainbow Coalition).

On 3 December 2002, Kibaki was seriously injured in a traffic accident while on his way back to Nairobi from a campaign meeting at Machakos. He was hospitalized in Nairobi and then flown to London to be treated for multiple fractures. While he was recovering his NARC colleagues Raila Odinga and Kijana

Wamalwa (who was later appointed vice president) campaigned tirelessly on his behalf stating, 'The captain has been injured in the field...but the rest of the team shall continue.'

Everyone at State House was anticipating Kenyatta's imminent defeat. I was there with Moi when the early returns indicated a blowout was heading his way. Kibaki trounced Kenyatta, receiving twice as many votes. It was a disastrous election for KANU at nearly all levels. KANU had been the ruling party since Kenya's independence. It was an ignominious end after four decades of totalitarian government.

The president took it well. Word soon came from Kibaki's camp that he would like to take over power almost immediately. Moi graciously replied he had no problem with the request. On 29 December, two days after the results had been announced, thousands gathered in Uhuru Gardens for the inauguration. Kibaki was pushed onto the podium in a wheelchair, his neck in a brace and his right leg sticking out straight in front of him. The crowd cheered loudly as he was sworn in as Kenya's third president. When Moi stood up to speak they jeered. Even Kibaki had nothing positive to say about his old ally. Nor did he show any appreciation for the smooth handover. Moi, by contrast, maintained his dignity throughout the ceremony then left immediately for his farm upcountry. On a continent where long-established leaders rarely stepped away from power without a fight, Moi's statesmanlike exit was impressive.

I phoned him the next evening. He didn't seem upset, although as a politician he was experienced in masking emotion. He simply said, 'I went to the inauguration to hand over power and I did that.' He was proud of the fact that the transition had been smooth.

It did not go unnoticed by other African politicians that here was a lesson to emulate. Zambia's former president Kenneth

Kaunda praised Moi for abiding by the election results and stepping down without demur. Kaunda had set the tone in 1991 when he was voted out in his country's first multiparty elections. He had been the head of state for twenty-seven years since independence.

Like all leaders, Moi's tenure was marked by both success and failure. Unlike Somalia, Sudan, Ethiopia and Uganda, Kenya hadn't suffered civil war or rebellion. But Kenya had become a land of polarized people with most getting by on less than a dollar a day while an elite clique of politicians and businessmen enjoyed huge, frequently ill-gotten, wealth.

'If we got this wrong, there would have been civil strife. This country would have gone down the drain,' observed John Githongo, the anti-corruption activist, of the remarkably orderly transfer of power.

There was another transition. In 2002 my long-term partner, Majid Warshow, informed me he had accepted a job offer from the Aga Khan Hospital on the other side of town. We took six months unwinding our practice. I then spent eight months as a solo practitioner while considering new partners. With Channa's help, I used this time to remodel the shabby office and hang the work of local artists on the walls. The patients loved the new look. I also needed to find a new echo cardiology technician. When Majid left for the Aga Khan he had taken our echo technician with him.

Choosing a new partner turned out to be easy. My favourite and best-qualified candidate was Dr Charles Kariuki. A colleague twenty years my junior, he had studied medicine at the University of Nairobi. He went on to do five-and-a-half years of cardiology training at the Royal Papworth Hospital in Cambridge and the London Chest Hospital, which at the time was one of the leading British hospitals for cardiac disease. He then qualified as an interventional cardiologist. It was an important subspecialty that had not existed when I arrived in Kenya and one that complemented my practice. Unlike the many Kenyans who became part of the brain drain and never returned, Charles had always planned to come back home. We've practiced together now for twenty years.

29

TWO MORE SONS

A year or so after setting up private practice I met Jackie Obare. She was the secretary to Imre Loeffler, the surgeon who had operated on Shem Musoke and Patrick Shaw. We bumped into each other often in the corridors or when I dropped by to talk to Imre. She had an exotic beauty and an intense gaze that I found appealing. Sometimes I invited her to join me for a meal. Then I took her on safari a few times and liked that she went out of her way to make sure I was comfortable and happy. Thus began an on-off relationship that endured for several years until I met Channa.

In March 1994 Jackie told me she was pregnant and intended to keep the baby. I was stunned. As always seemed to happen to me when confronted with important personal issues, I vacillated. I was instantly overwhelmed with guilt and self-reproach. Dad had taught me to honour certain moral absolutes. It was inexcusable. I had done wrong and cringed to think how appalled my parents, especially my father, would have been by this behaviour.

Sally Kosgei, the permanent secretary for foreign affairs and my travel companion on presidential trips, counselled me against this destructive thought process. She told me almost all the married men we knew in common had second or even third families. Kenyans didn't frown on having children outside marriage, she said reassuringly. Sally was only upset that she did not know about Aaron so that she could meet and play with him.

I took Sally's advice and after Aaron was born I bought Jackie a maisonette, which she rented out. She was a loving mother, patient and constantly attentive to Aaron. Jackie was calm and managing very well. I was a mess. A white spot appeared on Aaron's face. It was similar to the spots that had appeared on Nahum's face shortly after his birth. I instantly worried I had passed on a genetic flaw. Colin Forbes ordered a CT scan, and nothing wrong was found. Nevertheless I continued to feel unmoored.

When Aaron was about two, I began taking him on weekly Sunday trips to the Nairobi National Park in my old Land Rover Defender. The two of us would walk around the animal orphanage and I'd point out the animals in their pens and name them for him. One Sunday a kite swooped down and grabbed Aaron's sandwich out of his hands with its hooked beak. The incident so frightened him it took a while to calm him down and stop his tears. As I held him in my arms and comforted him, I felt a strong, protective love surge through me. I wondered how and when I would bring myself to express that love openly.

Jackie bore Jeremy, her second son, my fourth, in June 1997. I was surprised once again. She had told me earlier she was on birth control. Once more I was gripped by guilt and despair. I needed to talk to someone whose judgment I trusted. When I was in the States, I took Nahum and Joshua to visit Rochelle and Sol. While I was there, I told my sister the whole story. She was impatient with me. 'So what's the problem? We're going to love these children and treat them the same way as the other two boys.' Ever since that conversation she has enjoyed a special connection with Aaron and Jeremy.

I spoke to President Moi too. He listened quietly then asked, 'Do you love them and will you raise them and educate them according to your beliefs?' When I answered yes, Moi assured me that he'd do everything to support me as I struggled to resolve my identity crisis.

I also discussed the matter with Jackie's father. Her family were Luos from western Kenya. He had studied for the Catholic priesthood. I explained to him that I wasn't going to marry his daughter, but I wasn't going to abandon her either. That seemed to satisfy him. 'Are you going to raise these children as Jews?' he asked. I said that was my intent and Jackie had agreed with me. Her father nodded and smiled. The explanation satisfied him.

I emerged from these conversations with real hope that I might yet become what I had always aspired to be, a Jewish *paterfamilias* living in harmony with my four sons. At the time I had no idea how this could happen, but that's because I had not yet met Channa.

30

DEATH ON THE FARM

Among every tribe in Kenya there are tales of a time long ago when humans and animals talked to one another and more recent tales of hunting lion, buffalo and leopard or being hunted by them. I have collected some of my own tales from my time at the farm in Naivasha.

On a Thursday night in early 1994, I had just returned to Nairobi from visiting my two sons Nahum and Josh in the U.S. when I got a call from Hadson. Something terrible had happened. A rogue hippo had killed Roba Duba, an *askari* (watchman) who worked on the farm. He was a Boran from the wild and arid plains of northern Kenya near the Ethiopian border. Like many Boran he had drifted down to Naivasha in search of work. He and his wife and three daughters lived in a traditional one-room mud-and-thatch hut at the bottom of the property. He was one of a team of askaris who guarded the farm against opportunistic thieves, fish and game poachers and – although rarely – cattle rustlers.

On this night Roba and another askari would have been armed with a *panga* (machete) and a *rungu* (fighting club) and perhaps a spear as they went out on patrol with their dogs. In Kenya owning firearms is prohibited without a license, and a gun license is extremely difficult to get. There was another more frequent raider that the askaris continually watched out for – hippos. They emerged from the shallows of the lake every night to graze and, when they could, to raid the crops. Roba knew that in his situation hippos were more dangerous than humans. They were aggressive and charged without warning. The animals weighed three tons or more and could be bad-tempered without provocation. They kill about 3000 people a year in Africa. When the dogs started barking furiously, Roba and his partner went over to investigate pointing their flashlights in the direction of the noise. It was a hippo. The askaris ran as the hippo charged, but Roba tripped and fell. Within seconds the hippo was trampling him. He died instantly.

The day after Roba Duba's death I flew to the farm in a small plane I'd rented. Jackie drove up and joined me. She had come back into my life as Lesley was making her long, angry exit. Two game wardens from the Kenya Wildlife Service, Dware Mwai and Ole, joined us too. And so began our hunt for the hippo on a noticeably cool Friday night. The KWS men were in the lead vehicle and carried G3 rifles, but unfortunately they didn't have a spotlight or even a torch with charged batteries. A young cattle herder in my employ named Mohammad rode with them to identify the hippo. We followed closely behind in my Land Rover Defender, which had stronger headlights. It also was fitted with a powerful searchlight.

We searched until about 11 pm with no luck. The hunt resumed on Saturday night. At last they sighted the animal in thickish bush. The two wardens got out of their vehicle and tracked him on foot up a steep hill. A short while later I heard six sharp rifle reports, perhaps 100 yards away, then the sound of something big and heavy crashing down the hillside. The huge hippo bounced into view, its little tail wiggling, all four legs stiff and extended. It landed on its back, illuminated by a full moon, with its legs pointing to an inky sky like a dead bug in an insecticide ad. Its tail was now still. Steam curled up from its bloody snout and gunshot wounds. We were standing about 200 yards from where he'd killed Roba Duba.

The following morning at daybreak I was standing with Dware Mwai and Ole by the carcass when Roba Duba's widow approached me. She was very thin, about forty at a guess, and shrouded in a robe of mourning. She looked down at the animal and there was neither anger nor grief in her voice when she said softly, 'This hippo won't be making widows of any more Boran women.' Then she turned to me and asked, with a touch of nervousness, if she could have shillings 3000 (about $40) to buy, as was the custom, a goat to commemorate her husband on the fortieth day of mourning. Word had spread through the bush telegraph and other Boran women arrived in twos and threes to inspect the dead hippo. They did not ask for any of the meat, as other tribes would do, because hippos were considered to be a form of pork and the Boran are Muslim.

As they departed, Turkanas, Kikuyus and Luos appeared with gunny sacks to claim a share of the bounty. The KWS rangers explained the rules. The right hind leg and tongue, they said, were reserved for the KWS tracker dogs in Naivasha. A hippo's hide has great tensile strength and is ideal for making whips. In fact, the Swahili word for hippo and whip is the same - *kiboko*. But because making whips from hippo hide is prohibited, they said they would take the skin away and bury it. The hippo's teeth were removed to be taken to their superiors as proof that it was dead. Some of the teeth and the tusks as well as its massive skull eventually came to me. The tusks from the lower jaw were half a meter long. I put the skull in the garden on a large flat stone where it has rested ever since. I was offered the animal's heart too - a nod to my professional specialty. I declined, thinking it would be put to better use as a meal for a local family. Besides, it wasn't kosher. The rest of the meat was hacked off the skeleton and distributed to a never-ending line of people who stood patiently waiting all day. The excitement at the prospect of a few kilos of free meat was palpable. It felt like a carnival parade. They were laughing and joking as they strode home with their great chunks of hippo meat for that night's supper, as well as for salting and smoking.

I gave Roba Duba's widow six months of his salary and contacted my insurance company on their behalf. I soon received a polite letter in reply explaining that the company had been through all the fine print on hippo attacks and found that only hospitalization and funeral expenses were covered. I initiated a dialogue, wanting to do as well as possible for the family. They finally received a settlement equivalent to about $1000.

The hippo lived on - sort of. As my boys started school each year they took one of its tusks to class for show-and-tell day. Needless to say, the other kids were hard put to match up to the Silverstein brothers when it came to showing off unusual things.

Another animal that lives in confrontational coexistence with humans is the baboon. They are unafraid, vicious and cunning. You don't mess with them, particularly the alpha males with their powerful jaws and sharp canine teeth. Male baboons have been known to run off with lambs and baby goats and have even – on rare occasions – grabbed babies. Some years ago a particularly bold male baboon began raiding the garbage cans on the farm, easily evading all defensive measures we put in place. Soon he was leading other members of the troop to join him there at mealtime. He next expanded his range to the kitchen. He once helped himself to a bowl of fresh fruit, tossing aside orange rinds and apple cores as he ate. Susan, our cook, had to clear up the mess. Another day she walked into the living room to find him curiously poking at the television as if he were trying to switch it on.

The brash intruder's luck ran out, however, when he began to bother a man we knew as Yossi, a senior figure in the Mossad who had retired to a house further round the lake. I never learned what the baboon did to merit a death warrant, but Yossi clearly didn't take his antics lightly. He rang another of our neighbours, Tony Seth-Smith. Tony was a Kenyan-born professional hunter of renown and an honorary game warden. As such he had the authority to dispatch animals that were considered to be a danger to people. He was noted for his unerring marksmanship.

Yossi invited Tony for lunch, mentioned his problem and suggested he bring his shotgun with him. While they were eating, the cook spotted the baboon at the back door. Tony produced a single shell from his shirt pocket and shoved it into the chamber. Then he stepped into the kitchen, took aim at the swiftly retreating baboon and calmly carried out the execution.

'Why did you bring only one round?' Yossi asked.

'Because there was only one baboon,' he replied.

Stephanie Simborg was a twenty-five-year-old student from Marin, California who came to Kenya in search of outdoor adventure before entering Harvard Business School in September 1995. She was part of a hiking safari organized by the Wyoming-based National Outdoor Leadership School. The group was camping in pup tents at the base of Mt Longonot, the ancient volcano we could see from the farm. The area was scenic and full of wildlife. It was just before dawn and Stephanie was fast asleep when she woke with a start. Something was biting her elbow. As she later recalled, the animal had humanlike hands that were gripping her arm hard as it bit her. She thought it was a monkey or a baboon. She screamed and tried to pull her arm away, but the animal wouldn't let go. It dragged her out of the tent and lunged at her face. Everything happened in a few seconds. It was then she realized it was a hyena. She could hear its jaws clamping down on her. It felt as if her whole face had come apart. The Maasai askari, Oloimooga ole Rerente, heard the commotion and ran to the tent. He stabbed the hyena twice with his spear. It turned on him and knocked him to the ground then loped off into the darkness.

Stephanie required immediate evacuation. She had several deep bite wounds, and the hyena's uncharacteristic attack raised the strong possibility that it was rabid. She was put on a makeshift stretcher of bamboo poles and sleeping bags and driven across the plains to a dirt airstrip and flown out by the Flying Doctors in a helicopter. Twelve hours later at the Nairobi Hospital she was taken straight to the operating theatre. Dr Adriano Landra, a gifted Italian reconstructive surgeon and long-time resident of Kenya, led the delicate work on her injuries. I got her started immediately on rabies immunization injections as well as antibiotics for her bites. Luckily, she developed no disease or infection. Two days later her father, Walter Simborg, arrived. He too was a doctor and had been worried about the treatment his daughter would get in an African hospital. When he saw the beautiful job Adriano had done, he was thrilled.

In the meantime, word had spread through our community that a young Jewish woman from California was recuperating in the hospital from a hyena attack. A number of our synagogue members said prayers for her recovery and became a steady stream of visitors bringing her tasty dishes, fragrant soap, a hairbrush, flowers. 'It was like I had ten Jewish moms for the week. I was so touched by them,' Stephanie recounted later.

Back in the U.S. Stephanie had further surgery to reduce the scarring. She was determined not to let the experience get her down. 'Everyone I know has had a trauma, a major accident, or suffered a loss. If this is mine, I'll take it.' And she did. Her brush with death and the outpouring of love and concern from Nairobi's Jewish community opened Stephanie to a deeper grasp of her faith. Previously nonobservant, she began studying when she got home in preparation for a belated bat mitzvah, which she celebrated together with her mother. A hyena had kindled her Judaism.

Living among wild animals entails a measure of risk. The trick is not to invite trouble. It was a lesson a Maasai cattle herder named Zakaya paid a painful price for failing to heed. One afternoon several years ago, as our cows were wading around in the Lake Naivasha shallows having a drink, Hadson and Wakesa, another of my employees, heard what sounded like strange human grunts. Wakesa went to investigate and found Zakaya stretched out on the ground gasping and unconscious. He appeared to have been taken by surprise by a Cape buffalo which had inflicted serious injuries. He had a puncture wound in his chest, an ugly gash in his arm and one of his legs was broken. One lung was perforated, and multiple ribs were fractured.

Zakaya was known from time to time to drink on the job. Hadson and Wakesa surmised that he had been tippling once more, making him an easy target for the buffalo. Once again with the help of Tony Seth-Smith, Hadson bandaged Zakaya and loaded him into our old pickup for the long and painful trip to the closest medical centre, Naivasha District Hospital. Hadson thought Zakaya would not survive it. That night I called the hospital to ask for news of Zakaya's condition. The hospital physician called me back to report that the herder had a few broken ribs and some soft-tissue wounds that he would clean up in the morning.

This wasn't good enough for Channa. She was concerned and decided to go see what was happening first thing in the morning. She found Zakaya in one of the wards with about twenty other patients of all ages. He was lying on a bare mattress and was still in his dirty clothes. The ragged bandages that Tony and Hadson had applied had not been changed. He was pale and breathing rapidly. His chest wound was bubbling serous fluid in and out of what was left of his chest bandage. His daughter was at his bedside trying to feed him.

There was one nurse on the ward. She said that Zakaya was receiving an intravenous antibiotic called gentamycin. When Channa checked the dosage, it was grossly inadequate for an adult. His chest X-ray was of extremely poor quality. He obviously had a hemopneumothorax. His lung had collapsed due to the pressure of blood and air between the lung sac and the chest wall. This happens when the rib breaks and cuts blood vessels and lung tissue. It is dangerous because it can put pressure on the heart, compressing it so it cannot adequately fill and pump oxygenated blood throughout the body. Channa also worried about a possible hemopericardium. If that was the case the blood was seeping between the sac around the heart and the heart muscle itself constricting the heart from adequately pumping blood.

Channa found the doctor on call in the maternity ward. The doctor told Channa that she had scheduled time that afternoon in the operating theatre to debride (clean) and close Zakaya's wounds. Channa was horrified. The procedure could have killed him. The hospital staff clearly did not recognize the severity of Zakaya's injuries, which required chest tube insertion, oxygen, more X-rays and surgery, not to mention different types and doses of antibiotics. Channa had to rescue him. And quickly.

She paid his bill. Then with Hadson and Wakesa's help, she made the one-hour drive by car to Kijabe Mission Hospital where Zakaya could receive a higher level of care. Doctors at the mission hospital properly assessed his injuries, took him into the operating theatre where chest tubes were placed in both lungs, set his fractured leg, and admitted him to the ICU for two weeks. One month later he was released. Some weeks after that he returned to work. He had one complaint. He had a pressure sore, an ulcerative lesion, on one heel. It was probably the consequence of lying in bed for so long with his ankles crossed. I am pleased to report that since Zakaya's accident the Naivasha District Hospital has improved immensely. It is now sought out as a hospital for interns. It has an excellent training program.

In all, it was a harrowing episode for Zakaya. It should have taught him to cut down on his drinking. Alas a year later as we were driving past a cow pasture, we saw someone lying supine and motionless in the bushes. It was Zakaya. He was very drunk. We fired him.

Zakaya is not alone with his drinking problem. Alcoholism in Kenya and other African countries breaks up marriages, slashes productivity and leaves children without functioning parents. I am hoping that the new generation of Kenyans who are under forty, wired, connected and concerned for their physical and mental wellbeing, will take on the problem and solve this still much too neglected social epidemic.

I was involved in another hippo incident in 1997 that fortunately ended happily. My cousin Rena Kahn had asked me to host Yehuda Blum and his wife Moria, who was another of my cousins, during their trip to Kenya. Blum was a widely respected Israeli jurist and diplomat whose public career I'd followed from afar in the press. He had been sent to the Bergen-Belsen concentration camp when a child and had his bar mitzvah there. After the war he studied law at the University of London and went on to teach international law for thirty-six years at the Hebrew University in Jerusalem. Yehuda had helped draft the Camp David Accords in 1978. He then spent six years as Israel's ambassador to the United Nations. He also had taught law at several American universities and published a number of articles on international and world affairs.

It was tentatively agreed that the Blums would spend Saturday night at my house in Nairobi then we would drive together to the farm the next day. However, once our Jewish community learned that Blum was coming to town, they extended an invitation to Yehuda to speak at our Vermont Memorial Hall on Sunday night, and he accepted.

The visit to Naivasha thus became a daytrip. Once at the lake I showed them around the farm, then we sat on the veranda to enjoy the view and chat. The conversation ranged from the recent terrorist bombings in Tel Aviv and Jerusalem, to my observations on President Moi. We touched on Princess Diana's violent death, Great Britain's handover of Hong Kong to the Chinese and so on. Blum's observations in each instance were insightful and worth consideration. After lunch we decided to cruise around the lake in my inflatable rubber Zodiac. Hadson would man the outboard motor.

'Do you fish?' I asked my guests. They didn't. 'Well, Lake Naivasha is world-famous for its birdlife,' I said. 'We can enjoy some birdwatching, and I'll bring along a fishing rod. Maybe we can catch some black bass.'

The Blums managed apprehensive smiles as they clambered aboard the Zodiac and we set off. The weather was calm, but soon the wind started to pick up. Naivasha is notorious for its sudden storms. I suggested to Hadson we keep close to the shore. At this point a large clump of papyrus – maybe ten meters by ten meters – floated into view. Papyrus flourishes in Lake Naivasha's shallows as do hippos. As we approached it in the freshening wind, Hadson suddenly cut the engine. A look of concern came over him. Very calmly he said, 'I think you'd better put on your life jackets.'

'What for?' I wanted to know.

'That island is coming for us very fast.'

'Can't we move away?'

'No. We're not going to be able to.'

The papyrus was coming at us from both sides, pushing the Zodiac down. The water plants were folding the rubber craft in two. This had the effect of pushing us passengers upward. Water poured over the gunwales. All around us the hippos were snorting. We were invading their space, and they didn't like it. We couldn't see them, but I sensed from their snorts they were advancing toward us, low in the water, screened from view behind the floating green wall.

Always suggestible in a crisis, I considered our fate, imagining newspaper headlines declaring to a shocked nation that four people, including an eminent Israeli diplomat, had been killed on the lake by hippos. All of this passed through my mind in a matter of seconds. I looked at Yehuda and Moria. They were justifiably paralyzed with fear.

We were about thirty meters from shore in only about three meters of water. Yet I knew the lake bottom was very uneven in that area, and we could neither swim nor walk through the thick papyrus. Our only hope was help from the shore. Hadson and I began to shout, hoping that someone might hear. The wind now was strong, blowing onshore, and that helped carry our voices to five farm hands working near the water's edge. They looked up and came running to our rescue.

'Usijali!' they called. 'Don't worry. We'll get you out.'

We couldn't see them at first. Then all five gradually emerged through the papyrus, wielding pangas (machetes). They were chopping off the plants at the waterline as they approached while at the same time weaving a coarse mat from the severed stalks to serve as a makeshift floating bridge. When they reached the boat, two of the men stationed themselves in front and behind Moria and carefully guided her across the mat. She slipped off from time to time, but her two escorts were able to keep her more or less upright as they inched her safely ashore. They repeated the drill with Yehuda and then me. Hadson declined to abandon the Zodiac, which he was able to dislodge and carry safely to the landing undamaged.

We were soaked and shivering in the late afternoon. At the house I gave Yehuda and Moria British Airways first-class passenger pyjamas and warm blankets. The cook lit a fire for us and brought warm tea. This was not the first time I had been saved from either death, dismemberment or some other hazard by the local knowledge of the Kenyans. To their credit they often take it for granted although I do not.

Soon enough, Hadson pulled up in the pickup with the Zodiac in the back. He looked embarrassed as he stood by the front door. 'I'm sorry, Daktari. I lost one of your fishing lures.'

The view from the farm.

David and his closest friend Charles Szlapak.

Four sons on top of the Land Rover.

Josh (front left) and Nahum at Nahum's Bar Mitzvah in Nairobi.

David with Aaron and Jeremy at Jeremy's Bar Mitzvah in Nairobi.

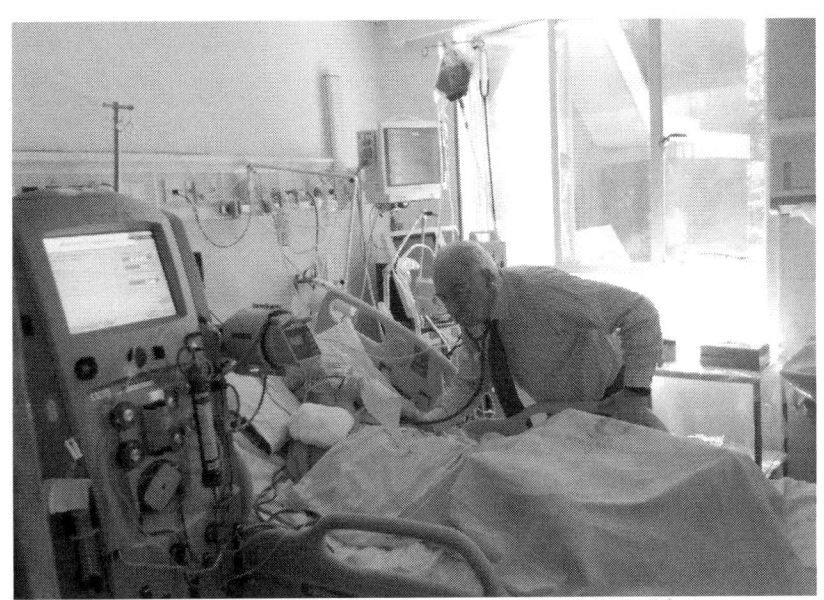

Attending an ICU patient.

David dictating a medical report in his office.

The skull and tooth of the rogue hippo that killed the watchman at the Naivasha farm.

With Hadson Sobet, the farm manager, in Channa's organic vegetable garden at the farm.

Enjoying a sundowner with Safi at the farm.

Enjoying sundowners with Charles and Margaret Njonjo.

David and Channa with all the sons at a family wedding, 2016.

David with siblings Allan and Rochelle.

Josh and Taylor, Benny and Max.

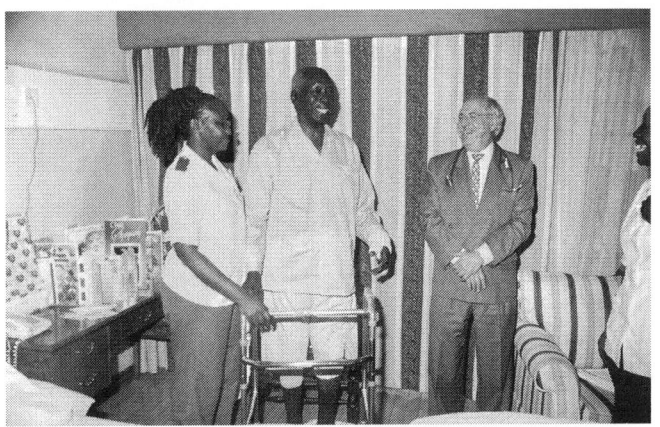

David with President Moi after knee surgery.

David delivers the eulogy at President Moi's funeral, February 2020.

Dr. Silverstein receiving his Distinguished Alumni Award from The University of Chicago Medical School.

Channa and David on safari in the Mara.

31

TRIPS TO CHINA AND ISRAEL

Beijing was one of my favourite cities so I was delighted when I was told in May 1994 that President Moi would be visiting Jiang Zemin, the recently elected president of the People's Republic of China. Moi had travelled to China twice before as head of state. In September 1980 after a long chill in Sino-Kenyan relations he had visited General Secretary Deng Xiaoping to patch up diplomatic relations. I had accompanied him on his second visit in October 1988 when he met with General Secretary Zhao Ziyang. He was considered a pro-Western economic reformer and lost his job the following year. He had been accused of supporting the June 1989 Democracy Movement protests in Tiananmen Square.

This visit began with a stopover in Hong Kong. We were taken to Shenzhen, the Special Economic Zone to the north of Hong Kong in Guangdong Province. From there we flew to Kunming in Yunan Province. After a lavish lunch with local officials, we visited the Kunming Pharmaceutical Factory. It was under license from Rhone-Pôlenc, the French pharmaceutical company (now part of Sanofi) and manufactured an effective injectable antimalarial using the old wormwood derivative, artemisinin.

This was a development of obvious interest to Kenyans for whom malaria is still a serious public health issue. In 2006

WHO recommended artemisinin combination therapy as the first-line medication in all endemic areas. The FDA (Food and Drug Administration) in the States gave its approval three years later. By that time resistance was already widespread. Even so artemisinin combination therapy is still the preferred treatment for malaria.

On the flight to Hong Kong Rev. Jones Kaleli took me aside. 'Daktari, I think I have malaria.'

'Really? What are your symptoms?'

'I have a runny nose. I'm sneezing. I have a sore throat, and I think I have a fever.'

It sounded like he had a common cold. I gave him an analgesic and antipyretic and told him he should be fine. He wasn't. After we returned to our hotel from visiting the pharmaceutical plant, I was summoned to Kaleli's room. He was in bed and running a high fever. Clearly it wasn't just a cold. It was indeed malaria. In fact I think he probably had both. I started him on IV fluids to counteract his dehydration and gave him quinine tablets. It was the only malaria medicine I had. Or so I thought.

My patient's health put me in mind of our pending departure for Beijing, which I *really* wanted to see again. If Kaleli didn't improve, I knew Moi would advise me to admit him to a hospital and stay behind to oversee his care. Selfish as it was, I intended to do my best to avoid that possibility. Back in my patient's room I found him highly confused and hallucinating as a consequence of his fever. He still had the drip in, but he had vomited up the quinine pills.

Then it came to me. The Chinese had given Moi several large cartons of their injectable antimalarial, and they were stored in my room. I thought *Let me try this stuff.* I'd never used it, but the pilot studies by its manufacturer Rhone-Pôlenc showed it was a safe drug. I read the instructions, gave Kaleli a 160 mg injection as indicated then joined the president for tea.

After I had briefed him on Kaleli's condition, Moi said, 'You know what he also needs? *Uji ya wimbi.*' Moi was referring to a nutritious millet porridge widely consumed in East Africa. Like many Kenyans, he was a staunch champion of its curative powers against a broad spectrum of illnesses.

It was discovered our traveling supply of wimbi had been left on the airplane, which was parked at the airport a good distance from the hotel. Two security officers were dispatched to retrieve it. After a very long interval they returned in the middle of the night with the wimbi in hand. The chef was roused and instructed to prepare it immediately. The patient took a few teaspoons of Moi's magic potion and fell asleep.

The next morning I gave Kaleli another injection. His temperature had come down. He was beginning to talk sense. The antimalarial was doing its job. He recounted to me one of his hallucinations from the night before. A delegation of elders from his village had come to him and said, 'This is not your time to come with us. You stay.' Even though a man of the church, like many Kenyans he retained a deep-seated belief in the ancestral spirits.

I reported his progress to Moi at breakfast, proud to show off how I had used an ancient Chinese drug to save his friend. Moi nodded and smiled. He was pleased. 'I *told* you uji ya wimbi would make him better.' We had to share the credit.

Beijing was as interesting as ever. Moi placed a wreath at Tiananmen Square. We visited the Ming tombs, the Forbidden City and the Great Wall. President Jiang hosted a banquet for us at the well-appointed Diaoyutai State Guesthouse, once home to Mao Zedong. Steak was on the menu, as well as abalone and mushrooms and asparagus. Ice cream, pastries and fruit were served for dessert. Jiang stood and raised his glass of champagne. 'To the prosperity of the Republic of Kenya. To the continued consolidation and strengthening of Sino-Kenyan friendly relations and cooperation. To the health of Your Excellency, President Moi and to the health of all friends present here – Cheers!' In Kenya Moi would have ginger ale in his glass to look like champagne. But here in China, champagne had been poured. He stood and raised his glass to Jiang and sat down again. He raised the glass to his lips, but he didn't take a sip.

Before our flight home President Moi and about twenty of us were invited to a twelve-course banquet at a restaurant featuring duck and regional specialties. The strange looking dishes that were placed before us troubled several in our group. Their palates were accustomed to fried and grilled meat, chips and wimbi. Sally Kosgei had mischievously stirred anxieties in New Delhi among the older and less travelled members of the delegation. She told minister Francis Lotodo, a political veteran from the fierce Pokot tribe, that snakes were a popular dish and dogs were a delicacy. The Chinese got their milk from buffalos, she added. All of that was true, of course. But Lotodo was confounded. In his day Lotodo had faced off President Jomo Kenyatta in Parliament. Now he was speechless. Cape buffalo were dangerous. No woman could milk them. Sally didn't mention that Asian water buffalos are as placid as cows.

Since I was the only one in the group who could speak a little Mandarin, and as I was the daktari, I was expected to be an authority on Chinese food and the creatures that might be on the menu that day. Several of the people in the restaurant, including Moi, asked me if anything they were eating included snake or dog. I assured them the meal was free of both. Francis Lotodo was served a milk-based beverage of some sort and asked me how the Chinese were able to milk buffalos. He was glad to learn his drink was safe but still would not consume it. Only Sally Kosgei and I used chopsticks.

On the trip over Kenya Airways had given us all red bed socks. Lotodo thought they were the best-looking socks he'd ever seen. He wore them that day at the restaurant and would later be seen wearing them all over Nairobi, even on State House visits to President Moi. I'm sure those socks were by far the fondest memento of his trip to the Middle Kingdom.

These trips marked the beginning of China's strategic ambition to supplant Western influence in sub-Saharan Africa. Since then China has had no qualms in creating African indebtedness by extending generous loans for infrastructure. Kenya is one of these countries. Over the past two decades China has lent $153 billion to the continent's public sector. It favours a lending model that marks revenue from natural resources such as copper, cobalt and bauxite as collateral against loan repayments.

This is the case in the Democratic Republic of the Congo, Ghana and Guinea. It may apply to Kenya and other countries too, but it is impossible to find out. The Chinese draw up loan contracts that are unique in the official credit market. Borrowers are forbidden to disclose the loan terms unless required by law. These confidentiality clauses undermine domestic accountability and prevent questions being asked by a country's citizens and its legislature. There are now more than a million Chinese living and working on the continent, and the Chinese are fast inserting themselves in Africa's economies.

On the night of 4 November 1995 I was at home in Nairobi when I heard the terrible news that Yigal Amir, an Israeli law student who was a right wing extremist, had assassinated Prime Minister Yitzhak Rabin. It had happened in a Tel Aviv parking lot adjacent to Kings of Israel Square. Rabin had been walking to his car having come from a rally in support of the Oslo peace process. The Oslo Accords had recognized both the State of Israel and the PLO (Palestine Liberation Organization) as the negotiating partners to achieve an ultimate peace. This was strongly opposed by a large section of Palestinians as well as some Israelis. Amir had fired two shots from a Beretta pistol killing Rabin instantly.

Moi was devastated. Rabin was a personal friend. Like many Kenyans, Moi had a deep respect for the Israelis and their leaders. He also felt a special kinship with Israel. He considered the Israeli presence in Africa a beneficial one. Added to this was a belief among the Kalenjins they were one of the ten lost tribes of Israel. During the fifteen years when the OAU dictated all African countries cut ties with Israel, Moi maintained a discreet relationship with the Israeli representative to UNEP (the United Nations Environment Programme) although his preferred channel of communication was the Mossad. One night in 1987 Prime Minister Yitzhak Shamir made an unofficial touchdown at Jomo Kenyatta International Airport at 2 am. Moi joined him on the plane and the two leaders chatted amicably for a few hours.

Rabin's funeral was arranged for two days later. Under ordinary circumstances President Moi would have attended. Unfortunately, he was scheduled to depart for Auckland, New Zealand for the annual Commonwealth Heads of Government meeting. As far as Moi was concerned, this was a command performance. He had to attend. The previous night Moi had heard on the BBC news that Rabin had been shot. He had immediately called his permanent secretary for foreign affairs, Sally Kosgei, to tell her that Rabin had died. He was terribly upset. Neither of them was able to sleep that night.

The next morning when Moi boarded the plane for Auckland, Sally came to tell him the funeral was scheduled for the next day. He would not be able to attend, but he needed to send a delegation. Word was sent to the pilot to keep the plane sitting on the tarmac. George Saitoti, the vice president, was summoned to the aircraft and told he must get to Israel in time for the funeral. It was a logistical nightmare, but Saitoti managed it.

Meanwhile the heads-of-state meeting in Auckland was about to become a newsworthy event imbued not with the gravitas of high-level diplomacy but tainted with broadsheet sleaze. Nicholas Biwott, a former cabinet minister and one of Moi's senior assistants, notoriously distinguished himself by allegedly assaulting a chambermaid while he was watching the pornography channel in his room. This did not go down well in New Zealand. Biwott was flown out of the country in a hurry and rejoined us in Singapore. He became known as the Bull of Auckland.

Throughout the trip Moi was monitoring the news from Israel closely. I could see it was frustrating for him not to be there to honour his friend in death. Then a thought occurred to me. On the thirtieth day of mourning Jews observe *shloshim* (meaning thirty in Hebrew), an observance for the deceased in some ways more meaningful than the funeral. I explained this to the president, and his face lit up. He pointed out that in the Kalenjin tradition there was a similar occasion on the fortieth day for observing remembrance. Moi told Sally Kosgei he wanted to attend Rabin's shloshim. She consulted with Aryeh Oded, the Israeli ambassador to Kenya, and it was arranged.

We checked into the King David Hotel in Jerusalem and were taken that night to the office of the acting prime minister, Shimon Peres. I was among those allowed to meet Peres as was Vaizman Aharoni, the man who memorably drove to Nairobi Hospital with his sidearm to protect the hostages who had been wounded during the Entebbe Raid. He was there to represent the Nairobi Jewish community. Peres was warm and welcoming. He said to ask if we needed anything. We replied that we had come to show our respects and to mourn the deceased.

Moi visited President Ezer Weizman in Jerusalem as well. He also met with Rabin's widow at her house after laying a wreath on her slain husband's grave. Before leaving, Moi had a cordial visit with Yasser Arafat on the West Bank. As the head of the PLO, he was considered a political ally of Israel.

32

TRAVELS IN IRAN

In December 1998 President Moi made an official trip to Iran. Prior to our departure several of my Israeli friends and patients, including the head of the Mossad in Kenya, warned me that Iran was too dangerous for a Jewish American man to visit even as part of a Kenyan delegation. I did not take their concerns lightly, but the opportunity to go to Iran intrigued me. Though I would be cautious, I was determined not to let this chance pass me by.

Our Fokker Friendship jet touched down late in the day at Tehran's Mehrabad Airport. We were taken to a hotel in advance of talks that night between Moi and President Mohammad Khatami. The meeting was at Sa'dabad Palace in the north of the capital. The two presidents first held a private consultation while our delegation was shown to a conference room. We took our assigned seats at a large elliptical table and waited for Moi and Khatami and their respective senior aides to arrive. Ordinarily I was excluded from such gatherings. This time Frost Josiah, the chief of protocol, surprised me with a seat at the table. I considered it an honour and was excited by the prospect of seeing first-hand what would transpire, especially given the nature of the host country.

As Moi and Khatami entered the room, the excitable Iranian ambassador to Kenya began pointing at me and talking in

Persian. I couldn't understand what he was saying, but his raised voice indicated trouble. He took Josiah aside and spoke to him in an animated whisper. Josiah then crossed to where I was sitting. 'The ambassador has accused you of being a spy,' he said into my ear. It reminded me of a similar allegation made by Hillary Ojiambo when I first came to Kenya and brought a smile to my face. Then I recalled that this was the Islamic Republic of Iran and became more than a bit concerned.

'Maybe you'd better sit outside,' Josiah suggested. It seemed a good idea under the circumstances. I withdrew to a large hallway and spent some forty-five minutes admiring the surroundings. The masterful Persian art on the walls, which was of museum quality, turned my exile into a pleasant interlude. IRNA, the official government news agency, later reported the night's presidential talks had centred on Khatami's desire to expand economic and trade relations with Kenya.

Back in my room later that evening, I was notified that President Moi wished to see me. He had heard I had been told to leave the meeting and was concerned. Moi was always sensitive to my feelings. He had already demonstrated on several occasions that he felt protective of me. That evening he sat me down and told me a story that had not been reported by IRNA.

Moi was a natural diplomat and liked to be involved as a behind-the-scenes intermediary. He had already chalked up a reasonably successful track record in Africa as a mediator by bringing various warring factions to the table. Beyond the continent, he sometimes used visits to rogue nations to try to parlay happy outcomes to difficult situations. In 1986 an Israeli navigator of an Israeli F-4 Phantom II jet had been taken into Lebanese custody after a raid over the city of Sidon. Ron Arad was believed to have been handed over to a Hezbollah unit and possibly passed on to Iranian Revolutionary Guards. There had been no reliable reports of his condition or whereabouts since then despite continued and intensive Israeli efforts to learn the truth. Now that he was in Iran and as a friend of Israel, Moi felt it was important to try to get information on Arad, and at least ascertain if he was still alive. I suspect the Israelis had probably asked him to do it.

Moi told me he had brought up the subject of Arad in a private conversation with Khatami before their public discussions. Did Khatami know Arad's whereabouts? Would he be in a position to help determine his fate? As it turned out, President Khatami was not forthcoming. The Israelis continued investigating the navigator's disappearance until they were forced to conclude he must have died soon after the Lebanese took him into custody.

The next day included a visit to the tomb of Ayatollah Khomeini, the leader of the 1979 Iranian Revolution which saw the overthrow of the last Shah of Iran, Mohammad Reza Pahlavi. He had been adulated as a spiritual and political leader by Iranians, but for many he was remembered for his role in the Iran – Iraq War of 1980-1988, force-marching wave after wave of child soldiers onto enemy lines, killing hundreds of thousands of young Iranian boys.

The third day we were scheduled to fly north to Tabriz, a historic city dating back to the 9th century. That morning the Iranians announced there were no available government aircraft for the trip. The solution, they said, would be to fly with the Kenyans on Moi's plane. The Kenyans were happy to agree to the plan. This meant four or five of our delegation would have to take a commercial flight. When I was told one of them would be me, my jaw dropped.

The Iranians hated the Israelis, but they hated Americans too. There had been recent anti-U.S. demonstrations in the streets with shouts of 'Death to America! Death to Israel!' Mindful of this, I sought out Frost Josiah. 'You're aware of the demonstrations? You know I carry an American passport and have a Jewish name. Have you thought this out carefully? I'm prepared to fly commercially, but I want to make sure you're aware of all the implications of that and any possible consequences if something goes wrong.'

Frost took my issue to Harry Katharima, a former chief of protocol and now the permanent secretary for foreign affairs. Katharima in turn took it to Moi who personally restored me to his plane's passenger manifest. Before we departed he called me to his room. 'Some of my people just don't think,' he said in Kiswahili and shook his head in disbelief. 'If I fall down, who's there to pick me up? You're coming with me.'

Tabriz was an enlightening experience. For all the fevered fundamentalism the Iranian government and mullahs showed the world, the bazaar at Tabriz revealed another side of the country. The stalls were an Aladdin's cave of finely made traditional crafts and fine jewellery. The centrepiece attractions were the stunning handwoven carpets renowned as some of the finest carpets in the world. Others were stocked with fashionable clothes from the U.S. including women's lacy underwear and stiletto shoes. The more modern Iranian women covered their heads with a hijab while those who were more conservative wore an all-enveloping chador. They were strikingly beautiful and openly curious about the African men. The Kenyans were just as curious in return. American music was playing everywhere. The Iranian embrace of Western goods and culture, their casual acceptance of us as we wandered through the souk, coupled with a civilization dating back six millennia, gave me hope.

When we returned to Tehran, our visit was extended by a day because our hosts were eager to show Moi an armaments factory. The Iranians by this time had introduced ammunition production into the conversation. Everyone was given a full-colour brochure detailing the arms available for export. I was mildly surprised to be given one as well. I kept it as a souvenir. I had been barred from the other meetings, but during the arms discussions no one objected to my presence in the room.

On the flight back to Nairobi I developed a migraine and was relieved to get home in the early evening so I could take a pain pill and go to bed. I was asleep by 8 pm. Three hours later the phone rang. It was the casualty medical officer at the hospital ER. Annoyed, I pointed out I was officially away until the next morning. He apologized and said there was a patient with chest pain who insisted I was the only doctor he would see.

I reluctantly got dressed and climbed into the car. When I arrived at the hospital, the patient turned out to be the Iranian ambassador, who had denounced me so vehemently as a spy. He assaulted me now with embraces and kisses. 'Thank you for seeing me,' he said. 'I'm sorry to drag you out this late after your long trip. You see, you're the only doctor I can trust.' The ambassador recovered quickly. After that I was invited to all Iranian Embassy social events. I took it as a sign I was no longer in danger of being accused of spying.

Iran today is a theocracy, an Islamic dictatorship and a major exporter of terrorism. As far as I can tell, most Iranians dislike their leaders and would rather have a secular state that recognizes the U.S. and Israel. Should détente come to pass sometime in the future, I hope Iranians will revert to the lifestyle enjoyed under the Shah. It is still followed by the easygoing residents of Tabriz: poetry, wine, well-dressed men and women, silken carpets and a lemon-scented bazaar. May that day come soon.

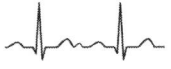

Whenever the president required medical treatment, I would try to coincide it with an official overseas meeting to dampen speculation about his state of health. Usually he only needed routine checkups, but in June 2000 I diagnosed Moi with an entrapment syndrome. Simply put, it is pressure on a nerve that can result in a range of outcomes from numbness to pain to muscle wasting. A common example of this is carpal tunnel syndrome, usually due to repetitive motion, where the median nerve is impeded as it passes through the wrist's carpal tunnel on its way to the hand.

Moi was suffering muscle atrophy in both his hands due to entrapment syndrome in his elbows. His ulnar nerves in both arms were being crowded by adjacent tissue. It can be fixed with a straightforward surgical procedure. An operation was duly scheduled to be performed in London. On our way there we were to make a brief stop in Crans Montana, a Swiss mountain resort, where Moi had been invited to address an international economic forum.

I enjoyed dinner with Sally Kosgei at the hotel on our first night. Her position as the permanent secretary in the foreign affairs ministry meant she invariably came on these trips. We were by then seasoned veterans of countless trips and enjoyed sharing stories. Sally was amusing and told a good tale. A favorite topic was the changing faces of the delegations as government officials came and went. We also used to trade stories on how presidential travel had impacted our lives, for better or worse. I mentioned how my family and friends thought of the trips as a paid holiday, unaware of how stressful and tiring they could be. In my practice, for example, it meant that I was kept up at ungodly hours in distant time zones, monitoring the progress of my critical patients back in Nairobi. Of course, neither of us would have ever wanted to give up our front-row seats to Kenyan history in the making.

The next day we toured the resort's alpine museum and cheese cellar. Moi was a farmer at heart and so took an interest in the Swiss dairy cows. We also visited the Cave St-Michele vineyards for a wine tasting. Moi politely sipped the crisp white wines though his palate preferred the sweet ceremonial kosher wines from Israel that he and Charles Njonjo discovered and enjoyed at my house. During the wine tasting I noticed the president was short of breath. I wasn't surprised. He was hypertensive and had been nursing a cold. We were 9600 feet above sea level, and it was cold.

The next morning I listened to his heart and detected rapid atrial fibrillation, an irregular and fast heart rhythm. I confirmed the diagnosis with my portable ECG machine. My immediate concern was the possibility of blood clots developing in his heart's left atrium. They could break off and go to his brain causing a stroke. I went into town in search of blood thinners. Several pharmacists, not understanding my mixture of English and broken German, mistakenly believed I wanted narcotics and refused to help me. Finally I secured heparin, a blood thinner.

I administered it to Moi, who said he felt fine. He was nearly seventy-seven and robust for his age. Even so I was more than mildly concerned by the turn of events. I phoned Dr Steve Jenkins in London. He was a friend and an excellent cardiologist. I told him I wanted to enlist his help the moment we landed in England. Twenty years earlier Steve had done me the favour of taking on my patient load, *locum tenens*, when I was called away from Nairobi. I also contacted Dr Maurice Slapak, the brother of my dear friend Charles Szlapak. He was a retired transplant surgeon who also lived in London. I asked for his assistance too.

Maurice knew the London medical community well. He said he would be happy to make the necessary arrangements for Moi's expected treatment of electric shock (cardioversion) to restore his normal heartbeat.

We checked into the Mayfair Intercontinental. Moi went to his room, and I called a meeting in mine. After discussing the issues and options with Jenkins and Slapak, I went to Moi and explained the situation to him in private. To make sure I wasn't putting him through an unnecessary procedure, I took a second ECG. It confirmed my finding. There was no question he needed the treatment. Moi wasn't upset by what I told him. He said I should do whatever I needed to do.

Jenkins told Moi to eat nothing after midnight and instructed me to have the president at London's Cromwell Hospital first thing in the morning. Everything went according to plan. Moi was put under total anaesthesia. This differed from my Nairobi practice where I use pain medication if needed and conscious sedation so that the patient has complete airway control and can follow commands but has no memory of the event.

Dr Jenkins administered two jolts of electricity to shock Moi's heart back into a normal sinus rhythm. He was then put on a course of oral anticoagulants. I breathed a great sigh of relief when we returned to Kenya. The trip certainly hadn't been the paid vacation my friends talked about. The responsibility of keeping the president in good health could be extremely stressful. That was certainly the case on this trip. I was happy to be home and return to my clinic. All had ended well. Moi never required shocking again for this cardiac arrhythmia. His entrapment syndrome was repaired on a subsequent visit to London.

33

THE CHESONI SAGA

Throughout my career I have been lucky enough to enjoy harmonious professional and personal relations with my Kenyan medical colleagues. The one exception happened in 1999 when my patient Chief Justice Zacchaeus Chesoni succumbed to a fatal cardiac arrest in the hospital's ICU. I was charged with mishandling the case. Once the facts were made plain, I was fully vindicated. It was a long time ago, but the anguish I experienced is still vividly etched in my memory.

Zach Chesoni was a personal friend who had been my patient since September 1975 when he had presented at Kenyatta National Hospital with vague complaints of chest pain. On examination I detected a leakage of the aortic valve. At the time there was no echocardiogram machine in Kenya. His heart size was normal. He had no symptoms other than mild chest discomfort, which was clearly of muscular origin and related to stress. The following year he came back complaining of significant chest pain. An X-ray and fluoroscopic examination – the only diagnostic tools then available to me - showed considerable dilation of the aorta. It was an aortic aneurysm. Left untreated, it would kill him.

I was worried and told him he needed surgery. He wasn't happy at this prospect. I understood how he felt, but I feared that if he didn't agree to the procedure, his time on earth was limited. Zach told me he had a relative who was a resident physician at the Mayo Clinic in the U.S. and he would like to go there. He asked me to call Charles Njonjo, then the attorney general, and explain the situation to him.

Charles listened patiently as I explained that Zach's rapidly expanding aneurysm might rupture. It was a surgical emergency which we couldn't yet manage in Nairobi. He immediately assured me that not only would his office cover Zach's expenses, but I should move quickly. I was hugely relieved. Zach flew at once to the Mayo Clinic where my diagnosis was confirmed. Dr Dwight McGoon, a famous pioneer in cardiac surgery, performed an aortic valve replacement as well as a resection of the aortic aneurysm.

On Zach's return to Nairobi, I put him on the blood thinner warfarin together with a beta-blocker, often used not only as an anti-hypertensive but also to prevent further aortic aneurysms. He recovered well, and I didn't see him again for a review for nearly fifteen years. By then he was head of the Electoral Commission, which was overseeing Kenya's first multiparty elections in twenty-six years. It was a momentous event for the country and stressful for everyone.

We now had echocardiography available. When I examined the images, I was alarmed to see Zach had developed a very large sinus of valsalva aneurysm at the base of his aorta. It measured eight centimetres. When an aneurysm grows beyond four or five centimetres there is a grave risk of a rupture or further dissection of the aortic wall. I wrote Zach a letter urging him to return to the Mayo Clinic for surgery immediately and faxed a copy to his son Solomon, a doctor doing postgraduate training in the States.

For reasons I never understood Zach never made the trip. Perhaps he feared going under the knife once more. Possibly his finances were a problem. He had a strong sense of duty and loyalty to President Moi. He may have hesitated to leave his important post at this critical juncture in Kenya's political evolution. He also kept his visits to me to a minimum. I suspect he thought that somehow he could tough it out.

I repeated Zach's echocardiogram two and a half years later in May 1994. The aneurysm had grown to nine and a half centimetres. I was very clear his heart condition needed urgent intervention. Unfortunately Zach ignored this. Five months later he was back in my office. At his request, I approached President Moi, who sanctioned an operation at government expense. Still my friend chose not to go abroad. We occasionally encountered one another at State House events. Zach would greet me with a big smile. 'Daktari, I'm still alive!' I didn't have the heart to tell him he was laughing in the face of death.

By April 1997 the aneurysm measured ten centimetres. I wrote at his request to the head of the public service. 'I strongly recommend that Justice Chesoni goes overseas for further consultation and intervention.' Once again Zach did not go. He did come in for regular reviews, and I tried to keep his blood pressure as low as possible in order to keep the shearing pressure of the ballooning blood vessel to a minimum. An echocardiogram now showed the aneurysm at ten-and-a-half centimetres. Besides his blood thinner, he was also on five antihypertensives including a beta-blocker. Zach would come by almost every week on Friday afternoons when I was off duty just to have his blood pressure checked by the nurses. Then came his last visit and the ensuing nightmare that started in August 1999.

It began 24 August when he came to me with pain in his left knee. As he had a history of gout and his white-blood-cell count was mildly elevated, I suspected this was a recurrence.

On examination I found it to be warm and swollen. But my chief concern was his low blood pressure, which consistently measured at 90/60 mmhg. One reading was 80/70. I urged him to come in for hospital admission. He categorically refused until his wife Mary convinced him to go. I gave him an injection of diclofenac, a non-steroidal anti-inflammatory drug, and put him on a dosage of the same compound three times a day.

When I visited him that evening, he was alert and keen to go home. His blood pressure had come up to 110/70. It was a good sign, but I still wanted to keep him in the hospital for another twenty-four hours. He was, after all, Kenya's chief justice. Extra caution seemed reasonable. The next morning he looked even better. His white-cell count was within normal limits. He had no fever. He was in excellent spirits and cracking jokes.

By this time the press was beginning to wonder why the chief justice was still in hospital. Zach and Mary told me they were growing weary of the reporters' constant inquiries. They asked if he could go home. I told them that out of an abundance of caution I wanted to keep him until his blood pressure reading was consistently at 100/70 or higher for twenty-four hours. This probably meant one more day of hospitalization. Zach was disappointed but reluctantly agreed.

Channa, who was soon to become my wife, had recently returned to Nairobi on a break from her work in Portland, Oregon. We had accepted an invitation by the owners of Chui Lodge in Naivasha to celebrate my birthday there. I told Zach about our plans and reassured him I would be available at all times on the phone. Dr Mark Joshi, a consultant cardiologist, would be in attendance as well as those employed in my practice. Zach said he was fine with that as 'no one is indispensable'. I wondered whether he was referring to himself or to me. As

Channa and I left town, I was confident of Zach's excellent care and continued recovery.

The next day Channa and I drove to Lake Bogoria Hotel at the invitation of President Moi. En route, I called Dr Jimmy Mbogori, who worked for me. He reported Zach was somewhat confused. His white-cell count was normal, but Mbogori had noted some stiffness in his neck. Out of concern the onset of his confusion and neck stiffness might be a brain haemorrhage caused by the blood thinner warfarin he was taking or some sort of meningitis, Mbogori had transferred Zach to the high-dependency unit where he could receive a higher level of care. A subsequent CT scan had ruled out any bleeding.

Zach's blood oxygen was low, but his chest X-ray was normal and a repeat 2D echocardiogram showed no change in his heart function. After reviewing the patient again, Joshi and Mbogori provisionally concluded that Zach may have developed encephalitis from an unknown cause. A lumbar puncture produced xanthachromic (yellowish) CSF (cerebrospinal fluid) that usually is associated with a subacute bleed. With bacterial meningitis you expect to see an elevated white-cell count in the CSF, visible as pus. Zach's white-cell count, however, was surprisingly low which suggested that he was not able to mount a defence or else the infection was very recent.

Another consideration was a nonbacterial infection such as viral or fungal meningitis. This was why we were monitoring the patient's neck. Neck stiffness is a common symptom of inflammation of the lining of the brain (meninges), the hallmark of meningitis. There had been no neck stiffness until then. However, the gram stain, revealing gram-positive diplococci bacteria, firmly established that Zach was infected by bacterial pneumococcal meningitis, one of the most common forms of bacterial meningitis. Given this diagnosis Jimmy Mbogori, in conjunction with my colleague Shem Musoke, immediately started Zach on Rocephin (ceftriaxone), the drug of choice for bacterial meningitis in 1999. It continues to be commonly used to this day.

As soon as Channa and I arrived at Lake Bogoria late that afternoon I phoned Jimmy Mbogori, who briefed me on Zach's condition. There had been some early reports, mostly out of the U.S., of the pneumococcal organism's resistance to penicillin and, more rarely, to drugs such as ceftriaxone. In the remote possibility that Zach's infection was resistant to the ceftriaxone, I also started him on vancomycin, another antibiotic. I called President Moi to update him on his chief justice's status and to inform him I would be driving back to Nairobi at sunrise to be at the patient's bedside.

Sometime after midnight I was called because Zach's blood oxygenation was falling. I had him transferred to the ICU. He was intubated, which meant inserting a tube through the mouth into the wind pipe, and then put on a ventilator.

Channa and I rushed back to Nairobi as quickly as we could. When I arrived, I saw at once that Zach had responded well to our treatment. I was mildly relieved. The next day his chemically-induced paralysis (necessary at times for adequate ventilation) and sedation were stopped. After two days Zach was well enough to receive visitors, one of whom was President Moi.

It was about this time that Dr John Matseshe, a gastroenterologist and Zach's cousin, flew in from Illinois. He at once presented himself to the media as the man in charge of the chief justice's treatment. Matseshe provided the reporters with daily updates, explaining that the patient was responding well to his (Matseshe's) treatment. I thought this was inappropriate, but as he was

Zach's close relative I didn't think it wise to call him on it. My responsibility was to the patient not Matseshe.

Zach was indeed doing well. The various bacteria cultures showed he had contracted a meningitis due to a very sensitive pneumococcus. When subsequent cultures came back indicated that penicillin was effective, I stopped the ceftriaxone and vancomycin and put him on penicillin. Zach continued to improve and I was able to take him off the ventilator by 1 September.

The next day we removed his endotracheal tube. Zach was fully alert and able to carry on a conversation with me. It was clear he had recovered. His kidney function had returned to normal. Plans were made to move him out of the ICU to the ward. His cousin, the gastroenterologist, continued to assure reporters that under his splendid care the chief justice was making excellent progress.

By Friday, 3 September Zach's vital signs were normal and stable so Channa and I went to our farm in Naivasha for a relaxing weekend before her return to Portland. I left Dr Luke Musau in charge. He was a consultant anaesthesiologist who had been doing intensive-care work in my practice for the previous five years. I also asked Dr Joshi to be available for any cardiological problems should they arise. They understood that if Zach's condition deteriorated, I would be able to return within two hours during the day and, as travelling on Kenyan roads in the dark can be dangerous, first thing in the morning should a call come at night.

Nothing of concern transpired until 2 am Sunday morning when Zach spiked temperatures of up to 40° C and developed difficulty breathing. He was returned to the ICU at once and put back on a ventilator. The lumbar puncture was repeated. There was no evidence of any further meningitis infection. I worried about the possibility that some bacteria had seeded his artificial aortic valve or possibly even set up shop in the aneurysm itself. If that was the case, he would be at high risk of a fatal rupture of the aneurysm.

Dr Matseshe telephoned me shortly afterward to inform me he believed an urgent echocardiogram should be done. I didn't think this would alter the treatment available to us in Nairobi in 1999. Nevertheless I asked Mark Joshi to perform one. Zach's echocardiogram was unchanged from the previous one. He was put on new antibiotics to cover the possibility he had developed a new infection. By dawn he was stable once more.

Then came his sudden collapse. At 11 am, as I was driving back to Nairobi, Luke Musau rang to say Zach's heart rate had suddenly plummeted and his heart had stopped. I had been stuck on the road having encountered a horrendous traffic jam caused by an accident. When I got the call, I was still finding my way to the hospital using circuitous back roads. I got to the ICU five minutes after efforts to resuscitate Zach Chesoni from his second cardiac arrest were abandoned.

Zach's son Solomon Chesoni and his cousin John Matseshe were there at the bedside. I offered my condolences, and they thanked me for my efforts. I shared my concerns about Zach's aneurysm and aortic valve and their possible role in his death. I said a post mortem was essential to establish the cause of death. Clearly it wasn't meningitis as the infection had cleared. They said they did not want a post mortem.

My friend Zach Chesoni was buried at his farm six days later. I had a busy day and didn't get a chance to take a break. When I stopped by to see Aaron and Jeremy at their mother Jackie's house, I found Jackie and her sisters listening to the news. They looked up when I walked in. Was I okay? There was concern in their eyes. Something was definitely amiss. Jackie's sister Angela led me outside and explained. Thousands of mourners had turned up for Zach's funeral. It had been covered on national television and radio. John Matseshe had given a eulogy. In front of President Moi, the entire Kenyan judiciary, most of the cabinet and a strong representation of Western Kenya dignitaries, he had accused me of malpractice in treating his late and beloved cousin. I was stunned.

I was at a loss to understand why Matseshe had lashed out in this manner, but I was pretty certain I needed a lawyer. I called Charles Njonjo and asked my friend if the brilliant and well-respected Byron Georgiadis would be the right lawyer to represent me. The Oxford-educated Georgiadis, sometimes referred to as the 'silver-haired Perry Mason of East Africa', had a long string of wins to his name in high-profile cases. Charles believed he would be a solid choice even though he had recently retired from full-time practice. I called him at home that evening. To my relief he agreed to take the case. His first piece of advice was to keep quiet and leave the speaking to him.

The following day coverage of the funeral was splashed across the front page of the *Sunday Standard* under the headline, 'Wrong medicine killed Chesoni – family doctor'. Matseshe was quoted as saying that Zach '…would be alive today if the disease that killed him last week had been diagnosed on time.' The *Standard* went on to reveal the Chesoni family had decided against an autopsy because Matseshe '…was by the bedside, and the family knew what the top judge had died from.'

At the request of the Nairobi Hospital Medical Advisory Committee, Dr Samuel Gathua, a consultant chest physician, drew up a detailed review of the Chesoni file with findings that absolved me of professional misconduct. In my heart of hearts I thought this would be the end of the matter, but I was wrong.

The next morning the Nairobi Hospital's Standards Audit & Ethics Committee issued a statement pointing out that Chesoni had received the correct diagnosis and treatment and regretted the family had declined a post mortem. The relentless Matseshe called his own press conference and stoked the fires of doubt by refuting the hospital's statement.

The following week the board ordered a preliminary-inquiry committee to review the matter and prepare a report. That pleased me. It would give me an opportunity to refute the allegations. By this time I was angry and ready to do battle. I had rehearsed my presentation for the investigators and was buoyed up by the many letters of support I'd received from patients and friends.

George Anyona, a high-profile MP, raised a question in parliament about Zacchaeus Chesoni and Cecil Miller, a prior chief justice. In a weird coincidence Miller had died of meningitis under my care exactly ten years earlier to the day. Anyona asked the government to institute judicial inquiries into the causes, circumstances and conditions of the deaths of the two late chief justices. Then came another shock. The *East African* ran the front-page headline, 'Chesoni probe points finger at Silverstein'.

Meanwhile the Medical Practitioners and Dentists Board was forming a tribunal to determine whether I had violated professional ethics in the treatment of the chief justice. If the answer was yes, I risked losing my license. The timing of the tribunal coincided with the introduction of new members to the board. Several had been appointed by the health minister. Others were elected in a secret ballot. Campaigning for positions on the board was commonplace and considered appropriate. What was unusual and unwelcome on this occasion was the promise from a group of candidates that if elected, they would ensure that Dr Silverstein was found guilty and that an African doctor would be selected to care for President Moi. I kept my thoughts to myself and took strength in the knowledge that among the people appointed to the new board by the minister were some very capable doctors with whom I enjoyed mutual respect. Foremost among them was Professor Julius Kyambi, the new chairman.

There was no question that during this time the clinic traffic slowed down. Byron quipped, 'When shit gets thrown at you, you get dirty.' However, for the most part my patients were very supportive. One patient whom I had pulled through a difficult and long ICU admission for meningitis made an appointment to see me to offer himself as a witness to vouch for my expertise in treating this condition. I was touched.

I wrote letters to leading infectious-disease authorities around the world, providing them with the case history without comment and soliciting their professional response. All replied that from their expert perspective the chief justice's case was handled in an exemplary fashion.

I was impressed with the way Byron Georgiadis studiously absorbed the material I gave him, drawing on it to write detailed briefings in pencil. I explained to him that Zach Chesoni's widening aortic aneurysm was much more likely to have killed him than his meningitis, which we'd cured before he died. Without a post mortem, of course, there was no conclusive proof. We decided it was fruitless to pursue the issue before the tribunal. Better to keep our arguments as simple and straightforward as possible.

I paid a call on President Moi to explain all that had happened and to reassure him I had done everything correctly and to the best of my ability. He supported me wholeheartedly saying he had great faith in me. 'You will remain my doctor,' he said and commended me for taking up the battle rather than asking for political protection.

D-Day arrived on 18 February 2000. The tribunal was being held in the University of Nairobi faculty of health sciences boardroom. When I first came to Kenya this drab space lit by overhead fluorescent lights was used by the faculty for tea and coffee breaks. Standing in the same room a quarter century later, I managed a little smile at the recollection. Business that day was procedural. Testimony was scheduled to begin the following Monday.

The sixteen-member tribunal, led by Julius Kyambi, was at the front table. Their legal team, led by the distinguished Lee Muthoga and Martha Koome, was seated at a separate table. Muthoga was chair of the Law Society of Kenya. He later served as a judge at the International Criminal Tribunal for Rwanda. Two decades into the future Koome became the first woman to serve as Kenya's chief justice. I sat with Byron Georgiadis and his assistant, Fiona Elms, at a third table.

The Chesoni family, including Zach's widow, sat behind us. Mary, like Zach, had been my patient for many years. Their attorney was Steven Adere. He had a remarkably loud voice. He must have been nervous going up against a legal legend such as Byron, who had once been his mentor. My chair was uncomfortable. Everyone else's appeared to be too. The atmosphere was tense.

Byron was the first to speak. In a long preamble, he lectured the room on how such a medical tribunal should be conducted, rather cheekily appropriating the board's authority to himself. Byron's presumption might have rankled some of the tribunal members, but I think he succeeded in setting the tone for the inquiry. And that was his objective.

The tribunal began taking evidence at 9 am on Monday morning by which time I had finished my hospital rounds. First to testify was John Matseshe. Muthoga led him through a series of questions related to Zach's care and asked for an explanation of the so-called 'red flags' that he claimed to have discovered on arrival at his cousin's bedside.

The witness performed reasonably well until Byron cross-examined him. On the first two allegations against me - that I had delayed a correct diagnosis and overseen incorrect treatment of the chief justice - Byron simply buried the doctor in data drawn from the articles and text books I had provided him. By the end, he had demonstrated beyond any reasonable doubt that I had performed in accordance with the most up-to-date and highest standards of patient care. It was a virtuoso performance in which Georgiadis delivered a global and detailed knowledge of the facts, presented in a compelling manner that had the effect of diminishing John Matseshe's medical knowledge.

Then Byron went after Matseshe's third allegation which was that I had abandoned my patient without proper medical supervision. Here Matseshe seemed to lose control of himself. His lips were quivering. Sensing the moment, Byron pounced.

'You have a chip on your shoulder, don't you?' he asked.

'Yes! I have a chip on my shoulder. If you trained as a Black man in America as I did, you would also have a chip on your shoulder.'

Byron immediately fell quiet allowing Matseshe's words to hang in the air so the panel members could consider without distraction what they had just heard from my prime accuser. He was holding up a mirror to my detractors, showing them what it looked like to demonize someone for the colour of his or her skin, or the kind of passport they held. It was an old evil with which they were all acquainted. After Byron had roundly refuted the alleged facts of his accusations, all that was left was anger and Matseshe's determination to punish me for all that he had endured. His allies on the tribunal, if they were listening, would have to consult their own motives in calling for my head.

The next day it was my turn to be grilled. Byron carefully turned down the heat with a calm and businesslike review of my training and experience. Together we reviewed the history of the Chesoni case. I explained that when the chief justice had come to me with gout, I had persuaded him to allow me to admit him to the hospital because I was concerned by his very low blood pressure. I had kept him beyond his expected discharge date because the low blood pressure persisted. The meningitis had been a secondary development. Its diagnosis had been delayed because he never developed the triad of meningitis symptoms - high fevers, mental confusion and a stiff neck - until very late in the course of his illness. I backed this up with literature as well as with the correspondence I had conducted with authorities in the field. As I looked around the room, I sensed a lot of people had become noticeably friendlier toward me as they listened to the science and the explanation of how I made my decisions.

Doctors Jimmy Mbogori, Luke Musau and Mark Joshi, the colleagues taking care of the chief justice in my absence, were also questioned. They gave cogent responses consistent in every detail with my testimony. Seven people in all gave testimony. Zach's daughter Atsango Chesoni was one of them. She had nothing substantive to say about the medical science at issue but took the opportunity to speak from her heart. Her sorrow was real, and I was disturbed to have it exacerbated by Matseshe's accusations. The tribunal concluded Friday morning, and I returned to the hospital. After evening rounds I left for the synagogue as was my usual Friday practice. On the way my car phone rang. It was Daniel Yumbya, the tribunal's secretary. He told me a verdict had been reached and I was to come immediately for it to be announced. He must have heard the anxiety in my voice for he added, 'Just relax.' I reached the health sciences board room around 6.45 that evening. This was not a court of law so Byron's presence was not required. The Chesoni family had asked to be notified as well when a decision was made so they could attend. But after several unsuccessful attempts to reach them, at 9 pm Julius Kyambi finally stood to read the verdict. I was innocent of all three charges. I had been vindicated as I predicted, although by a paper-thin margin of nine to seven as I later heard from Julius. The Ministry of Health constitution required a two-thirds majority to find me guilty. That night I slept well for the first time in months.

There was a strange twist to the affair that didn't come to light until nearly two decades later. On a trip to Israel with the now retired President Moi in March 2018, I met Zach Chesoni's son, Jon, who was the Kenyan ambassador there. Sitting together in an airport VIP lounge at the beginning of the visit, he reminded me of that troubling time. He said that the family had struggled to come to terms with his father's death. They were in enormous turmoil. Subsequently, as a young diplomat in Uganda, he had listened to the entire tribunal proceedings and realized the allegations against me were not right. I had taken excellent care of his father, he said. He thanked me for keeping Zach alive for as long as I had and for helping to get him admitted to the Mayo Clinic in 1978. If his father had been heading the tribunal, Jon confided, his sharp judicial mind would have seen through the allegations immediately and dismissed the case out of hand. He would have been unhappy to see the misery I was put through, he added.

Some years later I was awarded the Order of the Burning Spear, Kenya's highest civilian award. Had Zach lived I believe he would have congratulated me and told me 'justice has prevailed'. I miss him to this day.

34

CHANNA MAKES US WHOLE

Channa Commanday was a native Californian who lived in Portland, Oregon. She was a highly qualified nurse who worked in emergency clinical settings and administration in the U.S. and abroad. In other words, she looked after the dying and wounded, the malnourished and traumatized in war zones and refugee camps. She also provided leadership in emergency medical health systems. A marriage in her twenties to a skilled luthier and bluegrass musician who was also a mental health counselor had ended in an amicable divorce. Now single again, she was making regular trips to Nairobi to teach emergency medicine courses at the hospital. I had taken her trauma course, and it was excellent. What little I knew of her prior to the U.S. Embassy bombing I'd gleaned from encounters at the synagogue or Charles Szlapak's Shabbat dinners and once or twice on social occasions.

Channa was competent, gutsy and undeniably sexy. She had worked in Somalia and the dark forests of the Congo. But most impressive, to my mind, was the time she had spent in refugee camps in Tanzania establishing some sort of order among the hundreds of thousands of Hutu who had streamed out of Rwanda in the aftermath of the genocide. She told me her one style statement while she was there was to paint her toenails red.

One night Lesley and I had dinner with Charles Szlapak and

Channa in the garden of the Fairview Hotel. It was Lesley's last visit to Kenya, and we were finding it difficult to be with each other. Channa's sunny presence was a welcome relief. I liked the way her eyes sparkled when she talked. And I liked the way she was both mischievous and serious all in the same conversation. I remember that I was careful not to look at her too often.

Gradually, Channa entered my life. In early July 1998 she accompanied me to Court Parfet's Muthaiga mansion where we chatted on the veranda as I wrote a funeral eulogy for my friend Dr Shani Gellert, who had just died. The divorce from Lesley was about to become final. It had been a long time in the coming. I had done a good job of bottling up the hurt and frustrations of those years when we had tried to live together and failed. Looking out over the Karura Forest in the lemony light of late afternoon, I found it easy to talk about it all. Channa had a way of gently opening the doors to my soul. Being with her made me sharply aware of how closed I had become, a prisoner to my own secrets. It was my first intimation of Channa's healing powers. I couldn't know it then, but over the coming years she sought out the fissures and cracks that had appeared in the family and made them good again. For the twenty years and more she has been my wife, Channa has been our peacemaker.

Channa had an office next to our consulting rooms. One day she called me in as I was walking past. 'Hey David, have you got a second? I've heard something – and I hope it's true because you deserve love in your life – that you have an African family.'

I was speechless. She'd caught me completely off guard. 'Yes, it's true. I have two sons with a Kenyan woman.'

'That's wonderful. Do you have photos of the kids?'

Again I was floored. I had never admitted the boys' existence to anyone at work let alone shown them photos. 'Yes, I do,' I said.

I happened to have my briefcase with me. I put it on her desk and brought out the snaps of Aaron and Jeremy that I always kept there.

Channa held them in her hands and stared at them for a long time. When she looked up she said, 'How can you raise these beautiful children in secret?' That encounter was something of a gamechanger in my life. I began to think hard about what I was doing.

On the Friday after the terrorist bombing I took Aaron with me to Naivasha for the weekend. At two years old, Jeremy was still too young to leave his mother. I also invited Channa. Late that night she arrived in the company of three young doctors from the States who were helping Channa teach emergency medicine. The four of them had been visiting the Arap Moi Children's Home in Nakuru, which was housed in a former synagogue. I thought that a Shabbat dinner was a good way for Channa to meet Aaron, who was not yet four. They hit it off.

Channa returned to Oregon via France where she visited her sister Karen. I followed, accompanying Moi on a state visit. We met up in Paris where, as part of Moi's delegation, I had been assigned a room at the Ritz. It wasn't much bigger than a cubbyhole, but we had a wonderful time together. A romance was born.

Things were beginning to look like they could become serious between us when Channa brought up the subject of the boys again. 'Pretty soon they're going to be big enough to ask questions. They'll want you to go to their sports days at school and 1000 other things that a father does with his sons. They deserve for you to be known as their father.'

I took her chiding to heart and sat down with each of my close friends in turn to tell them about Aaron and Jeremy and their mother Jackie. I persuaded Channa to come with me on some of these visits to give me support. It was extremely painful for her, but she did it anyway.

My four sons met one another for the first time when Jackie dropped off Aaron and Jeremy at the house one afternoon. They immediately recognized Nahum and Joshua, whose pictures hung on Jackie's walls. I told Nahum and Joshua that the younger boys would call me Daddy and that they should refer to them as their brothers. Nahum said he was used to that because Black kids in the U.S. often called one another brother. The four of them had a great time playing soccer together before Aaron and Jeremy went back to Jackie's. Even then I didn't tell them the truth.

At the end of December 1999 I flew back to the States to take Nahum and Josh for the holidays and join Channa at her friend's millennium wedding. I gave her a diamond ring the night I arrived. She asked which hand and finger she should put it on. I said it was for her to decide, but I recommended the left ring finger. But I didn't pop the question. The old commitment phobia was holding me back. I was hoping the ring would persuade her to come and live with me on some sort of trial basis. But Channa was too smart for that sort of malarkey. She didn't accept my lame explanation.

In April 2000 Channa put her foot down on another matter. We had taken Nahum and Josh skiing on Mt Bachelor in Oregon. One afternoon she said, 'I'm going to buy some things at the supermarket. When I come back, the boys will know they have two brothers.' And that's how I finally found the nerve to tell them.

'You remember those guys who called me Daddy?' I said, 'Well, I *am* their Daddy.'

Nahum was unfazed. 'You know, Daddy, I sort of expected it.' Then he added, 'It's cool. Now we have two brothers.'

Channa's friends and family were suspicious of me. I was ten years older than her, had four sons and lived far away in Africa. It took them a few months to realize I made her happy. Then they accepted me and welcomed my intentions. At the end of our skiing trip her friends held an engagement party for us in Portland. Many of Channa's dearest friends and even some of her old boyfriends attended, along with Nahum and Josh and her godchildren. A week later, we flew to Kenya to start the next big chapter of our lives. And Channa was still insisting that we were not really properly engaged.

That August I took her to Kiwayu, a luxurious retreat north of Lamu. The camp sat on a secluded beach looking over a small bay not far from the border with Somalia. It was hands down one of the most romantic getaway spots in East Africa. We were enjoying a glass of wine and watching the moon and stars when Channa announced, 'I have a present for you,' and produced a footballer's kneepad. This woman never ceased to surprise me. Channa saw I was flummoxed and laughed. 'I don't want you to hurt yourself when you get down on the sand and propose.' And so I kneeled and ask her to marry me. It was as easy as that.

When we got back to Nairobi, Channa immediately made the construction of a cottage for my mother her first priority. Rochelle, Allan and I had been apprehensive over how Mom would manage without our father. To our initial relief, she seemed to handle Dad's death well. Her antidote to melancholy was to keep busy. It had always been second nature for her. She was active in advancing Jewish education, her professional métier. She hosted meetings at the family house and kept up a busy event schedule.

Unfortunately, things began to change for her in the spring of 1995. It first became apparent in the midst of a family tragedy.

That May Rochelle's son Aron died in a bus crash in Turkey. He was on his way back to Maryland for his medical school graduation after spending the summer in Israel. He was twenty-six. The Sobels were devastated. Mom went at once to console them. During *shiva,* the prescribed seven days for mourning the dead, she suddenly decided that she had to go back to Chicago to attend a cousin's wedding. It was deeply inappropriate and against Jewish law for a grandmother in mourning to behave in this way. Yet Rochelle could not dissuade her, making the pain of Aron's loss that much sharper.

After that Mom began to deteriorate mentally. It was heartbreaking to watch her mind gradually fade away. By 1997 it was apparent that she could no longer live alone in Chicago. She still was driving but got lost ever more frequently, even on familiar streets. Rochelle and Allan finally took away the car keys and put the house up for sale.

Rochelle found her a hotel apartment in Rockville near her house. It was the same one where Lesley and our boys had stayed when they first arrived in Maryland. My sister arranged to have some of Mom's furniture from the old house installed in the apartment, hoping the familiarity of her own things would make her more comfortable and ease her disorientation. At about the same time, Lesley was becoming uneasy about Mabel living with her. She planned to return to work at the National Security Agency. She felt a Kenyan nanny living under her roof could threaten her security clearance. Besides Nahum and Josh were at school and didn't need a fulltime nanny. We reassigned Mabel to looking after Mom in her new apartment. This solved Lesley's issue, and Rochelle was relieved of a major daily concern as she dealt with the grief of Aron's untimely death.

Heartbeat: An American Cardiologist in Kenya

After a couple of years it was my turn to look after Mom for a while so I brought her and Mabel out to Kenya. My house was wholly unsuited for her needs. The bedrooms were upstairs and as her confusion had increased, she could easily have fallen down the stairs. It was Julius and Barbara Kyambi who hit on an answer – a separate cottage in a corner of the garden. She would be safe there, and I could arrange for around-the-clock care. It was an excellent idea. Once again I hired Heini Lustman as our architect. He worked with Channa's designs to create a beautiful home.

Mom loved the place. Although her dementia progressed, her paranoia abated. She reverted to the warm and loving person I'd always known. Her cottage became an after-work social centre for the staff. They would come by to sit with her and hold her hand as they watched television together. They made sure she got fresh air and exercise as well, taking her on walks around the neighbourhood. Mom became a familiar fixture. If she missed a day, the neighbours would call me, wondering where she was. Once a month Channa took her to the hairdresser to have her roots touched up. Even in the fog of dementia she refused to go grey.

Mom's presence was a reminder of my family obligations. Channa and I had been engaged for some while, but were too busy to sit down and think about a wedding. The question of when and where we got married was decided for us by her family. On a visit to California we invited them, as we always did, to come to Kenya. Channa's parents, Maurice and Ruth Commanday, were direct with their reply. The only thing that would bring them to Africa, they said, was our marriage.

We decided on 9 September 2001. It was a Sunday, well before the Jewish high holidays so that everyone would be able to come. We chose Kongoni Game Valley Lodge on Lake Naivasha as the venue. It was an old colonial stone bungalow set on a hillside overlooking the lake. Zebra and impala invariably came to graze on the lawn. It was one of our favourite spots and just a short drive from my shamba. We rented the entire lodge to accommodate all the guests.

After twenty-five years in Kenya, I had a lot of friends and associates, both among my patients, colleagues at the hospital and the many civil servants and politicians in President Moi's government. Channa was widely connected as well. We figured if we invited everyone we'd be looking at 600 guests or more. It was an unmanageable number. We pared the wedding invitations down to sixty family and friends. The guests of honour were President Moi and Charles Njonjo. Those of our close friends who could come included Julius and Barbara Kyambi, the Sheth family, Court Parfet, Colin and Margaret Forbes, Sally Kosgei, the former Eldoret mayor Joe Lesiew, Bethuel and Honorine Kiplagat and Charles Szlapak, his daughter Eliana, her husband Mark and their children, and several friends from abroad.

Not only Channa's parents but all her siblings came for the wedding. Besides Maurice and Ruth, there were Channa's sister Ramah and son Agam Neiman as well as her sister Karen and husband Jean-François Jouannaud, and her brother Frank. My clan skipped the ceremony with one exception. My cousin, Rena Kahn, made a point of attending all family gatherings. On this occasion, Rena's stalwart family loyalty may have saved her life. She lived in New York City and worked in lower Manhattan next door to the twin towers of the World Trade Center. Had Rena not decided to make the long journey to Kenya, the following Tuesday she almost certainly would have observed her custom of meeting a friend for coffee on a lower floor of the center's North Tower before starting work at the office. She would have been sitting at a table, chatting about nothing in particular, when American Airlines Flight 11, the Boeing 767 hijacked on its way from Boston to Los Angeles, slammed into the North Tower.

We had perfect sunny weather for the outdoor ceremony. Although we didn't plan it, our wedding outfits complemented each other perfectly. Channa looked stunning in a sleeveless gold-brocade top with a long ivory chiffon skirt. A soft blue scarf was draped over her head and shoulders. I wore an ivory suit with a blue shirt and gold silk tie.

The guests were assembled by 11 am. President Moi and his twelve-strong entourage all wore *kippot* (traditional Jewish skullcaps) that had been given to them by Channa. We seated them in the shade on big bales of straw covered in brightly coloured *kangas* (traditional African cloth). Moi greeted his fellow guests then sat down and held hands with Charles Njonjo. A devout Christian, he was a bit hesitant about the *kippah* (Hebrew, skullcap). But as soon as he saw Charles wearing one he put his on too. Reverend Zeev Amit, an Israeli friend who had been the rabbi of the Nairobi Hebrew Congregation some years earlier, had flown in from London to conduct the service.

A Jewish wedding ceremony is steeped in symbolism and history. According to one tradition, just as the Israelites led by Joshua passed seven times around Jericho, so too did my Jewish bride circle her groom seven times beneath the *chuppah*, the canopy of prayer shawls spread over the wedding party to symbolize God's presence. With each step the power of Channa's love loosened the figurative wall enclosing my heart until the barrier was breached, as was Jericho's, and we were joined as one. When I broke the glass underfoot, it reminded us at our moment of joy of a solemn moment in history, the destruction of the first and second temples.

After the ceremony there were three toasts. Charles Njonjo, referring to my domestic vicissitudes, spoke of the 'potholes' encountered along the way to this day. The quip bypassed Moi, who said, 'When we came here there were a lot of potholes also.' Raising a glass of water, he then proclaimed, 'Let's have a toast for Channa and David and all the people in your blessings and your prayers.'

Channa's father delivered a loving and funny speech which was capped with a remark addressed to Moi. 'Your Excellency, we agreed on the bride's dowry, but now I don't know what to do with all those cows.' Channa and her father were very close, and he was deeply moved to see his radiant daughter so enveloped in love. The memory of his warmth and playful sense of humour that day was soon to be tinged with grief. Maurice Commanday fell ill three months later. He died in July 2002. Channa and I are grateful that he passed on knowing that his daughter was in safe hands.

There was only one mix-up that day. Unaware that Moi and Njonjo had developed a taste for our ceremonial wine, when the presidential aides discovered we were serving fish poached in wine they insisted that all fish served at the head table be steamed in water instead. As we were toying with this tasteless dish, Njonjo turned to me, 'That bottle of kosher wine you had, where did you leave it?'

'Down at the chuppah,' I answered.

'Well! You see me? You see the president? Bring it up!' Two bottles of kosher wine were promptly placed on the table, and the two old friends happily helped themselves. We had seated Moi between Channa and Margaret Njonjo. He usually departed weddings early. Not this time. He sat through the meal, the dancing Maasai warriors and even the speeches. He and

Njonjo finished off a bottle of wine between them. By 4 pm the presidential security detail was growing nervous. It was well past time to leave, but they couldn't say that to the president. So I cautiously addressed Moi. 'Mzee, we really love having you here. If you can stay, please do. But if you have to go, we understand.'

Grinning through what clearly was a pleasurable afternoon buzz, the president pulled himself together, rose and announced it was time to depart. As the entourage made its grand exit, a light rain began to fall from the nearly cloudless sky – a sun shower. In African tradition it is the mark of a blessing.

Channa was visiting her mother in the States when my mother collapsed in her bathroom in May 2006. I woke up around 4 am to mournful African singing. I was confused and ran out of the house to see what was going on. The askari was running across the lawn ahead of me. We found Mabel sitting on the edge of the bath cradling Mom against her bosom. She was rocking gently as she sang a Swahili hymn, not softly but loudly as if she was in church and wanted God to hear her. I took her from Mabel and gently laid her out on the bed. I felt for her pulse and couldn't find it. Then I tried to resuscitate her with CPR unsuccessfully. After that I put her in the car and drove to the hospital. They wanted to do CPR again when I got there. I told them it was too late.

At first I was numb. I informed Allan and Rochelle and busied myself with the logistics of arranging the funeral and flying her body back to the States. She had left instructions she wanted to be buried beside Dad. We travelled to Chicago together. Mom in a casket in the hold and me up front. It all seemed very unreal.

I got a pad and pen out of my briefcase and tried to write

a eulogy. That's when the grief began to hit. Putting her life on paper brought home what a tremendous influence she had been on me. She was the one who made me memorize so much of what we studied. Dad laid out the program and Mom was the one who made it happen. Most of all, she provided her three children with a warm, safe home filled with happiness and love.

Delivering the eulogy was painful. The longer I spoke, the more emotional and tearful I became. In my mind I was seeing Mom, the family matriarch, telling me to finish my homework if I wanted to go out and play ball with Allan. Then suddenly she was elderly again and the boys playing ball in the garden were my sons as she looked on. The four of them liked being around her. Nahum and Aaron called her Bubby. Josh and Jeremy preferred GrandSarah. They loved her a lot.

35

UNUSUAL BAR MITZVAHS

Bar mitzvah means 'Son of Commandment' and is a rite of passage for every Jewish boy who has turned thirteen. The ceremony marks the day when he assumes the responsibilities of a man. Bar mitzvah is bestowed on the boy himself. He becomes the Son of Commandment. It is one of the most significant moments in a Jewish male's lifetime.

In the summer of 2002 it was time for Nahum's bar mitzvah. I wanted to make this important day as special as I could for my firstborn son. Properly preparing a boy for his bar mitzvah takes time. Rochelle suggested I contact Paul Blank, a colleague of hers at the Jewish day school where she taught. I called Paul and offered him a trip to Kenya if he would bring my sons with him for the purpose of readying Nahum for his big day. Paul agreed and arrived in early July with both Nahum and Josh. He had until late August to impart what Nahum needed to learn. As it turned out, he did an excellent job of it.

Others of us pitched in to help. Rochelle and Nahum worked together on his speech. She warned him that preparing for his coming-of-age ceremony would be hard work. Nahum replied, 'Well, at least I'm not a Maasai,' referring to the Maasai tradition of circumcising boys when they reached puberty. Channa used photos to create visually arresting invitations. As the years rolled on she did this for all my sons. Vaizman Aharoni lent a hand as a tutor to Nahum and a guide to Paul in our community customs. I worked with Nahum on the *haftorah* - the reading from the prophets - which I taught him to sing in Hebrew in just the same way as I had been taught for my own bar mitzvah. We invited Lesley to join in the celebration but she angrily declined.

Nahum did an excellent job. He projected well and clearly. There was no stammering, which had been an issue when he was younger. This was his first really big personal success, and he developed tremendous self-confidence as a result. His three brothers spoke as well. Josh, eleven, and Aaron, seven, read from written notes. Jeremy was just four and didn't know what he wanted to say until he was standing in front of the congregation. He belted out, 'Congratulations on your bar mitzvah, Nahum, and Shabbat shalom to everyone!' He received enthusiastic applause, not least for his brevity at the end of a three-hour service. Channa gave a short speech to note that those who had come together to honour Nahum on his special day were of many ethnicities and religions. This inclusive global community would protect and support him from now on. She delivered a similar message to Nahum's three brothers at their bar mitzvahs.

A week later we took them for a visit to the Arap Moi Children's Home in Nakuru. Charles Njonjo, who had been a guest at the ceremony, paid to have the onetime synagogue's Star of David refurbished and reinstalled as a bar mitzvah present for Nahum. Nahum was very good with children and developed a great connection with the little ones who lived there. He donated a quarter of his bar mitzvah gift money to the orphanage. This became a family tradition. His three brothers did the same when the time came for their bar mitzvahs. Every summer Nahum and Josh spent a week or two working at the orphanage as part of a community commitment required of them by their school in the U.S. The matron of the orphanage, Justine Oduya, became a warm friend and attended all four bar mitzvahs.

Joshua's bar mitzvah took place 30 July 2004 to coincide with the 100th anniversary of the Jewish community in Nairobi. We flew out Paul Blank again, who by this stage was becoming part of the family. As with Nahum, Vaizman Aharoni and I helped Paul to tutor Josh. We chose a reading from Deuteronomy, *Va'etchanan*, the fifth book of the Torah. It began with Moses pleading to God to be allowed to enter the Holy Land after leading the Jews through the wilderness for forty years. God denies his request and instructs him to prepare Joshua for assuming the mantle of power from Moses. Josh did a stellar job in reading this and chapters from the Book of Isaiah in front of the 300 guests who had congregated at the synagogue. He concluded his speech by imploring the audience to keep the synagogue going for another 100 years so that he could get married there. As it turned out, Josh married Taylor in a ceremony shared by the family over Zoom as it was at the height of the COVID-19 pandemic.

According to Jewish law, a child takes on the religion of the mother not the father. There is a practical reason for this. We all know who our mothers are, but short of genetic testing which only recently become available, we have had to *believe* we know our father's identity. Thus the rules for converting to Judaism are important. In 2005 when Aaron was eleven and Jeremy eight, both boys made it clear they considered themselves Jews. They accompanied me every Friday night and Saturday morning to the synagogue for Shabbat and never ate pork or sea food. I discussed conversion with Orthodox rabbis in the U.S., Israel and South Africa. They all said Aaron and Jeremy would have to live in Israel for a full year. This wasn't a viable proposition.

I next looked into a Conservative conversion. I wanted to have the boys converted *now* so they could have bar mitzvahs, the next big Jewish milestone in their lives. The Conservative Jewish movement follows Jewish law but is more liberal, allowing for modernization according to the evolving situation of the Jewish people. Paul Blank found a Conservative rabbi in Maryland. Since the boys were not yet at the age of bar mitzvah, she was willing to assist in the conversion process. Rochelle wanted to make it a big family event with a celebration at the synagogue and at the Sobel's house. We set 5 April 2007 as the date. The Sobel children and grandchildren all came with their children plus their friends and my friends. Charlie Clements came. So did Alan Frankel, a friend from my early days in Nairobi.

According to Jewish law, the boys needed a ritual circumcision. This was my job. All that was necessary was to draw three drops of blood with a needle while saying a prayer. Aaron put up with it under protest. Jeremy screamed, but I got it done. I worked with Aaron on his speech while Channa assisted Jeremy.

At the appointed hour, we congregated at Etz Hayim Synagogue in Arlington, Virginia. Here a *bet din* - religious court - of three rabbis sat to examine Aaron and Jeremy. The boys did a beautiful job. They were asked simple questions to assess their knowledge of Judaism. Did they know the prayer over wine and bread? Of course, they did. Did they know any of the Hebrew songs from the synagogue? They sang *Lecha Dodi,* which is sung at the start of the Sabbath. It celebrates the imagery of the Shabbat queen being welcomed in.

Then they were brought to the *mikvah* (bath) for the ritual immersion performed during the conversion. My sons were concerned about this stage of the ceremony but were reassured when they learned they could wear bathing suits. I jumped in the water with them and shared their sensation of cleansing. In my case, it was the cleansing of the stress and worries over whether I'd ever be able to create a nuclear family with my beautiful wife, Channa, and my four Jewish boys. That time was now.

That evening, Rochelle threw a big party at her house. Each boy read his speech. Each boy thanked everyone who had encouraged and helped them on their conversion voyage, particularly their mother Jackie. After the speeches, Channa and I, Rochelle and many of the other members of the Potomac Jewish community rose to praise my sons and say how proud we were of them.

Aaron turned thirteen in October 2007. We began at once to prepare him for his bar mitzvah. We decided to hold it during the Christmas holidays to give Nahum and Josh and our American relatives a convenient date to join us. Aaron was excited that his elder brothers would be coming. He wanted his Uncle Sol, a notorious homebody, to come too. He asked Sol what it would take to entice him to Kenya. Sol didn't hesitate. 'A giraffe.' On the previous Passover, celebrated at the Sobels' house, Aaron had brought his uncle a huge carving of a giraffe. When he found the *afikomen*, the hidden matzo, and could ask for anything he wanted, Aaron said to Sol, 'I want *you* for my bar mitzvah.' So Sol came with Rochelle and other members of their extended family.

Channa organized the event. Vaizman Aharoni helped me prepare Aaron, showing him how to manage his *tefillin* – phylacteries – and to sing the Kiddush. I taught Aaron his *haftarah* from the Books of the Prophets. Rochelle helped him write his speech.

Jackie and her family turned out in force and were warmly welcomed to the synagogue. Nairobi's entire Jewish community was invited too as were our work colleagues and Aaron's school friends. It was standing room only. We invited Michael Ranneberger, the American ambassador, who said he'd be there, 'If Kenya isn't on fire.' This was because Kenya was holding general and presidential elections two days before Aaron's bar mitzvah.

After Aaron's speech, as the guests were showering him with candy, their pagers starting going off. From a distance came gunshots that foreshadowed violence throughout the country. Rioting had erupted in the streets of Nairobi triggered by the election results. It had been a hard-fought campaign pitting the incumbent, Mwai Kibaki, against Raila Odinga, who had become leader of the coalition Orange Democratic Movement. As of Friday night, Odinga had been leading by approximately one million votes. Then came a radical shift in the late returns. Kibaki caught up with Odinga and soared past him to victory. Convinced the counting had been rigged, Odinga supporters had hit the streets to vent their anger. Our guests Charles Njonjo, the Kenyan diplomat Bethuel Kiplagat, and Gen. Lazaro Sumbeiywo considered crossing the street to make a statement at the Voice of Kenya studios to calm the rioters. They decided against it as the violence was already too far gone for the crowds to react to appeals for calm.

The synagogue quickly emptied. Channa and I brought all eight of my American relatives and guests to our house. It was decided to evacuate them as soon as we could. Early Sunday morning, with at least fifteen people already dead in the escalating violence, heavy black smoke curled up from Nairobi's slums and the normally teeming streets were crowded now with soldiers and police. We succeeded in reaching the airport and put everyone on a flight home. Jackie gathered with her family and close friends. Channa and I took the four boys and my South African cousin Theo Schkolne to the shamba, following the example of the urban Kenyans who retreat to the farm in times of trouble.

The violence lasted two months. Politicians issued sharp-bladed pangas to young men in the countryside with orders to go on the attack. As many as 1400 Kenyans, mainly Kikuyus, Luos, and Kalenjins died. At the end of February, Kofi Annan, the former United Nations Secretary General, announced a deal he'd brokered between the warring sides. Mwai Kibaki was declared president. Raila Odinga was to serve as prime minister. It had been a frightening time for all of us.

Jeremy's bar mitzvah was in August 2010. It was memorable for another entirely unexpected crisis. The bar mitzvah itself went smoothly. By then we'd had a good deal of practice. Once more Vaizman Aharoni assisted me in preparing my boy. Though quite shy at that age, Jeremy performed very well, just as his three elder brothers had. Channa staged the program beautifully. My brother-in-law Sol also attended. Once most of the guests had left Kenya, Sol, Rochelle, their grandson Sammy, Theo Schkolne and the four boys all flew with Channa and me to Little Governors' Camp in the Maasai Mara. We arrived around lunchtime. That afternoon we went on a game run.

I was worn out by the time dinner was over and decided to make it an early night. Channa thought it was a good idea too. While I was in the shower, I heard her talking to the camp manager. I couldn't catch what he was saying, but he was clearly agitated. I joined them as soon as I could. Channa was being briefed by the manager about a serious emergency. A private camping site had been attacked by bandits. The party was a group of Kenyan farmers who were celebrating the sixtieth birthday of Johnny D'Olier, a neighbour from Naivasha. The men had burst out of the darkness brandishing AK-47s and shooting indiscriminately.

There were unconfirmed reports of gunshot injuries. That was about the only information the manager had to share with us. He said he was assembling a medical convoy to go to their aid. He wanted to know if Channa and I would be willing to help if there were indeed injuries.

Channa, the veteran trauma nurse, replied, 'We'd better go immediately. We can turn back if we hear there are no injuries. Time is of the essence in trauma.'

Medical supplies were loaded into a Range Rover and we set off. With us were the Governors' clinical officer and an armed askari. 'I must warn you,' the manager said, 'we don't know where these bandits are. They could be anywhere out there in the bush.' It took us an hour and a half lurching over a tortuous trail to reach the other camp. When we got there we found the camp in pitch darkness. The first rule of an emergency response is to secure the scene from further danger. This was impossible to do. We had no idea where the bandits were. They might have left or they might have been lurking nearby poised to attack again. There was a great deal of fear and confusion as people emerged from where they had been hiding.

A married couple, Pat and Sara Neylan, had sustained serious gunshot wounds. A bullet had shattered Pat's right femur. Sara had been hit in her buttocks and pelvis. Johnny D'Olier had been shielding his teenage daughter when gunfire came from the direction of where the Neylans were hiding. He ran to help them and was shot from behind in the pelvis and the back of his head. He had died instantly.

The Neylan's situation was grave. They had both lost a fair amount of blood. They were cold and clammy to the touch and going into shock. Channa got intravenous drips going on both of them to get their blood pressure up to near normal. While she was doing this, I radioed the Flying Doctors to arrange the Neylans' evacuation to a hospital. The nearest site for the plane to land was the grass airstrip at Kichwa Tembo, a large tourist camp across the river from Governors'. The Flying Doctors said they preferred the airstrip at the Mara Serena Safari Lodge because it was tarmac. Though a two-hour drive for us, it was a much safer place to land at night. The Flying Doctors asked that we summon all available motor vehicles from camps in the area so that they could line up along the strip with their lights on to guide in the aircraft.

Pat was loaded into someone's car. Sara was laid flat on a mattress in the back of a pickup. Channa sat with her while I sat in the front. We didn't have any strong pain medicine so Pat and Sara had to suffer even more on the long, bumpy ride. The plane landed at Mara Serena about twenty minutes after we got there. The Flying Doctors nurse Alex Gikandi quickly administered the appropriate medication to relieve their acute pain, and within minutes the plane was in the air headed for Nairobi with the Neylans safely aboard.

We got back to Little Governors' around 3 am. The manager asked if there was anything he could do for us. Channa said she'd love a cognac. He poured each of us a glass. We fell asleep as soon as we hit our beds, somewhat later than we'd planned. The next morning Rochelle said brightly, 'So how did everyone sleep? I haven't slept that much in years!' We then related the whole story to the Sobels, who had slept through it all. We told the boys nothing of the night's drama until much later. We went on a morning and an afternoon game drive that day and watched the splendour of a group of elephants crossing the plains on their way to the river to drink.

That same day, with the gang still on the loose, tracker dogs flown in from Ol Jogi Ranch in Laikipia took up the trail. A

Maasai who had guided the men was arrested. He told his interrogators that the gang were Kuria from across the border in Tanzania. The leader was a well-known criminal who was wanted for theft, carjacking and murder. Weeks later he was shot dead when robbing a petrol station in Mwanza, Tanzania. The other gang members were arrested in Tanzania and handed over to the Kenyan authorities but later escaped.

Barry Gaymer, the D'Oliers' neighbour and friend, flew Johnny's body to the morgue in Nairobi. Johnny's wife Ellie and the two children were flown back to Naivasha by a friend, Donno Dunn. Governors' Camp gave the rest of the party accommodation so that they could recover in safety. Pat and Sara spent almost a month in the hospital undergoing several operations. They then flew to South Africa for further operations which were successful. They called us about five years later. 'We're so happy to be alive. And it's all because of you two. We can't thank you enough.'

36

ON THE FRONTLINE OF THE WAR ON TERROR

It is not only tribalism that erodes national security in sub-Saharan Africa. Kenya borders the Horn of Africa and is on the frontline of the war on terror. Sadly it is a country that is far too often on the receiving end of attacks. On several occasions they have been on Israelis and Israeli properties. On the morning of 28 November 2002 I received a call from Yaakov Amitai, the Israeli ambassador to Kenya. There had been a two-pronged terrorist attack on Israeli targets in Mombasa. A trio of suicide bombers had attacked the Israeli-owned Paradise Hotel at Kikambala, twenty miles north of Mombasa. Almost simultaneously a charter plane of tourists returning to Tel Aviv was nearly shot out of the sky by surface-to-air missiles as the aircraft took off from Mombasa's Moi International Airport. 'I need you to assess the situation,' Amitai said.

This was the third bombing I had been involved with since coming to Kenya. It underscored the realization that this sort of thing was becoming a fact of life. The Islamic thrust into East Africa, which had retreated after the ban on slavery more than a century ago, had returned with a sinister Jihadi twist.

The first attack happened at the Norfolk Hotel on New Year's Eve in 1979. It was revenge for Kenya's assistance to Israel during the Entebbe raid to rescue the Air France hostages four years earlier. The Norfolk was a high-profile hotel with a colourful history dating back to before World War I. It was targeted because its owners, the Blocks, were a prominent Jewish family. A bomb was detonated in a bedroom above the dining room where guests were ushering in the New Year. Twenty people of several nationalities were killed in the blast, most of them instantly. Another eighty-seven were wounded with the majority coming to Nairobi Hospital.

I was working at the hospital that night, the only senior doctor there. Two junior casualty medical officers were on duty as well. The first patient to be triaged was a young Belgian boy with half his head blown away. There was nothing that could be done for him. When the surgeons arrived I moved to ICU. I stayed there through the night and into the next afternoon, stabilizing the casualties before they went into surgery and managing them when they came out of theatre. Given the severity of a lot of the injuries, it was miraculous that we had only two deaths. I later learned that almost all deaths from terrorist bombings occur immediately.

The Popular Front for the Liberation of Palestine were responsible for the attack although they never claimed it publicly. The bomber was a Moroccan with a Maltese passport named Qaddura Mohammed Abd Al-Hamid. He booked into a room the night before, requesting one over the dining room. He checked out and departed on a flight to Saudi Arabia on the day of the bombing. In due course he was hunted down and 'neutralized' in a forest in Europe.

The Kikambala attack happened only four years after the explosion at the American embassy. This time round it was on a smaller scale. Even so Channa and I knew that it would be a distressing scene. When the news broke, we steeled ourselves for a long few days of intense activity and swung into action. I caught a Kenya Airways flight to Mombasa as soon as I could. Channa, who was by now my fiancée, had already left on a separate flight to Mombasa. Her first responsibility would be to find and triage all of the victims at the city's three major hospitals.

My flight was full of Kenya-based Israelis already mobilizing in response to the emergency. One of the passengers was a bearded man who told me he was a specialist in handling human remains according to Jewish law and customs. He was going to make sure that every last bit of each body was collected and buried in Israel.

A group calling itself the Army of Palestine that was based in Lebanon claimed credit for the bombing. The attack had been timed to coincide with the fifty-fifth anniversary of the 1947 partition of Palestine which led to the creation of the state of Israel. That year 29 November also marked the start of Chanukah, the Jewish Festival of Lights. Muslim terrorists often chose Jewish holidays to strike Jewish targets. They did so to show their victims they have nothing to celebrate.

Israeli and American terrorism experts suspected the attack was the work of al-Qaeda, probably under the direction of Fazul Abdullah Mohammed, the man who had driven the lead vehicle in the 1998 bombing attack on the U.S. embassy in Nairobi. Mohammed had risen high in al-Qaeda's ranks since then. By 2002 he was on the FBI's most-wanted terrorists list with a $5 million reward on his head. He later became an important figure in al-Shabaab, a militant Islamist group based in Somalia that had links to al-Qaeda.

The Paradise Hotel attack at Kikambala began around 8 am. A group of tourists had just arrived from Israel on an Arkia

Airlines charter. Some were in the lobby where a group of Kenyan performers were welcoming them with songs and dances. Others had already checked in and were heading for their rooms. It was at this point that three men in a green Mitsubishi Pajero sport utility vehicle pulled up to the gate. They were visiting someone in the hotel, they said. The guard stepped away to confirm this was true, and one of the men jumped out of the car and ducked under the barrier. He ran into the lobby and detonated his suicide vest. The Pajero's driver then gunned the vehicle through the gate and crashed into the reception desk as he and the third attacker exploded their bombs.

Fifteen people were killed and eighty injured in the attack. Twelve of the dead were among the Kenyans who had been performing for the arriving tourists. Two of the three slain Israelis were brothers, Dvir and Noy Anter, aged fourteen and twelve. They had come to Kenya for a holiday with their parents Rami and Ora Anter and their younger sister Adva. Rami Anter worked in a rope-making plant in Ariel. It was their first family vacation together.

After checking in, the Anters went to their rooms. After freshening up Ora and the children headed back downstairs to order coffee. Then came the explosions. As Rami explained at his sons' funerals three days later, 'I threw open the window and saw Ora and Adva but not the boys. I went to find them. But I couldn't save them. I couldn't. Everything was burning. Things were exploding. I took Ora aside, away from the fire. I tried to do something so she wouldn't bleed and die with the children.'

The attack on the departing airliner, an Arkia Boeing 757, was almost simultaneous. The terrorists fired two shoulder-mounted surface-to-air missiles at the aircraft as it was taking off. They were positioned at Changamwe, just over a mile from Moi

International Airport. Thankfully they missed. The pilot saw the missiles streaking past his window. He considered making an emergency landing at Nairobi but decided to continue to Tel Aviv where he was escorted in by Israeli fighter jets.

Once in Mombasa I went straight to the Aga Khan Hospital where Channa had already triaged all the victims in the hospitals and briefed me on the injured. She'd accounted for everyone who had been brought to the city hospitals including Ora Anter, who was undergoing treatment in the Aga Khan ICU. Ora had not yet been informed of her sons' deaths. I examined her first and went on to speak to the other Israelis who had been wounded. We conversed mostly in Hebrew and also English with those who preferred it. The Voice of Israel had broadcast word that President Moi's personal physician was on the scene. They found this reassuring.

Ambassador Amitai, who had telephoned me from Kampala, arrived that evening and joined us at the Aga Khan Hospital. He displayed remarkable calm and empathy as he spoke at length with the distraught Rami Anter. President Moi also flew to Mombasa. 'Kenya is safe. Israelis should feel safe, and all other tourists should feel safe. We will protect them,' he said, standing outside of one of the hospitals.

Moi's assurances notwithstanding, the Israelis sent four C-130 Hercules planes – the same make and model that was used in the Entebbe raid - to evacuate all Israelis who wanted to cut short their barely begun holiday and return home. At least one plane was staffed and set up as a medical unit to provide specialized care to anyone who needed it. One Kenyan woman with a complicated leg injury was taken to Israel on this flight - along with the hospitalized Israelis - because she needed advanced burn treatment and plastic surgery.

Finally, in the small hours of the morning, Channa and I were able to go to a hotel for what remained of the night. In the bedroom we had one last casualty to deal with. That morning Channa had gone from the hospital directly to the airport without even a shilling on her. It seemed a lifetime ago. We were bone tired after eighteen hours on our feet dealing with one crisis after another. We couldn't wait to wash off the dirt and blood and fall asleep. Before leaving Nairobi I had run home to pack an overnight bag for both of us. It had taken less than two minutes to grab the essentials and throw them into a small duffel bag. As an afterthought, I grabbed my running kit too, in case there was time. In my mind I was already in Mombasa. Channa watched as I unpacked my toiletries and pyjamas and threw them onto the bed. Last but certainly not least, I held up her passport. I had had the foresight to bring it in case she needed to travel with the patients to Israel. She shook her head in disbelief. 'So Dr Silverstein. No hairbrush. No nightgown. No clean underwear. Nothing…How do you feel about sharing your toothbrush?'

Soon after our return to Nairobi, I received a phone call from Aryeh Glozer, an Israeli businessman. He was my patient and a personal friend. Aryeh was kind and generous, always willing to assist any Israeli or friend in need at the drop of a hat. I knew he was close to a number of Mossad agents. They often stayed with him on their visits to Kenya. He said he was calling on behalf of someone who wished to speak with me. This could only mean one of his Mossad friends.

We met and talked in my car, which I had parked not far from State House. The man was indeed a Mossad agent, and he had a problem. His team had collected the terrorists' missile launchers and other equipment that had been abandoned at the launch site. Now they wanted to take it all back to Israel for forensic evaluation. Unfortunately, the local police commander in Mombasa refused to release the items from his custody. Could I break this impasse?

Yes, I could. I called Abraham Kiptanui, the State House comptroller and requested an urgent meeting with President Moi. 'Sure,' Abraham replied. 'Come right away.' The meeting had been arranged through the president's personal secretary, Judy Maloba. I seated the Mossad agent in the anteroom to Moi's office then walked through to have a private word with the president. Moi asked me a few questions then summoned the Mossad agent.

'*My* police have the launcher?' he asked.

'Yes, Your Excellency,' said the agent.

'And they are *not letting you take it?*'

'Yes, sir. That's correct.'

'Leave it to me,' Moi said. 'It will be sorted out.'

As we were leaving, I heard the president call for Kiptanui to get the police commissioner on the telephone. The next day, the Mossad man rang to thank me for my help. There had been 'a dramatic personality change' in the Mombasa police commissioner. 'He even offered to help carry the launcher,' he said.

In the aftermath of the Kikambala incident Israeli Prime Minister Ariel Sharon issued a terse warning that the bombing would be avenged. 'Our long arm will get those who carried out the terror attacks. No one will be forgiven.' Sharon was as good as his word. It required seven years, but all three fugitives sought by the Israelis in connection with the attack were captured or killed. The mastermind of the Kikambala and Mombasa attacks, Fazul Abdullah Mohammed, was shot dead at a roadblock in Mogadishu on 7 June 2011. At the time of his death he was the head of al-Qaeda in Africa.

Thanks to my involvement in helping the Israelis, my personal safety now became a concern. By then I was also head of the Jewish community as well as the president's physician. Friends and acquaintances worried that the terrorists would single me out for kidnapping or murder because I was a high-profile Jew in Kenya. The first alarm bells sounded with reports of a car parked in the street where Channa and I lived. The people in the car were taking pictures of the house. It could have been nothing or it could have been something. Terrorists are always looking for soft targets. They aren't necessarily going to act at once, but they can collect and save the information for another day.

I mentioned it to Moi. He nodded his head as he listened. 'There is a concern,' he said and made a phone call.

For several months, until after Moi had stepped down from the presidency at the end of the year, I was assigned administration police as close protection. An armed policeman was in my Nairobi residence during the day and accompanied me in the car as I moved around the city.

Since then there has been a continuous spate of roadside bombs and shootings, conducted by the Somalia-based al Shabaab. They get little or no media coverage, but they succeed in terrorizing people and rendering northeastern Kenya near the Somali border unsafe to work and travel in. However there have been two infamous attacks by al-Shabaab that made international headlines. Both occurred in Nairobi. One was at the Westgate Mall, a popular shopping centre with restaurants and other leisure activities that attracted people with money to spend, especially on the weekends. The other was at the DusitD2, a five-star hotel nestled at the bottom of a dead end beside an office complex.

The Westgate incident lasted four days and was on a scale of horror reminiscent of the U.S. embassy bombing. The venue was probably chosen because it was Israeli owned and frequented by expatriates, especially Israelis. On Saturday, 21 September 2013, four masked gunmen, probably al-Shabaab, entered the mall and roamed through it shooting people at their leisure. They kept the security forces at bay for hours because they had taken hostages. There were conflicting reports about the number killed since part of the mall collapsed due to a fire that started during the siege, but at least seventy-one people died including the four attackers. Some 200 people were wounded in the mass shooting.

Channa and I were not involved in Westgate. We were in the Aberdare National Park staying at a lodge as the guests of Colin Church, a former Kenya Wildlife Service chairman, and his wife Nicole. Also with us were Charles Njonjo and his wife Margaret. We heard the terrible news while sitting on the veranda watching elephants and buffalos silently file out of the forest. The contrast between man's inhumanity and the animals drinking peacefully at the water hole remains in my mind to this day.

I was involved in the DusitD2 incident not as a doctor but as the rosh kehilla, the head of the Jewish community. This al-Shabaab attack by five or six gunmen took place on 15 January 2019 and resulted in twenty-two deaths and about thirty injured. Five of the attackers were also killed. Ostensibly the motive for the attack was opposition to Kenyan military involvement in Somalia and President Trump's recognition of Jerusalem as the capital of Israel.

Among the deceased was an American called Jason Spindler. He was an idealistic forty-year-old Jewish man who had a PhD in law and was a Peace Corps veteran. He was also a survivor of the 9/11 attack in New York. As the CEO of a consultancy and investment firm he had founded, Jason had just arrived in Kenya to assist young entrepreneurs with their start-ups. He was having a cup of coffee in the hotel's veranda restaurant when a bomb was detonated by a suicide bomber.

On the morning after his murder I was called on by his non-Jewish Kenyan friends to make sure that whatever rites were required by Jewish law would be performed before his body was repatriated to Texas. They gave me his parents' phone number, and I called them immediately. His father, Dr Joseph Spindler, was a highly respected rheumatologist. His mother Sarah was also a medical professional. They were devastated but managed to make sense when discussing plans for repatriating Jason's body to the States and the rituals to be performed in Kenya. They arrived in Nairobi two days later, and we hosted them for dinner. The next day I conducted a memorial service for Jason at the synagogue. My sermon addressed the passages in the Bible that were read by all Jews the world over on that particular Sabbath. I read aloud Exodus 17:14 which stated that God said to the Jewish nation, 'Thou shalt erase the memory of *Amalek* (the archetypal enemies of the Jews after the Exodus) from under heaven (the earth).' I proposed that this seemingly merciless commandment was appropriate for terrorists who lived to kill. They were beyond redemption.

37

ROSH KEHILLAH

Rosh kehillah is an ancient Hebrew title, literally meaning the head or leader of the Jewish community. The rosh kehillah, who can be a man or a woman, is elected and serves voluntarily, representing and providing leadership in religious affairs and all matters pertaining to the Jewish community. In Kenya the rosh kehillah is the person who speaks on behalf of the community in dealings with the Israeli Embassy and all arms of the Kenyan government.

The rosh kehillah or a representative speaks at public forums such as interfaith conferences, the UN Day of Remembrance of the Holocaust, other memorial occasions, charity events and celebrations. At the synagogue the rosh kehillah chairs a council that directs all Nairobi Hebrew Congregation activities including membership; social, educational and religious events; supervising the maintenance of buildings and cemeteries; and budget oversight. Our celebrations and services include Shabbat, Jewish holidays, bar and bat mitzvahs, sometimes weddings and, sadly, death rituals and burials.

I have the honour of being the longest serving rosh kehillah of the Kenyan Jewish community since Sir Charles Bowring, the Acting Governor of the British East African Protectorate, laid the synagogue foundation stone in 1912. I continue to this day as the rosh kehillah.

People who have not visited Kenya may imagine Nairobi as an African capital with not only the political and business powerbrokers and middle class but a large population of people living in low-income settlements struggling to make ends meet. This is not the full picture. Nairobi is a regional hub for finance, business and transport. The United Nations has its regional headquarters here as do many aid agencies, some of which cover more than twenty countries from Nairobi. The World Bank and the IMF are based here as are religious leaders of all faiths and denominations. All in all, there is a well-established international presence of highly skilled men and women from all over the world. Part of that group is our Jewish community, which fluctuates between 100 to 400 members at any given time.

During my tenure as the rosh kehillah I have made a point of referring often to the Holocaust in speeches. The 1994 genocide in Rwanda occurred in this part of Africa. As I write, a repeat of that event is being played out in northern Ethiopia where the Tigrayan people are being massacred and deliberately starved in the hundreds of thousands at the hands of the Ethiopian leadership. Rwanda and Ethiopia are both reminders that what happened to the Jews of Europe during World War II can all too easily be repeated as a final solution for an unpopular ethnic group while the world stands by and watches.

In November 2005 a UN General Assembly resolution designated 27 January as International Holocaust Remembrance Day. It commemorates the 1945 liberation by the Soviets of the Nazis' largest and most notorious death camp, Auschwitz-Birkenau. In 2020 Israel hosted a world gathering in Jerusalem to commemorate the event's seventy-fifth anniversary.

In 2008 then UN Secretary General Ban Ki-moon said at this sombre occasion, 'We must go beyond remembrance and make sure that new generations know this history. We must apply the lessons of the Holocaust to today's world. But we must also do our utmost so that all peoples may enjoy the protection and rights for which the United Nations stands.' This did not happen in Rwanda in 1994 nor in Ethiopia's Tigray in the civil war that started in 2020. Today we must be even more vigilant.

On numerous occasions I have been invited to speak on Holocaust Remembrance Day. Each time I delivered the same message - until 2010. That year Pope Benedict XVI elevated Pope Pius XII (Eugenio Pacelli) to the status of 'venerable', the last step before 'blessed' on the road to becoming a saint. I knew the story of Eugenio Pacelli and the Nazis before and during World War II. Appalled and angered, I decided to make my views on the matter forcefully known to the Remembrance Day gathering in Nairobi.

The event was held in a large auditorium in the UN grounds at Gigiri in Nairobi. The 200-strong audience included senior Kenyan government officials, the German and Israeli ambassadors as well as other members of the diplomatic corps, religious leaders, members of the Jewish community and a large number of Kenyan students, some of whom were from Catholic schools.

'The Holocaust – *Shoah, Churban* – is the most tragic period of the Jewish diaspora history, and indeed of modern mankind as a whole,' I began. 'The motto and cry of this commemoration day, and the message of its survivors is *al Tishkach* (We must never forget.) What must we never forget? That there was a Holocaust.'

I went on to chronicle the various genocides from biblical times to the present including the African genocides such as Rwanda in 1994 and the systematic killing of the Darfuri people in western Sudan that began in 2003. During World War II the leaders of the Allied countries, including President Roosevelt of the United States, were well aware of what was happening to the Jews but decided to withhold this information. They wanted to forestall an influx of Jewish refugees. Pope Pius XII remained silent too for fear of alienating Hitler. He used the excuse that it was difficult to confirm the details and the Vatican policy was that of neutrality.

I spoke of contemporary Holocaust deniers as well. They included the Iranian president at the time, Mahmoud Ahmadinejad, and Bishop Richard Williamson. Two years earlier the Catholic bishop had been convicted of Holocaust denial in a German court. He had stated that gas chambers had not existed in the concentration camps and no more than 300,000 Jews had died there.

I went on to express my outrage that the current head of the Catholic Church, Pope Benedict XVI, had beatified Pope Pius XII as the initial step toward sainthood.

When I sat down Jacob Keidar, the Israeli ambassador, leaned over to tell me that Archbishop Giovanni Tonucci, the apostolic nuncio to Kenya, was in the audience.

'Do you think I offended him?' I asked Jacob.

'Well he hasn't walked out. Yet.'

Two weeks later, Archbishop Tonucci sent an official letter of protest to Achim Steiner, then the director-general of the UN Office at Nairobi. Ambassador Keidar obtained a copy of the letter and read it to me over the phone. The gist of his complaint was that my speech was an inappropriate and unfair attack on Pope Benedict XVI. I strongly disagreed. Clearly a discussion between the two of us was in order. It was a Friday morning when I phoned Tonucci's office and was informed that the nuncio was about to catch a flight to Rome. Some twenty minutes later the nuncio's office called back to say he wasn't leaving until that night. He would like to meet me beforehand. Could I please email him a copy of my speech. This I did.

That afternoon at the nuncio's office I encountered some of Kenya's Catholic bishops, most of whom I knew as patients. They all greeted me with warm smiles and handshakes. I was then ushered into the nuncio's study, the inner sanctum. Tonucci came in a bit later, and we engaged in small talk over cups of tea. He then brought out the document and went over it paragraph by paragraph. He was not shocked by the allegation that the U.S. and Britain had abandoned the Jews and left them to their fate.

When he reached the section where I attacked Pope Pius XII, he said, 'I expected that and it is understandable. But why did you attack my pope in front of young students?'

I explained, '"Thou Shalt Never Forget" is the theme of Holocaust Remembrance Day. As children of the survivors, we have vivid memories of the trauma our parents and grandparents lived with for the rest of their lives. Their soulful eyes spoke to us far more than words or the tattooed numbers on their arms. The young students in the audience haven't studied the Holocaust at school so how can they remember something they don't know about? They must be taught so they will never forget. Certainly, it is not right that Pope Pius XII, who insisted on staying neutral when millions were being butchered, is being beatified by your pope sixty-five years later.'

Tonucci pointed out that the sainthood machinery grinds very slowly. I thought this a weak defence. By the time I left to attend the Shabbat service at the synagogue, we were no closer to mutual understanding. The Vatican has since opened its archives on this tragic period. Scholars will now be able to examine them from the nuanced perspective of professional historians.

I have been the rosh kehillah of Nairobi's Jewish community since 2017, previously from 2003 for four years and before that from 1989 for five years. During these years I have given many speeches and sermons, usually tied to the *parsha* of the week. That is, the section of the Torah that Jews all over the world read on a specific Sabbath according to a universal schedule. Many of my sermons deal with the universality of God. I feel very strongly about this. I view it as a lesson that Judaism could help teach the world. In my sermons for the High Holidays I rely extensively on the Books of Jeremiah and Jonah.

In the same spirit, I have played an active role in the ongoing integration of our African Jews into the community. Without any encouragement from the rest of us, many of them have been attending our synagogue for decades. They practice their chosen faith with great sincerity despite the obstacles they face.

The situation has troubled me deeply. I have devoted both time and money to making them feel welcome among us. I was surprised by the stiff resistance to my efforts, put up by some Israelis who were not religious, as well as the very few old timers from Kenya's colonial days. The older Kenyans' attitudes could be explained, if not forgiven, by a residual racial prejudice. However the local Israelis have no such excuse. Perhaps they are missing the influence of the moral conscience of Israeli public opinion that would persuade them otherwise.

Their attitude is all the more untenable for the fact that the majority of them are Sephardic Jews, descendants of those exiled during the Spanish Inquisition in 1492. They fled to the Ottoman Empire, which extended to North Africa and the Middle East. Some 500 years later with the onset of armed conflict at Israel's birth in 1948 they relocated again, this time to Israel. Here they encountered discrimination because of their darker skin colour.

Having endured such bigotry, I would have hoped they would be even more sensitive and try to assist the Africans in their present plight to learn more about Judaism and becoming Jewish.

We celebrated the centennial of our recently renovated synagogue in September 2012. I was asked to deliver a speech, which I wrote while on an Arctic cruise with Channa. The voyage had started on Norway's Spitsbergen Island at Longyearbyen. It is the northernmost settlement in the world. As we navigated the Svalbard Archipelago, from time to time we would go ashore aboard a Zodiac inflatable, accompanied by naturalists from the National Geographic Society.

On one of these excursions I noted a beautiful flower known as purple saxifrage. Pollinators such as bees and other insects are not always available at hyperborean latitudes. In that case, saxifrage plants self-pollinate and rely on the wind to waft their seeds into a protected niche of calciferous rock or perhaps the bones of a beached whale. The smallest advantage determines survival.

As I pondered my speech, I considered some parallels between the survival prospects of the purple saxifrage and the future of our small Jewish community. East Africa is known as the Cradle of Mankind because it is one of the sites where apelike creatures evolved over the millennia into *Homo sapiens*. For hominids to survive and flourish in this hostile environment was quite an accomplishment, if not a miracle. Likewise, for a small Jewish community founded in a remote region to persevere for more than a century is indeed a special achievement.

I compared the Darwinian forces that favour hardiness and adaptability in regions such as the Arctic to the tolerance of our Christian and Muslim Kenyan neighbours, who have respected our religion and culture and welcomed us as friends. I wrote about the importance of hard work and the strong leadership with which our community has been blessed. I then turned my focus to the Arctic and the polar bear, imperilled by global warming and dependent on visionary thinking to secure its future. The purple saxifrage is also endangered, for the same reasons as the polar bear.

Will such thinking be needed to ensure that the Nairobi Hebrew Congregation will survive in the longer term? The answer I believe is yes. I have agreed to serve as rosh kehillah once more for several reasons. Our community has been shrinking. We have not even been able to form a *minyan* (a quorum of ten male Jewish worshippers) for most of our services. Africans who attend were excluded from being counted because they had not undergone a formal conversion. I have taken on this obligation to ensure that what is correct and ethical will be done.

The Congregation should welcome unexpected gifts, such as embracing these African Jews. An inclusive policy would make our community attractive, not only to the Jews of Nairobi but to Jews from all parts of the world. We could also assist other African devotees who are keen for an orthodox conversion – as long as the rabbinate concurs with sincerity. An infusion of indigenous Kenyans into our membership, along with the participation of the next generation of youth, many of them products of conversions, will ensure our survival into the next centennial.

It was not only the survival of our community that I had in mind but also what was morally and ethically correct according to Jewish law. Contrary to popular opinion, thousands upon thousands of people have converted to Judaism over the last two thousand years despite periodic persecution by other religions such as Christianity in Europe or Islam in the Middle East.

Some time ago we received a visit from Shlomo Riskin, then chief rabbi of Efrat in Israel. Rabbi Riskin is a liberal thinker despite his strict adherence to *Halacha* (Jewish law). I was able to have several of our African followers converted to Judaism at a ceremony that the rabbi conducted in Uganda. Recently I received a letter from Rabbi David Stav, chairman of Tzohar, an Israeli organization of more than 800 religious Zionist Orthodox rabbis who want to bridge the gap between religious and secular Jews in Israel. Rabbi Stav confirmed in his letter that Rabbi Riskin's conversions, no matter where he performs them, are universally recognized by Tzohar.

Armed with Rabbi Stav's letter we are now including our African Jewish brothers in our *minyan* (quorom) and recognizing their children and grandchildren as Jewish.

38

MOI'S LAST DAYS

When Moi retired from politics in 2002, our travels together on state business came to an end, bringing a long and enjoyable chapter in my life to a close. There was a point when the international trips became routine. In late 2002 on a night flight returning to Kenya from Washington via London, I was in first class two rows from the president. I was dozing when I was awakened by the familiar voice of former U.S. President Bill Clinton. He and Moi were discussing opportunities for the Clinton Foundation and the Moi Foundation to work together following Moi's imminent retirement. I peeked out of a corner of my eyeshades to confirm it indeed was Clinton then rolled over and fell back to sleep once more. Presidents no longer excited me. I needed my sleep. I can't say I miss the official trips. Fun, enlightening and often exciting at first, over time they became physically exhausting as well as personally and professionally disruptive. It was a relief to finally remove them from my list of responsibilities.

When Moi was no longer president our relationship changed, especially as he entered his nineties. He and I became more informal and friendlier with each other. He regularly moved back and forth between Nairobi and his farm in Kabarak near Nakuru. As soon as he was back in the capital, I would be called to see him early the next morning. He was no longer rushed so there was time to talk, usually about his favourite topics - religion, domestic and international politics. As the years went by, he spent more and more time at his farm and I flew there at least every one to two weeks. There were more medical issues as he aged, mostly arthritis or problems with his teeth or his eyes.

When he was in Nairobi, Channa and I would regularly arrange dinners with Mzee and some of his closest friends. Each time I would change the venue. Initially the dinners were at our house, then we sometimes held them at the Serena Hotel, the Fairview or other restaurants. Latterly, our venue became Sally Kosgei's house. Charles and Margaret Njonjo were a must for these get togethers. The other regulars were Jerry and Muringo Kiereini and Sally Kosgei. We had other guests on occasion, such as Richard Leakey, the Israeli ambassador, and Abraham and Mary Kiptanui.

At the end of one of these meals Charles pushed back his chair and stood up. 'As the eldest of this group, I would like to make a speech.'

Moi pushed back his chair and stood up too. 'You are wrong. I am the eldest. You have forgotten I was driving cattle on foot over long distances in 1936.' He began talking about how we were all connected. He started with Margaret's mother, Mrs Bryson, who had taught him how to write. He recalled with sadness how she had drowned when the ship she was sailing on from Ireland to Kenya sank in the Atlantic Ocean. He praised Charles for marrying a wonderful woman who came from an exceptional family. Although he had known the Kiereinis for a very long time, he thanked Charles for bringing Jerry even closer to him. He also thanked Charles for recommending me to be his personal physician. He then turned to Sally and recalled meeting her as a 'small girl' studying at university. He concluded with a toast that our longstanding friendships would never end.

If I miss anything from my two decades as the president's personal physician, it was the small and unrequested privileges accorded me. Petty annoyances were quickly resolved. Our phones and electricity in town and at the farm always worked. When they didn't, the service was reconnected immediately. I never stood in bureaucratic queues. I was always taken care of by senior personnel. I didn't seek favours. They were accorded because of my connection to the president.

Requests to intervene on someone's behalf always made me uncomfortable, and I nearly always declined. There were occasional exceptions when I saw that a friend or colleague was being treated unjustly. In my opinion, this was not an abuse of power. There is one example that stands out in my memory. One of my medical colleagues was arrested for the alleged manslaughter of a politician's wife. She had died of a common complication from a difficult surgery that he had performed. He was remanded in jail under terrible conditions. I was outraged by this and spoke to Attorney General Amos Wako and President Moi. They agreed to help me transfer him immediately to Nairobi Hospital. I was able to keep him there for the next several days under the guise of medical management for a possible heart attack until his lawyer, Byron Georgiadis, got him released on bail. He was soon cleared of all charges. I believed that using my position to get justice was not an abuse of power.

Charles Njonjo was of a like mind. I once asked him what he missed most from his days in power. His answer surprised me. 'I don't miss the politics, *Kijana* (young man). I don't miss the power. The only thing I miss is the ability to pick up the phone and change people's lives, protect them from injustice and help them get what they deserve. I can't do that anymore.'

In 2017 I noticed with concern that Moi was having increasing difficulty in walking. I brought out Dr Hadi Manji, a Kenyan-born neurologist at the National Hospital for Neurology and Neurosurgery in London. He reviewed Moi's extensive medical history and conducted tests. Nothing explained his muscle weakness. I was not the only one who was concerned. On New Year's Eve that year I received a call from Moi's youngest son Gideon. He asked if we could meet. I assumed he meant after the holidays, but no, Gideon wanted to see me at once. He arrived at the farm the next morning in his helicopter. His father's physical deterioration, Gideon told me, had him deeply distressed. He said that he wanted everything possible done to arrive at a definitive diagnosis and treatment, no matter where in the world we needed to go to get it.

I explained to Gideon that pressing the case further might well be an exercise in futility, reminding him his father was in his nineties. He persisted and urged me to consider going outside of Kenya where more advanced medical technologies would be available. His first suggestion was Germany because we had had a very good experience in Essen with Moi's aortic aneurysm repair by Professor Christophe Broelsch. I agreed that Germany offered fine facilities and expert care but suggested we consider Israel, where his father could receive top-notch treatment and visit holy places. Mzee was always moved by his trips to Israel and had often mentioned how much he wanted to return for a religious visit. Gideon was excited and asked me to proceed with it at once. 'Israel is the land of miracles,' he said.

Dr Manji returned in mid-January and examined Moi once more, noting his significant decline in mobility in just a few months. We conferred and decided to focus on Moi's spine as the possible source of his spreading weakness, or perhaps the nerves that spread into the body from the spine or alternatively, their connections to muscle tissue. Our diagnostic tool would be an MRI. Late the next evening we conducted an extensive series of scans requiring several hours to complete. Moi stoically endured the torture of lying on the hard table for hours, and then thanked us all for our trouble. Our hopes for a definitive diagnosis, however, remained unrealized.

Then a personal crisis hit me. Rochelle's husband, Sol Sobel, was suffering from kidney cancer. He was far more than a brother-in-law to me and his illness touched me deeply. Sol had been a father figure for Nahum and Josh while they were in America and I was in Kenya. He was a precious friend whose warmth and wisdom made my visits to the Sobel family home a highlight of my trips to the States. In early February he went into a sudden and steep decline. I flew at once to Maryland. I reached Sol's bedside a few hours before he died, just in time to say goodbye. I feel his absence to this day.

Getting Moi to Israel was a nightmare. We selected one of the country's very few private hospitals and forwarded all of the president's medical records. I also recruited my well-connected friend Aryeh Glozer to help with arrangements. No luck. The hospital informed us that in their view there was nothing more to be done for Moi than what we had already done. Taking a patient for whom they could do nothing further, they said, made no sense and would only hurt their reputation. Fortunately, Aryeh and I both knew a senior doctor at Tel Aviv's Ichilov Medical Center. It is Israel's third largest hospital and one of its finest, capable of performing the latest and most sophisticated nerve conduction studies. But first we had to get Moi there.

We determined that transporting him the roughly 3000

miles from Nairobi to Tel Aviv by private jet was our best choice. It certainly wasn't the easiest. The comptroller's office neglected to send Shino Aviation, our air charter service, the required advance payment, jeopardizing the whole trip. Only Gideon's personal intervention with the government bureaucracy saved the operation.

I asked Channa to come with us. She is an experienced nurse practitioner, familiar with medical evacuations and very good at logistics. She was very fond of Moi as he was of her, especially having experienced her nursing skills when he underwent the abdominal aortic aneurysm surgery in Germany. Her expertise would be critical at several junctures of the expedition.

Departure was scheduled for early morning in the hope of avoiding press attention, particularly as Moi would be in a wheelchair. Unfortunately, several social media sites covertly covered the departure, which was complicated by equipment problems. The apparatus meant to hoist Moi aboard was incompatible with the aircraft. The nursing team and security detail had to carry him up the stairs and into the plane. Similar difficulties awaited us in Tel Aviv, but with the assistance of Jon Chessoni, the acting Kenyan ambassador and son of my late friend Chief Justice Zach Chesoni, we got Moi out of the airport and to his hotel near the medical center. The accommodation – the best available – was modest by presidential norms, but Mzee was exhausted from the trip and happy for a bed. He fell asleep almost at once.

The next day the medical center admitted Moi into one of its very few single rooms while Hadi Manji, Gideon Moi and I met with the heads of the center's departments of neurology, orthopedic surgery and rehabilitation. An extensive set of advanced diagnostic tests was then performed. The results, once again, were inconclusive. There was nothing more to do except a muscle biopsy, the results of which would not be known for several weeks.

It was about this moment that the internet lit up with stories that Moi was dead or dying accompanied by photos taken at the airport as we struggled to get the president aboard the aircraft. Newspapers were taking an interest in the story. It threatened to go viral unless we interceded. John Lokorio, the State House comptroller, asked Lee Njiru, Moi's longtime head of the presidential press unit, to dispel the rumours. Lee assured his old contacts Moi was well. They backed off.

Even though the biopsy was a relatively simple procedure, it became an administrative conundrum. My morning began at 6.45 am in the hospital shop where I encountered the president's butler, Paul Kirui, buying fruit juice for Mzee's room. When I asked Paul where he was at that moment, he replied Mzee was on the Minus One floor, one level below us.

'Why is he *there*?' I asked.

'He's there for an autopsy.'

Panic gripped me. It couldn't be that all the rumours were true and I was the misinformed one!

'Yes, you arranged it,' Paul said.

My heart returned to my chest. 'I said that I'd arranged for a *biopsy*.'

'Oh, yes, that's the word.' He smiled politely. 'Sorry for my English.'

More confusion greeted me at Minus One where I encountered Mzee on a gurney. With him were Frederick Kibichii, his personal nurse, as well as his aide-de-camp and security personnel. It transpired that the Israeli nurses spoke very little English and were having trouble communicating with Moi.

As the head of the hospital had arranged the procedure informally the night before, Moi was not on the surgical schedule. The nurses did not know when or who was doing what. Nor had a surgical consent form been signed. To add to their confusion, they were not accustomed to patients such as this tall African man of undeniable stature who was surrounded by an entourage of men who, in contrast to the informality of Israelis, were all wearing tailored suits. Fortunately, my Hebrew was good enough to overcome these obstacles, and the procedure went ahead without more issues cropping up.

The comptroller's office back in State House again failed to send the required funds so Gideon's wife, Zahra, covered the hospital costs with her personal credit card. We thus were able to spring him free from the hospital. The first stop was the InterContinental Hotel in Tel Aviv where we made Moi comfortable in the presidential suite on the top floor. Its breathtaking view of the Mediterranean Sea immediately energized him. He became enthusiastic about everything Israeli, especially Israeli fresh fruit, dried figs, dates and breads. It is a cuisine not unlike that described in the Bible. He loved the sparkling 'Israeli water', which was really Perrier but written in Hebrew, and said he wanted to continue drinking it. When he returned home I made sure he did.

Early the next morning after breakfast we set out for Jerusalem on the spiritual leg of his journey. As we pointed out various sights to Mzee, his voice changed and became charged with energy. He was becoming progressively more animated. We all were excited as we entered the narrow, walled lanes of the Old City of Jerusalem. Just before we reached our first stop, a young Israeli security officer joined us as anticipated and warmly greeted Mzee. Our guide for the Church of the Holy Sepulchre in the Old City of Jerusalem was Shmulik Avyatar, once the chief of the Mossad in Kenya. He was now in his late seventies and pursuing a second career as a tour guide. Like Moi, Avyatar was deeply religious.

The stone complex dates from the 4th century. Avyatar explained that it encompasses two of Christianity's holiest places, Golgotha where Jesus was crucified and His tomb. We climbed a slight rise to the site of the crucifixion. Then we moved to a large slab where Jesus' body was prepared for being interred. Moi said to me in Swahili, 'Look Daktari! This is where Jesus was put after his death.' Everyone wanted to touch the stone, and Mzee was no exception. I took several photos of him with the rock slab, his face lit with excitement. There was a long line of tourists waiting to see Jesus' tomb. Moi was shown to the head of the queue by two Greek Orthodox clerics wearing long black vestments. I thought it would be too taxing for him to negotiate the tunnel into the crypt, but I was wrong. He lingered for a long time. When he emerged, he was beaming.

Our second stop was the Wailing Wall. It is one of the very few structures that has survived from the Romans' destruction of the second temple in 70 AD. Although Moi had visited the Wailing Wall before, it was still a special moment for him. By now he was tiring. After a brief visit with Israeli diplomats, we returned to Tel Aviv. The trip had inspired him and he radiated happiness. He retired without dinner. The next morning after I had conducted my usual, brief physical exam he announced that we had to make the pilgrimage again and bring along Charles Njonjo. At that Channa suggested we call Njonjo. She got through to Kenya and put him on the phone with Moi.

'Charles,' he bellowed into the mouthpiece, 'I'm in Israel, and I just saw where Jesus was buried. I touched the rock where

He was placed before burial. You must come here on our next trip so you can enjoy this also.'

It was Saturday, Shabbat. We were scheduled to leave early on Sunday. A diplomatic team from the Kenyan embassy came by in small groups for short visits with the president, and to have their pictures taken with him. Channa and I busied ourselves with organizing everything for the flight. Mzee's happiness was evident on the long flight home. As I identified points of interest along the way, he nodded and smiled with excitement as if he'd imbibed some elixir that had led him into a new realm of being.

After a few weeks I received a letter from our colleagues at the Ichilov Medical Center. Having analyzed the results of the biopsy report in minute detail, they said they were able to eliminate all of the ominous neurological diagnoses we had considered. It appeared, simply enough, that Moi's muscle loss was primarily due to disuse. He wasn't getting enough exercise because he had fallen into the habit of accepting the assistance of the strong men around him. This is not unusual among the elderly. It was great news. At least we could now act rather than wonder what to do. For this I give credit to Gideon for his insistence that we take Mzee overseas for medical treatment. From then on with aggressive physiotherapy and the special equipment we had brought back from Israel we were able to help him recondition.

In the year following this trip his spirits remained high and his condition continued to improve. But even as a man of science I'd think it hasty not to consider how in the Church of the Holy Sepulchre a man of such abiding faith might have experienced something wonderful and beyond explanation. Besides, Israel is the home of miracles.

Mzee continued to improve fairly dramatically with the help of a full-time physiotherapist. By this time I was flying in weekly to see him at Kabarak, occasionally bringing close friends such as Charles Njonjo and Sally Kosgei. He received visiting dignitaries too and always enjoyed his family coming to see him. The mornings were best for him. In the afternoons when he tired he became somewhat confused. I continued to enjoy our conversations with his great insights and memories just as we had been doing for more than forty years. His physical condition had improved, and he was able to walk between parallel bars.

In December 2018 I received a phone call from his nurse Fredrick that his oxygen saturation level had dropped lower than usual. Gideon decided to have him flown by helicopter from the farm to Nairobi. After landing at his home at Kabarnet Gardens, he was brought to the hospital. Moi looked very tired and was far less communicative although he recognized everybody. I had the radiographer waiting in his room and a chest X-ray was taken immediately. By this time his oxygen saturation had dropped to sixty-five percent on room air. The normal level at Nairobi altitude is ninety-three percent and above. The chest X-ray showed the entire left lung was opacified. A subsequent CT scan showed that there was a collection of fluid causing his lung to collapse. It also showed pneumonia in the left lung. The pressure was relieved with the insertion of a chest tube to drain the fluid, and his breathing improved. My next concern became the cause. We took repeated samples of fluid as well as doing a bronchoscopy to rule out the most likely cause, which was cancer. None of the procedures showed any evidence of cancer.

Over the next several months, Mzee developed diabetes and we admitted him to the hospital repeatedly. He remained very brave, stoic and trusting despite his discomfort. As I watched his gradual decline, I felt very conflicted. It was my policy to discuss advance directives for end-of-life care with patients while they were mentally competent to understand their prognosis and make their wishes known. This entailed asking whether they would want to be kept alive by being put on artificial ventilation or be subjected to tube feeding, dialysis or painful investigations. Or would they like to be treated in a hospice fashion to make sure they were comfortable and didn't suffer during their final journey.

To this day, I feel guilty that I did not have this conversation early. It was my responsibility to initiate a discussion, particularly as Mzee never brought it up himself. For some reason, probably because he was who he was and because of the cultural differences, the conversation never happened. Autonomy - the right of competent adults to make their own decisions - is one of the first principles of medical ethics. With the increasing fallibility of his cognitive functions, Moi reached the stage where decision-making passed on to the next of kin. I had the end-of-life conversation with Gideon on several occasions and later with all the sons. It was made clear to me that in their cultural setting the input of the daughters was not necessary. The family wanted everything done to keep Mzee alive. Gideon, who was closest to their father, acted as the family spokesperson and his proxy.

Mzee's oldest son Jonathan died from pancreatic cancer on 20 April 2019. After that Moi deteriorated rapidly. Jonathan had been much closer to his mother Lena and had a very difficult relationship with his father. Gideon had initially decided against telling Mzee about Jonathan's rapidly growing cancer. I suggested that he tell him as Jonathan's condition was incurable and his death would come soon. I offered to go with him. He agreed that we do this when he returned from a trip out of the country. Unfortunately this never happened. Jonathan developed clots in his legs that went to his lungs. He died just three weeks after the cancer diagnosis had been made.

The morning after his death it was on social media. We were sure Mzee would hear about it either from the television or from one of his friends. It was agreed I would fly to Kabarak to join the whole family there. As Gideon was still overseas it fell to Raymond, who was now the oldest son, to break the news to Mzee. While we waited for him to arrive, Mzee and I had tea together and chatted about this and that. Raymond and Mzee had their conversation in Kalenjin. The old man was understandably very shocked. He kept on asking again and again if it was really true that Jonathan was dead. The difficult relationship that had endured for the past thirty years must have made the loss of his eldest son even harder to bear. The funeral was attended by hundreds. Mzee was in no position to go, physically or emotionally. Charles Njonjo and I and other close friends sat with him and watched the service on television. He was then driven to the private burial.

After that Mzee's deterioration became more rapid. He developed recurrent infections and required blood transfusions. His lungs began accumulating fluid once more. Chest tubes had to be reinserted on several occasions. By October 2019 he was too sick to be at Kabarak. We kept him at his home in Kabarnet Gardens where I saw him daily. He was admitted to hospital for a week mid-October then re-admitted for another eighteen days the following week. He was at home for only three days before being admitted for the final time on 9 November. After that he stayed in hospital until he died on 4 February 2020.

During this time Charles Njonjo regularly came to be with his old friend. He was one of the few visitors Moi really looked forward to seeing. When Moi deteriorated and became less communicative, Charles would sit by his side silently holding his hand. On leaving he would say a short prayer, intoning it so softly only Moi could hear him.

To ensure we were optimizing treatment and not missing any possible diagnosis, Gideon asked that we bring in a chest specialist from San Francisco whom he knew from Kenyan contacts. He came in November and reviewed the entire situation. He had a few technical suggestions but was in agreement with the treatment Moi was receiving.

Gideon was spending most of his days and some of his nights in the hospital, obsessing about what new technology might improve Mzee's physical condition and mental alertness. In his great effort to save his father, he researched all possible treatments including stem-cell therapy. Although I did not think this would change the inevitable decline, I discussed this with Mzee's London neurologist, Dr Manji. He too didn't see any medical benefit in the treatment. Gideon was introduced to Dr Hussayn Salem, a London-based molecular biologist with a special interest in gene and cell therapy. His team included two professors from Europe. They agreed to fly out, but there was going to be a delay. Immediately before their expected arrival, Mzee had a cardiac arrest.

I was called at 9.30 pm on 21 November. The ICU team had started resuscitation measures including CPR (cardiopulmonary resuscitation). I jumped into the car with my driver James Muiruri and made it to the hospital in record time, calling an anaesthetist to assist as we drove. Resuscitation was ongoing when I entered the room. Gideon, the aide-de-camp and the two security staff were standing with their arms around each other in prayer.

It took about thirty minutes to resuscitate Mzee and stabilize him sufficiently to move him to the ICU. He never regained complete consciousness. At this stage he required a tracheostomy and regular kidney dialysis. There were moments when he was lucid and communicated, but they were brief. He would sit in a chair and watch inspirational videos of Christian evangelists such as Billy Graham, who was a personal friend of his.

When Mzee seemed to be stable, Gideon called Dr Salem and asked whether his team could come. They arrived on 18 January 2020. They called their procedure regenerative therapy. It entailed removing blood, centrifuging it, and mixing it with beads of gold-quartz particles to activate various proteins to promote cell regeneration. I didn't think it would do any harm although I was sceptical it would do any good. Mzee didn't get better, but he didn't get worse either. Then on 3 February he suddenly deteriorated, undoubtedly due to an infection that spread into his blood (septicaemia). That night he was rushed to the ICU. He was in septic shock. He passed away the next morning.

President Moi's exact age was not at all clear. His official birth date was 2 September 1924. However, from talking to his contemporaries, his students when he was a teacher, his family and those who knew him as a young man, my best estimate is that he was born between 1914 and 1918. He was well over 100 years old when he died.

When I look back at his final eight months of life from my own cultural perspective, I wish his final journey could have been shorter and more comfortable. It hurt me to see him in distress. But there were some positive aspects. His presidential duties had left little time to be with his family. That family relationships were not stellar was no secret. During Mzee's prolonged deterioration the family seemed to pull together. This new closeness was evident at the funeral at Kabarak when Raymond handed over Mzee's ivory rungu to Gideon. Raymond was the head of the family, but Gideon had assumed his father's political mantle.

When Moi died, I was devastated by the loss of a close friend and someone I had looked up to as a patriarch for forty years. He had advised me wisely when I sought his counsel. I invariably heeded what he had to say. He never drew me into his political and business affairs. Nor did he assume to interfere in my medical practice. There was not a single occasion when he sought a second opinion about his health unless I had already suggested it. I think I can fairly say our relationship was on a footing of mutual respect. He was a devout Christian but also well versed in Judaism. We spent many hours discussing the Bible and had the habit of counselling each other by quoting biblical passages. I was honoured when Moi's sons asked me to deliver a eulogy at their father's funeral in Kabarak.* I said all this and much more when I addressed the gathered mourners. Daniel arap Moi provided a solid presence in my daily life. I ended the eulogy by putting on my prayer cap and reciting the Jewish memorial prayer for the departed, *El Maleh Rachamim*, in Hebrew and then in English. I miss him still.

A video of the eulogy can be found using the link below: http://tinyurl.com/moi-glimpse

39

ANOTHER MYSTERIOUS DISEASE

In December 2019 a mysterious disease in Wuhan, China was brought to the world's attention. It became known as COVID-19, a coronavirus that had the year of its identification attached to its name. Medical colleagues looked at each other and said, 'This is like nothing we've ever seen before.' We didn't know what caused it or how to treat it, least of all how to prevent patients from dying. At first the only source of reliable information I could find was in the *New York Times* and on CNN. It was a few months before COVID-19 was recognized as a pandemic. From the outset my instinct told me this unexplained virus would become an existential threat to the entire world.

My practice had brought me face to face with other deadly viruses – HIV/AIDS and Marburg. As frightening as they were, protocols existed for their treatment. Not so with COVID-19. Since the turn of the 21st century, there has been a rapid evolution of previously unknown respiratory syndromes, many of them related to mutations that allow the virus to jump species and attack humans. These emerging diseases presented as isolated cases in patients who had been travelling outside Kenya. We had the ability to make the diagnosis and send specimens to specialized viral laboratories in Nairobi and overseas. The first epidemic was SARS (severe acute respiratory syndrome) with an initial outbreak in China in 2002. It was a relatively rare disease that petered out seven months later. More than a decade later Chinese scientists managed to trace the origin of the virus to cave-dwelling horseshoe bats in Yunnan Province. It had jumped to humans via Asian palm civets. There was a fatality rate of eleven percent among the 8,469 cases recorded. Luckily for us it never reached Kenya.

Next came H1N1 from a subgroup of influenza A, the same virus group that caused the Spanish flu pandemic a century earlier. It was a reassortment of bird, swine and human flu viruses with a Eurasian pig flu virus added to the mix. Hence its better-known name - swine flu. The first two cases were discovered in the U.S. in 2009. From there it spread to 208 countries. The risk of serious illness was no greater than with normal flu. Nevertheless, the pandemic may have caused as many as 284,000 deaths by some estimates. We definitely saw several cases of swine flu at the hospital. Our diagnoses were confirmed in specialized viral laboratories in Nairobi and overseas. That – and supportive care - was about the most we could do for these cases as only the old-generation antivirals were available. Although the patients looked very ill initially, for the most part they did well.

By now these viruses were appearing more frequently and seemed to be more virulent. The coronavirus MERS (Middle East respiratory syndrome) emerged in 2012 from the Arabian Peninsula. The first case was detected in Jeddah. By January 2021 only 2500 cases had been diagnosed. The mortality rate was thirty-five percent. It is thought MERS originally came from bats, but humans caught it from contact with camels or from each other. Many Kenyan businessmen travelled to the

Middle East, especially to Dubai and Abu Dhabi. And many businessmen from the Middle East came regularly to Kenya. I treated only two cases. One survived.

What was triggering these outbreaks? Was it changes in the environment or the fact we had become a global village where diseases spread rapidly around the world? Perhaps it was germ warfare brewed up in a laboratory. Or simply scientific advances in isolating and characterizing the viruses' DNA and RNA, the polymeric molecule essential to coding and decoding genes. I had no idea. Neither did the rest of the medical community.

The first case of COVID-19 was confirmed in Kenya on 12 March 2020, nearly three months after the original Wuhan cases, and a day after the World Health Organization announced that this public health emergency of international concern was now recognized to be a pandemic. Kenya's patient zero had been in the U.S. and travelled back to Nairobi via London. I heard about it on the news and felt a visceral excitement mixed with apprehension. We had no idea when the tidal wave would hit us or how we would be able to cope.

Kenya was woefully short of chest specialists, hospital physicians and emergency care nurses. Only twelve percent of health facilities had the standard items needed to prevent infections. These included basics such as gloves, infectious-waste storage and disinfectant. In the entire country there were only 537 intensive-care beds and 256 ventilators. Nearly all of these were in the cities and towns. Seventy percent of Kenyans lived in rural areas and were looked after by community health volunteers and nurses who provided immunization and other primary healthcare services. What would happen to these people when they fell sick?

I thought it would be like COVID-19's 21st century predecessors. Before it disappeared people would die. But not on our patch. We live in a tropical climate and arguably have a robust immune system due to exposure to a wide variety of pathogens. On top of that, three out of four Kenyans are under the age of thirty. With any luck Kenyans might escape relatively unharmed. Meanwhile I had to make some personal decisions. I was fired up for the new challenge but well aware of the danger if I took on COVID-19 patients. The literature that was appearing in the West and China indicated a marked increase in morbidity and mortality in the elderly. I dithered until Channa made the decision for me. 'You're seventy-five. There's no way you're going to get involved.'

At about the same time a notice was circulated at Nairobi Hospital that all outpatient clinics situated on the premises would be closed with immediate effect. Elective surgeries were to be cancelled and elective admissions were to be discouraged. It was two weeks after the first COVID-19 case. I closed my office to all but emergencies and headed to the Naivasha farm with Channa, leaving my much younger colleague Dr Christopher Kahuho in charge. We stayed there for seven weeks, far longer than the brief interlude I had anticipated.

I knew I couldn't stay sane unless I established a routine. I arose with the dawn to go for a five-kilometre jog. Along the way I'd stop to look at the giraffe and herds of impala and eland and take photos. It was fun. I'd never allowed myself the time to do it before. There had been unusually heavy rains and the lake had risen far beyond its riparian line. The acacia trees closest to the shoreline were standing in water. So was our workers' camp and the pump house for the irrigation system. Channa's carefully tended farm – the coops for 300 chickens, the organic vegetable garden and the fodder fields – soon were all submerged.

There was another change to the landscape too. Many of the workers from the neighbouring flower farms had been laid off.

Now unemployed, they had taken to fishing from the shoreline. It was the only way they could sustain themselves and their families. They were a security risk, but on the other hand I was impressed by their entrepreneurial ingenuity. After breakfast I'd call those of my patients who had requested consultations. I was treating many with COVID-19 and giving others advice about prevention. This was before vaccines were available. People were washing their hands manically and taking more showers than necessary.

Late morning I'd scan the web for the latest posts about COVID-19. Most of the opinions were based on anecdotal data and impressions. The pandemic had been on the map for only a brief period, but already new scientific studies were appearing almost daily. Often they contradicted the previous studies. It was too early to be able to apply the scientific gold standard of large numbers of patients being treated with either a medication or a placebo and neither doctor nor patient knowing which until the study ended. Besides, such was the lethal potential of COVID-19 it would have been unethical not to treat someone who had been diagnosed as positive for the virus.

I began taking after-lunch naps then birdwatching from the comfort of our veranda. I had a clear view of a pair of hadada ibis building a nest in a croton tree very close to the house. They were stocky grey-and-brown birds with a noisy call. The nest, constructed with sticks bound together with grass, was suitably sturdy for this raucous pair. Soon after it was done the female laid eggs, and they took turns sitting on them. One morning four little bald heads popped over the edge of the nest hungrily opening and shutting their beaks. The mother and father took turns feeding the chicks, heralding their arrival with a screeching *ha-dee-da*. They often fed the smallest ones first, presumably to ensure they fared well. We were experiencing torrential rains at night, and each time I woke up expecting to find the nest dashed to the ground and the chicks lying next to it dead. By this time I was attached to the little family, and it was a relief to see the parents had managed to keep their chicks safe and warm through each of the storms.

One day the bravest and strongest of the chicks launched itself into the unknown and came to a shaky landing on the ground. It took a few unsteady steps and flew for a short distance. Then it slowly came back to the base of the tree and climbed up the trunk with much flapping of its wings, grabbing the bark with its beak when it lost its balance. In due course all of the fledglings did the same. With each take-off the nest became more dilapidated until one morning we found its remains strewn on the ground. There was no sign of the ibis family. For the next two days they returned one or two at a time and perched on a branch as if to salute us and give us a proper goodbye.

It was time for me to go too. By now it was very clear we were in the midst of a pandemic. As much as I had enjoyed the slow pace of Naivasha life, I was missing the hands-on aspect of being a practicing doctor. At the beginning of June 2020 Channa and I packed up and returned to Nairobi.

When the second wave of COVID-19 began in October 2020, we were receiving so many extremely ill people they were backed up in the emergency room waiting to be admitted. As they lay there gasping for breath, we had to tell them there was no room in the hospital. Ringing round other hospitals in the city, we learned their emergency rooms were overflowing too. So the patients stayed there on gurneys, struggling to suck air into their lungs. Taking care of them under these conditions was extremely challenging. One of us would stay in the ER for long periods of time juggling from one patient to the other trying to readjust their masks and oxygen-flow rates. Many patients would have fared better on a non-invasive ventilator. They were invaluable, but we had precious few. The PPE (personal protective equipment) had to be changed between each patient on every visit. Occasionally a bed freed up on the ward either by a discharge or death. We managed to brief the families too as they were not allowed in to see their loved ones. We relegated them to the waiting rooms or advised them to wait outside where they were less likely to be infected.

The hero in my practice was Dr Kelvin Muthamia who spent days and nights in casualty. His courage and determination to save as many patients as he could kept him going. Thankfully, he never contracted COVID-19 despite the constant exposure. There were many heroes employed by the hospital including younger doctors, nurses, technicians and cleaners under the supervision of Dr Ruben Okioma, the hospital's Deputy Director of Medical Services, who was in charge of the ICU and all COVID-19 patients.

Very often the patients who were brought in by worried relatives protested they weren't feeling that bad and wanted to go home. They'd been sick for a week or so with flu-like symptoms, they said, but it wasn't that serious. In truth many of them were critically ill. COVID-19 was proving to be a stealthy virus of a type we hadn't seen before. COVID-19 pneumonia was causing silent hypoxia, an insidious type of oxygen deprivation that was hard to detect. Pneumonia is an infection that fills the lungs with fluid or pus. Normally people have chest pain and breathing problems. This wasn't necessarily the case with COVID-19 pneumonia. Patients were unaware their oxygen levels were falling. In Nairobi, which is at an altitude of 1,795 meters, oxygen saturation should be ninety-three percent or higher. Patients who were admitted with oxygen readings as low as sixty-eight percent were still chatting on their phones when we hooked them up to monitors. We soon became adept at recognizing the syndrome. Many patients had gone untreated for days, perhaps weeks, when they arrived. Distressingly often they were in critical condition. In those early days when we were still figuring out the best treatment, one third of the patients admitted to the ICU died. Nearly all of the patients who were admitted to the wards with less severe symptoms recovered.

The chronic lack of beds wasn't solved until a COVID-19 facility across the street was built and opened in November 2021. The UN had suggested collaboration with our hospital to construct a 135-bed annex exclusively for COVID-19 cases, many of which would be UN personnel evacuated to Kenya from other African countries. By then we had a much better idea of what we were dealing with and how to treat it. Out of more than 3000 patients treated, more than ninety percent of them survived.

Timely treatment was one of the most important factors in recovery. There were publications documenting the benefit first of dexamethasone in sick patients with low oxygen levels and subsequently of an intravenous antiviral drug called remdesivir. Dexamethasone had been in medical use since 1958 and was readily available and cheap. Remdesivir was very expensive and not available in Kenya until August 2020. Most of my colleagues and I were convinced that it did make a difference if given early enough to our sick patients. And as it turned out, remdesivir was indeed the most effective antiviral.

One evening I got a call from my colleague Chris Kahuho to tell me a heart patient I had admitted two days earlier had tested positive for COVID-19. The first thing the next morning I got tested. Kelvin Muthamia, a young doctor who accompanied me on my rounds, brought me the result. I knew immediately from his face I was positive. I called Channa and told her she needed to get tested as soon as possible. She was positive too. We were fortunate. Neither one of us had a fever nor did our oxygen concentration drop below ninety-two percent. We slept in separate bedrooms for the first time in our marriage. Channa would sneak into my room during the night to make sure I was still breathing. We had a daily ritual of giving each other intravenous drips of remdesivir. By the end of the first week we were feeling markedly better. After a period of quarantine, I started doing half days at my clinic.

As long as they were able to talk, I called my patients every day, sometimes several times. They were very appreciative, knowing I was there for them any time day or night. I was the doctor who made the decisions for the team, but because of my age I was barred from going into the COVID-19 wards or COVID-19 ICU. It was frustrating and made me feel impotent. I knew how much a bedside visit reassured patients that we were doing everything possible to heal them. I could not begin to imagine the loneliness of dying without family or friends around.

As the months wore on and this unpredictable virus mutated into new strains, it was continually taking us by surprise. Most people got better. Some didn't. Someone who seemed to be rapidly deteriorating would pull through while another on her way to recovery would suddenly die. Usually this was caused by what was known as a cytokine storm. Cytokine molecules are part of the body's immune response to infection. If they are suddenly released in large quantities they can cause so much inflammation in the body that there is multisystem organ failure. More than once a patient and I had chatted on the phone in a relaxed way only to be informed a few hours later she had suffered cardiac arrest and all attempts at resuscitation had been abandoned. I felt a terrible sadness when this happened.

During that year I was involved with the treatment of nearly ninety COVID-19 cases with variants ranging from Alpha to Delta and Omicron. Tragically we lost close to a quarter of them. Some were colleagues and close friends. Others I got to know after they had been admitted. There were business magnates whose unlimited funds made no difference in their ultimately unsuccessful fight. There were those who had been brought on emergency medical evacuation on a trip of last resort. They came from all over Africa and as far afield as Afghanistan. Most of them had been sick for some time and were exceptionally ill. When I had to give a family sad news, they invariably thanked me for the close relationship I had developed with them and the deceased family member. In fact, they ended up comforting me more than I comforted them. They all said that irrespective of where they might have been in the world, they could not have received better treatment. I was humbled by how gracious they were in their time of sorrow.

There were happy stories too. A former government minister and his wife, both in their eighties, miraculously survived against all odds. A fifty-seven-year-old missionary from the U.S. was evacuated to Nairobi from Uganda. He was on a ventilator for four months with a very low level of brain function before we finally managed to get him flown home. Eleven months after being admitted he was able to talk again and take his first tentative steps walking. When you see things like this, you begin to think miracles do happen.

At the time of writing there have been 615 million cases of COVID-19 and 6.45 million deaths worldwide. Kenya has recorded over 338,000 cases and 5,675 deaths making the mortality rate 1.7 percent compared to a global mortality rate of one percent. Unlike the West less than seven percent of our population is fully vaccinated.

40

THE NEXT GREAT PANDEMIC

The past decade has seen huge improvements in Kenyans' prospects for a healthy life, but our battles against illness are far from over. Despite the best efforts of the medical world, the incidence of infectious diseases in Africa remains high. Antibiotics, antifungals and antivirals underpin the successful treatment of many infectious and other diseases, but overuse and inappropriate use has resulted in widespread resistance to many of the first-line drugs we have traditionally relied on. We have been forced to use second- and even third-line drugs which are less effective. Too often they cause life-threatening side effects such as kidney failure and damage to the nervous system.

It is devastating for a doctor when a patient succumbs to a curable disease for wont of a drug to combat the germ that is raging through her body. Sadly it occurs regularly. The first time it happened to me was many years back. Mary was a twenty-year-old English woman on safari in Kenya with her mother. She was admitted to the Accident and Emergency Department extremely dehydrated with severe upper abdominal pain and vomiting.

My initial diagnosis was gastritis, an inflammation of the lining of the stomach and possibly the duodenum. However Mary's blood tests pointed toward pancreatitis. They showed elevated amylase and lipase, the enzymes produced primarily in the pancreas to break down or digest starches and fats. Normally pancreatic enzymes enter the gut through a tube called the pancreatic duct, but when severe inflammation in the pancreas occurs the enzymes leak into the blood stream and surrounding tissues, digesting the tissues around the pancreas rather than digesting starches and fats in the duodenum. This condition can be fatal with a mortality rate of five to ten percent depending on the severity. About seventy percent of pancreatitis cases are caused by gall stones. The other cases are usually caused by excessive alcohol consumption which, I presumed, was the case for Mary. An ultrasound and CT scan of the abdomen confirmed she had a markedly inflamed pancreas but no gall stones. I treated her with intravenous fluids and she stabilized.

On her third night in the hospital Mary's oxygen level and blood pressure dropped. Alarmed by her mysterious rapid deterioration, I transferred her to the ICU. Pancreatic damage can cause massive fluid leaks into the abdomen. I began pushing IV fluids into her at a faster rate. Following the now outdated guideline used at that time for treating severe pancreatitis, I started her on the broad-spectrum antibiotic cefotaxime after taking blood cultures. This was intended to prevent a bacterial infection developing in and around the inflamed pancreas. Instead the antibiotic killed many of the protective germs. This allowed the dangerous, drug-resistant bacteria that exist in all hospital ICUs to become the predominant microbes in her body. As they spread she developed repeated pneumonias. Then her kidneys, lungs and cardiovascular system began to fail. We intubated her and put her on a ventilator to ease her laboured breathing. As new infections emerged, we added many different antibiotics. Nothing seemed to work. There were many times when we thought we were going to lose her. Then to my delight

Mary started a slow but miraculous recovery. After three-and-a-half weeks she was stable enough to leave us and be flown back to her home outside London.

A week after her repatriation, her mother wrote to say she had been admitted to hospital again with pneumonia. The sputum culture showed extensively drug-resistant pseudomonas. Doctors had told her mother it was due to a 'very resistant African bug'. Mary had continued to deteriorate. She died in the hospital a month later of infection.

Microbes are organisms invisible to the naked eye that thrive in the air and water, the soil, in animals and in us. Some make us sick and others are important to our health. They can even protect us from harmful microbes. There are three types - viruses, fungi and bacteria. Viruses have no cells so strictly speaking they are not alive. They have genetic information called RNA or DNA within their shell. Viruses damage our cells when they inhabit them and multiply. They cause diseases as mild as the common cold and as severe as Ebola. They are not affected by antibiotics. Fungi can be single or multiple cells. Yeast, molds and mushrooms are all fungi. Most exist happily in our bodies but some can cause damage. Bacteria are single-cell and less than one percent are harmful. Of the three types of harmful microbes, only bacteria can be treated with antibiotics.

Worryingly, some of the treatment options for bacterial infections that once were reliable are no longer effective. When that happens, more potent antibiotics have to take their place. The more antibiotics are exposed to killer germs, the more the germs mutate to develop resistance. All too often the worst-case scenario occurs and our arsenal of available antibiotics becomes obsolete. These bacteria are referred to as being pan-resistant or XDR (extensively drug resistant).

High-grade resistance to microbes inevitably increases the death rate. A pneumonia with an XDR bacteria transforms a manageable infection into a wrecking ball on the loose in a patient's body. XDR tuberculosis is resistant to the two most powerful anti-TB drugs, isoniazid and rifampicin. Less than sixty percent of those treated for multidrug-resistant TB are cured. Twenty percent die. Thanks to a renewed focus on combating TB by the government and its partners, Kenya is no longer one of the top thirty countries with a high burden of multidrug-resistant TB, although the disease continues to be a severe problem.

A global study conducted in 2019 found that 7.7 million people had died from infections resistant to antibiotics. More than four million people had died from lung and blood infections. Another million had succumbed to peritoneal and abdominal infections. The highest mortality rates were in sub-Saharan Africa. Killer pathogens have become so commonplace over the past few decades that they have entered our everyday language. We call them superbugs. We are seeing increasing resistance in the last twenty-five years and longer to gram-negative organisms, initially in patients in the ICU but now even in community acquired infections. Even gram-positive infections such as Staphylococcus aureus have become resistant to our usual antibiotics. They are often referred to as MRSA (methicillin-resistant Staph. aureus). Although more prevalent in the west, we are seeing some in Kenya. Recently we have had an influx of MRSA infections coming to Nairobi Hospital from the regional wars where soldiers have been treated with multiple antibiotics prior to arrival. There is high resistance in Kenya to bacterial diarrheas such as Salmonella, Shigella dysentery and typhoid. In ICUs many patients die not from the condition for which they are being treated but from hospital-acquired infections.

Heartbeat: An American Cardiologist in Kenya

Bacteria were the first forms of life on the planet 3.5 billion years ago. Aggressive mutation is hardwired in their genomes, making them formidable opponents for antibiotics. They developed antibiotics to kill other bacteria competing with them for survival and other bacteria mutated so they could survive the onslaught of the antibiotics their competitors manufactured. Bacteria that are resistant to most clinically used antibiotics have been discovered in New Mexico's Lechuguilla Cave, an underground ecosystem that has been isolated from the earth's surface for more than four million years. Even though the bacteria had never been exposed to humans, they were resistant to multiple types of antibiotics that doctors currently use to treat patients. Similarly the genetic material of bacteria found in samples of permafrost up to 30,000 years old contains elements resistant to penicillin, tetracycline, aminoglycoside and glycopeptide antibiotics.

By comparison penicillin is less than the blink of an eye in microbial history. It was discovered in 1928 by the Scottish physician Alexander Fleming. Although it proved to be one of the most important medical breakthroughs of the century, it initially received little acclaim. Then in 1940 an Oxford University team led by Howard Florey and Ernst Chain succeeded in isolating a purified compound. Fleming used this to successfully treat a patient with streptococcal meningitis and published the clinical trial in *The Lancet*. Having been ignored for more than a decade, penicillin now began to get noticed. After failing to persuade the British government of its potential, the Oxford team travelled to Washington DC with samples of the mold smeared on their pockets. They feared that if they used glass vials they would break.

Under the auspices of the U.S. War Production Board, the Department of Agriculture worked feverishly to produce 2.3 million doses of penicillin in time for the invasion of Normandy.

A viscous concentrate of corn solubles known as corn steep liquor was used to culture the penicillin. A rotting cantaloupe melon provided the starter mold for the process. It can safely be said that it changed the face of warfare, saving the lives of thousands of servicemen who otherwise would have died of their wounds on the battlefield as happened in World War I. Fleming, Florey and Chain were awarded the Nobel Prize in Physiology or Medicine in 1945.

Antibiotics are used extensively in hospitals not only to treat disease but as a preventative measure to reduce the risk of infection during procedures and surgeries. Medical practice relies on antibiotics to ward off infection during organ transplants, joint replacements and cancer therapy as well as the long-term treatment of diabetes, asthma, rheumatoid arthritis and other chronic diseases. Eventually the drugs we have been using over the course of a century will no longer be useful to us. Whether this happens years from now or decades on depends on the actions we take today. Resistance rates can be slowed down or even reversed in some cases. There are several ways we in the world of public health can do this. Vaccination campaigns against disease reduces the demand for antibiotics as the caseload of patients with infections shrinks. Improved infection control in hospitals, clinics and dispensaries keeps pathogens at bay.

Correct diagnosis of infections is critical but not always achieved, particularly in rural clinics and dispensaries. Often there isn't the equipment to conduct microbiological bacterial culture and drug-sensitivity tests. Many clinicians rely on the old-fashioned way of reading the clinical signs and symptoms. They then turn to broad-spectrum antibiotics to hedge their bets which in turn breeds resistance. A recent study of fourteen public hospitals across Kenya showed that only half the patients received the appropriate antibiotic treatment. Furthermore, less than one percent of antibiotic prescriptions were written on the basis of lab results.

In Africa and many parts of Asia and Latin America it is shockingly easy for the public to get hold of antibiotics. People who buy them over the counter without a prescription are very likely to use them incorrectly, either purchasing the wrong antibiotic or failing to complete the course once they feel better. The more we use antibiotics in an unregulated way, the more microbes can develop resistance. This will not improve until legislation regulating the sale of prescription drugs is tightened and there is a reporting system to oversee all pharmacists.

Unfortunately the sale of drugs without a prescription is almost impossible to enforce. Added to this is the custom of buying only a partial course of antibiotics because it is cheaper. Or asking for an antibiotic to treat a common cold. Street hawkers calling out 'Capsule! Capsule!' are a common sight peddling their wares at bus stops. Antibiotics must be used as indicated and only when it is wise and necessary to do so. As doctors we fail when we give patients antibiotics just because they want or expect them even when they are unnecessary. In some cases prescribing the wrong antibiotic can make a patient's condition worse.

There is another battlefront to contend with too. In most of Africa there is no surveillance system for the use and subsequent resistance of antimicrobials in poultry and livestock. Animals and poultry raised for commercial food production are routinely dosed with antibiotics in their feed to enhance growth and control disease (primarily in the tetracycline, aminoglycoside and penicillin groups). Chicken farmers are the greatest culprits. Most of them buy antibiotics directly from feed dealers or the veterinary drug suppliers. Kenyan agrovets, the dealers in agricultural supplies, sell the antibiotics over the counter to pastoralists and dairy farmers who have home-diagnosed their animals or use them because they believe the antibiotics will promote growth. Legislation requires veterinary antibiotics to be dispensed on prescription through a vet, but it is too expensive to police.

The cycle of transmission leads quickly to humans. Chicken manure is absorbed into the soil. Rain leaches it into rivers that are used to irrigate vegetables. The antibiotics contaminate drinking water as well. And livestock manure is dug directly into the soil as fertilizer. An example of another dangerous transmission route starts in rubbish dumps such as the giant one we have at Dandora on the outskirts of Nairobi. Marabou storks scavenge improperly disposed of medical waste. This is then transmitted to other birds which in turn transmit it to domestic poultry destined for the dinner table.

In February 2012 I was appointed chair of the hospital's AMS (antimicrobial stewardship) committee. As antimicrobial stewards, it was our responsibility to ensure our patients received 'the right antibiotic at the right time in the right dosage by the right route (oral, intravenous or intramuscular) and for the right duration'. It was a challenge I undertook with serious intent for the next eight years. I am happy to say that the incidence of hospital-acquired infections as well as multidrug-resistant infections dropped significantly at our hospital during my tenure. Although no longer the chair, I am still an active member of the programme.

Using the research and data collection of our multidisciplinary team of doctors, nurses, pharmacists and microbiologists, we have been able to ascertain which microbes are the most resistant to antibiotics. We continually monitor to assess which drugs work against them and how resistance is building in our environment. Based on these findings we have established policies and guidelines for the use of antimicrobials and educated hospital staff about these protocols.

Some of our 'big gun' antibiotics are at risk of no longer being effective so we restrict their usage just as we do with the strongest narcotics. We do not allow them to be dispensed without a strong rationale. The guideline for the treatment of serious infections is to use a shotgun blast of antibiotics to keep the patient alive until an analysis of the culture comes back from the lab one to three days later. Once the bug is identified, we administer the specific antibiotic that can kill it without damaging the other bacteria.

In 2014 the Kenya government began to establish a national AMS program. I was appointed to the Ministry of Health's advisory committee. I used this position to leverage my stature in the medical community, among politicians, opinion leaders and through public lectures to highlight what the community needs and deserves in strict control of antimicrobial usage.

This proved to be useful when combating the irresponsible use of Canem-O. It was an oral brand of carbapenem, an important drug that is a last-line defense against multidrug-resistant pathogens. Canem-O was manufactured in India and was not approved for sale in either the U.S. or Europe. However there were no restrictions on its distribution in Africa. In 2016 it was being widely marketed and cheaply sold over the counter without prescription, particularly in Mombasa. It was popular with the general public for a range of minor ailments, even an infected toe.

When carbapenems fail, we are forced to use toxic and often expensive antibiotics that can damage the patient's kidneys and nervous system. In due course a superbug could become resistant to these toxic second- and third-line antibiotics as well. This scenario could manifest a pan-resistant bacteria resistant to all antibiotics, making the infection deadly. I discussed this injudicious and unethical use of our most powerful class of antibiotics with the AMS guru, John Bartlett from Johns Hopkins University. We agreed the situation was potentially catastrophic. I was determined to get the drug off the Kenyan market.

After failing to get a response to my letters to the Ministry of Health, I wrote directly to the head of the local distributor for Canem-O. This was met with silence. Clearly another line of approach had to be taken. I googled the company one Sunday afternoon while sitting on the veranda and spotted a corporate Achilles heel almost immediately. Imported cardiac medication accounted for a large percentage of the company's turnover. I began to write a second letter. I would hate to see the company's sales drop, I said, but a boycott of one of its most profitable lines of business by Kenya's cardiologists might be in order if the contents of my previous letter were not given serious consideration. Two days later I received a letter of commitment to withdrawing Canem-O. Within the week it was no longer available in Kenya. Now you have to be in our ICU with a life-threatening infection before carbapenem is considered. And it must be vetted by the AMS committee before a prescription can be written.

We must continue to prepare the groundwork to combat future pathogenic threats from an arsenal of ever-mutating microbes. But just when the pace needs to be accelerated, research on antibiotics has slowed down. It is extremely costly to develop new antibiotics, and there is the likelihood that bacterial resistance will occur before they can realize a profit. Some antibiotics never even reach the market because resistance has already developed by the time they get FDA approval. Pharmaceutical companies prefer to invest in drugs for chronic diseases that patients will use for a lifetime such as statins for coronary heart disease or new diabetic medication.

In 2020 the onset of the COVID-19 pandemic triggered another wave of overuse of antibiotics, even though they are useless against any virus. As a result hospitals are experiencing a resurgence of resistant bacteria as well as fungi and viruses. I do not believe the resolution to this problem will be the continued development of new antibiotics. It will require scientists to think outside the box. They will have to develop new vaccines - as they did with COVID-19 - or antibodies (as opposed to antibiotics), proteins that can be given to bind the killer bacteria or the substances they release. We must experiment with novel ways to give medications and fluids in the ICU to eliminate the tubes on which bacteria breed (intravenous cannulas, dialysis catheters and other prosthetic materials). Perhaps we can even dragoon microbes to fight other microbes on our behalf. We must develop rapid tests to determine the bacteria causing the infection and the appropriate antibiotic in the shortest period of time.

It is estimated that by the year 2050 antimicrobial resistant infections will cause ten million deaths annually! Compare that with the 6.6 million deaths from COVID-19 in the last three years. In a recent study on the Global Burden of Disease that reviewed 2019 data, bacterial infections ranked second only to cardiovascular disease and above cancer as the leading cause of death globally. Sub Saharan Africa had the highest rate of death from bacterial infections.

Everyone must do their part. Do not run to the pharmacist asking for an antibiotic for a common cold or cough. Do not pressure your doctor for an antibiotic when they question the need. Mild infections don't kill, but antibiotic-resistant organisms do.

We can't be complacent. All evidence points towards a future plagued with infections we may not be able to contain. Climate change will be causing mass migrations that will transport pathogens from one population to another. Likely they will mutate along the way. And as the global population increases, there will be more zoonotic diseases caused by the close proximity of people and livestock and the closer proximity of people and wildlife. We can never stay ahead of the mutation curve, but we cannot allow ourselves to fall too far behind. It is my belief that microbes are one of the greatest of all threats to the future of mankind.

41

CHARLES NJONJO SAYS HIS LAST SHALOM

Channa and I were shaken by Moi's death. It had left a gap in our lives. We were soon to lose someone else too. I had known Charles Njonjo for forty years, first as a patient and then a dear friend. He took an instant liking to Channa when I introduced them shortly after she and I had started dating. The friendship was cemented at our wedding. In his speech as father of the bride, Maurice Commanday commented that as he lived in America, he was delighted to see so many wonderful friends who would look out for his daughter in Africa. Charles immediately called out, 'Don't worry! I'll take care of her!' After that he always called her Ward. He took his self-appointed role seriously. From time to time, I would be pulled aside. 'Are you treating Ward properly? You have to take special care of her.' I dared not do otherwise.

At an early stage in our private practice our relationship changed from one of doctor and patient to friends. I had great respect for him and, I believe, it was reciprocated. He did me the signal honour of relaxing in my presence and being his true self. We shared the same sense of humour, enjoying banter that bordered on insult. There were afternoons sitting on the

Njonjos' long veranda we laughed so hard we were wiping the tears away. Money was a running joke between us. Charles teased me about my Jewishness. I told him the Kikuyus were worse. He was, in fact, unfailingly generous. When he came over for a meal, before leaving he would wander into the kitchen and take out 1000-shilling notes to give to whoever had been working that evening.

I saw Charles often in the hospital. Not always as a patient, but when he came to visit a friend. He would send for me and have me walk by his side along the corridors. He'd look around at the admiring hospital staff who had stepped aside to let us pass then give me a nod. 'Now they'll take extra care of my friend while he's here.' The hospital staff adored him and bent over backwards to please him. Charles was a beer connoisseur who liked to enjoy a sundowner at the bedside of his various sick friends. The staff were happy to turn a blind eye to the stock of beer in the mini-fridge in the patient's room.

Many years ago the politician Julius Kiano was admitted unconscious after a heart attack. We had resuscitated him successfully in the emergency room, but due to the long delay in transit he had suffered irreversible brain damage. His heart had started beating again, but I was concerned that a man of his age was unlikely to recover with any meaningful faculties. I told Charles what had happened, and he immediately came to visit his long-time friend. Kiano was lying motionless attached to several tubes. I had already warned Charles that he was unresponsive and to be prepared for the worst. Charles took some coins from his pocket and jingled them by Kiano's ear. As I had expected, there was no reaction. Charles turned to me. 'He's not going to make it, David. A Kikuyu always reacts to the sound of money.'

Throughout his nineties he retained his sharp mind and fitness. He came regularly to my office for check-ups, walking into the surgery and announcing to the room at large, 'Where is Kijana (the young man)?' I had always reassured Mzee that 100 would be a shoo-in, but at times I was concerned despite his unflagging enthusiasm for life. As he approached his century, the Njonjo family planned an unforgettable celebration. The last item on Charles' bucket list was to see a gorilla family in its natural habitat. The family flew on a chartered plane to Uganda then switched to a helicopter that ferried them to Bwindi National Park next to the volcanic Virunga Mountains. The next morning Charles was carried through dense undergrowth up the slopes of the park's ancient tropical forest in a sedan chair. His reward was a close encounter with a silverback male and his family. Charles spent a companionable hour sitting next to them while they went about their business of grooming, playing and eating. Five days after his return he celebrated his birthday in a sparkling marquis on the lawn of Muthaiga Club with 300 guests, many of whom had flown in from other continents. It was a beautiful event, and I was relieved that my promise he'd make it to 100 had been kept.

After that his health began to fail him. He got tired and was forgetful, but he still bantered with me and flashed his mischievous smile whenever I visited. There were many times when he had to be admitted to hospital. These sojourns became frequent enough that Margaret, Channa and I took the decision to create a mini intensive-care unit at home where he could be looked after by a team of round-the-clock nurses. At first I visited him every week, then it became twice a week. During his last days I went round to the house after or before work on an almost daily basis, depending on his condition. Margaret said his eyes lit up whenever the nurses announced Kijana was climbing the stairs to his bedroom.

That last year of his life he never left the house to socialize except to visit us a few times at our new home in Muthaiga and, on one memorable occasion, for a long weekend at our farm. It was December 2020, and the second wave of the COVID-19 pandemic was at its height. The previous six months had been difficult. Both Channa and I had worried about his state of health as we saw him retreat within himself. It had been touch and go as he grew ever more frail. Then unexpectedly Charles improved. 'Well Kijana, when are you inviting me to that shamba of yours?'

He was turning 101 in six weeks' time. For months the family had been planning another birthday party. Now with a great deal of the world locked down in some form or other, including Kenya, they had decided to cancel it. The Njonjos' five-day interlude on the shores of Lake Naivasha was as good as it was going to get. Channa, Margaret and I intended to make it not only good but excellent. We wanted Charles to enjoy the beauty of the Rift Valley and its wildlife one last time. It would be a memory that Margaret would be able to savour in years to come.

Channa and I were standing at the airstrip at Oserian, a neighbouring flower farm, as the Caravan light aircraft came to a halt. Charles was carried down the steps by the pilot and his son David, who was in the plane solely to ensure his father arrived safely. Two nurses accompanied Charles and Margaret to take care of him during his stay with us. It was a wonderful interlude. Channa prepared one delicious meal after another. We did several game drives. Stopping to watch the buffalo, giraffe and herds of impala reminded Charles of the many weekends he spent with Court Parfet at Solio Ranch. In the evening we drove to the top of the hill behind the house and toasted each other with a beer for Mzee Njonjo, gin and tonics for Margaret and Channa and a single malt whiskey for me as the shadows lengthened on the slopes of Mt Longonot and the Kinangop. After five days Channa and I and our dog Bosco joined them on the flight back to Nairobi.

It was 30 December 2021, a year later, when I was summoned urgently to the house. Charles had a low-grade fever and was struggling to breathe. Despite being on oxygen, his oxygen saturation had dropped precipitously. Listening to his chest confirmed he had severe pneumonia in both lungs. I put him on intravenous antibiotics and increased his oxygen supply to the maximum. The following morning, on New Year's Eve, I arrived at 7.45 am to review his progress. His breathing was shallow and rapid, and he was obviously very uncomfortable. He had become angry with the physiotherapist when he had tried to suction out secretions in his lungs by feeding a tube through his nose to the back of his throat.

I spent most of the day at his bedside, leaving briefly to make the rounds of my ICU patients and returning that evening. He was clearly worse. For the first time, I did not get a smile to acknowledge my presence. The end of the year had come on a Friday, the beginning of the Jewish Sabbath. Channa arrived with the braided challah bread that is eaten on Shabbat and the sacramental kosher wine that Charles and Moi had enjoyed drinking together. The nurses helped him to sit up in his reclining chair. I asked my old friend if he would like me to say the Shabbat prayers as I had done so often in the past. His eyes brightened for the first time that day. 'Yes,' he said very clearly, 'Bring my cap.' Margaret had his *kippah* at the ready and placed it on his head.

I poured a small amount of wine into a glass and gave it

to him. With trembling hand he slowly brought it to his lips, refusing any assistance. As he drank, we said, '*L'chaim*. To life.'

'*L'chaim!*' Charles responded and asked for another glass of wine.

After a third glass, I said a prayer over the challah as was our custom. 'Blessed art Thou king of the universe who brings forth bread from the earth.' I broke off a piece of challah and gave it to him. He tasted it and said it was delicious.

By now Charles was exhausted. Channa and I said goodnight to which he replied, 'Shabbat shalom.' They were the last words I heard him speak.

On the morning of New Year's Day I arrived early at the house. His pneumonia was progressing. I arranged for a family meeting with Margaret, their daughter Mary and her husband Carey Ngini, and their son David. We also managed to reach their elder daughter Nimu, who was in France with her husband Volker Bassan and children.

It was time to make the transition to comfort care. Charles' directives on his last days were already known to all of them. He did not want to be hospitalized. He did not want to suffer. Once his condition was irreversible, he wanted to be left to die peacefully. Everyone tearfully agreed that we must honour these directives. I changed the oxygen mask for oxygen nasal prongs and put him under mild sedation. Within an hour he no longer was struggling to breathe. He was much more comfortable, and the family could see his face clearly.

That night Margaret slept next to Charles as she always did. Theirs had been an extraordinary marriage, a coupling of two kindred spirits who loved each other deeply to the end. Another woman might have been overshadowed by Charles' strong personality, but Margaret kept her own identity. He supported her in whatever she did. To anyone who saw them together, it was immediately apparent she had her own opinions, which she articulated with a light touch. They were an indomitable couple. Margaret had written his speeches, planned his events, and tended to his every need as he aged. At dinners with friends there was always much laughter as Charles entertained them with funny stories of incidents from the past. Margaret would nod in confirmation of what he said or set him straight when he veered off the point. In short, she had quietly made sure that Charles was always the most he could be.

It had been an unexpected courtship. Margaret was the daughter of Irish missionaries and had been brought up in a remote area not far from Moi's childhood home. Moi used to come to their house during school holidays and help out by washing the dishes. In return Margaret's mother had helped him with his reading and writing. Moi had been deeply fond of her. At State House he kept her photo in his desk drawer.

Margaret was thirty when she met Charles. She was teaching French at Kenya High School. She also sang in the choir at All Saints' Cathedral. Charles regularly attended mass and sat in the front pew. The pair never spoke but could not help noticing each other. Charles was twenty years older than Margaret so perhaps she thought nothing of it. He was the chair of the Kenya High School board of governors as well. When Margaret was sent to the Sorbonne University in Paris for a linguistic sabbatical, he hosted a farewell dinner for her at the New Stanley Hotel. He wrote her letters in green ink for the year she was in France, addressing her as *Dear Miss Bryson*. The couple married soon after her return.

Now, fifty years later, Margaret was saying goodbye to the man she had spent her life with. She was not alone. Her son

David was in his room next door coming in and out. Her younger daughter Mary spent much of the night also sleeping next to her father. The older Nimu attended through FaceTime. Just before daybreak Charles Mugane Njonjo took his last breath. I was called to the house to declare him dead.

Naturally, Charles had left advance directives about his interment too. His family were well aware he wanted to be cremated, which is contrary to Kikuyu tradition. He had also talked about it to me and other friends as well as his lawyers. He had made it clear that his death should not be announced until after his cremation. He did not want his family to be pressured by the Kikuyu community to bury him.

That same morning John Lee, the funeral director and an old acquaintance, sent a hearse to transport Charles across town to the Hindu Crematorium in Kariokor. He was accompanied by the family and a small group of friends who had been informed of his death an hour earlier. There could not have been even thirty of us. Charles was laid on a pyre with a white sheet as his shroud. On his head was the blue-and-white *kippah* he had been wearing when Channa and I had last spoken with him. We filed past to pay our last respects, some saying a short prayer, others giving the man we loved one last message of farewell.

Carey Ngini was the master of ceremonies. He called upon Attorney General Paul Kihara Kariuki to say a Christian prayer. Muhoho Kenyatta, representing President Uhuru Kenyatta, described the close ties linking the Kenyatta and Njonjo families. David Njonjo said thanks for the love and wisdom he had received from his father and for the closeness they had enjoyed during the last year of his life. I sang the Kaddish, the Hebrew memorial prayer. I also spoke of Charles' final words, *Shabbat shalom,* the Sabbath of peace.

Channa and I, like many others there, were tearful. We were saddened by the loss of this wonderful man who had been a steadfast friend to us for so many years. A patriarch to many, a mentor to others, he had valued loyalty highly and returned it too. In the public arena he would be remembered as a shrewd politician, and in due course his career would be writ large in Kenyan history. What would not be mentioned was the fact that after decades of enjoying influence and power and overcoming political intrigue and setbacks, he had emerged a contented family man. And now my friend Charles had been sent to his final resting place to enjoy eternal peace.

42

LOOKING BACK ON IT ALL

To paraphrase Soren Kierkegaard, the Danish philosopher, we live life looking ahead and understand it looking back. The stories in this book tell the tale of my life. Or, if you will, they map out the experiences and choices that have shaped me into the person I am today.

My stories from childhood and med school are not unusual. I was protected as a boy and not encouraged to stray from the path trodden by my family. My grandparents' generation had experienced hardship and danger that took exceptional courage to survive. Grandfather Zedi Kahn as well as Mom and Dad lived with the shadow of East European pogroms and the Holocaust. It's hardly surprising they were thankful for the opportunity to prosper in the stable environment of Chicago's Jewish enclave of Lawndale. At the time they moved there, most of the past and present generations of my extended family were rabbis or teachers. We were proud of our Jewishness. Our moral compass was steered by readings in the Hebrew Bible. We mixed mainly with each other and socialized at weddings and bar mitzvahs and on religious holidays.

While we were growing up Rochelle, Allan and I basked in our parents' unconditional love and never questioned their credo that success was reached through hard work and study. Dad was my role model. My love for him was so strong at times it felt almost visceral. It was natural I would follow in his footsteps into the medical world and, in due course, set my sights on becoming a cardiologist.

My first steps away from the family hub were the Vietnam War, Israel and the Cook Islands. Those trips were the stirrings of a realization that I wanted to see and experience the world in a different and more intense way. I don't know if I believe in good luck and bad luck. It's more down to recognizing when a door is opening and then stepping through it. Luck or not, Kenya gave me that opportunity to enter a new world. I have been here for nearly fifty years and have never once regretted my choice to make it my home. From the time I set foot in Africa, most of the stories in this book venture towards the edges of my personal map. They recount extraordinary happenings with fascinating people.

When I arrived in Kenya, it was little more than a decade after independence from Britain. I sensed immediately the excitement of possibility. Kenya allowed me to fulfil my dream of working in a cardiac cath lab and later establishing a thriving practice with two exceptional cardiologists. First with Majid Warshow and later with my current partner, Charles Kariuki.

As a doctor, I have encountered lethal tropical illnesses such as Marburg haemorrhagic fever, better known as the Green Monkey disease. I have ventured to the frontiers of medical knowledge during global pandemics of AIDS and COVID-19. There has been the satisfaction of healing thousands of patients and discovering new protocols along the way. White coats and strange instruments and machines are intimidating. I have done my best to treat every patient with compassion and humour. A joke and lightness of touch helps to relax someone who is anxiously awaiting a prognosis.

People often ask me what it feels like to have death as a constant in my working life. A doctor becomes acquainted with aspects of his patients they may not show to even their family or friends. He sees them when they are vulnerable and at their most fearful and thus can get some measure of who they really are. Patients who were gravely ill have touched me profoundly with their humility and courage. I have felt great sadness when they haven't recovered despite the best efforts of our medical team. This holds particularly true for children and young adults whose lives were still ahead of them. Death is there for all of us. My team and I do our best each day. Given this knowledge I am able to sleep well and awake with enthusiasm again to practice medicine each day.

There is good and bad in every man. We all have personalities that are shaded and complex. Kenyan politicians are no different. As his private physician, I had privileged access to President Moi for forty years. During that time, the glue of our long and rewarding friendship was mutual kindness and respect. He was exceedingly loyal to me in all situations, as I was to him. He was godfather to my firstborn son Nahum and a guest of honour when Channa and I were married. I confided in him at times of personal crisis and valued his wise counsel. Some of Moi's colleagues questioned why he had chosen a Jew and not a Christian to be his doctor. He told them, 'The Jewish people have a special relationship with God. It's not our job to interfere with that.' The stories I have told about Daniel arap Moi are what happened between us or when I accompanied him on his travels as seen through my perspective. I certainly was not privy to the decisions and actions that took place in his public life except for what was reported in the media. The same held true for most of his domestic life.

Moi was not impulsive. He took the time to listen to different opinions on issues although he had little patience for outright dissent. Sometimes he would task a minister to send up a trial balloon. If it got knocked down he would publicly reject it. Once he had made up his mind there was no stopping him, such as the acceptance of multiparty democracy. You could not budge him or change his mind.

As president he was an authoritarian leader but a populist too with a sure grassroots touch. He drank tea with ordinary people and stopped by the side of the road to hand out money and give a short speech. He maintained contact with local leaders who briefed him on what people were feeling and thinking across the country. They were his political eyes and ears. He was exceedingly generous to thousands of these Kenyans. I am still approached by people of all ages and different backgrounds who tell me that had it not been for his generosity they would not have been educated.

As the attorney general, Charles Njonjo was a civil servant so he didn't get out and about. His information network largely consisted of urban professionals and businessmen. Charles placed great value on loyalty both in the giving and the receiving. He wouldn't tolerate infidelity either in marriage or politics. He made his thoughts very clear when it came to my poor track record for romantic entanglements. Even so he was always supportive when I ran from commitments to women. It was different when I introduced him to Channa. There was an instant connection. Even then he kept me on a tight leash, cautioning me not to stray. Channa and I had many wonderful times together with Charles and his wife Margaret. Some found him intimidating. We were lucky enough to know his gleeful, playful side.

Much changed in my life once I met Channa. Over the past

twenty-three years, she has shown me the face of enduring love and helped me to grow through the security of our togetherness. I am blessed with a deep love for my wife and for my four sons – Nahum, Joshua, Aaron and Jeremy. My distant relationship with Lesley meant that I became a holiday father to Nahum and Joshua while they were growing up. Aaron and Jeremy lived in Nairobi, and I was able to spend far more time with them. Yet I did not present them to the world like Simba in *The Lion King* because my relationship with their mother Jackie was secret. I was fiercely protective of all four boys. This was my excuse for my ambivalence in introducing the boys to each other. Channa, in her wisdom, led the way in uniting us as a family. I now understand that I had allowed my pride and guilt to be barriers, fearing what other people might think. For many years now, Channa and I have enjoyed the closeness of a tightknit family that relies on each other for support in the hard times and celebrates each one's rites of passage through bar mitzvahs and university degrees to marriage and, in Joshua's case, grandsons.

Despite the inherent challenges of learning difficulties and being mildly affected with tuberous sclerosis, Nahum, now thirty-three, shone in sports and maths and charmed everyone he met. He has a chef's diploma from the Culinary Institute of America but has never practiced as one. When dark days troubled him in his early twenties, Channa and I brought him over to Kenya. He stayed with us for nine months doing construction jobs. He returned to the States to start his own real estate business. Nahum is hardworking and hopeful, even while bad fortune and at times bumpy roads plague his adult life journey.

Josh, who is now thirty-one, graduated in psychology from Indiana University and promptly moved to Colorado to be a personal trainer while he decided what he really wanted to do.

He is now a software engineer working for Apple in Austin, Texas. Taylor, his wife, is a coder too, and back to work after a hiatus as a full-time mother. They have two sons, Benjamin, who was born in January 2021, and Max who arrived sixteen months later. We dote on both our grandchildren in keeping with the longstanding tradition of all grandparents.

Aaron is three years younger than Josh and the only one of the four brothers who is following in my footsteps. He is a resident in internal medicine at the Massachusetts General Hospital. My almost daily early morning calls to him on my way to the hospital are very special times for us and reminiscent of my relationship with my own father. We discuss the complicated cases we're treating and offer each other advice.

Jeremy, my youngest son, recently completed a master's degree in finance at Washington University in St. Louis, Missouri. Unfortunately for him, his time there coincided with the COVID-19 pandemic and almost all his classes were on Zoom. This deprived the students of the friendships and business contacts that give young graduates a head start on the career ladder. Despite this setback, Jeremy has landed a good position in finance at Moody's in New York.

Looking back at the map of my life from the vantage point of seventy-nine years, I feel proud of my professional accomplishments and commitment. The responsibility for my lengthy emotional development and its consequences is mine alone. We all chart our own course. We should be grateful for the mistakes we make and hardships we encounter as they help us learn and grow. Life is to be savoured and enjoyed along the way. Life is for living. I have well and truly lived mine, listening to my own heartbeat.

L'chaim! To Life!

EPILOGUE

COVID-19 caused immeasurable heartbreak and much loss. For me, it was also a time of gratitude. In early 2020 at the beginning of the COVID-19 pandemic, our hospital closed the private doctors' offices for a time. This gave Channa and I the opportunity to spend many weeks at the farm, something I wouldn't have done otherwise. Relieved of all my usual responsibilities, I was able to work consistently on the book. While I wrote, conducted telemedicine over the phone and read up on the emerging disease of COVID-19, Channa was dealing with the disastrous rise in the level of the lake which was flooding our farm. Oblivious to our labours, a pair of nesting hadada ibis hatched and fed their chicks in a tree a few yards from where I sat on the veranda. The young ones flew their nest just before we returned to Nairobi. Now, two years later as I write this, the parents are back and building a new nest, continuing the precious circle of life.

My life has embraced all that circle contains. In the words of Margaret Njonjo, 'To life, to love, to laughter and to loss'.

ACKNOWLEDGEMENTS

More than thirty years ago my dear friends Charlie and Ruth Cronheim mentioned that my interesting life merited a book. Ruth gave the idea momentum by volunteering to help me retrieve my memories. She interviewed me whenever we got together in the States, during her trips to Kenya and when we sailed on their yacht in the Mediterranean until she became too busy with family and life to go on. I didn't give it any more thought until I was rummaging in the back of a cupboard and came across an old yellow plastic bag containing twenty-five tapes. My seventieth birthday was around the corner. It was time to get serious about the memoir.

The arduous task of transcribing everything was tackled first by Pearl Dastur. Later the ever cheerful Jerusha Muita and Agnes Mwangi took over the task, bantering with each other about which female character they would play in the imagined movie version as sheet after sheet of paper stacked up beside them.

Armed with these reams, I hired an experienced writer who took my dry and lengthy dictations and began to mould them into the semblance of a book with narrative detail and flow. Although greatly appreciated, this talented writer has asked to remain a ghost. We next asked our anthropologist friend Geoffrey Clarfield, who writes humorous and informed magazine articles, if he would continue the project. As a North American Jew who had lived in Kenya for many years, I knew he would enter my world with an insider's perspective. Geoffrey gave the Kenya sections of the manuscript heft and depth and brought clarity to my relationship with Israel and Jewishness. He also entertained Channa and I with folk music and great stories once work was done for the day.

By now I was exhausted from all the work I'd put into making the book happen, especially the psychological effort of delving into the flawed parts of myself that I wasn't proud of. I considered abandoning the whole idea, but Channa wouldn't let me give up. She approached our good friend Mary Anne Fitzgerald, a brilliant and accomplished journalist and author who knew most of Africa inside out thanks to her past reporting with the *Financial Times* and *The Sunday Times* of London. She graciously agreed to take me on. Kathy Eldon, another dear friend, read my latest draft and urged me to change the book from an autobiography to a memoir. I didn't know the difference, but over lunch with the three of us, Kathy convinced me to condense large sections of my early life. Over the next two years Mary Anne whipped my raggedy and politically incorrect memoir into shape. She did a superb job, pulling together all our previous attempts and distilling them into a proper book injected with my voice and humour. Mary Anne has become an even dearer friend to Channa and me - a testimony to her grace and perseverance.

Shel Arensen and his son Blake, the editors and publishers of *Old Africa* magazine and gentlemen both, took the manuscript on its final journey to being put between covers. Thanks to Julia Seth-Smith for the beautiful book cover. Their extensive knowledge and long experience with publishing made it a pleasure to work with them as did their patient and kind explanations of how everything worked. Any mistakes or offensive passages that have survived their rigorous editing are entirely mine.

Heartbeat: An American Cardiologist in Kenya

I want to acknowledge all my medical colleagues including the residents and students who I mentored over five decades and who have made the practice and teaching of medicine one of the most exciting experiences of my life. Special mention goes to my partner of twenty years, Dr Majid Warshow, and Dr Charles Kariuki, my partner for twenty-one years and still counting. My colleagues over the years also deserve special mention. They include my dear friend Dr Shem Musoke, famed for surviving Green Monkey disease, and Dr Christopher Kahuho and Dr Kelvin Muthamia.

In a busy cardiologists' practice one becomes dependent on the nurses and technicians who can make the experience either wonderful or miserable for everyone. I have been blessed with the former and want to express my gratitude to Mary Mutua, Winnie Makena and Jacinta Nkoyo, who have worked for me for close to forty years, and the others too numerous to name. My thanks to Anne Morris, Leonard Mureithi and James Muiruri. They are all well acquainted with my intolerance of clinical ineptitude and my often outrageous humour and mercifully still come to work every day.

The most precious teachers and friends are my patients, past and present, who have entrusted me with their vulnerabilities and secrets. You give me plenty of reason to continue improving the practice and looking forward to each day at work. You are interesting, entertaining, challenging, sometimes difficult and often hilariously funny. I thank you and your families for being in my life.

A difficult part of writing my memoir was not being able to include all the many friends who moulded me in my formative years. In the field of medicine from my early career onwards: Dr Simeon Rubenstein, Dr Robert Thompson, Dr Bernice Hecker,

Dr John Barton, Dr Charlie Clements, Prof. Julius Kyambi and his late wife Dr Barbara Kyambi. Charles Szlapak and Dr Chandu Sheth, my dearest and closest friends who attended both of my weddings on two different continents, still accepted me despite my idiosyncrasies and shortcomings. They continue to be my superegos and confidants. Dr Austin Moede has been sending me monthly envelopes of cuttings from his voracious readings in Americana, medicine, religion and lifestyle, expanding my horizons for over thirty years. Aryeh and Mari Glozer nurtured us with their open door and kosher pickles even when Aryeh was on his courageous medical journey, sadly now ended.

Among the many reasons to thank Margaret Njonjo is her gift of wisdom. Many is the time I sat with her as she told me stories of events that took place before I came to Kenya and corrected me where memory had been misleading. Sally Kosgei's total recall of places, dates and details was equally invaluable.

The other driving force in my life is family. The close relationship with my parents and siblings, Rochelle and Allan, are described in some detail, but the love I have for all of them goes far beyond what I have written. My four sons light up my life: Nahum, Joshua, Aaron and Jeremy, as does my daughter-in-law, Taylor, and my two grandsons, Bennie and Max. I am pleased and proud of them all beyond measure. I want to acknowledge their biological mothers, Lesley Meltzer and Jackeline Obare, for bringing them into this world.

Lastly I want to thank my wife Channa. She not only read every word of every version of this book but helped me write and rewrite every chapter. She supported and encouraged me and pushed me to finish what I had started so many years ago. Throughout our marriage we have shared an intense love that neither of us thought could exist. She helped me raise our boys and create a nuclear family held together by love and respect. She is the metronome of my heartbeat.

INDEX

A
Abbema, (Eliana and Mark) 318
Adamson, George 205-209
Adamson, Joy 207-207
Adamson, Terence 205-208
Adere, Steven 306
Aharoni, Vaizman 98, 286, 324-325, 327-329
Altman, Dr Larry K. 33, 53-56, 244
Amin, Idi 89-93, 96, 98-99
Amit, Reverend Zeev 319
Amitai, Ambassador Yaakov 333, 337
Annan, Kofi 329
Anter, (Adva, Dvir, Noy, Ora and Rami) 336-337
Arad, Ron 288
Arafat, Yasser 212-213, 230, 286
Atieno, Sylvia 3
Avyatar, Shmulik 359
Aya, Wilson Ndolo 252

B
Bagshawe, Dr Antonia 149-150, 170
Bartlett, Dr John 388
Bassan, (Nimu and Volker) 396
Begin, Prime Minister Menachem 214
Ben Aryeh, Yossi 270
Ben Gurion, Prime Minister David 214
bin Laden, Osama 4
Biwott, Nicholas 285
Blank, Paul 323-326
Bloch, Dora 98
Block, Jack 178, 334
Blum, (Moria and Yehuda) 275-276
Blumenthal, Dr Paul 233
Bowry, Dr Ravi 171
Boy, Juma Boy 125-128
Brazeal, Ambassador Aurelia 255
Bristow, Des 221-222
Broelsch, Professor Christophe 355
Broughton, Sir Delves (Jock) 157-158
Bruce, Dr Robert A. 58
Burstein, (Harry and Chana Gitel) 9, 14-15
Bush, President George H.W. 214, 251, 255
Bush, President George W. 247, 251
Bushnell, Ambassador Prudence 4, 259

C
Carr-Hartley, Sue 3
Carter, President Jimmy 259
Charrier, Jean 148-150, 152-153
Chemai, Ambassador Samson 237
Chepkwameka, Dr 70
Chesoni, Chief Justice Zaccheaus 295-305, 357
Chesoni, Atsango 308
Chesoni, Mary 298, 306, 309
Chesoni, Dr Solomon 296, 302
Chesoni, Ambassador Jon 309, 357
Cholmondeley, Tom 158
Church, Colin 185, 341
Church, Nicole 341
Clements, Dr Charlie 50-51, 58-60, 62-63, 232, 326, 410
Clinton, President Bill 251, 255, 352
Cohen, Ambassador Herman 253
Cohen, Pasco 97
Colvile, Gilbert 158-159
Commanday, Channa 3-4, 6-7, 36, 155, 173, 217-218, 224, 237, 261-263, 265, 273-274, 298-301, 311-321, 323-324, 326-331, 334-335, 337-338, 340-341, 349, 353, 357, 360-361, 371, 373, 376, 391, 393-396, 398-399, 402-404, 406, 408, 410
Commanday, Maurice 317-320, 391
Commanday, Ramah 318
Commanday, Ruth 317-319
Constable, Ambassador Elinor 251, 255
Cronheim, Charlie 115, 257, 407
Cronheim, Ruth 257, 407

D
D'Arbela, Professor Paul 93
D'Olier, (Elli and Johnny) 329-332
Delamare, Diana 156-164, 220-222
Delamere, Hugh 158
Desai, Dr Ramesh 103
Duba, Roba 266-269

E

Earl of Erroll (Josslyn Hay) 157-158, 163
Eban, Abba 188
Elms, Fiona 306
Engel, Eli 93

F

Fitzjohn, Tony 207-209
Fleming, Alexander 383-384
Floyer, Mrs 71
Floyer, Professor Michael 26, 28, 70-71, 73-74
Forbes, Dr Colin 234, 264, 318
Forbes, Margaret 318
Forssmann, Dr Werner 54-56
Frankel, Alan 326

G

Gaddafi, Col Muammar 187-194, 230
Gathua, Dr Samuel 303
Gaymer, Barry 332
Gellert, Dr Shani 312
Georgiadis, Byron 303, 305-309, 354
Gethi, Ben 94, 198
Gikandi, Alex 331
Githongo, John 261
Glozer, Aryeh 338, 356, 410
Gordon, Harold 114
Gordon, Marcia 114-115, 210, 237
Gordon, Saul 92, 114-115, 210
Goren, Rabbi Shlomo 29
Greenburg, Rabbi William 52
Griffin, Geoffrey 196-198
Griswold, Dr Herbert 87

H

Harbage, Col Mike 150
Harvey, Dr William 53
Hecker, Dr Bernice 106, 409
Hempstone, Ambassador Smith 251-255
Holmes, Dr King 240
Hunt, (Don and Iris) 161

I

Irrigation Pete 107-108

J

Jackson, Reverend Jesse 212
Jenkins, Dr Steven 293-294
Johnson, Dr Bruce 145, 150
Jorgensen, Dr Tom 97
Joshi, Dr Mark 298-299, 301-302, 308
Josiah, Ambassador Frost 287-288, 290
Jouannaud, (Jean François and Karen) 318

K

Kahn, Rabbi Moshe Zeev (Zedi) 11-12, 14, 18, 400
Kahn, Rena 275, 318
Kahugu, Dr Wallace 76
Kahuho, Dr Christopher 371, 375, 409
Kaleli, Dr Rev. Jones 280-281
Kamdar, Dr Hasmukh 134
Kanyotu, James 94
Kariithi, Geoffrey 109
Kariuki, Dr Charles 261, 401, 409
Kariuki, J.M. 197-198,
Kariuki, Paul Kihara 398
Kassarjian, Romeo 232
Katharima, Ambassador Harry 290
Kaunda, President Kenneth 212, 261
Keidar, Ambassador Jacob 346-347
Kenyatta, Muhoho 398
Kenyatta, President Jomo 68, 70, 75, 77, 94, 101, 104, 107-111, 197, 215, 256, 282, 165-166, 181, 215, 236
Kenyatta, President Uhuru 259-260, 398
Khatami, President Mohammad 287-288
Kiano, Dr Julius 392
Kibaki, President Mwai 72, 110, 169, 176-177, 179, 185, 188, 249-250, 255, 259-260, 328-329
Kibichii, Frederick 358
Kiereini, Dr Eunice Muringo 104, 353
Kiereini, Githae 104
Kiereini, Jeremiah 104, 170, 177, 353
Kilele, Walter 220-222, 224
King Jr, Martin Luther 59
Kiplagat, Ambassador Bethuel 182, 318, 328
Kiplagat, Honorine 182, 318
Kiptanui, Abraham 2-3, 182, 339, 353

Kiptanui, Mary 182, 353
Kirui, Paul 358
Klippel, Dr Jack 132
Knight, Professor Ed 67
Koech, Dr Davy 245-246
Koinange, Mbiyu 109
Koinange, Dr Wilfred 130, 151
Koome, Martha 306
Kosgei, Sally vii, 263-264, 282-283, 285, 292, 318, 353, 361, 410
Kreiss, Dr Joan 240
Kuschel, Dieter 76
Kyambi, (Dr Barbara and Dr Julius) 182, 305-306, 309, 317-318, 410

L
Landra, Dr Adriano 271
Lee, John 398
Leakey, Richard 185, 237, 353
Lesiew, Joseph 318
Likimani, Dr Jason 75-76, 105
Loeffler, Martha 142
Loefler, Dr Imre 200, 263
Lokorio, John 358
Lotodo, Francis 282
Lustman, Heini 222-224, 317

M
Mabel 234, 236, 316, 321
Machel, Graca 213
Machel, Samora 210-213
Mahihu, Eliud 108-109
Mahugu, Ambassador Njuguna 215, 217
Maloba, Judy 339
Mandela, Nelson 175, 213-217
Mandela, Winnie 213, 215-216
Maniar, Dr Sharad 134-136
Manji, Dr Hadi 355, 357, 365
Mariam, President Mengistu Haile 188-190
Masembe, Dr John 151
Matiba, Kenneth 180, 255
Matseshe, Dr John 300-304, 307-308
Mbogori, Dr Jimmy 299-300, 308
McGoon, Dr Dwight 296
McKenzie, Bruce 94, 99
Meir, Prime Minister Golda 188, 214

Meltzer, Lesley 228-238, 267, 312, 316, 324, 404, 410
Meyerhold, Dr Andrew 207-209
Miller, Chief Justice Cecil (Dusty) 179-181, 304
Miller, Justice Jay 237-238
Mngola, Dr Eric 105, 108
Moede, Dr Austin 410
Moi, Gideon 355-367
Moi, Jonathan 363-364
Moi, President Daniel Arap 2-3, 101-111, 150-151, 165-194, 199-203, 211, 215-217, 227, 229-230, 233, 244-245, 247, 249-255, 258-261, 265, 275, 279-290, 292-294, 297, 299-300, 303, 305, 309, 313, 318-321, 337-340, 352-367, 391, 395, 397, 402-403
Moi, Raymond 364, 366
Moi, Zahra 359
Mtulia, Professor Idris 215
Mugabe, President Robert 212
Muhindi, Dr David 196-198, 204
Muigai, Ngengi 256
Muiruri, James 365, 409
Mungai, James 109
Mungai, Ngenga 250
Murumbi, Joseph 102
Musau, Dr Luke 301-302, 308
Musoke, Helen 182
Musoke, Dr Shem 148-151, 161, 166, 182, 263, 300, 409
Musomba, Brigadier John 168
Muthamia, Dr Kelvin 374, 376, 409
Muthoga, Lee 306-307
Mwangale, Elijah 178, 180
Mwinyi, President Ali Hassan 215

N
Nderi, Ignatius 198
Neiman, Agam 318
Netanyahu, Prime Minister Benjamin 95, 100
Netanyahu, Benzion 100
Netanyahu, Lt. Col. Yonathan 95-96, 99, 100
Neylan, (Pat and Sara) 330-332
Ng'ang'a, Amos 177
Ngini, (Carey and Mary) 396, 398
Ngugi, Elizabeth 242

Ngugi, Naomi 3
Njiru, Lee 193, 358
Njonjo, Charles 93-94, 97-98, 102, 108, 110, 151, 163, 167, 175-185, 252, 293, 296, 303, 318-320, 324, 328, 341, 353-354, 360-361, 364, 391-399, 403
Njonjo, David 394, 397-398
Njonjo, Josiah 175
Njonjo (Bryson), Margaret v, 93, 98, 163, 176, 181, 184, 253, 320, 341, 353, 393-397, 403, 406, 410
Njonjo, Nimu 396
Nkoyo, Jacinta 216, 409
Nsanze, Professor Herbert 240
Nyachae, Simeon 177
Nyerere, President Julius 212

O
Obare, Jackie 263-265, 267, 302-303, 314, 327-328, 404, 410
Obel, Dr Arthur 245
Oded, Aryeh 285
Odinga, Jaramogi Oginga 169, 255
Odinga, Raila 169-170, 255, 259, 328-329
Oduya, Justine 325
Ojiambo, Professor Hillary 70, 77, 87, 104-105, 288
Ojiambo, Dr Julia 70
Okioma, Dr Ruben 374
Onyango, Gradus 72-73, 203
Osogo, James 151
Oster, Dr Chuck 145

P
Parfet, Claude 156, 161, 232
Parfet, Court 98, 154-156, 160-161, 177, 232, 252, 312, 318, 394
Partridge, David 156, 161
Patel, Dr Ashvin 64, 71-72
Patel, Dr R.I. 234
Patel, Dr S.R. 233
Patel, Dr Yashvent 71-72
Patel, Sureka 71
Patterson, John Henry 99-100
Peres, Prime Minister Shimon 90, 286
Perlez, Jane 246
Petersdorf, Dr Robert 36
Ping, Xiao 48

Pinto, Dr Joel 108
Piot, Professor Peter 240-241
Plummer, Dr Francis 240-241
Pope Benedict XVI 345-346
Pope John Paul I 107
Pope John Paul II 244
Pope Paul VI 105
Pope Pius XII 345-347
Porcher, Dr William 43
Presley, Frank 6
Preston, Dr Richard 149

R
Rabin, Prime Minister Yitzhak 89, 95, 284-285
Ranneberger, Ambassador Michael 328
Ravn, Kristian 152-153
Reese, Dr Philip 74
Ribeiro, Dr Rosendo 130
Riskin, Rabbi Shlomo 351
Ronald, Dr Allan 240
Rowe, David 204
Ruto, President William 170

S
Saitoti, George 285
Salem, Dr Hussayn 365
Sayers, Bill 223-224
Schkolne, Theo 329
Selassie, Emperor Hailie 188
Seligman, Henry 213
Seth-Smith, Tony 270, 273
Shamir, Prime Minister Yitzhak 284
Sharon, Prime Minister Ariel 339
Shaw, Patrick 195-204, 222, 263
Sheth, Dr Chandu 144, 165, 182, 224, 318, 410
Sheth, Nanalal 224, 318
Sheth, Dr Pratima 182
Silverstein, Dr Aaron 26, 264, 302, 313-314, 322, 324-328, 404-405, 410
Silverstein, Alec 9
Silverstein, Dr Allan 15, 17-19, 225-226, 235, 315-316, 321-322, 400, 410
Silverstein, Eva 9
Silverstein, Jeremy 264, 302, 313-314, 322, 324-326, 329, 404-405, 410
Silverstein, Joe 9

Silverstein, Joshua 184-185, 235-236, 264, 266, 314-316, 319, 322-325, 327, 356, 404-405, 410
Silverstein, Nahum 184-185, 233-236, 264, 266, 314-316, 332-327, 356, 402, 404, 410
Silverstein, Nochem/Norman/Brzoza 9, 10, 233
Silverstein, Dr Norman 8-22, 24-26, 31-32, 47, 61-62, 64, 224-226, 263, 315, 321-322, 400
Silverstein, Rochel 9
Silverstein, Rubin 9
Silverstein, Ruth 9
Silverstein, Sarah Peshe (Kahn) 10-22, 24, 26, 31-32, 64, 315-317, 321-322, 400
Simborg, Stephanie 270-272
Simborg, Dr Walter 271
Skirpal, Sergei and Yulia 135
Skolnik, Abe 15
Slapak, Dr Maurice 293-294
Sobel, Aron 316
Sobel, (Silverstein) Rochelle 12, 14-15, 19-21, 184, 227-229, 231-232, 236, 264, 315-316, 321, 323, 326-327, 329, 331, 356, 400, 410
Sobel, Dr Solomon 227, 231-232, 264, 316, 326-327, 329, 331, 356
Sobet, Hadson 236, 256-257, 266, 272-274, 276-278
Spindler, (Dr Joseph and Sarah) 342
Spindler, Jason 341
Spurrier, Dr Alfred 130
Stav, Rabbi David 351
Sterling, Leroy 21-22
Sumbeiywo, Elijah 167-168
Sumbeiywo, Lazaro 167-168, 328
Szlapak, Charles 231, 233, 293, 311-312, 318, 410
Szlapak, Rachel 233

T
Talwar, Dr Virendra 171
Thompson, Dr Robert 106, 409
Tonucci, Archbishop Giovanni 346-347
Tukei, Peter 145

W
Wakesa, John 272-274
Wako, Amos 354
Warshow, Dr Majid 86, 116-117, 159-161, 226-227, 261, 401, 409
Wasunna, Dr J. 108
Wasunna, Professor Ambrose 117
Waterman, Sheila 145
Weizman, President Ezer 286
Wekullo, Dr Vera 5,
Western, David 183-185
Wicks, Chief Justice Sir James 110
Williams, Mr Brynn 104, 121, 125
Williamson, Bishop Richard 346
Wunderlich (Delorie), Anne 117, 160

X
Xiaoping, General Secretary Deng 279

Y
Yumbya, Daniel 309

Z
Zakaya 272-274

Made in the USA
Monee, IL
18 December 2023

575984ce-6565-4141-b747-44a0cdeab539R01